Tocqueville and the Frontiers of Democracy

Alexis de Tocqueville is widely cited as an authority on civil society, religion, and American political culture, yet his thoughts on democratization outside the West and the challenges of a globalizing age are less known and often misunderstood. This collection of essays by a distinguished group of international scholars explores Tocqueville's vision of democracy in Asia and the Middle East; the relationship between globalization and democracy; colonialism, Islam, and Hinduism; and the ethics of international relations. Rather than simply documenting Tocqueville's own thoughts, the volume applies the Frenchman's insights to enduring dilemmas of democratization and cross-cultural exchanges in the twenty-first century. This is one of the few books to shift the focus of Tocqueville studies away from America and Western Europe, expanding the frontiers of democracy and highlighting the international dimensions of Tocqueville's political thought.

Ewa Atanassow is a Junior Professor at ECLA of Bard, a liberal arts university in Berlin. Her research focuses on democracy and nationhood in the liberal tradition of political thought, with emphasis on Tocqueville.

Richard Boyd is Associate Professor of Government at Georgetown University, where he teaches courses on liberalism, international ethics, and the history of political philosophy. He is the author of *Uncivil Society: The Perils of Pluralism and the Making of Modern Liberalism* (2004).

Tocqueville and the Frontiers of Democracy

Edited by

EWA ATANASSOW
ECLA of Bard University

RICHARD BOYD
Georgetown University

 **CAMBRIDGE**
UNIVERSITY PRESS

CAMBRIDGE UNIVERSITY PRESS
Cambridge, New York, Melbourne, Madrid, Cape Town,
Singapore, São Paulo, Delhi, Mexico City

Cambridge University Press
32 Avenue of the Americas, New York, NY 10013-2473, USA

www.cambridge.org
Information on this title: www.cambridge.org/9780521263757

First published 2013

Printed in the United States of America

A catalog record for this publication is available from the British Library.

Library of Congress Cataloging in Publication Data

Tocqueville and the frontiers of democracy / [edited by] Richard Boyd, Georgetown
University, Ewa Atanassow, European College of Liberal Arts (Berlin)
    pages cm
ISBN 978-1-107-00963-9 – ISBN 978-0-521-26375-7 (pbk.)
1. Tocqueville, Alexis de, 1805–1859. – Political and social views.   2. Democracy.
3. Democratization.   I. Boyd, Richard, 1970–   II. Atanassow, Ewa.
JC229.T8T593   2013
321.8–dc23   2012042450

ISBN 978-1-107-00963-9 Hardback
ISBN 978-0-521-26375-7 Paperback

Cambridge University Press has no responsibility for the persistence or accuracy of URLS
for external or third-party Internet Web sites referred to in this publication and does not
guarantee that any content on such Web sites is, or will remain, accurate or appropriate.

Contents

List of Contributors

Ewa Atanassow is a Junior Professor at ECLA of Bard, a liberal arts university in Berlin. Her research focuses on the question of nationhood and nationalism in Tocqueville and more broadly on the intersection of ethics and politics in the liberal tradition of political thought. Her articles and reviews have appeared in *Journal of Democracy*, *Kronos*, *Nations and Nationalism*, and *Perspectives on Political Science*. She is currently working on a book-length account of the vexed relationship between the modern nation-state, as defined by cultural particularity and aspirations to sovereignty, and the global universalism of the democratic creed.

Paul Berman writes about politics and literature for *The New Republic*, *The New York Times Book Review*, and other journals. He is the author of two books on the history of the generation of 1968 in different parts of the world – *A Tale of Two Utopias* and *Power and the Idealists* – and the author of two books on the Islamist movement and the challenges it presents – *Terror and Liberalism* and *The Flight of the Intellectuals*. He is the editor of several anthologies, including *Carl Sandburg: Selected Poems*, published by the American Poets Project of the Library of America.

Richard Boyd is Associate Professor of Government at Georgetown University. He is the author of *Uncivil Society: The Perils of Pluralism and the Making of Modern Liberalism* (Rowman & Littlefield, 2004) and numerous journal articles and book chapters on the intellectual history of classical liberalism, civil society, French literature, and contemporary political theory. He is currently completing a book manuscript on liberalism, capacities, and citizenship.

We are especially grateful to our editor at Cambridge University Press, Robert Dreesen, for his sensible guidance and unflagging support for the original book proposal, as well as to Abby Zorbaugh, Jeri Litteral, and Susan Kauffman for ably shepherding the manuscript through the editorial process. David Golemboski offered exemplary research assistance in compiling the bibliography and tracking down scores of missing references. Marija Uzunova caught many errors and incongruities in her careful reading of the page proofs. We also want to acknowledge the two extensive sets of comments from anonymous reviewers and those from Thomas Bartscherer of Bard College, whose generous and insightful suggestions greatly improved the form and substance of our efforts.

While working on this book, both of us welcomed our first children to this world, thus each crossing for the first time the "frontier" of parenthood. To our daughters, Dara and Liliane, we would like to dedicate this volume.

List of Contributors

Ewa Atanassow is a Junior Professor at ECLA of Bard, a liberal arts university in Berlin. Her research focuses on the question of nationhood and nationalism in Tocqueville and more broadly on the intersection of ethics and politics in the liberal tradition of political thought. Her articles and reviews have appeared in *Journal of Democracy*, *Kronos*, *Nations and Nationalism*, and *Perspectives on Political Science*. She is currently working on a book-length account of the vexed relationship between the modern nation-state, as defined by cultural particularity and aspirations to sovereignty, and the global universalism of the democratic creed.

Paul Berman writes about politics and literature for *The New Republic*, *The New York Times Book Review*, and other journals. He is the author of two books on the history of the generation of 1968 in different parts of the world – *A Tale of Two Utopias* and *Power and the Idealists* – and the author of two books on the Islamist movement and the challenges it presents – *Terror and Liberalism* and *The Flight of the Intellectuals*. He is the editor of several anthologies, including *Carl Sandburg: Selected Poems*, published by the American Poets Project of the Library of America.

Richard Boyd is Associate Professor of Government at Georgetown University. He is the author of *Uncivil Society: The Perils of Pluralism and the Making of Modern Liberalism* (Rowman & Littlefield, 2004) and numerous journal articles and book chapters on the intellectual history of classical liberalism, civil society, French literature, and contemporary political theory. He is currently completing a book manuscript on liberalism, capacities, and citizenship.

Nestor Capdevila is Professor of Political Philosophy at the Université de Paris Ouest Nanterre La Défense. He is the editor and translator of *Bartholomé de Las Casas* and the author of *Las Casas, une politique de l'humanité: l'homme et l'empire de la foi* (Editions du Cerf, 1998); *Le concept d'idéologie* (PUF, 2004); *Tocqueville et les frontières de la démocratie* (PUF, 2007); and *Tocqueville ou Marx: Démocratie, capitalisme, révolution* (PUF, 2012).

David Clinton is Professor of Political Science and Chair of the Department of Political Science at Baylor University. He is the author of, among others, *The Two Faces of National Interest* (LSU Press, 1994) and *Tocqueville, Lieber, and Bagehot: Liberalism Confronts the World* (Palgrave Macmillan, 2003) and the editor of *The Realist Tradition and Contemporary International Relations* (LSU Press, 2007).

Robert T. Gannett, Jr., is an independent scholar and community organizer, currently serving as the executive director of the Institute for Community Empowerment in Chicago. He is the author of *Tocqueville Unveiled: The Historian and His Sources for "The Old Regime and the Revolution"* (Chicago, 2003).

Ran Halévi is a political historian, Directeur de recherche at the Centre National de la Recherche Scientifique (France), and senior Fellow at the Centre de Recherches Politiques Raymond Aron in Paris. Most of his work focuses on the Old Regime and the French Revolution. He is the coeditor of the Pléiade volume on the Orators of the French Revolution, the author of books on the origins of democratic sociability in eighteenth-century France (1984), the first French revolutionary Constitution (1996), François Furet (2007), and numerous articles on Louis XIV's political thought, political moderation under the absolute monarchy, politics and modern honor, the genesis of constituent power, and, more recently, Israeli democracy.

Alan Kahan is Professor of British Civilization at the Université de Versailles/St. Quentin. His recent research focuses on the comparative history of liberalism in nineteenth-century Europe and on the relationship between intellectuals and capitalism. Kahan is the translator of Tocqueville's *The Old Regime and the Revolution* (1998, 2001) and coeditor of *The Tocqueville Reader* (2002). His most recent books are *Alexis de Tocqueville* (2010) and *Mind vs. Money: The War Between Intellectuals and Capitalism* (2010). He is currently working on a study of Tocqueville, Religion, and Democracy.

Ralph Lerner is the Benjamin Franklin Professor Emeritus in the College and in the Committee on Social Thought at the University of Chicago. His many scholarly works include *The Thinking Revolutionary: Principle and Practice in the New Republic* (Cornell, 1987); *The Founders' Constitution* (coedited with Philip B. Kurland), 5 vols. (Chicago, 1987); *Revolutions Revisited: Two Faces of the Politics of Enlightenment* (North Carolina, 1994); *Maimonides' Empire of Light: Popular Enlightenment in an Age of Belief* (Chicago, 2000); and *Playing the Fool: Subversive Laughter in Troubled Times* (Chicago, 2009).

Susan McWilliams is Associate Professor in the Politics Department at Pomona College, where she teaches courses on liberal political theory and American political thought. She received her BA in Russian and political science from Amherst College and her MA and PhD in politics from Princeton University. She is coeditor (with Patrick Deneen) of Wilson Carey McWilliams's, *The Democratic Soul* (Kentucky, 2011) and *Redeeming Democracy in America* (Kansas, 2011). She is currently preparing a book manuscript on the theme of "travel" in political theory.

Joshua Mitchell is Professor of Government at Georgetown University. He is the author of *Not By Reason Alone* (Chicago, 1993), *The Fragility of Freedom* (Chicago, 1995), and *Plato's Fable* (Princeton, 2005). His book *Tocqueville in Arabia* is forthcoming. Professor Mitchell was Chair of the Government Department at Georgetown from 2002 to 2005, Associate Dean for Faculty Affairs at Georgetown's Qatar campus from 2005 to 2007, and Provost and Acting Chancellor of The American University of Iraq – Sulaimani from 2008 to 2010.

Robert Pippin is the Evelyn Stefansson Nef Distinguished Service Professor in the John U. Nef Committe on Social Thought, the Department Philosophy, and the College at the University of Chicago. He has published extensively on the modern German philosophical tradition, the problem of modernity, theories of self-consciousness, the nature of conceptual change, and the problem of freedom. His interdisciplinary interests involve the relation between philosophy and literature, modern art, and contemporary film. He has recently finished a book about political psychology and the American identity in the classic Hollywood westerns.

Jennifer Pitts is Associate Professor of Political Science at the University of Chicago. Her interests include the history of modern political and social thought, with a focus on Britain and France of the eighteenth and nineteenth centuries. She is the author of *A Turn to Empire* (Princeton,

2005) and editor and translator of *Alexis de Tocqueville: Writings on Empire and Slavery* (Johns Hopkins, 2001). She is now writing a book on European debates about international law and legal relations with non-European societies in the eighteenth and nineteenth centuries.

Céline Spector is currently Professor in the Philosophy Department of the University of Bordeaux 3 and Member of the Institut Universitaire de France. Her research interests include the history of political thought – particularly the eighteenth century and its legacy. She has published several books on Montesquieu and Rousseau, including *Montesquieu: Pouvoirs, richesses et sociétés* (PUF, 2004 [rééd. Paris, Hermann, 2011]); *Montesquieu et l'émergence de l'économie politique* (Paris, Champion, 2006 [awarded the Prix de l'Académie des Sciences morales et politiques]); Jean-Jacques Rousseau, *Principes du droit de la guerre: Ecrits sur le Projet de Paix Perpétuelle de l'abbé de Saint-Pierre*, coedited with B. Bachofen (Paris, Vrin, 2008); *Montesquieu: Liberté, droit et histoire* (Paris, Michalon, 2010 [awarded the Prix de l'Académie Montesquieu 2011]); and *Au prisme de Rousseau : usages politiques contemporains* (Oxford, Voltaire Foundation, 2011).

Cheryl B. Welch is Senior Lecturer on Government at Harvard University. She is the author of *Liberty and Utility: The French Idéologues and the Transformation of Liberalism* (Columbia, 1984) and *De Tocqueville* (Oxford, 2001). She is also the editor of *The Cambridge Companion to Tocqueville* (2006) and an editor of *The Tocqueville Review/la Revue Tocqueville*. The author of numerous articles on French and English political thought, liberalism, and democracy, she is currently working on two projects: a book on the moral dimensions of international political thought in the nineteenth century and a study of the fate of utilitarianism in nineteenth- and twentieth-century Francophone thought.

Short Title Abbreviations of Tocqueville's Major Works

English Editions

DIA   *Democracy in America*. Translated and edited by Harvey Mansfield and Delba Winthrop. Chicago: University of Chicago Press, 2000. Cited by volume, part, chapter, and page numbers: e.g., DIA I.2.iii, 174–175.

DIA (G) *Democracy in America*. Translated by Arthur Goldhammer. Edited by Olivier Zunz. New York: Library of America, 2004.

DIA (L) *Democracy in America*. Translated by George Lawrence. Edited by J. P. Mayer. New York: Harper Perennial, 1969. Cited by volume, part, chapter, and/or page numbers: e.g., DIA (L), xiii.

DIA (N) *Democracy in America*. Critical bilingual edition. Translated by James T. Schleifer, in 4 volumes. Edited by Eduardo Nolla. Indianapolis: Liberty Fund Inc., 2009. Cited both by the conventional divisions of Tocqueville's work into volume, part, and chapter, as well as by page numbers to this edition; e.g., DIA (N) II.3.xviii, note v, 1110.

JA   *Journey to America*. Translated by George Lawrence. Edited by J. P. Mayer. New Haven: Yale University Press, 1959. Cited by page.

JEI   *Journeys to England and Ireland*. Translated by George Lawrence and K. P. Mayer. Edited by J. P. Mayer. New Brunswick, NJ: Transaction Books, 1988. Cited by page: e.g., JEI, 116.

OR I and OR II   *The Old Regime and the Revolution*. Vol. 1: *The
                 Complete Text*. Vol. II: *Notes on the French
                 Revolution and Napoleon*. Translated by Alan S.
                 Kahan. Edited by François Furet and Françoise
                 Mélonio. Chicago: University of Chicago Press, 1998
                 and 2001. Cited by volume and page: e.g., OR I, 157.
R   *Recollections*: *The French Revolution of 1848*.
                 Translated by George Lawrence. New Brunswick, NJ:
                 Transaction Publishers, 1995.
SLPS   *Selected Letters on Politics and Society*. Translated by
                 Roger Boesche and James Toupin. Berkeley:
                 University of California Press, 1985.
WES   *Writings on Empire and Slavery*. Translated by
                 Jennifer Pitts. Baltimore: Johns Hopkins University
                 Press, 2001.

French Editions

LCS   *Lettres Choisies, Souvenirs: 1814–1859*. Edited by F.
                 Mélonio and L. Guellec. Paris: Gallimard, 2003.
OC   *Oeuvres Complètes*. Edited by J. P. Mayer et al.
                 17 vols. in 28 parts to date. Paris: Gallimard, 1951– .
                 Cited by volume, part, and page numbers: e.g., OC
                 3:1, 120
OP   *Oeuvres*. Edited by André Jardin, *Edition Pléiade*. 3
                 vols. to date. Paris: Gallimard, 1991– . Cited by
                 volume and page numbers: e.g., OP1, 56.

Acknowledgments

One of the main inspirations for this volume was a conference on "Tocqueville and the Frontiers of Democracy" jointly held at the University of Chicago and Roosevelt University in the spring of 2009. We would again like to express our heartfelt thanks to Thomas Bartscherer, Anton Barba Kay, Dan Bertche, Pamela Edwards, Anne Gamboa, Brett Keyser, Margaret Litvin, Robert Pippin, Nathan Tarcov, and Stuart Warner for their inestimable help in staging that originating event, as well as to the Jack Miller Center, Harvard University's Program on Constitutional Government, Montesquieu Forum of Roosevelt University, and University of Chicago's Center for International Studies Norman Wait Harris Fund, Department of History, France Chicago Center, Franke Institute for the Humanities, and John U. Nef Committee on Social Thought, all of whose financial and logistical support were essential to its success.

This volume's major themes were strongly affirmed by moderators, discussants, and attendees at the Chicago event who did not contribute chapters, particularly Paul Cheney, Nathan Tarcov, and Stuart Warner. Along with the original conference participants, we are grateful to the majority of contributors who joined this discussion belatedly, in some cases on very short timelines, and whose participation amply enriched and deepened the conversation. It goes without saying that this volume would not have been possible without all of its contributors' hard work. We admire their diligence, open-mindedness, and equanimity, particularly when it came to revising their chapters in view of our seemingly endless barrage of editorial criticisms. This volume stands as a testament to their scholarly dedication and subtle understandings of Tocqueville's social and political thought.

We are especially grateful to our editor at Cambridge University Press, Robert Dreesen, for his sensible guidance and unflagging support for the original book proposal, as well as to Abby Zorbaugh, Jeri Litteral, and Susan Kauffman for ably shepherding the manuscript through the editorial process. David Golemboski offered exemplary research assistance in compiling the bibliography and tracking down scores of missing references. Marija Uzunova caught many errors and incongruities in her careful reading of the page proofs. We also want to acknowledge the two extensive sets of comments from anonymous reviewers and those from Thomas Bartscherer of Bard College, whose generous and insightful suggestions greatly improved the form and substance of our efforts.

While working on this book, both of us welcomed our first children to this world, thus each crossing for the first time the "frontier" of parenthood. To our daughters, Dara and Liliane, we would like to dedicate this volume.

Introduction: Tocqueville and the Frontiers of Democracy

Ewa Atanassow and Richard Boyd

Introduction

Few thinkers in the history of Western political thought are as widely cited as Alexis de Tocqueville. Among the legions of U.S. pundits and policy makers who have invoked the Frenchman's authority, Ronald Reagan, George W. Bush, and Bill Clinton all bolstered their speeches with choice quotes from Tocqueville's *Democracy in America*. Tocqueville is embraced across the political spectrum in the United States and Europe for his advocacy of civic engagement and civil society, his praise of religion's salutary role in public life, his warnings about the growth of the centralized state, and his sometimes biting observations about the leveling tendencies of democratic culture. His thoughts on democracy in America seem to resonate just as strongly today as when they appeared in the first half of the nineteenth century.

Even so, Tocqueville's ubiquity may actually detract from the subtlety of his message. It is difficult enough to characterize Tocqueville's domestic political theory – as a nostalgic conservatism, skeptical liberalism, communitarianism, or radical participatory democracy – but the confusion is only amplified when one looks beyond the relatively settled frontiers of American or Western-European democracy.[1] His insights into the challenges of a globalizing age are among the most neglected and misunderstood parts of his political theory. Despite a recent surge of interest

---

[1] For a sense of the manifold ways that Tocqueville's ideas have been interpreted by both the Right and the Left in contemporary American political discourse, see especially Chad Alan Goldberg, "Social Citizenship and a Reconstructed Tocqueville," *American Sociological Review* 66 (2001), 289–315.

in Tocqueville's writings on empire, foreign policy, and European affairs, his thoughts on international relations are overshadowed by his famous book on America.

Thus it should come as no surprise that Tocqueville has been invoked in so many contradictory ways. In a recent *World Affairs* article, for example, the Hudson Institute's Seth Cropsey and Arthur Milikh argue that Tocqueville's focus on the structural preconditions of democracy bodes poorly for the fate of the Egyptian revolution. Without supporting factors such as genuinely representative political parties, a large and inclusive middle class, and administrative decentralization, the prospects for democracy in Egypt and other parts of the Middle East look dim. According to the authors, the mere "hatred of a tyrant" should not be confused with a true and legitimate "love of liberty." In their view, at least, a Tocquevillean perspective on the Egyptian revolution and other steps toward democracy in the Middle East lead to pessimistic conclusions.[2]

This recent "Tocquevillean" skepticism about indigenous democracy in the Middle East may seem ironic given the neoconservative appropriation of Tocqueville during the U.S.-led invasion of Iraq. Widely hailed as the intellectual architect of American interventionism, political-theorist-turned-Pentagon-advisor Paul Wolfowitz cited Tocqueville as a blueprint for democratization and constitution-building in Iraq. After first appealing to the authority of the illustrious Frenchman, Wolfowitz enthused to an Iraqi audience that "There are people in the world who say that Arabs can't build democracy . . . I think that's nonsense. You have a chance to prove them wrong."[3]

Critics of U.S. foreign policy plead that Tocqueville himself would hardly approve of such idealistic efforts to export American-style democracy. Left-leaning columnist Nicholas von Hoffman complains that neoconservatives distort Tocqueville's message:

De Tocqueville explained that the American democracy which he had studied firsthand . . . was shaped by and grew out of the culture, religion, etc., of the Americans. He believed that democracy is not a collection of rules, laws and

---

[2] Seth Cropsey and Arthur Milikh, "Democracy in Egypt: Applying the Tocqueville Standard," *World Affairs* (May/June 2011). http://www.worldaffairsjournal.org/articles/2011-MayJun/full-Cropsey-MJ-2011.html (accessed July 21, 2011).

[3] As cited in David Ignatius, "A War of Choice, and One Who Chose It," *Washington Post*, November 2, 2003, p. B01. http://www.washingtonpost.com/wp-dyn/articles/A49310-2003Oct31.html (accessed July 20, 2011).

procedures which are pressed down on a people or a nation; that a political system needs to have organic unity with the society in which it operates.[4]

Lawrence Harrison of the Fletcher School similarly objects that surely "Bush advisers such as Paul Wolfowitz and Condoleezza Rice have read Alexis de Tocqueville's classic *Democracy in America*. But they – and Senator McCain – must have forgotten its overriding lesson: When it comes to the viability of democracy, more than anything else, culture matters."[5] Revisiting the issue in the wake of the Arab Spring, Harrison maintains his pessimism: culture still matters.[6]

We mention these exchanges not to take sides or to reignite old quarrels but because they so vividly illustrate the animating premise of this volume, namely that although academics and policy makers share a broad sense of Tocqueville's importance for international politics and comparative democratization, there is no consensus whatsoever as to what his lessons consist of. Even as contemporary political scientists, sociologists, economists, and moral philosophers struggle to come to grips with the preconditions for democracy's spread throughout the world, the questions Tocqueville originally raised have taken on new urgency. Indeed, they have become the defining issues of our time: What is democracy, and how does it emerge? Is it an inevitable stage of societal development, as many hope, or the fragile artifact of a particular cultural and historical experience, as others fear? Must democracy be actively encouraged, even by military force and conquest, or allowed to develop spontaneously according to its own logic? What are the main challenges for fostering democracy in nations in which it has not yet been established? What is the relationship between democracy and free markets, commerce, or globalization? Is democracy compatible with Islam or other non-Western religions and cultures? Are nationalism and religious fundamentalism

---

4 Nicholas von Hoffman, "Our Idealist in Chief Promotes a Lovely War," *New York Observer*, November 17, 2003. http://www.observer.com/2003/11/our-idealist-in-chief-promotes-a-lovely-war/ (accessed July 20, 2011).

5 Lawrence Harrison, "Want Democracy in Iraq? Culture Matters," *Christian Science Monitor*, July 1, 2008. http://www.rath.us/random-stuff/interesting-articles/want_democracy_in_iraq_culture_matters.txt (accessed July 5, 2011); for a more developed version of this thesis about how culture matters, see especially Lawrence Harrison and Samuel Huntington (eds.), *Culture Matters: How Values Shape Human Progress* (New York: Basic Books, 2000).

6 Lawrence Harrison, "After the Arab Spring, Culture Still Matters," *The American Interest*, September 1, 2011. http://www.the-american-interest.com/article.cfm?piece=1021 (accessed January 4, 2012).

merely transient phenomena, or are they with us to stay? These and other questions press us to think long and hard about the political, geographical, cultural, and moral frontiers of democracy.

Contributors to the present volume shift the focus away from Tocqueville's well-known and relatively sanguine thoughts on America. Instead they wrestle with his more pessimistic observations about the agonistic process of democratization in nineteenth-century France and other parts of the world that lack America's fortuitous circumstances and mores. Although these chapters all strive to take seriously Tocqueville's own writings, they also move beyond the scholar's narrow preoccupation with what Tocqueville thought or did and apply his political reflections to dilemmas of international justice, democratization, and cross-cultural exchanges. In doing so, they address not only an urgent set of contemporary problems but also a deficit in the scholarly literature.

Tocqueville Scholarship and Comparative Democratization

With the preponderance of these themes in Tocqueville's writings, it is surprising that they have – with a few noteworthy exceptions – been sidestepped by traditional Tocqueville scholarship. One of the pioneering works to delve into these topics was Seymour Drescher's 1968 *Dilemmas of Democracy: Tocqueville and Modernization*, which explores the Frenchman's view of the rocky path of economic development. Responding to the then-fashionable school of modernization theory (what passes today as "globalization" or "economic development") sponsored by the likes of Seymour Martin Lipset and others, Drescher uses Tocqueville to challenge the orthodox view that "modernization" is inevitably a progressive force. Drescher calls attention to the condition of many groups – African Americans, industrial workers, rural peasantry, colonial subjects, and convicts – whose "social condition did not fit well into the nineteenth-century scheme of providential equality."[7] Not only is modernization far from unidirectional, but it also gives rise to new inequalities and exclusions.

Another seminal work to plumb the international aspects of Tocqueville's thought is Michael Hereth's 1979 *Tocqueville: Threats to Freedom in a Democracy*. Although Hereth is mainly concerned with the process of democratization in America and France, he is sensitive to how

---

[7] Seymour Drescher, *Dilemmas of Democracy: Tocqueville and Modernization* (Pittsburgh: University of Pittsburgh Press, 1968), 15.

Tocqueville's writings on America are inextricably linked, for example, to problems of imperialism, colonialism, and slavery – all noteworthy themes in the present volume. Hereth's study of Tocqueville the "political man" demonstrates that the latter's flirtations with nationalism, a militaristic foreign policy, the subjugation of the Algerians, and the replacement of chattel slavery in French colonies with a "new aristocracy" are all premised on a "claim to domination and leadership by Europeans over people who have not been stamped with European-Atlantic civilization."[8]

Tocqueville's controversial endorsement of empire has been well known at least since the publication of André Jardin and Melvin Richter's seminal articles in 1962 and 1965, respectively; however, the subject has come front and center in mainstream Tocqueville scholarship only in the past decade or so with the appearance of Jennifer Pitts's translation of Tocqueville's *Writings on Empire and Slavery* in 2001, as well as sustained engagement with Tocqueville's imperialism (and the apparent contradiction it poses to his liberalism) by Richter, Pitts, Tzvetan Todorov, Cheryl Welch, Roger Boesche, and others.[9] Despite the newfound attention to these themes, enduring dilemmas remain – for example, whether Tocqueville's imperialism and liberalism are compatible, and if so, on what metric; how the Algerian question relates to broader views on the civilizational vocation of European nations; and how his imperialism springs from deep reservations about bourgeois or commercial society. These themes are well covered in the present volume.

Maybe the most explicit attempt to reckon with Tocqueville's insights into the challenges of democratization was the *Journal of Democracy*'s tenth anniversary symposium on "Democracy in the World: Tocqueville Reconsidered," published in January 2000, in which a number of eminent scholars reflected on Tocqueville's implications for understanding the fall of communism, U.S. foreign policy, the uneven path of economic

[8] Michael Hereth, *Alexis de Tocqueville: Threats to Freedom in a Democracy* (Durham: Duke University Press, 1986 [1979]), 130–165.
[9] André Jardin, "Tocqueville et l'Algérie," *Revue des Travaux de l'Académie des sciences morales et politiques* 115 (1962), 61–74; Melvin Richter, "Tocqueville on Algeria," *Review of Politics* 25 (1963), 365–399; Tzvetan Todorov, *On Human Diversity: Nationalism, Racism, and Exoticism in French Thought* (Cambridge, MA: Harvard University Press, 1998); Alexis de Tocqueville, *Writings on Empire and Slavery*, edited and translated by Jennifer Pitts (Baltimore: Johns Hopkins University Press, 2001); Pitts, *A Turn to Empire: The Rise of Imperial Liberalism in Britain and France* (Princeton: Princeton University Press, 2006); Cheryl B. Welch, "Colonial Violence and the Rhetoric of Evasion: Tocqueville on Algeria," *Political Theory* 31 (2003), 235–264; Roger Boesche, "The Dark Side of Tocqueville: On War and Empire," *Review of Politics* 67 (2005): 737–752.

development in the contemporary world, the challenges of economic inequalities for sustaining democratic governance, as well of some of the side effects of democracy and economic prosperity on culture, manners, and society.[10]

Although this symposium's distinguished contributors brought Tocqueville to bear on many a twenty-first-century concern – exploring, among other topics, the problem of executive power in Russia, the nature and prospects for democracy in Latin America, and European federalism – the world seems to have changed profoundly since its appearance. Problems scarcely visible at the turn of the millennium have emerged in the meantime. For example, are there unique challenges presented by the spread of democracy to non-Christian or non-Western parts of the world? If, as Francis Fukuyama suggests in his contribution to the *Journal of Democracy* symposium, Tocqueville sees the March of Equality as providential or divinely ordained, does its purview extend into the non-Christian world? And if the spread of self-government presupposes an underlying democratic culture supportive of the value of equality, then what about parts of the world in which aristocratic values are deeply entrenched, as in the Middle East, or are in the process of being established by the extreme inequalities of globalization, as in many parts of Asia?

Some of these issues are posed directly and fruitfully in the recent edited collection, *Conversations with Tocqueville: The Global Democratic Revolution and the Twenty-First Century*.[11] In this timely set of essays, the editors Aurelian Craiutu and Sheldon Gellar lay out a stimulating framework for what they term "Tocquevillean analytics," which various experts then apply to different nations, regions, or historical periods. Individual Tocquevillean studies of Russia, Guatemala, Latin America, Western Europe, Africa, Burma, China, and Japan are illuminating, but the volume's major conceptual innovations are developed by the coeditors in their chapters on "Tocquevillean Analytics and the Global Revolution" (Gellar) and "What Kind of Social Scientist was Tocqueville?" (Craiutu). Responding to criticisms of Tocqueville as a crude or unsystematic social scientist, Craiutu mounts a persuasive defense of Tocqueville's coherence, distancing himself from recent characterizations of Tocqueville's social

---

[10] Marc Plattner and Larry Diamond (eds.), "Democracy in the World: Tocqueville Reconsidered," *Journal of Democracy* 11 (January 2000).
[11] Aurelian Craiutu and Sheldon Gellar (eds.), *Conversations with Tocqueville: The Global Democratic Revolution in the Twenty-First Century* (Lanham, MD: Lexington Books, 2009).

science as a precursor to ostensibly more sophisticated positive theories.[12] And as Gellar points out in his helpful "checklist" for a Tocquevillean analytics, there is indeed a discernible method at work.

Building on themes broached by Drescher, Hereth, Richter, and others – and in broad sympathy with Craiutu and Gellar – the present volume's approach is nevertheless distinctive. Rather than assuming that Tocqueville offers a single, systematic, and readily identifiable framework for making sense of the process of democratization, our contributors are engaged in a more open-ended dialogue about Tocqueville's relevance. There are profound disagreements about what a "Tocquevillean approach" looks like, the degree and sincerity of Tocqueville's support for democracy, and the relative optimism or pessimism of his conclusions. Authors begin with an even more elementary set of questions. What does Tocqueville mean by "democracy," and how does his unique (and arguably somewhat idiosyncratic) take on the process of democratization relate to the processes of globalization underway in the contemporary world? Which of his categories, themes, and insights seem to apply especially well? Which not so well? It is often assumed that democracy unfolds within the context of Westphalian nation-states, but how might Tocqueville's account of democratization problematize the very notion of nationality and national borders, eliding the usual frontiers of democracy? Are the obligations of democratic nations the same within their borders as across them? And if culture, tradition, and religion all matter in the process of democratization, is it fair to conclude that the propagation of democracy is culture-bound, limited by the frontiers of the Occidental or developed world? We submit that Tocqueville's writings offer fresh insights into these and other issues of pressing interest to citizens, scholars, and policy makers.

The Meaning of Democracy and the Democratic Revolution

Pundits and political scientists speak approvingly of democracy and applaud its spread throughout the contemporary world. Western observers cheer developments of the past four decades in the former Soviet

---

[12] See, for example, Jon Elster, *Alexis de Tocqueville, The First Social Scientist* (Cambridge: Cambridge University Press, 2009), and Richard Swedberg, *Tocqueville's Political Economy* (Princeton: Princeton University Press, 2009). For an earlier and very different normative account of what a Tocquevillean political science might look like, see especially James W. Ceaser, *Liberal Democracy and Political Science* (Baltimore: Johns Hopkins University Press, 1990).

Union, Eastern Europe, Asia, and the Middle East. However, one need not scratch too deeply beneath the surface of the rhetoric of democratization to find basic conceptual ambiguities. What does democracy really mean? In the strict sense of the term, democracy as a political system obviously has something to do with free and fair elections. Democracy allows the popular will to shape public policy, giving ordinary citizens a say in choosing their own governors. And yet above and beyond the formal requirement that a democratic regime must stand for reelection, calls for democracy today seem to be aimed more broadly at the equitable distribution of a society's resources, offices, and opportunities. In this expansive sense of the term, democracy is juxtaposed to various species of authoritarianism, oligarchy, kleptocracy, political oppression, corruption, monopoly, exclusion, and inequality.

Tocqueville's thoughts are generally congruent with contemporary expectations about democracy or democratization, but his own understanding is nuanced. Democracy may be first and foremost political – having to do with institutional questions of political participation, voting, representation, and civic engagement. However, more fundamentally, democracy for Tocqueville refers to a uniquely modern *état social*, or social condition, distinguished as much by its moral, social, economic, or even phenomenological dimensions.

As Nestor Capdevila explains in Chapter 1, Tocqueville initially defines democracy over and against its historical antecedent aristocracy. And yet as Capdevila points out, this "external frontier" between democracy and other regimes is necessarily hazy to the point of being "metaphorical." Rather than clear-cut boundaries, democracy is characterized by a kind of hybridity. The line separating democracy as a social condition from socialism, liberalism, capitalism, or even despotism is ambiguous. One can speak of social democracy, liberal democracy, democratic despotism, authoritarian democracy, and so forth. The sense of equality at the heart of democracy is compatible with many regimes, both liberal and illiberal. What is more, the struggle to define democracy is also a political struggle internal to democracy – a contest between "different understandings of the democratic present" and of what it means to be democratic (p. 33). Although by contrasting democracy with revolution, Tocqueville sought to define democracy in a way that would exclude radicalism, his analysis suggests that contesting democracy's meaning is essential to the dynamism of democratic society. For Tocqueville, then, it remains an open question as to which understanding of democracy will ultimately prevail. This explains the "essential indeterminacy" of democracy's providential movement through the world (p. 52). Will we enjoy equality under liberty, or suffer equality combined with servitude?

Tocqueville accepts democracy, yet he insists on maintaining a conceptual distinction between democracy and revolution. The notion of a perfect democracy is revolutionary and must be resisted as such. Here Capdevila captures the elusive reality that democracy's purview must always be limited: "democratic discourse is universal: all human beings are equal. But there are always some inequalities remaining" (pp. 43–44). Within a political community, for example, "internal" distinctions of gender, race, family, profession, or social class may cease to be relevant in some contexts, but they do not as a consequence disappear. Analogously, democracy as an "external" concept contains within itself an immanent universalism that is necessarily incomplete. Presumably democracy unfolds on the world stage – cutting across traditional frontiers among nations, civilizations, or religions. Again, however, these frontiers – while blurred or breached – do not vanish, and Tocqueville clearly supposes that the struggle for democracy takes place within the porous borders of discrete political communities.

While agreeing with Capdevila about the difficulty of drawing a bright line between democracy and aristocracy, Ran Halévi argues in Chapter 2, that Tocqueville's fundamental orientation – both personal and political – rests on his conviction that aristocracy as a social system was destined to give way to democratic equality. The frontier between these two social worlds is near-absolute, and the liminal passage between them is permanent and conclusive. Once a people crosses the democratic Rubicon, there is no turning back. Erstwhile aristocratic institutions such as lawyers, juries, civic associations, or even wealthy industrialists may perform quasi-aristocratic functions, as Tocqueville suggests, but they have nothing to do with a true aristocracy. Interpreters have repeatedly – and incorrectly, in Halévi's view – sought to paint Tocqueville as a nostalgic aristocrat. In reality, Tocqueville sees the French Revolution as marking a clear delineation between an irretrievable past and a dawning democratic age.

Several implications would seem to follow from Halévi's thesis. First, if the social and political frontier between aristocracy and democracy marks a historical turning point, and, moreover, if democracy demands a congruence between social conditions and political institutions once this frontier has been crossed, then it seems to follow that societies steeped in inegalitarian traditions face difficult transitions to a democratic future.

If laws cannot remake mores, or can do so only imperfectly, as Halévi argues following both Montesquieu and Tocqueville, then one wonders if democracy as a political system is a realistic possibility for nations whose social lives remain profoundly undemocratic. As Halévi points out, the Bourbon Restoration and July Monarchy both failed because they rested on unstable juxtapositions of civil equality and aristocratic political institutions. One might argue that democratic institutions today suffer from a similar instability. At a minimum, democratic revolutions face an uphill battle – one that is resisted, frustrated, and thwarted at every turn and is prone to further revolutions and violence – when democratic political institutions outstrip the underlying equality of conditions that would support them.

On a more optimistic note, Halévi emphasizes that because the origins of aristocratic society are anything but natural, they require psychological acceptance on the part of the ruled. Although originally born of force or conquest, "aristocratic rule, enjoying the tacit consent of the people" must be represented as "the natural order of things" to maintain authority (p. 66). The "distinctive constituents" of an aristocracy are force and landed property, on which inequalities of birth, wealth, and enlightenment are subsequently established. Absent such an authentic aristocracy, the last vestige of support for inegalitarian political orders is the threadbare illusion that domination is somehow natural or God-given. This mythical legitimacy rapidly evaporates in the face of new technology, the experience of other neighboring nations, and the dawning notion of equality. The near-simultaneous passing of this illusion in so many parts of the world today may be precisely what Tocqueville had in mind when he spoke of democracy as providential. Much to the consternation of despots, the jinni of democratic equality will not go back in the bottle.

Revolutions are the most identifiable symbols of democratization. Revolutions underscore a rupture – often violent, bloody, and painful – between disparate regimes, time periods, and ways of life. It is only a slight exaggeration to say that history itself is composed of revolutions, with the otherwise inconspicuous passage of time punctuated by key dates and eras such as 1688, 1776, 1789, 1918, 1989, prerevolutionary, postrevolutionary, antebellum, and so forth. Describing those exceptional moments when a new nation is born, Tocqueville (perhaps thinking as much of France as America) saw in them the whole physiognomy of the future. "Peoples always bear some marks of their origin," Tocqueville keenly observes, and these "circumstances of birth and growth affect all the rest of their careers."[13]

Paradoxically, however, in *Democracy* as well as the *Old Regime*, Tocqueville stresses how nations and national character resist even the most concerted efforts of revolutionaries, founders, and political innovators to change the course of a nation. Much to their surprise, readers of the *Old Regime* learn that many of the characteristics the French have mistakenly attributed to the Revolution of 1789 actually date back to the periods of Bourbon centralization. And in the previously cited passage from *Democracy in America*, it is revealing that Tocqueville implicitly dates the founding of the American regime not to the epochal political events of 1776 or 1787 to 1789 but rather to the original colonial settlement.

The eyes of historians and political scientists may be drawn to symbolic events such as the Boston Tea Party, the storming of the Bastille, the fall of the Berlin Wall, or the demolition of statues of Saddam Hussein, but the real work of democratic revolution goes on silently and incrementally for decades if not centuries. This aspect of Tocqueville would caution us to be sober in our emphasis on the decisiveness of "democratic revolutions." If Tocqueville is to be believed, the widely publicized visions of Orange, Jasmine, or Twitter Revolutions as the apotheosis of democracy may be will-o'-the-wisps, drawing the eyes of even the most careful observers away from democracy's more prosaic development.

And yet whatever their real impact, as Ralph Lerner ably demonstrates in Chapter 3, the eyes of historians and political thinkers are nonetheless captivated by precisely such revolutionary dramas. Whether they are ultimately causes or effects, revolutions do serve to symbolize the profound social and political changes that have given us the modern world. In his appreciation of the symbolic importance of revolutions, Tocqueville seeks, even sometimes disingenuously, to draw our attention to a stylized version of the historical record most edifying for the future. Revolutions – rightly understood – can showcase a nation at its best.

Lerner begins by observing that the disagreement between Tocqueville and Burke over the French Revolution is unexpected. There was "much in Burke's moral taste that would have appealed to Tocqueville's humane liberalism" (p. 78). These two great political minds are both critical of

---

[13] DIA (L) I.1.ii, 31.

revolutionary excesses, of the dilettantism, immoderation, and irreligion of the revolutionaries. And yet Tocqueville stops just short of savagery in his criticism of Burke's alleged errors and misunderstandings. How can this be? Do the two really disagree that fundamentally about the record? As Lerner suggests, it is Tocqueville's artful attempt to make the French past inspiring for the future – more than any disagreement over the historical facts, or ideological antipathy between Burke and Tocqueville – that explains the peculiar dialogue between the latter and former. In Lerner's words, Tocqueville's retelling was meant "to unearth and salvage those possibly redeeming moments, casting them not as a history but as a story" (p. 82).

Insofar as the circumstances of an historical founding have a bearing both on our present self-understanding and future political possibilities, then how we understand our history cannot be a matter of indifference. This is especially true if Tocqueville is right about the tendencies of democracies to lose touch with the past. As Lerner notes, particularly in revolutionary times, a nation "needs a story reaffirming its worth by helping it distinguish whatever is substantial and enduring in its sense of peoplehood from the accidental and transient events that fill its everyday horizon and distort its vision of itself" (p. 86). Democratic revolutions, then, are moments pregnant not just with occasions for drafting new constitutions or fundamental laws but with the more fundamental opportunity to author an enduring, and potentially inspiring, image of the nation itself.

Democratization in a Non-Western Context

Along with Montesquieu, who influenced him so profoundly, Tocqueville is often credited as one of the founders of modern political sociology.[14] Central to this enterprise is his insight into the role of what he calls "circumstances, laws, and mores" in facilitating democracy. American democracy was made viable by its auspicious geographic and geopolitical situation; by the fact that Americans left behind the feudal baggage that plagued European society; and, maybe most importantly, by the mores and practical experience of liberty that the Anglo-Americans brought

---

[14] Raymond Aron, *Main Currents in Sociological Thought*. 2 vols. (New York: Anchor Doubleday, 1968); Robert Nisbet, *The Sociological Tradition* (New York: Heinemann, 1966); Irving Louis Horowitz, *Behemoth: Main Currents in the History and Theory of Political Sociology* (New Brunswick, NJ: Transaction Publishers, 1999).

along with them to the new world. The flip side of this observation, however, is pessimism for other nations less fortunate.

As Tocqueville notes in an early foray into comparative political sociology, the nations of Latin America enjoyed many of the same geographical advantages as the Anglo-Americans. They even went so far as to copy the political constitution and laws of the American regime.[15] Given these constants of circumstances and laws, then, what explains the fact that democracy in North America thrives while it languished in other parts of the world? The answer for Tocqueville lay in the ineffable quality of American mores, or what sometimes goes by the term *national character* – easy to identify but difficult if not impossible to transplant or replicate.

Indeed, for much of the rest of the globe in Tocqueville's day – particularly his native France – circumstances, laws, and mores looked more like hurdles than handrails for democratic self-government. The significance of Tocquevillean habits and institutions has not been lost on contemporary social scientists such as Robert Putnam, Francis Fukuyama, Ernest Gellner, and countless others who have identified civic engagement, local liberties, moral rectitude, social capital, and trust as preconditions both for good governance and economic development.[16] For example, Putnam's influential comparative work on variations between Northern and Southern Italy demonstrates not only the ways in which cultural differences act as constraints on civic capabilities but also, and more optimistically, how mores and civic habits can themselves be reshaped gradually in the face of more democratic political institutions. Likewise for Fukuyama, trust – both in other people and in political institutions – proves to be a decisive factor in economic development and the well-functioning of liberal democratic institutions.

Assuming neo-Tocquevilleans are correct about the advantages conferred by a healthy civil society, it remains difficult to assess whether this ultimately bodes well or ill for democratization in the contemporary world. The obverse and more pessimistic version of the claim sticks out uncomfortably. That is, if civil society is indeed the most decisive variable, then what are the prospects for nations in Central and Eastern Europe whose indigenous civil societies were suppressed or destroyed by

15 DIA (L) I.1.viii, 165.
16 Some of the most influential recent expressions of the social capital argument include Robert Putnam, *Making Democracy Work: Civic Traditions in Modern Italy* (Princeton: Princeton University Press, 1993); Francis Fukuyama, *Trust: The Social Virtues and the Creation of Prosperity* (New York: Free Press, 1995); and Ernest Gellner, *Conditions of Liberty: Civil Society and its Rivals* (New York: Viking, 1994).

decades of Communist rule?[17] What about nations in the Middle East
or Africa that suffered under centuries of colonial domination followed
by decades of indigenous authoritarianism? Tocqueville himself seemed
to believe that democracy was fated for nations that were part of the
Christian, Western world, but what does this mean for non-Western or
non-Christian nations?

Within the broader categories of laws, circumstances, and mores identified earlier, Tocqueville singles out religion as an especially powerful
source of mores and a reliable grounding – at least in the American
case – for the transition to democracy. He was certainly aware that
Catholicism formed one of the galvanizing points of reaction against
the rising tide of democracy in the eighteenth and nineteenth centuries,
but even these manifestations seemed unwittingly to have hastened –
rather than thwarted – democracy's providential march throughout the
world.[18] Regardless of the political postures of its adherents, Christianity,
in Tocqueville's view, has a fundamental affinity for democratic values
of equality, moderation, compassion, and universality. All of the "Christian nations of our day," Tocqueville specified, are moving more or less
quickly toward democracy.[19] But the unstated flip side of this formulation seems to be that non-Christian nations will have greater difficulty in
adopting a democratic social condition and political system. Is this really
the case?

A fruitful starting point for gauging democracy's prospects in the non-
Christian world is Tocqueville's probing assessment of Islam, Hinduism,
and other world religions. As Alan Kahan reveals in Chapter 4, Tocqueville was fascinated by Islam and Hinduism. He read carefully the
major theological texts of these non-Western religions and reckoned with
their similarities and dissimilarities to Christianity. Rather than indulging
a purely philosophical or theological curiosity, however, these efforts are
politically inspired. Kahan explains that Tocqueville took an interest in
the teachings of Islam in the context of the French colonial project in Algeria, and likewise his study of Hinduism was informed by the question of
British colonialism in India. As Kahan suggests, Tocqueville's considerations fall broadly under three headings: namely, the connection between

---

[17] For an assessment of this difficulty, see especially Marc Morjé Howard, *The Weakness
of Civil Society in Post-Communist Europe* (Cambridge: Cambridge University Press,
2003).
[18] DIA (L) Introduction, 10–14, 17.
[19] DIA (L) Introduction, 12.

religion and materialism, the psychological relationship between religion and liberty, and links between religion and the state.

Without discounting Tocqueville's skepticism about Islam, Kahan makes a finer distinction: many of the problems Tocqueville identified with Islam are contingent rather than essential. Islam's core values overlap with salutary Christian ideals of charity, justice, equality, and a moderate acceptance of materialism. The stumbling block is Islam's conflation of sacred and civil law. This more than anything else informed Tocqueville's conviction that Islam was not likely to be a fruitful soil for liberty. And yet, as Kahan reminds us, this political objection to Islam is a generic problem that Tocqueville had identified in earlier iterations of Christianity, including French Catholicism. Thus it seems entirely possible that a reformed Islam, one which allows for a "separation of mosque and state," could be conducive to liberal democracy (p. 103).

Hinduism is another story. Hinduism, on Tocqueville's reading, is necessarily an aristocratic, or rather pseudo-aristocratic, religion that is poorly suited to address the needs of modern democratic society. The problem is Hinduism's connection to the caste system. Unlike other world religions such as Islam that are compatible with the democratic value of equality, Hinduism simply does not allow for the fundamental equality of all human beings. Because of this, according to Tocqueville, it was not likely to prove compatible either with democratic equality or political liberty.

In hindsight, Tocqueville's dismissal of the prospects for what is now the world's largest democracy appears spectacularly wrongheaded. Yet in fairness, as Kahan argues, Tocqueville's point is actually more nuanced. Notwithstanding his views on the incompatibility of Hinduism and democracy, he was remarkably upbeat about the fate of India itself, observing with approval some of the earliest efforts at revolt against British colonial rule (p. 108). In his view, the prospects for democracy in India existed despite Hinduism, and not because of it. India's democratic future hinged more on what the Indians could derive from the British rather than any indigenous Hindu resources.

Tocqueville's thoughts about the world religions are fascinating and instructive. But the danger is that considering only what Tocqueville thought or wrote – correctly or mistakenly – about Islam or Hinduism may end up telling us more about Tocqueville's prejudices than the prospects for democracy in the twenty-first century. Cognizant of this difficulty, Kahan wisely guides us beyond Tocqueville's doctrinal commentary and toward the deeper affinities of these political theologies for structural factors such as materialism, secularism, law, the state, education, tradition, and economic development.

In Chapter 5, Cheryl Welch tackles the question of how these and other independent variables operate in a non-Western context. In a wide-ranging survey of the literature on democratic development in East Asia, Welch documents how scholars in other disciplines have drawn – sometimes unwittingly – upon Tocquevillean concepts and categories. One of the most consistent themes in recent literature on East Asian politics, as Welch notes, is a "sensitivity to how moeurs change, persist or resurface in new guises, and especially to how they relate to the changing role of the state in different societies" (p. 117). Just as Tocqueville was concerned to highlight the ways in which American mores underpinned its success with democracy, so too East Asian scholars have discovered a wide range of Tocquevillean affinities between Confucianism and liberal democracy.

As Welch cautions, however, there is a danger in importing unreflectively Tocquevillean categories to the East Asian context – assuming, for example, that civil society will operate the same way vis-a-vis the state, or that it must be composed of the same kinds of institutions and actors as in the United States or Western Europe. One of the most important take-away points of Welch's chapter is that despite a number of remarkable overlaps, we cannot expect to apply rigidly Tocqueville's blueprint for democratization to the non-Western world. Just as institutions and laws cannot be blindly copied, Tocqueville's method also needs to be adjusted to fit different cultural circumstances. What is required is a more richly imaginative way of understanding Tocqueville's relevance. Suggestively responding to this difficulty, Welch unearths deeper rhetorical commonalities between Western and East Asian approaches to democratization: namely, a recourse to "human exemplars" as a way of destabilizing settled beliefs, the use of "just so" counter-narratives to instill confidence in the possibilities of democratization, and an appeal to the family as a way of assuaging concerns about rapid social change (p. 124).

In some of the most famous passages of *Democracy in America*, Tocqueville credits the Enlightenment of the New England Puritans with setting the tone for democracy in America. The Puritan emphasis on literacy and education – both primary and secondary – did much to foster an enlightened, virtuous, and critical citizenry. Tocqueville was notoriously silent about the role of higher education in America – arguably one of his greatest lacunae, given the quasi-aristocratic excellence of the American university system – but he did see "educating democracy" to be of central importance.

Assuming this connection between education and democracy, as Joshua Mitchell argues in Chapter 6, we can learn much about the prospects for democracy in the Middle East from recent efforts to establish American-style universities. Mitchell's firsthand glimpse into the workings of universities in Qatar and Iraq underscores several Tocquevillean themes. For example, attitudes toward democracy are deeply intertwined with beliefs about status, honor, and tradition. Democracy demands that institutions of higher education remain independent of political forces within the state or civil society that would capture them and transform the dispassionate search for truth into the mere propagation of ideology. And beyond the walls of the university, the success of democracy in the Middle East hinges not just on diffusing ideas about human rights or establishing free markets but even more fundamentally on fostering newly democratic attitudes about honor, family, dependency, hierarchy, entrepreneurship, and economic competition.

In Mitchell's view, the contemporary Middle East faces a dire predicament. Younger generations are on the verge of becoming "delinked" from traditional ways of life. Westernization has delivered all the fruits of technology, wealth, and the information age to their doorstep. As Mitchell notes, "They are haunted by this fact, and see in America the specter of the complete delinkage they fear, quite irrespective of whether they detest American foreign policy or embrace it" (p. 136). And yet Mitchell's pessimistic conclusion is that notwithstanding this delinkage, nations in the Middle East remain so steeped in tradition, hierarchy, patronage, and clientelism that the process of market capitalism – which requires the widespread acceptance of individualistic values – cannot take root. The dilemma he sketches allows for no easy resolution. Delinking is necessary if these nations are to become fully democratic and integrated into the world economy, and yet this very process is existentially disruptive, and threatens to give rise to what Mitchell calls "re-enchantment movements" (p. 150).

The Challenges of Globalization: Markets, Nationhood, and Democracy

We have already distinguished between political democratization – or the rise of representative political institutions – and the broader sense of democracy as a "social condition" characterized by commercial prosperity, economic mobility, and the widespread diffusion of wealth. As we have suggested, Tocqueville sees these two thrusts of democracy to be related but by no means necessarily connected to one another. Indeed one of the consistent themes of his writings on both America and Europe is the compatibility of economic prosperity with political servitude.

This distinction is important to keep in mind because the contemporary world is conspicuous for the divergence between political and economic freedom, an apparent disconnect between the liberalization of markets and the democratization of political institutions. Notwithstanding the beautiful dreams of eighteenth-century philosophers such as Montesquieu, Thomas Paine, Adam Smith, and David Hume or the prognostications of modernization theorists of the twentieth century, the propagation of free markets has, at least so far, failed in many instances to yield political democracy.[20] Many nations in Asia and the Middle East have proven that economic development can thrive amidst political repression. Moreover, whether true or false, one of the main allegations against the globalizing force of capitalism is that its effects are notoriously uneven, aggravating rather than alleviating the miseries of the developing world while increasing the prosperity of multinational corporations or wealthy nations that are in a position to take advantage of disparities.

Terms such as *globalization, economic development, modernization,* or the Fukuyaman vision of liberal democracy's triumph at the "end of history" obscure the fact that the spread of free markets is not a sufficient condition for the growth of political democracy. China, Singapore, Russia, Saudi Arabia, Qatar and the Emirates, Chile, and many other nations managed at various periods of the twentieth century to generate substantial economic growth and affluence for at least some of their citizens without giving rise to full-blown political democracy. What, then, is the connection – if any – between capitalism and political democracy? And what is the relationship between that providential march of democracy described by Tocqueville and the phenomenon that passes today under the label of globalization? Can Tocqueville's treatment of the former tell us anything useful about the latter?

In Chapter 7, Susan McWilliams wrestles with this question of the relationship between Tocquevillean democracy and globalization, highlighting the contradictory paths taken by contemporary trends. At first glance, Tocqueville would seem to be less preoccupied with the

---

[20] On this commercial republican vision of commerce "softening" or "polishing" mores and giving rise to civilization and liberty, see especially Albert Hirschman, *The Passions and the Interests: Political Arguments for Capitalism before its Triumph* (Princeton: Princeton University Press, 1977).

phenomenon of globalization than, say, Karl Marx or Max Weber. Yet McWilliams takes note of many similarities between the universalizing movement he calls democracy and the contemporary phenomenon of globalization. Both tend, as we have seen previously, to diminish the significance of traditional boundaries and borders. The twenty-first century is characterized by unprecedented mobility.[21] Frontiers vanish, and traditional borders either disappear altogether or are easily crossed. The scale of economic and political life rapidly expands, and we gain the possibility of living and acting politically in a truly boundless fashion.

While this globalized village may seem auspicious for human freedom, McWilliams sees a problem. As Mitchell also appreciates, this new world order is psychologically, spiritually, and existentially unsettling. Exponentially increasing the scale and rapidity of contemporary political life generates anxiety, dissatisfaction, fear, and ultimately a longing for new sources of authority. "Because those feelings of anxiety are awful if not unbearable, people in conditions of relative borderlessness will yearn for some orienting principle or authority in their lives," McWilliams worries (p. 155). Tragically, one logical outcome of the democratic pursuit of boundlessness is an eventual retreat toward new incarnations of authority; global citizens crave new masters and, ironically, hasten to throw up boundaries.

One of the key empirical questions for our own day is whether the rise of global markets and an international juridico-political order is destined to sweep away national borders and the distinctiveness of nationhood. Whether as hope or as fear, for many, globalization spells cosmopolitanism. And here again Tocqueville's writings demonstrate both the complexity of the question and the naivety of cosmopolitans who assume that national borders and nation-states are destined to evaporate in the face of global markets. As Ewa Atanassow argues in Chapter 8, the phenomenon of globalization is dialectical and cuts in two apparently opposed directions. On the one hand, the forces of globalization do seem destined to undermine differences within nations. Democratic modernity "tends toward universality and growing interdependence between various parts of the world that lay bare 'for the first time' one unified humanity" (p. 179). On the other hand, however, "the coming together of diverse cultures and forms of life leads to affirmation of local specificity and resurgence of particularism" (p. 179). As a consequence of

---

[21] See, for example, Seyla Benhabib, *The Rights of Others: Aliens, Residents, and Citizens* (Cambridge: Cambridge University Press, 2004).

globalization, individuals and cultures become superficially more alike. And yet this very likeness, and the increased contact and interdependence between different ways of life, provoke questions of identity and self-definition and therewith the desire to become more, and not less, distinctive. Rather than being atavisms of the nineteenth century, condemned to be swept away, nationality, nationalism, and national pride are part and parcel of the process of democratization, and thus are likely to persist in the globalizing world.

Atanassow's argument – following Tocqueville – is that this is not only a sociological reality but also a consequence of the naturalness of honor and pride to the human soul. Honor is not just a peculiarity of feudal aristocracy, but an inherent feature of all societies. For Tocqueville, honor is the moral bond that holds society together and constitutes its cultural identity. Whereas aristocracy fixed social identities once and for all and assigned distinct roles in society, democracy throws everything into flux and casts doubt on social identities. Under these conditions, the nation stands as the sole moral horizon and source of cultural distinctiveness. Hence the freer democratic citizens become from the bonds of social memberships, the more likely they are to turn to nationalism as a form of cultural and political self-affirmation. "As the frontiers between classes blur, those between nations crystallize" (p. 182). Linking together Tocqueville's thoughts on the predicament of the Native Americans in the face of European colonization with his observations about the sources of indigenous resistance to British rule in India and French colonial rule in Algeria, Atanassow argues that the longing for national honor and cultural particularity represents a countercurrent that will frustrate the universalism of globalization in the foreseeable future.

Hardly original to the twenty-first century, questions about the relationship between polity and economy and how commerce affects civic life are timeless themes in the history of Western political thought. As Céline Spector observes in Chapter 9, Tocqueville's ambivalence about the triumph of commercial civilization stands in vivid contrast to his predecessor Montesquieu, who optimistically linked commercial civilization and moral progress. As Spector points out, Montesquieu was instrumental in repudiating notions of universal monarchy or land empire based on military conquest and therewith the traditional celebration of heroism and martial virtue. He replaced this with a modern vision of a maritime commercial empire extending across the seas, woven together by trade and animated by the pursuit of prosperity rather than glory. While in his earlier writings Tocqueville seems to have been persuaded by the latter vision, Spector shows his ambivalence toward Montesquieu – an ambivalence that prompted Tocqueville to take "Montesquieu's analysis in a new direction" (p. 215).

There are political reasons for this, of course, the key among which is Britain's evolution from a commercial empire of the kind Montesquieu advocated to a more conventional hegemony. But at least in part, Spector suggests, this change of heart stems from Tocqueville's deeper skepticism about the Montesquieuean vision of the civilizing, polishing, and enlightening attributes of commerce. Rather than viewing the softening of mores as the great virtue of a commercial society and a safeguard against the tyranny of princes, as did his eighteenth-century predecessors, Tocqueville regards the softening of mores and the dilution of honor, courage, and grandeur as a singular threat to liberty. He observes with ambivalence the fact that great revolutions – but also acts of heroism and grandeur – will become rare in the democratic age. Faced with the choice between liberty and prosperity, modern democratic citizens are likely to exchange freedom for material well-being. In this context, the political glory and honor potentially afforded by imperial conquest may serve as antidotes to the mediocrity and softness to which commerce necessarily gives rise. Once the French had embarked upon the military conquest and subjugation of the Algerian colonies, it would mark a shameful and civically destructive blow to their national ego for them to abandon their imperial project.

Democracy, Imperialism, and Foreign Policy

Tocqueville's imperialism is a complex topic that raises practical as well as ethical questions. As we have seen, Tocqueville sometimes speaks of democracy's progress as "providential" or fated. Of course, as we have also seen, spreading democracy throughout the world is in practice a politically tenuous project. However, if we accept that the transmission of democracy is at least desirable – if not altogether fated or inevitable – then what legitimate means may democratic nations bring to bear in their efforts to nudge other nations toward the blessings of liberty? Do they have the right to interfere in the sovereign affairs of other nations to help them navigate the difficult transition? Under certain extreme circumstances, such as civil war or genocide, do they have a moral obligation to do so?

Tocqueville's writings are so richly theoretical that we often forget he was a political man deeply engaged in most of the great domestic issues of his day. He was also immersed throughout his political tenure in France's foreign policy and served as foreign minister under the Second Republic.[22] As such, his diplomatic career and writings offer great insights. David Clinton argues in a fascinating reconstruction of Tocqueville's foreign policy in Chapter 10 that geopolitical circumstances – not categorical moral principles – dictate foreign policy. Rather than being governed by hard and fast rules, the question of whether nations ought to play a leading role in foreign affairs and act as "vindicators of liberty" depends on the "empire of circumstances," such as their relationship with neighbors, their internal political life, and other geopolitical factors. As Clinton points out, the "givens" of a nation's international position – whether it is effectively strapped into the "cockpit of international politics" – structure both the kind of political system it can adopt (centralized versus decentralized) and the means to which it ought to be deployed (p. 229).

We tend to assume that nations have to be actively discouraged from pursuing aggressive foreign policies and flexing their muscles on the world stage. However, Clinton's discussion of Tocqueville serves as a reminder that the mirage of isolationism must also be resisted. Sometimes nations need to take a leading role in international affairs and conduct a proactive – if not imperialistic – foreign policy. As Clinton suggests, the United States of the 1830s, with its geographical isolation and decentralized government, had the luxury of holding itself aloof from the European conflicts of its own day, but the United States in 2013 arguably shares more in common with France of the 1830s and 1840s – that is, a strong state inextricably caught up in the era's major diplomatic conflicts, and for which Tocqueville urged a vigorous and honorable international vocation.

One of the mainstays of the secondary literature on Tocqueville and the process of democratization more generally is that illiberal and exclusionary policies such as colonialism, slavery, the removal of indigenous peoples, and other forms of imperialism exist in contradiction to the general drift of democracy. As Rogers Smith, Judith Shklar, and others have argued in the case of American democracy, illiberal practices

---

[22] See, for example, Edward Gargan, *Alexis de Tocqueville: The Critical Years, 1848–1851* (Washington, DC: Catholic University Press, 1955); Mary Lawlor, *Alexis de Tocqueville in the Chamber of Deputies: His Views on Foreign and Colonial Policy* (Washington, DC: Catholic University Press, 1959); and David Clinton, *Tocqueville, Lieber, and Bagehot: Liberalism Confronts the World* (New York: Palgrave Macmillan, 2003).

such as nativism, slavery, imperialism, sexism, and racism are exceptions that prove the more general democratic rule of American political development.[23]

Nonetheless, as Jennifer Pitts suggests in Chapter 11, it may be the case that these imperialistic exclusions are actually part and parcel of the process of democratization. Pitts's analysis of Tocqueville's later correspondence on America reveals an increasingly pessimistic attitude toward democracy. In his view, the violence and incivility of American society, the degradation of its public life, rampant political corruption, and a loss of national character were effects of democracy's inability to impose sufficient internal control over its population (p. 255). Unlike his more perceptive American correspondents of the 1840s and 1850s, who blamed slavery and the power of Wall Street elites for these adverse developments, Tocqueville simply did not fathom the link between slavery and the political corruption he lamented, between inequalities of power and the disposition toward American expansionism. Rather than seeing these pathologies as arising from the undemocratic aspects of American society, Tocqueville blamed the inherently corrupting dynamic of democracy itself. "For all the subtlety of his analysis of democratic society in America and in France," Pitts notes, "as a political thinker Tocqueville was in important ways strikingly inattentive to the connections between democracy and domination, and to the dangers of empire for democracy" (p. 244).

Shifting focus from the American continent and toward France's own problematic engagement with empire in North Africa, we find that imperialism was more central to Tocqueville's political thinking than many of his interpreters have acknowledged. It is generally accepted that Tocqueville's endorsement of French colonialism in Algeria may be traced back to his nationalistic privileging of France's political interests. However, as Richard Boyd argues in Chapter 12, there is also a nostalgic component to his fascination with empire – one that sets Tocqueville at odds with many of his fellow nineteenth-century liberals. Unlike other French liberals who despised Bonaparte and abhorred the tragedies of the First Empire, Tocqueville is captivated by imperial glory. Confronting a

[23] See, for example, Rogers Smith, "Beyond Tocqueville, Myrdal, and Hartz: The Multiple Traditions in America," *American Political Science Review* 87 (1993), 549–566; and Judith Shklar, *American Citizenship: The Quest for Inclusion* (Cambridge, MA: Harvard University Press, 1991).

domestic French political scene afflicted by malaise and even decadence, empire appears "therapeutic," in Boyd's words, calculated to stimulate a sense of public involvement and civic engagement in a nation that lacks the fortuitous traditions of the Americans.

Tocqueville's defense of the conquest of Algeria has been roundly criticized both in terms of *jus ad bellum* and *jus in bello*, but it nonetheless raises hard questions about the legitimate prerogatives of liberal interventionism. Nations may need to take an active role in the world not so much for their own good as for the good of others. That such interventions are often selective or self-serving is undeniable, but the underlying moral dilemma remains. Depending on the circumstances, a thoroughgoing commitment to individual liberty and human rights could very well require abridging the collective liberty and national self-determination of other nations. In this respect, Tocqueville is open to an interventionist possibility categorically denied by classical liberals such as Benjamin Constant and Madame de Staël, not to mention by many contemporary liberals today.

Yet the dilemma is more complex still. As Tocqueville points out, the psychological well-being of nations has a major bearing on their political culture. The humiliation of being conquered cannot help but have psychic ramifications for decades if not centuries. But if Tocqueville is right that national pride and honor truly matter for politics, then what does this say about the fate of nations colonized by the West and systematically deprived of their liberty by more powerful nations? If sublime feelings of national pride and honor really do matter, then Boyd concludes that Tocqueville's empirical observations about the psychological relationship between imperial and subject nations may cut in exactly the opposite direction he intends. That is to say that there is an inherent contradiction in conquering nations to make them free.

Democracy's Old and New Frontiers

As we have seen, the project of extending democracy's frontiers into every last corner of the globe most often considers democracy's frontiers in a strictly geographical or political sense. Among the most vivid and identifiable frontiers we confront in the twenty-first century are the borders between nation-states. One of the animating convictions of this volume, however, is the notion that the frontiers of democracy may be understood in something other than a strictly geopolitical sense. Taking the metaphor of the frontiers of democracy seriously means reckoning with the passage of democracy across various historical, literary, psychological, gendered, sociological, and other social frontiers that are in their own way just as significant for the propagation of democracy.[24]

The metaphor of a frontier of democracy is appropriate given Tocqueville's well-known fascination with the American frontier of the nineteenth century. Perhaps fueled by his uncle Chateaubriand's novels about the wilds of the Americas and the kind of savage independence that prevailed there or merely by a youthful spirit of adventure, Tocqueville and Beaumont's voyage to America was centered on their desire to explore the American frontier – a difficult task, they discovered, given the rapid expansion of American civilization westward.

As Jennifer Pitts reminds us, this very same frontier was premised on the extension of the power and scope of the American state across the previously unexplored and unsettled lands of the Western territories. This project of imperial expansion and manifest destiny was fraught with contradictions, resting as it did on the forcible displacement of Native Americans and tied with attempts to expand the economic footprint of slavery beyond its traditional center in the American South. As we have seen, rather than the expansion of the American empire being at odds with various forms of exclusion, it was actually premised either explicitly or implicitly on those very same subjugations and exclusions.

At the same time, however, and more optimistically, the westward expansion of the American empire and the frontier experience served as a veritable laboratory of democracy. The frontier was a great social equalizer or leveler. As the Englishwoman Mrs. Frances Trollope complained during her roughly contemporaneous sojourn in the United States, the rough-and-ready character of the American West lent it an inherently democratic character.[25] Whether it was the democratization of public space necessitated by travel on steamboats and stagecoaches, the breakdown of formal hierarchies and manners, or the possibilities of rapid social mobility and the invention of new identities – the American frontier dissolved inherited ranks and privileges even in the face of the most concerted efforts to make them stick.

---

[24] Works exploring the passage of democracy across the frontiers of gender and the family include Laura Janara, *Democracy Growing Up: Authority, Autonomy, and Passion in Tocqueville's "Democracy in America"* (Albany: SUNY Press, 2002), and Jill Locke and Eileen Hunt Botting (eds.), *Feminist Interpretations of Alexis de Tocqueville* (University Park: Penn State University Press, 2009).

[25] Frances Trollope, *Domestic Manners of the Americans* (London: Penguin Classics, 1997).

Thus it is fitting that Robert Pippin should choose the films of John Ford as a way to examine more critically Tocqueville's thoughts on democratic equality. As he explains in Chapter 13, one of the most common criticisms of U.S. democracy is the way in which it discourages common projects and throws every individual back upon her own devices. Tocqueville alleges that it breaks down the ranks and hierarchies of traditional aristocratic orders, leading to leveling, mediocrity, and a pathological equality. However, there is a different and more optimistic way of seeing the functioning of U.S. democracy, a view that Pippin distills from *Stagecoach*. Rather than a world of anomie and social disintegration, as Tocqueville might have predicted, we find strangers from different social classes coming together under conditions of adversity to work for common goals. The frontier's dissolution of the ranks, orders, and prejudices of social class is a liberating and heartening phenomenon. Ford's film seems intended to answer affirmatively the question: "*can* such a collection of people without much of a common tradition or history, without much of what had been traditionally assumed to be the social conditions of nationhood, become in some way or other a unity capable of something greater than the sum of its parts?" (p. 298).

In contrast to what we might take to be Tocqueville's pessimism about democracy's ability to supply political unity, Ford's *Stagecoach* reveals the kind of nobility that may emerge from democratic equality.[26] Notwithstanding profound differences of social class, background, history, and regionalism, the stylized passengers in Ford's stagecoach actually manage to act honorably. Contrary to Tocqueville's dim expectations, northerners and southerners work together, bourgeois behave courageously, social classes (and the prejudices that accompany them) dissipate under the wide-open vistas of the frontier, and a common humanity is revealed by means of a new birth. We are confronted, then, with a much more optimistic view of the potentialities for democratic equality.

It is not just American film or American public space that allows us to track the progress of democracy. The very language in which a nation expresses itself may also provide glimpses into democracy's inner workings. As Paul Berman details in Chapter 14, the very activity of writing about democracy requires the invention of a wholly new and uniquely

---

[26] For a similar effort to excavate a distinctively modern version of honor and human dignity, see Sharon Krause, *Liberalism with Honor* (Cambridge, MA: Harvard University Press, 2002).

democratic form of literary expression. Taking as his starting point Tocqueville's chapter on the workings of juries in *Democracy in America*, Berman argues that Tocqueville's stylistic method is not merely beautiful – investing a seemingly dry, legalistic subject like juries with poetic brilliance – but stylistically democratic, even subversive. In contrast to the traditionally aristocratic art form of poetry as practiced in the nineteenth century by Royalists such as his uncle Chateaubriand, Tocqueville's poetic prose follows in the footsteps of stylistic innovation pioneered by the likes of the republican Victor Hugo (whose enjambed sentence scandalized his legitimist audience and provoked a riot) and polished and perfected in the American context by that great democratic poet Walt Whitman.

Berman's broader point is that democracy is something much more than a matter of political institutions. Democracy needs a language all its own, one that is fully equipped to capture democracy's inherent fluidity, transgressiveness, and agitated impatience with traditional formalities and boundaries. It must above all else be a language that is attuned to the usages of the people, a participatory language, if you will. Democratic poetry has to be able to cut across boundaries and to blur distinctions. Berman's careful dissection of Tocqueville's elegy to the U.S. jury system signals the direction such a democratic poetry might take in our own day and draws attention to that poetry of everyday life that Tocqueville so brilliantly foretold for the Americans in *Democracy*.

Berman offers a welcome redirection of the study of democratization away from politics and government and toward the grassroots forces that are woven into the fabric of everyday existence. Many discussions of democratization assume that democracy spreads nation by nation, from top to bottom. Politically speaking, it is commonplace to classify nations as either democratic or nondemocratic based on their national governments. When translated into the contemporary political world, Tocqueville's heuristic unwittingly gives way to a binary rather than seeing democratization as a more fluid Guizotian process of development. Yet as Robert Gannett appreciates in Chapter 15, this traditional view neglects the role of cities and local communities as the real laboratories of democratization. Based on his decades of experience as a community organizer in the City of Chicago, Gannett shows how democracy's metaphorical frontiers extend to regions, municipalities, and even neighborhoods within a nation. Democratization is an ongoing process that waxes and wanes, spreading at different speeds and by successive degrees of approximation through disparate groups and populations.

Gannett points out that even in ostensibly democratic nations such as the United States, urban neighborhoods are among the last true frontiers where democracy strives to be achieved by some while being suppressed by others. Rather than a settled condition or a state of being, *un état social*, democracy is also and more importantly a process – ongoing, agonistic, and confronted by perpetual forces of resistance. As Gannett reveals in his juxtaposition of the campaign strategies of Barack Obama and the inspired efforts of a neighborhood organization in Chicago to resist the vested interests of boss politics, this relationship between locality and freedom is hardly written in stone. Gannett's glimpse into the behind-the-scenes workings of Chicago politics problematizes one of Tocqueville's key assumptions: namely, that U.S. local communities stand steadfastly behind local liberties, whereas centralized national governments are potentially at odds with them. As in Tocqueville's own vision of the nineteenth century, neighbors struggle to advance the cause of local liberties and participatory democracy in the face of bureaucracy, whether that centralized state is found in Washington, DC or the local governments of Chicago or Springfield, Illinois.

Conclusion

Several key thematic conclusions emerge from Tocqueville's wide-ranging contribution to our understanding of the frontiers of democracy. First, there is the decisive empirical question of just how deeply circumstances and mores – the givens of political life – constrain our ability to stretch the frontiers of democracy. On this particular score there seem to be two very different lines of Tocquevillean thinking. On the one hand, as our contributors have ably demonstrated, and for better or worse, circumstances and mores function as anchor points for democratic possibilities. Absent the support of religion, habits of civic association, and the actual experience of local liberties, the transition to democracy in many parts of the world is likely to be tempestuous and hard going. With the primacy of circumstances and mores over laws, the frontier of democracy looks impervious even to the most enlightened constitution writers and lawmakers. On the other hand, and notwithstanding these difficulties, there seems to be a common acknowledgment – on Tocqueville's part, as well as the volume's contributors' – that the transmission of democracy throughout the world is in the longer term irresistible. Whether and how it can be combined with political liberty, and in what context, nonetheless remains an open question.

The second lesson bears on the standing of sovereign states in a global system. As many of the chapters describe in great detail, Tocqueville is clearly aware of the contemporary tendency for democracy – broadly understood as the universal dissemination of equality – to erode traditional borders and weave the world together in a more uniform and integrated way. He would hardly be surprised by the adoption of various species of moral and political cosmopolitanism as the default philosophy of the twenty-first century. At the same time, however, Tocqueville is emphatic that sovereign and territorially bounded nation-states are very far from withering away. For reasons that stem from historical traditions, political expediency, and even human psychology, the nation-state is likely to remain the locus of political identification and agency for the foreseeable future. Indeed, as several contributors observe, the very same globalizing tendencies that threaten to erode traditional national borders and identities give rise – by way of response – to the resurgence of those very same identities. The problem, of course, is that while in some sense broadly democratic, neither the globalizing thesis nor its particularizing antithesis is guaranteed to be congenial to political liberty.[27]

Finally, Tocqueville's arguments offer lessons, or at least hints, for how nations already fortunate enough to enjoy the blessings of political liberty ought to relate to undemocratic or presently democratizing nations. Notwithstanding his cautionary warnings about the difficulties of transplanting democracy or creating political liberty de novo, Tocqueville still operates under the assumption that nations such as the United States or France have a vocation in the world of international relations. That this vocation, for Tocqueville himself, merges into odious nineteenth-century forms of colonialism and imperialism is regrettable, of course. However, this should not overshadow his deeper conviction that democratic nations have a role to play in disseminating the fruits of political liberty throughout the world. Inauspicious circumstances, undemocratic mores, intransigent traditions, and even the concerted political resistance of elites – all

---

[27] Although Tocqueville's view of the causes is more psychologically and sociologically nuanced, this characterization does bear a resemblance to the dialectical nature of the modern world described by Benjamin Barber in terms of "Jihad" versus "McWorld." See Barber, *Jihad vs. McWorld: How Globalism and Tribalism are Reshaping the World* (New York: Crown Books, 1995).

of these make this a project fraught with complications and uncertainty. Yet somewhere midway between a dreary sociological determinism and a naïve providential teleology, there is room for prudent political action and a new political science to rethink and expand the elusive frontiers of democracy.

PART ONE

THE MEANING OF DEMOCRACY AND THE DEMOCRATIC REVOLUTION

CHAPTER 1

Democracy and Revolution in Tocqueville: The Frontiers of Democracy

Nestor Capdevila

Tocqueville does not speak of "frontiers of democracy." So the use of this expression in reference to his work might appear arbitrary or even confusing. It seems to add the conceptual ambiguities of the notion of frontier, used in a metaphorical sense, to those of democracy. Yet it is possible to reverse this objection: the difficulties pertaining to the concept of frontier can focus our attention on an important aspect of Tocqueville's idea of democracy and help explore its complexity. This, I suggest, is precisely the case. Tocqueville's account of democracy is based on a necessarily revolutionary break with aristocracy. At the same time it reveals democracy's essential indeterminacy: Will the new democratic world be liberal, despotic, socialist? We all are, and we have to be, democrats, but we do not know exactly who we are. As democrats, we struggle against the aristocratic past but also against different understandings of the democratic present. This double conflict reveals the indeterminacy of democratic universalism. Democratic discourse is universal, but the actually existing democracy is often suspected of not being really universal.

The Idea of Frontier

How can the metaphor of the frontier illuminate this twofold struggle? In its most common and *proper* meaning, "frontier" signifies a dividing line between two countries. Beyond this line we have to speak another language, use a different currency; we cease to be citizens and become foreigners. The frontier delimits two territories and defines two identities, which are more or less modified when the frontier is displaced. The state of peace gives a kind of evidence to this line, which, when not contested, seems almost natural. Nevertheless, we know that this is not the case. Frontiers have been contested and can be contested again; they are the result of historical struggles that defined the extension and the identity of countries. Even in a state of peace the frontier is highly ambiguous. The country's different frontiers do not have exactly the same meaning: take, for example, eastern Germany and its western border during the Cold War. It is equally the case with a single frontier. Some people can cross a frontier only illegally; others, enjoying a kind of international citizenship and identity, are hardly aware of having crossed it (for instance, inside Europe). A legal border does not always correspond to a cultural or an economic one.[1] The ambiguities of the frontier show that what seems neatly delimited is subject to change and that a frontier can be contested so as to displace or even abolish it. If the frontier is a delimiting line, which does not delimit in an unambiguous and permanent way, it is possible to put the emphasis not on the line itself but on its contestability. The frontier, then, is less the line than the space where a line may be drawn and where different claims oppose each other.

What do we mean when we apply the notion of frontier to democracy? If we take its proper meaning, we distinguish neatly democracy from something else: aristocracy, revolution, socialism, totalitarianism, anarchy, and capitalism. However, once the distinction is made, we see democracy's ambiguous relation with these different others. Can we completely separate democracy from them? For instance, Tocqueville thinks that democracy needs some aristocratic elements – the power of lawyers, a senate, a certain inequality between man and woman – as well as respect for property and individual rights, market economy. He also suggests that democracy can be despotic. Others maintain that democracy is inconsistent with capitalism or despotism. The ordinary use of the notion of democracy always includes some elements that are not intrinsically democratic (e.g., inequalities of power and wealth) and that call into question the "nature" or "identity" of democracy itself. An excess of inequality threatens the equality of conditions, while socialist centralization threatens the liberty of individuals. If we believe ourselves to have a clear idea of what democracy is, we use the metaphor of the frontier in its proper sense. But if we think that its identity and meaning are unclear, the

---

[1] On the ambiguities of the idea of frontier, see Etien Balibar, *La crainte des masses. Politique et philosophie avant et après Marx* (Paris: Galilée, 1997), 131–156 and 371–395.

"metaphorical" is more appropriate. For instance, the Berlin Wall was a frontier of democracy because the legal frontier separated democracy from something else: socialism, communism, and totalitarianism. The fall of that wall displaced the frontier of democracy and extended the democratic institutions of the West to the countries of Eastern Europe. However, if we recall that the Soviet Union claimed to be democratic and to be based on "real" equality rather than a "formal" one,[2] then the wall would be a frontier of democracy in its metaphorical sense: the fault line between two claims about what constitutes "true" democracy. If we think that Soviet socialism was not of the true kind because it was not really democratic and we seek a true democracy beyond the Cold War opposition, we open a conceptual frontier of democracy, which does not simply coincide with the juridical and historical one.

American Frontier and Frontier of Democracy

Those who consider themselves as the political and theoretical heirs of Tocqueville would use the metaphor of the frontier in its proper meaning: as a line between democracy and its opposite. However, if we want to understand Tocqueville's own experience, the metaphorical is more suggestive. Tocqueville's account of the American frontier will help us to understand this experience. In his travelogue *Fortnight in the Wilderness*, Tocqueville describes his and Beaumont's journey to Saginaw, a small village at the fringe of European settlement. The two travelers wanted to see the most advanced point of civilization, where it struggles to conquer new territories and where the Americans come into contact with the native Indians and French Canadians. These three races, separated by "the profound lines that birth and opinion trace around human destiny," coexist without a "common bond."[3] The Canadian, the *bois-brûlé*, is the man of the frontier because he unites the European race and the Indian one, civilization and nature. Although he avoids drawing a line between the European and the Indian, he is nevertheless caught in the struggle between them. A rifle shot in the forest, says Tocqueville, is like "the long, fearsome war cry of civilization on the march." The American wants to push forward the dividing line between civilization and nature, while the

---

[2] B. Baïanov, Y. Oumanski, M. Chafir, *La Démocratie socialiste soviétique* (Moscow: Editions du progrès), 1969.
[3] Tocqueville, OP1, 405, 401; JA, 369, 365.

Indian resists, eagerly but hopelessly, its progress. Finally, through the French part of the Canadian's identity and the presence of the English who arm the Indians against the Americans, we perceive the rivalry of the Europeans for possession of this land. The frontier is less a line than the place where four forces struggle. Their historical struggle is framed by the larger conflict between civilization and nature.[4]

Tocqueville identifies himself with civilization when he expresses the conviction that the Indians will be destroyed. Even if he regrets it, he considers it a fact willed by God.[5] But when we consider that in the United States civilization takes the form of democracy, we perceive in the account of the Indian's experience some of Tocqueville's own feelings. In the travelogue, Tocqueville recounts being caught up in a tempest whose description symbolizes the resistance of nature to the progress of civilization. During the storm, he catches a glimpse of a praying Indian who seems to be overcome by "a superstitious terror."[6] In the introduction to *Democracy in America*, Tocqueville uses similar language to describe the process that is destroying his world. He claims to feel in its presence "a sort of *religious terror*."[7] The difference is that, while the Indian seeks divine help in the hope to reverse that process, Tocqueville seems convinced that the universality and the necessity of this evolution prove that it is willed by God.

Saginaw offers another analogy to the democratic revolution. We know that we live in a democratic world, but we do not know where we are going and what democracy will turn out to be. Tocqueville had a similar experience in the American forest. As a civilized man, he felt in it "a sort of *religious terror*." Lost in the darkness of the woods, he and Beaumont

---

[4] OP1 398, 408, 385; J 362, 371, 350. See also Ewa Atanassow, "Fortnight in the Wilderness: Tocqueville on Nature and Civilization," *Perspectives on Political Science* 35 (2006), 22–30.

[5] DIA I.2.i, 26–27; OP2, 28.

[6] OP1, 411; JA, 374.

[7] DIA, Introduction, 7. Cf. the drafts to the Introduction in which Tocqueville compares democracy or the democratic revolution to a flood (OP2, 937–938). See also his letter to his wife of May 4, 1858: "Nous faisons encore partie d'un monde qui s'en va. Une vieille famille, dans une vieille demeure de ses pères, encore entourée d'un respect traditionnel et environnée de souvenirs chers à elle et à la population qui l'environne, ce sont là des débris d'une société qui tombe en poudre et qui bientôt ne laissera point de trace. [...] Nous sommes à peine de notre temps," OC 14, 645–646; cited in "Tocqueville à travers sa correspondance familiale," in: L. Guellec, F. R. Ankersmit, A. Antoine (eds.), *Tocqueville et l'esprit de la démocratie. The Tocqueville Review / La revue Tocqueville* (Paris: Les Presses de Sciences Po, 2005), 408.

needed the guidance of an Indian to help them find their way.[8] What is the Indian's equivalent for the man who wanders in the democratic age? It is the "new science of politics" grounded in the study of American democracy. The American frontier offers an image of the frontier of democracy. Like civilization, democracy destroys its other, aristocracy. But we do not know what form democratic civilization will take. The American, the Canadian, and the English are pitted in a conflict whose outcome will determine the form of civilization's victory over nature. The same is true of democracy: will it be liberal, socialist, or despotic?

The two meanings of frontier – as a dividing line and as a place of contestation – describe the theoretical and political context of Tocqueville's *Democracy in America*. There is negative evidence of the difference between aristocracy and democracy. We see that the aristocratic world has been destroyed forever and that democracy will continue its geographical expansion. But Tocqueville seeks to know what democracy is positively. And from this point of view, what is often considered the best book on democracy is, for its author, probably a failure. The book begins with the question, "Où allons-nous?" ("Where, then, are we going?"), and ends with this confession of ignorance: "With the past no longer shedding light on the future, the mind advances in darkness."[9] In the course of the book we have learned a lot of things, but in the end we do not yet really know the most important one: What is democracy? Is democracy a new form of liberty or its negation?

From a Negative to a Positive Meaning of Democracy

The comparison with the American frontier highlights one aspect of Tocqueville's thinking that distances him from us. He is able to share the feelings of the Indian because he fears democracy. Tocqueville's book, which aims at promoting a liberal democracy, is grounded in the fear of a democratic destruction of liberty by the tyranny of the majority, or a new despotism. For us, however, since the end of the Cold War and the success of its interpretation as a conflict between democracy and totalitarianism,

---

[8] OP1, 390–392; J 355–357. Compare Beaumont's account: "On n'entre point dans ce monde nouveau sans éprouver une secrète terreur." "Nous marchions à travers les arbres de la forêt sans distinguer les traces du sentier que nous suivions sur la foi d'un sauvage (. . .); il était maître de nos existences." Gustave de Beaumont, *Marie, ou l'esclavage aux États-Unis. Tableau de moeurs américaines* (Paris: Librairie de Charles Gosselin, 1840), 169.

[9] DIA Introduction, 6; II.4.viii, 850.

the word *democracy* has lost this negative connotation.[10] Its meaning is
positive, universal. It is almost impossible for someone to say that he is
terrified by democracy and that he is not a democrat. For us, democracy
is not a flood but an order; it is not a threat to liberty but its precondition. From this point of view, Tocqueville is closer to François Guizot,
the liberal minister of the July Monarchy who compared democracy to
a "war-cry," than he is to us.[11] From a Tocquevillean point of view, it
would be possible to say that we are no longer frightened by democracy
because, ever since the end of the Cold War, democracy is positively recognized as a juridical and political order clearly distinct from revolution.
The contrast between our feelings and Tocqueville's can be expressed in
the double meaning of the idea of democratic revolution. If we put the
emphasis on revolution, this revolution is democratic because of its result:
democratic society.[12] Democracy as exemplified by the United States is
opposed to revolution as epitomized by France. However, it is also possible to consider that this revolution is democratic because it is produced
by democracy. Democracy is the subject of an ongoing, and perhaps
permanent, revolution that may threaten the most important values: liberty, property, religion, and family.[13] The first interpretation seems more
plausible today, but this was not the case in the revolutionary conjunc-
ture of the nineteenth century. For Tocqueville and Guizot, democracy
was closely linked to a revolutionary process whose end was unknown.
Democracy was frightening because it was impossible to say in advance
if the inequalities that seem to be indispensable to society would not be
destroyed by the blind quest for equality.

[10] Cf. Jacob Talmon, *The Origins of Totalitarian Democracy* (London: Secker and Warburg, 1952). The distinction, drawn by Talmon, between totalitarian and liberal democracy is more Tocquevillean than the opposition between democracy and totalitarianism
because liberty is not analytically linked to democracy.
[11] François Guizot, "De la démocratie dans les sociétés modernes, "*Revue française* 3
(1837), 197. Compare with Mazzini cited by Jens Andreas Christophersen, *The Meaning
of "Democracy" as Used in European Ideologies* (Oslo: Univesitetsforlaget, 1966), 108.
[12] DIA Notice, 400.
[13] "Does one think that after having destroyed feudalism and vanquished kings, democracy
would recoil before the bourgeoisie and the rich? Will it be stopped now that it has
become so strong and its adversaries so weak?" (DIA Introduction, 6). "En voyant
que la démocratie, après avoir détruit tous les privilèges, en était arrivée à n'avoir plus
devant elle que le privilège si ancien et si nécessaire de la propriété, j'ai pensé que, comme
l'océan, elle avait enfin trouvé son rivage. Erreur ! Il est évident aujourd'hui que le flot
continue à marcher, que la mer monte ; [. . .] mais pour arriver à quoi ? En vérité je
l'ignore et je crois que cela dépasse l'intelligence de tous," passage cited in André Jardin,
Alexis de Tocqueville, 1805–1859 (Paris: Hachette, 1984), 429.

Although we consider Tocqueville as a democrat, he does not spontaneously offer intrinsic grounds for accepting democracy. The main reason he gives is a *fact*: the impossibility of returning to aristocracy. The role of the new political science is to give the enlightened classes the power to control and instruct democracy. Sheldon Wolin suggests that this science "was intended as an antidemocratic science and to be antimodern in spirit."[14] The term *antidemocratic* is not convincing. It would be more precise to say that this science was conservative. It was not undemocratic because its defense of traditional values and advocacy of the power of superior classes had to be carried out within the framework of democracy.[15] The necessity to accept what Tocqueville spontaneously condemns and to become what he dislikes explains the particularity of Tocqueville's critique of democracy: " . . . it is because I was not an adversary of democracy that I wanted to be sincere with it."[16] Some friends can tell the truth, but here Tocqueville speaks truth to democracy because he is neither an opponent nor a friend of democracy. However, he cannot be completely outside democracy; he has to accept it. So this external critique of democracy is also an internal one. Tocqueville becomes one of these few friends who tell the truth. In his *Democracy*, Tocqueville also tells democrats a truth difficult to see and to defend openly. However, this truth can turn some opponents of democracy into "true friends." Representation, for instance, gives a political power to the people and at the same time excludes the people from the business of government. It is an acceptance of the dogma of the sovereignty of the people that can go together with a kind of hostility to, or limitation on, the power of the people.[17] On this ground an opponent of democracy, who fears the crowd like Tocqueville, can become a friend of it. In an unpublished note, Tocqueville acknowledges his own ambivalent relation to democracy,

---

[14] Sheldon Wolin, *The Presence of the Past: Essays on the State and the Constitution* (Baltimore: Johns Hopkins University Press, 1989), 71.

[15] This is probably why Wolin says that this science was not reactionary. Tocqueville could be included in the history of democratic elitism, Peter Bachrach, *The Theory of Democratic Elitism: A Critique* (Lanham, MD: University Press of America, 1980).

[16] DIA Notice, 400.

[17] In response to John Stuart Mill's 1835 review of *Democracy in America*, Tocqueville writes to Mill: "Je ne connais point d'ami de la Démocratie qui ait encore osé faire ressortir d'une manière aussi nette et aussi claire de la distinction capitale entre la *délégation* et *représentation*... Il s'agit bien moins pour les Amis de la Démocratie de trouver les moyens de faire gouverner le peuple, que de faire choisir au peuple les plus capables de gouverner et de lui donner sur ceux-là un empire assez grand pour qu'il puisse diriger l'ensemble de leur conduite et non le détail des actes ni les moyens d'exécution," LCS, 347–348.

stating that his instinct is aristocratic and that it is his reason that attaches him to democratic institutions.[18] The writing of *Democracy in America* has probably been for Tocqueville a personal transformation. His instinct, expressed in the religious terror of the Introduction, is mastered when Tocqueville understands that democracy can create a liberal order, which for him recapitulates the positive meaning of democracy.

Internal Frontier of Democracy

In his book, Tocqueville crosses the external borderline between aristocracy and democracy; however, as he remains aristocratic by instinct, the opposition between aristocracy and democracy is now expressed inside democracy and transformed into a democratic fact. When Tocqueville claims to be a friend of democracy and a democrat, another democrat may not believe him. To justify his suspicion, the opponent has to show that some of Tocqueville's analyses are made from an aristocratic point of view. Take for instance Tocqueville's idealized representation of historical aristocracy.[19] Yet it is only possible to disregard Tocqueville's democratic claim if his position is absolutely impossible to be expressed in the democratic language of equality of individuals and of the sovereignty of the people. Now, when Tocqueville published his book the use of the word *democracy* was already almost universal. The republican Laponneraye complained in 1835 that everybody claims to be a democrat, especially the enemies of democracy – the aristocrats – who want to retain what remains of their privileges.[20] This statement shows that the positive meaning of the word democracy is profoundly equivocal. Conservative, liberal, republican, socialist, communist, and anarchist positions can equally claim to be democratic. The concept of democracy is the locus of consensus and, at the same time, of political struggle between democrats about the necessity to put limits on democracy or to overcome those limits. This zone of contestation can be named the "internal frontier of democracy."

According to Tocqueville, democracy favors the use of abstract terms. When used by political opponents, these terms can become antithetical. For instance, Tocqueville distinguishes two passions for equality. In the first case, equality means that the inferiors are elevated to the rank of the

---

[18] "Mon instinct, mes opinions," OC 3:2, 87.
[19] Lucien Jaume, *Tocqueville* (Paris: Fayard, 2008), 375 and 387.
[20] Albert Laponneraye, *Mélanges d'économie sociale, de littérature et de morale*, II (Paris: Dépôt central, 1835), 177.

superiors. In the second, it means lowering the superiors to the level of the inferiors. Tocqueville does not simply distinguish between the two meanings: he brings them into opposition and champions the former against the latter. Everybody wants equality, but when dominated by the latter, "depraved taste for equality," individuals are ready to accept a master in exchange for being equal. By contrast, the first, "manly and legitimate passion for equality" reconciles equality with liberty.[21] We all feel both forms of the passion for equality, but this opposition has a political meaning. The socialist equality is an expression of the depraved passion for equality. The first passion can be that of the superior classes. The new political science allows the superior classes to take control of democracy that has been "abandoned to its savage instincts" and has acted against its real interests.[22] The bourgeoisie has elevated itself to the social level of the aristocracy, and the defeated aristocrat becomes a friend of equality when he seeks to elevate the inferiors progressively and carefully. Hence, the manly taste for equality may be the democratic expression of a very conservative position: indeed, if the raising of inferiors is slow enough, it almost amounts to stagnation.[23] However, it may also justify the acceleration of this process and, therewith, a more progressive policy. Even in this case, the more progressive position can be distinguished from another still more radical one, which could be disclaimed as an expression of the envy of the masses. What matters here is that the conceptual debate over the definition of equality and democracy is in fact a political struggle over the limits to the possible and desirable democratization of society.

Tocqueville struggles against what he considers to be a despotic democracy for the sake of a liberal one. He wants to show that the debased passion for equality is not the right way to love it. So if one wants to be a democrat, he has to love equality in the first way only. However, Tocqueville's opponent, who also claims to be a democrat, does not

---

[21] DIA I.1.iii, 52. The same idea was expressed by Disraeli in his 1835 "Vindication of English Constitution," in: *Whigs and Whiggism. Political Writings* (London: J. Murray, 1913), 228–229. Today equality is no less a contested concept: "L'égalité est en effet un concept sujet à controverses: ceux qui l'encensent et ceux qui le critiquent sont en désaccord sur ce qu'ils encensent et critiquent. Les philosophes ont en effet défendu diverses solutions, dont beaucoup sont discutées dans le présent ouvrage. Dans ces conditions ne serait-il pas sage de suivre la nouvelle mode et d'abandonner entièrement l'idéal égalitaire?" Ronald Dworkin, *La vertu souveraine* (Paris: Emile Bruylant, 2008), 44.

[22] DIA Introduction, 7.

[23] Edmund Burke, *Réflexions sur la Révolution française* (Paris: Hachette Pluriel, 1998), 74 and 215.

recognize himself in this polemical description. Rather, the possibility of a conservative implication of the manly passion for equality grounds the suspicion that this so-called lawful passion for equality cannot be the true one because it legitimizes, for a more or less long time, some essential inequalities. The violence of this internal struggle over the meaning of equality and democracy should not be underestimated. It may remain pacific, but it may also take the form of a civil war as it did in France in June 1848. With this opposition between the two passions for equality, Tocqueville interprets the political conflict between the superior and the inferior classes in the vocabulary of democracy.

At the beginning of the second volume of *Democracy in America*, Tocqueville expresses his hope that this book will appear to the reader as impartial as the first. It seems to him that his birth in an aristocratic family and in a democratic world and the use of the comparative method put him above the two opposite parties. However, his use of the concept of equality raises the question of the limits of his impartiality. According to Tocqueville, a lack of impartiality would be a personal failure.[24] This means that it would be possible to have an impartial view of what equality and democracy are. However, the opposition between the two passions for equality suggests another interpretation. The shared use of the concept of equality by the contesting parties qualifies them as members of a democratic society who can legitimately claim to be democrats. Yet, at the same time, the abstract notion of equality has opposite moral and political meanings. It becomes the place of a political struggle where the opponents confront their conceptions of the "nature" of democracy and equality. In this second understanding, the lack of impartiality is not a defect because the nature of democracy or equality is not something that is simply given and that has to be discovered but rather a historical and political construction. The proper meaning of the notion of frontier, which presupposes that we know what democracy is, gives way to the metaphorical.

The Conflict between "True" and "False" Democracy

Tocqueville offers two clear examples of a political intervention inside the concepts of equality and democracy. According to him, the inequality between master and servant is not inconsistent with democracy. In America this inequality is a temporary and reversible relationship of

---

[24] DIA Notice, 400.

dependence grounded in a contract between two individuals who recognize each other as equals.[25] Tocqueville thus instructs the conservative that, in this respect, his fear of democracy is not justified: democracy need not imply anarchy and disobedience. Nevertheless, it happens that, in the transition from aristocracy to democracy, the servants "revolt against an inferiority to which they themselves have submitted and from which they profit." They perceive a contradiction between equality and obedience because they have "a confused and incomplete image of equality."[26] If they had a distinct and complete idea of equality – in other words if they knew what equality really was – they would obey without shame. To these servants who rebel against their subordination in the name of equality, Tocqueville replies that they have all the equality to which they are entitled. The real object of their claim for more equality is something other than equality. Their contestation of obedience is not democratic but revolutionary. So what the conservative fears and the radical demands is not democracy but revolution. The same argument is used about the condition of women. When Tocqueville stresses that Americans recognize a full intellectual and moral equality between men and women, he defends this equality against the traditionalist view. At the same time, he shows that Americans maintain the exclusion of women from the political world. In this "they appear to me to have admirably understood the true notion of democratic progress."[27] To those who claim political equality in addition to the moral and intellectual one, Tocqueville replies that they have the wrong idea of democratic progress. It would be less democratic to give political equality to women than to continue to deprive them of it. Tocqueville could have said that political equality between men and women is not democracy but revolution. In a similar move, Tocqueville's claim to the right understanding of equality and democracy can of course be challenged by its opponents in a struggle that can reach a point of heresy, where one democrat denies another alleged democrat the name of democrat.[28] The difference is that Tocqueville's democratic defense of these inequalities would be rejected not as revolutionary but as aristocratic.

The grounds for this reciprocal critique are easy to understand. The democratic discourse is universal: all human beings are equal. However,

[25] DIA II.3.v
[26] DIA II.3.v, 552.
[27] DIA II.3.xii, 576.
[28] On the concept of heresy, see Nestor Capdevila, *Le concept d'idéologie* (Paris: PUF, 2004), 85–134.

there are always some inequalities remaining. So as democrats we have to speak of equality and accept some inequalities inside democracy. The gap between the universality of the concepts and their concrete use is best illustrated by Tocqueville's account of the treatment of slaves by their democratic masters. Democratic men "show a general compassion for all members of the human species." But, says Tocqueville, "the same man who is full of humanity for those like him when they are at the same time his equals becomes insensitive to their sorrows as soon as equality ceases."[29] The first sentence fits easily into the universal discourse of democracy grounded in the equality of men. The second explains the softening of manners by the equality of conditions within a state. The real object of compassion is not man as such but man as my fellow citizen and equal. So a democratic man can be gentle with his fellow-citizens and, at the same time, insensitive to the suffering of the Indians and the Blacks because they are not members of the people. Tocqueville suggests that the policy of dispossession and destruction of the Indians and of the enslavement and discrimination of Blacks is not consistent with the idea of human equality. However, he does not say that America is an aristocracy and not a democracy. He recognizes after all that the American people define their own limits and the concrete space where the general idea of equality must be applied. Democracy is the power of the people, and it is this very power that prevents equality from being extended to race relations: "as long as American democracy remains at the head of affairs, no one would dare to attempt such an undertaking, and one can foresee that the more the whites of the United States are free, the more they will seek to isolate themselves."[30] As Tocqueville adds in a footnote, slave emancipation was imposed in the British West Indies by the external authority of the mother country. The planters would not have abolished slavery had they governed themselves democratically.

Democratic Universalism

Does this interpretation of Tocqueville's argument overestimate the importance of some of his positions that, dominated by the prejudices of his time, prevent him from rigorously applying democratic principles – that is, from crossing the frontier between democracy and the aristocracy of gender, race, and class? Today we no longer say that democracy hinders the equality of gender and race. We think, on the contrary, that

---

[29] DIA II.3.i, 538.
[30] DIA I.2.x, 342 and note.

these inequalities are due to a deficit of democracy. Does this make Tocqueville's account problematic or even obsolete? This question about the theoretical value of some of Tocqueville's interventions can be answered in two ways.

First, Tocqueville shows that, although democratic man naturally speaks of equality as such, he loves in fact the concrete equality between individuals that belongs to a particular cultural and political space. And even within these limits, he seeks not equality as such but rather equality between individuals from certain – but not from all – points of view. Each of these limits may be contested in the name of equality. The problem with which we are faced is not that of democracy's external frontier, but rather of its internal one – that is, of the democrats' struggle within democracy to (re)define its nature. These internal struggles are due to two contradictions in the idea of democracy. The universal principle of equality is in tension with actually existing inequalities on the one hand and with the limit and particularity of the people on the other.

At times Tocqueville seems to admit that democratic universality overcomes national limits:

In democratic centuries, the extreme mobility of men and their impatient desires make them change place constantly, and the inhabitants of different countries mix with each other, listen to each other and borrow from each other. Therefore not only members of the same nation become alike; nations themselves are assimilated, and in the eye of the spectator all together form nothing more than a vast democracy of which each citizen is a people. This puts the shape of the human race in broad daylight for the first time.[31]

Democracy is universal, not only because the citizens of a state are ruled according to the principle of equality but also because it simultaneously unites all the nations into "one vast democracy" that encompasses all of humanity. Humanity and democracy are closely interdependent. The true democratic universality is a universal universalism. When we read this passage, we understand the trouble of those who think that Tocqueville contradicts himself when he defends the colonization of Algeria. Yet does he not avoid using the word *democracy* in this context? The colonial exclusion is clearly grounded in the primacy of the particularity of the people:

There is neither utility nor duty to allow our Muslim subjects exaggerated ideas of their own importance, nor to persuade them that we are obligated to treat them under all circumstances precisely as though they were our fellow citizens and our

---

[31] DIA II.1.xvii, 461.

equals. They know that we have a dominant position in Africa; they expect to see us keep it. To abandon it today would be to astonish and confuse them, and to fill them with erroneous and dangerous notions. Half-civilized people have difficulty understanding forbearance and indulgence; they understand nothing but justice. Exact, but rigorous, justice should be our sole rule of conduct toward the indigenous population when they act reprehensibly toward us. What we owe them at all times is good government.[32]

In fact, the two passages are easily compatible. The subject of the process of unification is the whole of the democratic peoples. We may suppose that the Indians (who are destroyed), the Blacks, and the Algerians plainly do not belong to this humanity. Tocqueville does not really go beyond European universalism.[33] This conclusion would have been much more difficult to reach if Tocqueville had considered the American revolution as unfinished because of the genocidal policy toward the Indians and the racist and proslavery policies toward the Blacks. He had serious doubts, but they never reached the point of heresy from which America would have appeared as a "false" democracy.

Even the more universal universality conceived by Tocqueville is still particular. Is this limit a frontier of democracy? In this case, democracy would have to overcome this limit to apply and realize its principles. True democracy would be that of humanity governing itself without any exclusion or domination. But one could argue that this limit is not a frontier. The idea of democracy has always referred to a partial whole: the *demos*, or the people. Democracy in this sense is a principle of exclusion that cannot be the form of the organization of humanity. Another word would be necessary to name this new form. It is impossible to say what would be Tocqueville's answer. The preceding passage suggests that he considered democracy as a process of increasing universalization of egalitarian principles. On the other hand, Tocqueville had a realistic vision of international relations. His career as a statesman shows that in his view international politics is not governed by democratic principles but rather by force. In 1839, on the occasion of the debates on the Eastern question, Tocqueville advocated a warmongering stance against Russia and global British hegemony, arguing that France must preserve an international status worthy of its past.[34] Similarly, one of his justifications for colonizing

[32] WES, 141.
[33] Immanuel Wallerstein, *European Universalim. The Rhetoric of Power* (New York: The New Press, 2006).
[34] OC 3:2, 255–265.

Algeria was France's need to maintain its position as a great power.[35] In a European context, as Minister of Foreign Affairs in 1849, he complains that by refusing to expel the German revolutionaries, the Swiss government applies the democratic principles to international affairs.[36] Perhaps, however, we need to distinguish the democratic revolution from its final outcome. As long as this revolution remains unfinished, international relations cannot and will not be fully democratic.

Political Concepts and Policy

This brings us to the second possible answer to the question of Tocqueville's relevance. The objection that, grounded in the Eurocentric prejudices of his day, Tocqueville's account of democracy is obsolete underestimates the fact that Tocqueville claims to be defining the true democracy, thus rejecting a competing claim. Moreover, the objection itself is based on an assumption about the nature of democracy. Although we may think that Tocqueville's definition is wrong, the competition between democratic claims to determine what is really democratic is an empirical fact that has to be taken seriously. How is this internal conflict possible? What does it teach us about the meaning of democracy as a concept and object?

Tocqueville uses the American example to ground the opposition between democracy and revolution. In the most democratic society, revolutionary theories have no success because the Americans are born equal and enjoy enough property. In Europe, democracy is and will be the outcome of revolution. In the course of their transition to democracy, the Europeans, and particularly the French, fail to distinguish what is democratic from what is revolutionary. So Americans and Europeans do not use the word *democracy* in the same way. Most of what is regarded as democratic in Europe is in reality revolutionary.[37] From the point of view of the external frontier, Tocqueville aims to convert antidemocrats to democracy by showing that what they fear is not democracy but revolution. However, he applies the same argument at the internal frontier

---

[35] "(...) si nous pouvions en arriver à tenir fermement et à posséder paisiblement cette côte d'Afrique, notre influence dans les affaires générales du monde serait fort accrue" ("Travail sur l'Algérie," OC 3:1, 215).

[36] "Jamais on ne vit mieux le naturel des démocraties, lesquelles n'ont, le plus souvent, que des idées très confuses ou très erronées sur leurs affaires extérieures, et ne résolvent guère les questions du dehors que par les raisons du dedans," OP3, 934.

[37] DIA II.3.xxi, 610–611.

as well, targeting those democrats who want to extend the revolution in a socialist direction. In both cases, Tocqueville argues as a democrat and gives the idea of democracy a positive meaning. The culmination of his appropriation of the word *democracy* comes with the revolution of 1848. In the drafts to his famous parliamentary speech denouncing the right to work, Tocqueville argues against the socialists who defend the right to work and attack the right to property claiming that he is "profoundly democratic" (*profondément démocrate*). He effectively forbids them to call themselves democrats because socialism is the negation of individual liberty, whereas democracy implies liberty.[38] This is an unexpected move: the aristocrat by instinct claims to be the true democrat in front of the defenders of the masses. We hesitate to give this declaration a true theoretical status. Is not Tocqueville here speaking as a politician, in an exaggerated rhetoric perhaps pushed by the fear of socialism? In fact, this antisocialist declaration is similar to those regarding women and servants. It is a political intervention in a conflict between democrats over the true nature of democracy and its definition, which denies self-proclaimed democrats their democratic credentials and excludes them from democracy. Just as in Tocqueville's political speeches, so too in *Democracy in America*, there is no clear separation between theory and politics because the political object, democracy, is not naturally given but is historically constructed. Democracy is an open concept of an open object.[39]

Tocqueville's argument is naturally relevant, if contestable, when addressed to a declared nonrevolutionary democrat: for example, a socialist like Considérant or a communist like Cabet. But it loses its relevance vis-à-vis an opponent who does not claim to be a democrat. The revolutionary Blanqui said that "democrat" is "un mot en caoutchouc."[40] It has no precise meaning because it is used by everybody and particularly by conservatives. This word is a trap for the radical critic of society. He has to use the forbidden but clearer words: *proletarian* and *bourgeois*. At first glance, we may consider Blanqui's rejection of the word

---

[38] OC 3:3, 192 and 195.

[39] On this, Walter Bryce Gallie, "Essentially Contested Concepts," *Proceedings of the Aristotelian Society* 56 (1955–1956), 167–198. For my interpretation, see Nestor Capdevila, *Le concept d'idéologie* (Paris: PUF, 2004), 299–312.

[40] Literally, a word out of rubber. Letter to Maillard, June 6, 1852, Auguste Blanqui, *Ecrits sur la Révolution. Œuvres complètes 1. Textes politiques et lettres de prison* (Paris: Galilée, 1977), 355. Compare with Tocqueville's own account of the democratic predilection for abstract words that he compares to a "box with a false bottom" (une boîte à double-fond), DIA II.1.xvi, 457.

democracy in the name of class struggle as a proof that he is not a democrat. It would be more precise to say that for Blanqui the idea of democracy does not offer a relevant viewpoint on the current condition of society. He wants to think in another way that is not expressed by the opposition democrat/nondemocratic. This position is best represented by Marx. Marx never analyzes modern society as democratic but as bourgeois or capitalist.[41] This epistemological distance from the idea of democracy pertains even to the future society: Marx calls it communism. Continuing with the metaphor of the frontier, we could say that we have reached a frontier of the concept of democracy. Does democracy offer a relevant vantage point from which to consider our society? Is there a point where the concept loses its theoretical relevance? And what are its theoretical alternatives?

Democracy and the End of History

Even if we remain within the Tocquevillean framework, the encounter with Marx raises an interesting question about the frontiers of democracy. Describing the present and future society, Marx uses two words – *capitalist* and *communist* – whereas Tocqueville uses only one: *democracy*. Marx's fundamental objection to bourgeois ideology is that the present society is not the end of history.[42] There will be a completely new classless society of which the proper name is communism. On the contrary, Tocqueville uses only one word because his reasoning is structured by the opposition between aristocracy and democracy. If aristocracy is destroyed, only democracy is possible and vice versa. If the destruction of aristocracy is irreversible, then democracy is the end of history. There is no future historical frontier of democracy. It seems easy to imagine what would have been Tocqueville's interpretation of Marx: the most radical and systematic attempt of his time to change the present world is thinkable within the frame of the democratic revolution, as a (pathological) form of democracy. If the proper name of the present society is not democracy but capitalist or bourgeois society, nothing logically prevents

---

[41] Nestor Capdevila, "Marx ou Tocqueville: capitalisme ou démocratie," *Actuel Marx* 46 (2009), 150–162.

[42] "Affirmer que la libre concurrence serait la forme ultime du développement des forces productives, donc de la liberté humaine, revient ni plus ni moins à affirmer que la domination des *classes moyennes* constitue la fin de l'histoire universelle – agréable pensée, du reste, pour les *parvenus* d'avant-hier," Marx, *Manuscrits de 1857–1858 (Grundrisse)* (Paris: Editions sociales, 1980), t. II, 144; MEW, t. 42, 552.

us from using the word *democracy* to name the future society. What can
be more democratic than a society without classes and without state?[43]

This argument in turn makes it difficult for Tocqueville to escape
completely Marx's point of view. Marx recognizes that in the contemporary society equality is a popular prejudice, but Tocqueville's study
of democracy had no influence on him. At the end of the first book of
Das Kapital, Marx speaks, like Tocqueville, of an America where private
property grounded in personal work is still alive. He saw in it evidence
that the Americans resist the development of the capitalist mode of production based on the appropriation of the labor of others. *Democracy
in America* is not relevant to the Marxian point of view because Tocqueville speaks of a society that, for Marx, is not only noncapitalist but
even anticapitalist[44] and that will be destroyed by the capitalist mode of
production. This possible Marxian critique of Tocqueville finds justification in some aspects of Tocqueville's analysis. When Tocqueville analyzes
the capitalist development of new inequalities, in terms that may seem
perfectly sound to a socialist, he speaks of the possible development of a
new aristocracy.[45] From a strictly theoretical point of view, it is possible
to maintain that the industrial aristocracy is a negation of democracy,
even if Tocqueville never accepted this argument, which would have
made him into a socialist. Certainly Marx could be fitted in the Tocquevillean framework insofar as his imaginary society is an attempt to
fulfill the democratic ideals.[46] On the other hand, Tocqueville's account
lends plausibility to the idea of a contradiction between democracy
and capitalism, which weakens the opposition between democracy and

---

[43] Tocqueville's father has written: "Dans les paroles de Saint-Martin [liberté, égalité,
fraternité] ne semble-t-il pas qu'on entend le langage tenu par le communisme, soixante-
dix ans plus tard?" Hervé de Tocqueville, *Coup d'œil sur le règne de Louis XVI, depuis
son avènement à la couronne jusqu'à la séance royale du 23 juin 1789, pour faire suite
à l'Histoire philosophique du règne de Louis XV* (Paris, 1850), 146.

[44] Recapitulating the bourgeois economist Wakefield's account of America, Marx speaks
of "den antikapitalistischen Krebsschaden der Kolonien," *Das Kapital*, I, VII, chap. 25
(Berlin: Dietz Verlag, 1989), 799.

[45] Cf. Villeneuve Bargemont's *Economie politique chrétienne, ou recherche sur la nature
et les causes du paupérisme en France et en Europe et sur les moyens de le soulager et
de le prévenir* (Paris: Paulin, 1834), which exemplifies the conservative critique of the
industrial revolution. See also the description of *der feudalen Sozialismus* by Marx and
Engels in the third part of their *Communist Manifesto*.

[46] François Furet, *Marx et la révolution française* (Paris: Flammarion, 1986), 40–41;
and "Le système conceptuel de la *Démocratie en Amérique*," in Tocqueville, *De la
Démocratie en Amérique* (Paris: Garnier Flammarion, 1981), 40–41. For a criticism of
this point of view, see J. Texier, "Marx, penseur égalitaire?," *Actuel Marx* 8 (1990),
45–66.

revolution.[47] So the Tocquevillean is again confronted with an internal frontier of democracy where some democrats accept the development of this new kind of inequality while others reject it.

The importance of the opposition between democracy and aristocracy in Tocqueville's comparative analysis seems to suggest that it is the main frontier of democracy. In reality, the destruction of aristocratic society is irreversible, which implies that the remaining and new aristocratic elements have to be expressed in democratic language and so become part of democratic society. The idea of frontiers of democracy is more interesting and useful when it concerns conflicts between democrats, which can reach the point of heresy when a self-proclaimed democratic position is excluded from democracy as either aristocratic or revolutionary. In Tocqueville's account, this conflict manifests itself above all in the necessity to distinguish democracy and revolution. In his attempt to define what is a true democracy, Tocqueville labors to differentiate democracy from revolution. At the same time, his notion of democratic revolution suggests that democracy is a revolution. The egalitarian ideal transforms society and continuously brings into question new relations of power and new inequalities. For Tocqueville, this tie between democracy and revolution is reinforced by the fact that the word "democracy" can have a negative connotation. This general revolutionary process assumes different aspects in light of different national histories, which have often known great revolutions. This is the second link between democracy and revolution. It is difficult to imagine a more democratic political act than the people's exercise of constituent power. However, to create a constitutional order means to put limits on the process of creation. Democracy is then opposed to revolution. Yet this necessary limit will continue to be challenged as long as the critical power of the democratic ideal does not seem to be exhausted.

---

[47] It is not clear that our world is Tocquevillean. Sheldon Wolin says: "Today it is difficult to imagine that any scientist or political sociologist in good repute would write a book about the irreversible tide of democracy or its incarnation in America, except either as a parody or, what amounts to the same thing, as an antithesis of the Soviet Union." And further, "one of the most striking recent changes stands Tocqueville on his head. It is the steady de-democratization of American society, both as 'social condition' and as a political 'civilization,'" *The Presence of the Past. Essays on the State and the Constitution* (Baltimore: Johns Hopkins University Press, 1989), 78. On the opposition between capitalism and democracy, see his *Politics and Vision* (Princeton and Oxford: Princeton University Press, 2004), 596–597; on contemporary America, see *Democracy Incorporated. Managed Democracy and the Specter of Inverted Totalitarianism* (Princeton and Oxford: Princeton University Press, 2008).

The metaphor of the frontier focuses our attention on the divergent meanings of the concepts of democracy and equality and thereby helps resist the tendency of some critical concepts to drift from utopia to ideology.[48] Although such resistance might seem dangerous from an antirevolutionary point of view, it is not inconsistent with Tocqueville's account, which warns not only against revolutionary democracy but also against conformism and democratic stagnation.[49] While seeking to settle the meaning of democracy, Tocqueville's analysis also suggests that the contestation of this meaning is constitutive of the dynamism of democratic society. Tocqueville does not imagine a world beyond the current one. But the essential indeterminacy of his notion of democracy and the ambiguous link between democracy and revolution continuously call into question the self-evidence with which the word is often used today. If democracy is the end of history, then in light of Tocqueville's experience, it is an end without an end.[50]

---

[48] The transition, never complete, from criticism to conservatism has been noted concerning Christian, liberal, and Marxist ideas. On this problem, see Karl Mannheim, *Ideology and Utopia. An Introduction to the Sociology of Knowledge* (London: Routledge, 1936).

[49] DIA II.3.xxi, 775 and 782.

[50] "L'idée d'une *autre* société est devenue presque impossible à penser... Nous voici condamnés à vivre dans le monde où nous vivons. C'est une condition trop austère et trop contraire à l'esprit des sociétés modernes pour qu'elle puisse durer. La démocratie fabrique par sa seule existence le besoin d'un monde postérieur à la bourgeoisie et au Capital, où pourrait s'épanouir une véritable communauté humaine. On l'a vu tout au long de ce livre sur l'exemple de l'Union soviétique... Mais la fin du monde soviétique ne change rien à la demande démocratique d'une autre société... [L]a disparition de ces figures familières à notre siècle ferme une époque, plutôt qu'elle ne clôt le répertoire de la démocratie," François Furet, *Le passé d'une illusion. Essai sur l'idée communiste au XXe siècle* (Paris: Robert Laffont / Calmann-Lévy, 1995), 572.

CHAPTER 2

The Frontier Between Aristocracy and Democracy

Ran Halévi

There is no more telling illustration of the elusive frontier between aristocracy and democracy than Tocqueville's own fate as a private person, as a public figure, and as a political author. Tocqueville is an aristocrat by heritage, manners, and inclinations and a democrat by reason, by political clairvoyance. This is precisely why he was destined to remain a solitary figure in the agitated drama of French political passions: too democratic for the royalist camp, too prone to endorse equality for the reactionary party, much too aristocratic for many of the Republican heirs of 1789, and a plain counterrevolutionary for the Bonapartists who were incensed by his damning portrayal of Napoleon.[1] Tocqueville's reflections on the fading fortune of aristocracy, on the irresistible course of the democratic process but also on the dangers this process posed to individual liberty and the very idea that "equality of condition" was the "generative fact" of modern society – these very unorthodox propositions – confined him to the rather lone eminence he was to experience throughout his public life, for they disproved the certitudes – and prejudices – of nearly every single political party of his day.

Tocqueville's interpretation, to begin with, upholds a fundamental premise that has long remained foreign to the French political tradition: following Montesquieu, he acknowledges the prevalence of mores over laws and political institutions in shaping the general spirit of a nation.

---

[1] Napoleon, he writes, deprived his countrymen "not only of liberty, but of the wish for liberty"; "towed by him, the French soon found themselves further removed from freedom than in any age of their history" (letter to Nassau W. Senior, OC 6:2, 286; "Discours de réception à l'Académie française," April 21, 1842, OC 16, 263, my translation).

"Mores and manners," cautioned Montesquieu, "are usages that laws have not established, or that they have not been able, or have not wanted to establish." For they belong to two different realms: the laws appertain to the legislator, whereas mores and manners, to the nation in general. Hence, it would be wrong for a prince – "c'est une très mauvaise politique" – indeed tyrannical, to seek to reshape mores by laws, especially in France where the influence of mores and the authority of manners govern in unison over society.[2]

If there were in the world a nation which had a sociable humour, an openness of heart; a joy in life, a taste, an ease in communicating its thoughts; which was lively, pleasant, playful, sometimes imprudent, often indiscreet, and which had with all that, courage, generosity, frankness, and a certain point of honor, one should avoid disturbing its manners by laws, in order not to disturb its virtues.[3]

These reflections should not have come as a surprise to readers of the *Persian Letters* in which Montesquieu lets Usbek carry his own voice: "Nothing [. . .] is more conductive towards tranquility in the state than mores, which always produce better citizens than the laws."[4] The relation between mores and commendable citizenship is thus plainly stated.

Tocqueville appears no less categorical. He grants institutions only "secondary influence" on the course of human destiny: in shaping American democracy, mores carry more weight than either physical causes or political laws. It is the mores that reveal the true character of a nation and the spirit of its laws; it is primarily by studying American mores that one can grasp the nature of American democracy.[5] And what Tocqueville takes for a "common truth" is by no means confined either to democracy or to America. "I am quite convinced," he imparts to a friend at the time he is laboring on the text that would become *L'Ancien Régime et la Révolution*, "that political societies are not what their laws make them but what they are prepared in advance to be by the feelings, the beliefs, the ideas, the habits of heart and mind of the men who compose them, and what native disposition and education made these men to be."[6] He would express again this viewpoint, practically with the same words, in the introduction to his inquiry into the origins of the French Revolution.

[2] Montesquieu, *The Spirit of the Laws*, trans. Anne Cohler, Basia Miller, and Harold Stone (Cambridge: Cambridge University Press, 1989), henceforth SL, book XIX, ch. 14, 16.
[3] Montesquieu, SL, book. XIX, ch. 5, 310.
[4] Montesquieu, *Persian Letters*, Letter cxxix.
[5] DIA I.2.ix, 292 ff.
[6] OC 15:2, 81, my translation [SLPS, 24].

Probing the nature of the Old Regime implies less the investigation of its laws and institutions than the learning of "the true instincts of the age," "its ideas, passions, prejudices, practices," the "sentiments" and political habits that the Revolution is alleged to have erased.[7] These notions defy at once absolutist ideology, the Enlightenment politics of will, as well as revolutionary *légicentrisme*. The idea that human nature can be remodeled, regenerated by absolute will, or by the power of reason, or by the authority of principles appears to Tocqueville both presumptuous and illusory.

But he offers no consolation either to the leading foes of radical Enlightenment – the faithful of the Catholic Church. French Catholics were less than enchanted to discover the instrumental function Tocqueville assigns to religion in American society. Whatever its dogma, religion is essentially a moral auxiliary of democracy, whose main purpose consists in restraining the immoderate usage of the power to will that liberty confers on individuals. And they were even more amazed to learn – in one of the opening chapters of *The Old Regime and the Revolution* – that the irreligious fury of the French Revolution had been but an historical accident as it were and that its transient effects were soon to fade away along the natural movement of the democratic process. On that account at least Tocqueville's optimism would be refuted by the course of French history: under the Third Republic, republicanism and anticlericalism would long remain intimately entangled. But even in Tocqueville's time such a pronouncement should have appeared quite extraordinary to those of his readers who still remembered the Jacobin accomplishments under the banner of human virtue and public salvation: the fierce persecution of priests, the devastation of countless churches, the extravagant politics of dechristianization, and the lasting stains left by these episodes on France's divided memory.

Indeed, both in *Democracy in America* as in *The Old Regime and the Revolution*, Tocqueville departs from his contemporaries' irreconcilable perception of the recent past. The Legitimists, who still nourish the hope of resurrecting at least some of the old royal prerogatives, are bluntly instructed that the former social state "has fallen and has confusedly carried away in its fall all the goods and all the evils it brought with it,"[8] that absolute monarchy can never be restored, and that although the Revolution failed to create lasting political institutions, its principles did

---

[7] OR1, Preface, 84–85.
[8] DIA II.4.viii, 675.

prevail over the old political legitimacy, of which no viable relic can be retrieved. The Republicans who, gripped by the ideology of *tabula rasa*, deny the Old Regime any viable hold, any noticeable imprint on the society that arose out of its debris, are advised that the French Revolution is as much a child of the absolute monarchy as the work of its own authors. 1789 was the convulsive conclusion of a long and veiled revolution that had preceded and made possible the Revolution itself – that is, of the erection of a centralized state, the political dispossession of the nobility, and the dislocation of the aristocratic society into a nation of individuals. The Republicans are also instructed that if liberty was the purpose of the Revolution, it was its principal casualty as well; that by destroying the French aristocracy, by eradicating the spirit of independence it had embodied for many centuries, the Revolution inflicted upon liberty unhealed wounds and thus contributed to reinforce the fateful predisposition of the French to accommodate themselves to despotism in its modern form.

In all his writings, Tocqueville remains the author so to speak of a single work: the study of the ongoing transition from aristocracy to democracy. By this he means more than just the succession of two different historical eras. Aristocracy and democracy, he writes in the closing chapter of *Democracy in America*, represent two contrasting social states, indeed "two distinct humanities," each possessing its own genuine character, virtues, vices, instincts, prejudices, and political institutions.[9] Tocqueville is not only the most insightful painter of these two human orders; he is also a living witness to a very particular moment in French history: the fading in France of the last vestiges of these aristocratic figures he happens himself to embody. In a letter to his wife a year before his death, he offers this gloomy remark:

We will not be replaced [. . .]. We belong to a world that is waning. An old family [. . .], still surrounded by long-established reverence and souvenirs treasured by its members and the population attached to it – these are but debris of a society reduced to dust of which there will soon remain no trace [. . .]. We barely belong to our time.[10]

This melancholic note by no means clarifies Tocqueville's understanding of what aristocracy really is. How does he interpret the historical fate of aristocracy in light of the democratic process? And where does

---

[9] DIA II.4.viii, 675.
[10] OC 14, 645–646 (my translation).

he really stand between aristocracy and democracy? Moreover, what is, according to Tocqueville, the nature of aristocracy as, in effect, a distinct form of humanity? Finally, Tocqueville evokes several aristocratic – or so-called aristocratic – features as useful correctives to potential democratic excesses: to what extent can democracy be tamed by aristocratic elements? What could be deemed aristocratic in a society that has never witnessed an aristocratic experience? These are the main themes I wish to explore in this chapter.

Tocqueville's Aristocracy

To the question of aristocracy's historical fate and its distinct attributes, Tocqueville provided abundant answers both in his oeuvre and correspondence. And he did that with such clarity and eloquence that one is left wondering about the effort deployed by some authors either to dub him as an apologist of the Old Regime (a label too loose to imply anything precise) or to portray him as a feudalist utopian pursuing an unavowed quest for the retrieval of aristocratic preeminence against the perils of democratic modernity.[11] In this latter version Tocqueville's aristocratic endeavor is spurred as much by his personal bias – his "feudal sensibility" – as by pragmatic purpose. "He never truly embraced democracy,"

---

[11] Garry Wills, "Did Tocqueville 'Get' America?" *The New York Review of Books*, April 29, 2004. This disquisition, based on random citations taken out of context, begins by offering a litany of things Tocqueville ignored in America, the books he failed to read, the towns he neglected to visit, the innovations he overlooked, and the prejudices he too earnestly embraced. And it ends up with a series of extravagant claims about Old Regime France: that French bureaucracy was not bourgeois as Tocqueville would have wished but at least in part aristocratic; that it did not enjoy "even the full support of the monarchy"; that according to Tocqueville, once the Revolution occurred, the bureaucracy's inertia "channeled the nation quickly back into a liberty-destroying equality"; and that this same bureaucracy both "caused a reaction against itself that was the Revolution, but then defeated the Revolution by its 'traditional' hold on the people." In short, the cause of the French Revolution was the bureaucracy (no mention here of absolute monarchy, political strife, philosophical radicalism) and its outcome bureaucracy again (not a word either about Napoleon and the closure of the revolutionary process). There is very little of Tocqueville in this poetic account. However, it does reveal something about its author who fails to notice that the fabric of equality in the closing centuries of the Old Regime had nothing to do with the social identity of French administrators and everything to do with the consequences of centralization: the political dispossession of Old Regime society by the absolute state and hence the disintegration of French social body into a society of individuals within the unaltered framework of aristocratic society. None of this seems of relevance to Mr. Wills, who concludes abruptly that for Tocqueville, "an aristocrat at heart" – which is certainly true – it was "the habits of the heart that prevailed." Because the text ends here, the reader, I suppose, should take this final chute for an article of faith.

writes one of his latest exegetes, "he never truly renounced aristocracy."[12]
Well, having refrained from providing a clear idea of what our commentator means – let alone of what Tocqueville meant – by these two notions,
such a ruling appears all but meaningless. This, however, cannot be said
of another assertion professed by the same author in his foray into the
less familiar wilderness of Old Regime France. Tocqueville, he says, by
exhuming this vanished world, sought to "restore the aristocracy and
justify it by arguing that it was the crucial element in a salutary scheme of
inequalities."[13] Once again, nothing in the crowded pages of this book is
produced to sustain such an assertion, which Tocqueville's own writings
corroborate nowhere and indeed rebut on countless occasions.[14]

Reflecting one day upon what he calls his own "fundamental instincts,"
his "serious principles," Tocqueville interposes this laconic note:

> I have for democratic institutions *un goût de tête*, but I am an aristocrat by instinct,
> that is I despise and fear the crowd. I passionately cherish liberty, legality, respect
> for the Law, but not democracy. *Voilà le fond de l'âme* [...]. I am neither of
> the revolutionary nor of the conservative party. However, all things considered,
> I feel closer to the latter than to the former. For I differ from the latter on means
> rather than on ends, whereas I dissent from the former both on ends and on
> means.[15]

But to capture Tocqueville's views of aristocracy, one should look beyond
his fundamental instincts. Perhaps the most comprehensive account of his
personal stance between aristocracy and democracy is laid out in a letter
written to an English friend in 1837:

> There are those who want absolutely to identify me with a party, but I belong to
> none; to credit me with [political] passions, whereas I have only opinions [...].
> I am ascribed alternatively aristocratic and democratic prejudices; I might have
> espoused either the former or the latter had I been born in another century and
> another country. But [...] I came to this world at the end of a long Revolu-
> tion that, after having destroyed the ancient state, has created nothing durable.
> Aristocracy was already dead when I was born and democracy did not yet exist
> [...]. Being myself an offspring of the ancient aristocracy [...], I felt neither
> hatred nor jealousy towards it. And the aristocracy being already shattered, I felt
> no particular inclination towards it either. For [people] are [naturally] attached

[12] Sheldon Wolin, *Tocqueville Between Two Worlds* (Princeton: Princeton University Press, 2003), 157.
[13] Sheldon Wolin, *Tocqueville Between Two Worlds*, 532.
[14] For an incisive critique of Wolin's thesis, factual errors, and misinterpretations, see Seymour Drescher, "Who Needs *Ancienneté*? Tocqueville on Aristocracy and Modernity,"
History of Political Thought 24 (2003), 624–646.
[15] "Mon instinct, mes opinions," OC 3:2, 87 (my translation).

only to things alive. I was intimate enough with the aristocracy to comprehend it, and distant enough to be able to judge it without passion. I could say the same of the democratic element. Neither family memory nor personal interest necessarily gave me a natural inclination toward Democracy. But no injury, no particular motive induced me either to cherish or to loathe it independently of what my reason commanded [...].[16]

No injury? Tocqueville's family paid a heavy toll to the revolutionary Terror. His forebear Malesherbes, the celebrated magistrate and later defender of Louis XVI at the bar of the Convention, was led to the guillotine along with his daughter – Tocqueville's maternal grandmother – her husband, their daughter, and son-in-law. These tragedies left an indelible imprint on Tocqueville's parents and markedly grieved his own childhood. Yet one should beware of confusing in Tocqueville's thinking democracy as a human and political experience with the convulsive effects in France of its tumultuous advent. Indeed, there is not a shred of anger in these sober lines – or of nostalgia for that matter.

Tocqueville is by no means a foe of the aristocratic legacy in French political culture – let alone of aristocratic values he very much admires. Here his own words are worth quoting, for they blur the impervious frontiers established by revolutionary ideology between the aristocratic past and the democratic present. Reflecting upon "the kind of freedom that prevailed under the Old Regime," he reckons how odd it may appear that a form of liberty so "irregular and intermittent, always contracted within the limits of a class, always linked to the idea of exception and privilege" should foster "such manly virtues." The nobles conserved, even in their political decline, "something of their ancestors' hauteur." This class "which led for centuries had acquired, during that long, uncontested experience of greatness, a certain pride of heart, a natural confidence in its strength, a habit of being respected, which made it into the most resistant part of the social body. It not only had manly mores, it increased the virility of other classes by its example." The loss of these fecund attributes, shattered along with the aristocracy itself, "deprived the nation of a necessary part of its substance" for many decades to come.[17] For their blessing, intimates Tocqueville, is by no means confined to aristocratic societies; they could offer a useful shield to freedom in France on its long and strenuous route to the democratic era. In fact, Tocqueville explicates here a view he had already intimated in *Democracy in America* when

[16] Letter to Henry Reeve (March 22, 1837), OC 6:1, 37–38, my translation [SLPS, 116].
[17] OR I, 173, 179.

discussing the forces and influences that may help in taming absolute power. In Old Regime France, these were not only institutions, corporations, orders, and provinces but also, transcending them all, opinions and mores that "raised less well known but no less powerful barriers around the royal power." By opinions and mores, Tocqueville clearly refers to what Montesquieu had called "the principle of honor" and this "aristocratic honor," which survived long after the nobility had lost its prime, "gave an extraordinary strength to individual resistance" to the throne. Moreover, it could be as useful in taming *any* power; it could indeed serve just as well in democratic societies "when the individual disappears more and more into the crowd and is easily lost in the midst of common obscurity." Yet now that it is gone, "who can say where the demands of power and the compliance of weakness could stop?"[18] The doom of aristocratic honor should then be considered as a loss not only to modern liberty but also to democracy itself in its relentless march. Again, one should read here neither nostalgia for a lost aristocratic age nor an insidious promulgation of aristocratic aspirations but the grim explication of a conspicuous historical circumstance.

Tocqueville thus conceives aristocratic honor as a precious contrivance for taming government, whatever its form. But he grants little credence to aristocratic political claims and indeed – as this citation makes clear – to the very idea of a possible survival of that fading human figure he happens himself to embody. If absolute monarchy had unwittingly dissolved the old French aristocracy, the Revolution was to obliterate, deliberately, the last vigorous remains of aristocratic spirit. Aristocracy henceforth belongs to an age that cannot be recovered. It represents, so to speak, the youth of man having since come of age. People, Tocqueville pointedly notes elsewhere, "no more come back to the sentiments of their youth than do men to the innocent tastes of their early years; they can regret them, but they cannot make them revive."[19]

"A Holy Undertaking"

The demise of aristocracy should not be accounted as the only reason why Tocqueville embraces democracy. Could he also have embraced it because the democratic process appears to follow a divine purpose? One is indeed struck by the "providential" language often used by Tocqueville to characterize what human reason alone, he contends, cannot fully grasp.

[18] DIA I.2.ix, 299–300.
[19] DIA I.2.vi, 226.

"The gradual development of the equality of conditions," he writes in a famous passage, "is [...] a providential fact, and it has the principal characteristics of one: it is universal, it is enduring, each day it escapes human power [...]." Or this other striking line: "To wish to stop democracy would [...] appear to be to struggle against God himself." Tocqueville even refers to "religious terror" in describing the impression produced upon him by the irresistible path of the democratic revolution.[20] For an author not particularly notorious for his piety (although he regards disbelief as an "accident," an "aberration of the intellect," and faith as "the permanent state of humanity"[21]), the constant reference to a providential design is not insignificant. Here as elsewhere God's will appears to bestow a transcendent authority to the verdict of history. "It is natural to believe," intimates Tocqueville in the closing page of *Democracy in America,*

that what most satisfies the regard of this Creator and Preserver of men is not the singular prosperity of some, but the greatest well-being of all: what seems to me decadence is therefore progress in his eyes; what wounds me is agreeable to him. Equality is perhaps less elevated; but it is more just, and its justice makes for its greatness and its beauty.[22]

These last words add yet another argument – and a decisive one – in favor of democracy's prosaic goods over obsolete aristocratic greatness. And here, again, religious references are called in as if to enhance pervading historical truths. "Christianity, which has rendered all men equal before God, will not be loath to see all citizens equal before the law [...]." And elsewhere Tocqueville goes as far as convening the authority of Jesus Christ – hardly ever mentioned elsewhere in his oeuvre – to endorse natural equality: "It was necessary that Jesus Christ come to earth to make it understood that all members of the human species are naturally alike and equal."[23]

Tocqueville's use of providential language seems to serve as a substitute for a rational interrogation of the origins of the democratic process and the secret of its unremitting progression. Tocqueville may well have believed that no philosophy of history could adequately account for the

---

[20] DIA, Introduction, 6–7.
[21] DIA I.2.ix, 284. On Tocqueville's realization, at the age of sixteen, of his own "universal doubt," see the brief account by André Jardin, *Alexis de Tocqueville, 1805–1869* (Paris: Hachette, 1984), 62 ff.
[22] DIA II.4.viii, 674–675.
[23] DIA Introduction, 11; II.1.iii, 413.

origins of the democratic revolution. He certainly did not share Hegel's
view of history as a universal ongoing progress of man's sovereign reason.
Once he had noticed that the democratic process was immune to any discernible "primary cause," that it transcended national character and the
variety of political regimes, that it was indeed universal and irresistible,
he might have candidly acknowledged its providential nature, hence, its
irreducibility to plain rational interpretation.

But whatever his viewpoint – and his purpose – in this regard, the
constant reference to Providence's decree appears suitably appropriate
to Tocqueville's political science as well as to his rhetorical intent. Tocqueville has little use for metaphysics or abstractions. He approaches
politics not from first principles but as a given reality one should comprehend and eventually endeavor to govern or transform. His study of the
democratic revolution does not stand as an inquiry about the best government, let alone as a gloss on the typology of modern political regimes.
His mode of thinking is indeed less attuned to historical causality than
to the latent workings of the historical process, its distinctive hallmarks,
and its possible effects, more to the human experience of the past than
to theoretical assumptions about man and society. He is as skeptical of
the idea of progress as of the notion of a "fixed" human nature, not
to mention "the state of nature" – a concept he hardly ever mentions.[24]
How then could he best convey, even while avoiding the grueling question
of historical causality, that the equality of conditions is the "generative
fact," the fundamental vehicle, the unique horizon of modern history and
that henceforth the choice is not between democracy and aristocracy but
between "democratic liberty" and "democratic tyranny"?[25] Perhaps the
most fitting language to impart that "solemn warning" is indeed providential oratory: it helps reinforce the claim that equality of conditions
appertains to God's intent and should therefore be acknowledged and
that pursuing aristocratic aspirations should hence be considered vain,
even blasphemous.

And what is true of equality is even more true of modern liberty.
Liberty being for Tocqueville the highest human value, the best regime is
that which secures best liberty's goods. In his essay of 1836 on "The Social
and Political State of France Before and After 1789," Tocqueville weighed
the aristocratic and the modern notions of liberty. The former, founded

[24] Harvey C. Mansfield and Delba Winthrop, "Editors' Introduction," DIA, xxvi–xxvii.
[25] Alexis de Tocqueville, *De la démocratie en Amérique*, "Forward to the twelfth edition,
1848" (Paris: Gallimard, 1961) t. I, xliv.

not on universal but on particular rights, preserves the independence of certain groups and inclines them, by the very energy they draw from that privilege, to carry out extraordinary deeds. The modern notion of liberty – in Tocqueville's words: "the democratic notion, and, if I dare say, *the just notion of liberty*" – is that which endows all men with equal rights to live independently and govern their own fate.[26] Thus, the "unjust" notion of liberty may produce grand accomplishments, while the "just" notion of liberty may expose the individual to new forms of servitude.[27]

Whatever its vulnerabilities may be, however, Tocqueville cautions that the path of modern liberty is irreversible: as social ranks diminish, equality naturally tends to prevail.[28] The French should recognize that truth and embrace equality – a "holy undertaking," he says – to ensure their independence and their dignity. Hence, they should abandon the old chimera of melding liberty with privilege. Tocqueville advises a few years later in the closing chapter of *Democracy in America*, "all those in the centuries we are now entering who try to base freedom on privilege and aristocracy will fail," and he concludes, "there is no question of reconstructing an aristocratic society, but of making freedom [emerge] from the bosom of the democratic society in which God makes us live."[29] As for those who still may hope to confound liberty with some selective aristocratic elements, "to make a choice among the institutions, the opinions, the ideas born of the aristocratic constitution of the former society," to abandon some, retain others "and carry them into the new world with them [. . .], they are consuming their time and their strength on an honest and sterile work;" for democracy and aristocracy are by no means assimilable.[30] That is precisely why, explains Tocqueville, the Restoration was doomed before it even set out its course: the Bourbons recreated aristocratic political institutions while maintaining democratic civil laws. Yet, "instead of seeking ostensibly to reinforce a principle which is dying among us, they should have devoted all their energy to securing order and stability to democracy."[31] Later, the July Monarchy and its chief political deviser, Guizot, would do even worse by trying to create – for the sake

---

[26] Alexis de Tocqueville, "État social et politique de la France avant et depuis 1789" [1836], in: *L'Ancien Régime et la Révolution* (Paris: Gallimard, 1952), 62.

[27] On this paradox see Pierre Manent, *Tocqueville et la nature de la démocratie* (Paris: Fayard, 1993), 62–63.

[28] "État social et politique . . . ," 63.

[29] DIA II.4.vii, 666.

[30] DIA II.4.viii, 675.

[31] Letter to Louis de Kergorlay, June 29, 1831, OC 13:1, 233–234.

of political stability and the benefit of the middle class – an artificial aristocracy based on voting franchise, a "bourgeois aristocracy" of a sort, or a "natural aristocracy" of the bourgeois age.[32] This self-promoted oligarchy, "egoistic, corrupt, and vulgar" – Tocqueville's words – was duly overthrown by the revolution of 1848 that embodied for Tocqueville the political advent of the people.[33]

Very early on, then, Tocqueville had acquired the certitude, as he confides in a letter during his trip to the United States, that democracy was an outstanding force that can be either a blessing or a curse wherever it proceeds: it could be tamed, but it could not be halted, let alone reversed.[34]

The Distinctive Constituents of Aristocracy

Now, given that the aristocratic era and aristocratic honor belong to a fading past, one may wonder why aristocracy is continually analyzed in a book devoted to the democratic process – what is more, in a society that had never been tested by an aristocratic experience. Aristocracy is indeed scrutinized practically everywhere in *Democracy in America*, especially in the second volume. One reason, rarely dwelled upon, is that *Democracy in America* pertains to much more than just democracy and America. Anyone familiar with the course of French modern history could read this oeuvre – and many of Tocqueville's contemporaries in effect did – as a lateral, but unmistakable, inquiry into the tribulations of the democratic process in modern France.[35] Moreover, Tocqueville's American readers may have been fairly perplexed to discover, in the opening pages of a book

---

[32] For Guizot, the American Revolution was led precisely by this sort of "natural and national aristocracy" of "the most elevated, rich and enlightened," endorsed and followed by the people; here he merely applies the same usual categories of his historical interpretation by transposing the "class logic" – which in France turned into a bloody conflict – to the more hospitable scene of the American Founding, François Guizot, *De la démocratie en France* (Paris: Victor Masson, 1849), 36–38; see also Lucien Jaume, *Tocqueville* (Paris: Fayard, 2008), 359–366.

[33] OC 12, 30 ff. See also Jean-Claude Lamberti, *Tocqueville et les deux démocraties* (Paris: Presses universitaires de France, 1983), Part I.

[34] OC 13:1, 233–234.

[35] I shall not try the reader's patience by drawing the inexhaustible list of themes, intuitions, working hypothesis that are probed or outlined in *Democracy in America* before being expanded or abandoned two decades later in *The Old Regime and the Revolution*. The best introduction to the "making" of *L'Ancien Régime et la Révolution* (although not directly concerned with the underlying interpretation of French history in *Democracy in America*) is Robert T. Gannett Jr., *Tocqueville Unveiled. The Historian and its Sources for "The Old Regime and the Revolution"* (Chicago: University of Chicago Press, 2003).

avowedly devoted to democracy and to America, a rather lengthy discussion on the fate and progress of the "equality of conditions" under the Old Regime, followed by an unbecoming assessment of the democratic revolution in France by the time of the July Monarchy: "[...] we have abandoned what goods our former state could offer; we have destroyed an aristocratic society, and having stopped complacently amid the debris of the former edifice, we seem to want to settle there forever."[36] In the concluding chapters of *Democracy in America*, France once again occupies practically every page in Tocqueville's forewarning on the various perils threatening modern liberty. Thus, if France in general and aristocracy in particular figure virtually everywhere in *Democracy in America*, it is for the obvious – if not always acknowledged – reason that this book may also read as an expansive prelude, as an intellectual laboratory, to *The Old Regime and the Revolution*.

Another obvious reason is that aristocracy offers the most cogent contrasting mirror to comprehend both the nature of democracy and its unwitting effects. Yet although this mirror yields extraordinary insights into the nature of aristocratic society as well, aristocracy never stands as an object of inquiry for its own sake. Indeed, Tocqueville, who has always been loose on definitions, never offers a clear characterization of aristocracy as he does for democracy (although he employs quite liberally the term *democracy* by assigning it a variety of meanings – as he does with *aristocracy*).[37] Democracy is characterized by the "generative fact" – the equality of conditions – that underlines both its nature and its progression. Should one then conclude that the generative fact of aristocracy is the *inequality* of conditions? Inequality of status is certainly an essential feature of aristocratic societies, but Tocqueville refrains from promoting it to the dignity of a generative fact or to ascribe for that matter any other generative principle to aristocracy.[38] Perhaps it is because aristocracy has indeed faded away, and its function thereby seems restricted precisely to highlighting by contrast the democratic process and its hallmarks, potency, or hazards.

This may also explain why the very notion of aristocracy in *Democracy in America* means different things in different contexts for different purposes. For one, nowhere does this notion, aristocracy, refer to what it

---

[36] DIA Introduction, 10.
[37] James T. Schleifer, *The Making of Tocqueville's "Democracy in America"* (Indianapolis: Liberty Fund, 2000), 325–339.
[38] Manent, *Tocqueville et la nature de la démocratie*, 29.

stands for in political philosophy, namely a type of regime. Sometimes it designates a political ruling class – the French medieval aristocracy. On other occasions aristocracy pertains rather to social or cultural eminence – that, for instance, of the French upper classes as late as the eighteenth century, at a time when the old aristocracy had long been turned into a caste dispossessed of political power.[39] Perhaps Tocqueville found it rather useful to avoid locking aristocracy in too rigorous a definition – which allowed him to use the term, as he did, with great latitude and without warning in one sense or the other. In short, he employs both meanings to portray – either in *Democracy in America* or in *The Old Regime and the Revolution* – two different epochs, two distinct historical configurations of French aristocracy in that long-term path from the aristocratic era to the democratic.

What he does offer, however – although scattered throughout his writings – is a rigorous account of how aristocracy comes into being, the resources by which it maintains its authority, its distinctive attributes, and the major threats that may imperil its survival.

Aristocracy, contends Tocqueville, is by no means a natural product of human consent. "It is impossible to imagine anything more contrary to the nature and the secret instincts of the human heart than a subjection of this kind." No people left to itself at any time would have by its own undertaking created an aristocracy in its midst. Men would have rather preferred submitting to an arbitrary despot than subjecting themselves to other men's command. Thus aristocracy, he writes, has always been the child of conquest.[40] But what begins as a deliberate act of force turns over time into a customary state of life. At that later stage aristocratic rule, enjoying the tacit consent of the people, comes to represent the "natural order of things." This is precisely how Tocqueville views French feudal society. The Germanic or Barbarian conquest of the fourth century concentrated in the same hands both property and political power. Inequality had certainly existed before – it was the natural corollary of property; however, from an adventitious historical circumstance, it has eventually evolved into a political right. The roots of aristocratic power then are the twin rules of force and property.[41]

[39] Tocqueville portrays that decline in the famous chapter ix, book II of *The Old Regime and the Revolution*.
[40] DIA I.2.x, 383. The spirit of conquest "was the father and mother of all lasting aristocracies," "Mémoire sur le paupérisme," OC 16, 120 (see esp. 117–124).
[41] DIA, Introduction, 4.

The "aristocratic age" is hence characterized by a social polarity between those who cultivate the land without possessing it and those who possess the land without cultivating it. Tocqueville offers neither an historical narrative nor a psychological account of how the initial, natural aversion to conquest receded throughout the ages and was transmuted, so to speak, into an innate disposition to consent and obedience. He does suggest, however, that the separate spheres in which these two different classes – the few and the many – lived and the rather modest expectations of the latter helped to habituate the poor to their subordinate condition, thus making it seem natural. "Limited in both capacity and want, untroubled about the present, or about a future that did not belong to them, they enjoyed a kind of vegetative contentment whose charm a highly civilized person can neither deny nor comprehend."[42] Hence, by the time the aristocratic age reached its full bloom, the hierarchy and distance between the two classes were definitely interiorized and assimilated accordingly to the natural order of things. One should add that for centuries in France, people envisaged the division of society between nobles and commoners as established for eternity by God's will.

The distinctive constituents of an aristocracy are thus force and landed property, to which Tocqueville would add three other fundamental elements: birth, wealth, and knowledge. These possessions have one thing in common: they cannot be shared; they belong to the few whom they endow with particular tastes, inclinations, and ideas, which place them apart – and above – the many.[43] The key to aristocratic rule consisted therefore of that inherent division of labor by mutual consent so to speak between those who were destined to command and those who were born to obey; it owed as much to the cultural chasm that held them apart as to the physical proximity and everyday intercourse that maintained them within sight:

The nobles, placed at an immense distance from the people, nevertheless took the sort of benevolent and tranquil interest in the lot of the people that the shepherd accords to his flock [...]. The people, not having conceived the idea of a social state other than their own [...] received their benefits and did not discuss their rights. They [...] submitted to their [chiefs'] rigors without trouble and without baseness, as they would to inevitable evils sent by the arm of God [...]. As the noble had no thought that anybody wanted to wrest from him privileges

---

[42] OC 16, 121, my translation.
[43] "État social et politique de la France," 45. The object of any aristocracy, he writes elsewhere, is "to concentrate enlightenment wealth, and power in its bosom and to keep them exclusively and by heredity," DIA II.3.xviii, 596.

that he believed legitimate, and the serf regarded his inferiority as an effect of
the immutable order of nature, one conceives a sort of reciprocal benevolence
that could have been established between two classes sharing such different fates
[...]. Thus organized, the social body could have stability, power, and above all,
glory.[44]

Guizot who deems that epoch a "feudal tyranny" does acknowledge
nonetheless some "reciprocal benevolence" between the classes; however,
this, he hastens to add, occurred not as a result of aristocratic rule but in
spite of it.[45]

Inequality of conditions, hereditary power, individual influence, a long
chain of dependence, voluntary consent to authority, reciprocal benevolence – those are the main characteristics, of which Tocqueville provides
many, of the political aristocracy that emerged in the centuries following
the conquest, before it was later progressively subverted and dispossessed
by the absolute monarchy. The Old Regime aristocracy to which Tocqueville devotes many extraordinary pages is in fact a post-aristocratic
aristocracy. Its power has been, henceforth, confined to social preeminence. But, it was by no means diminished: its political decline had given
way, as Montesquieu would suggest, to an extraordinary cultural bloom-
ing whose luster shone throughout Europe. And it preserved enough of
the old system of honor, as we have seen, to infuse its spirit of independence throughout the social body. Such an aristocracy establishes
its social and cultural ascendency on principles of its own making. It
remains the case, however, that once one removes the hereditary power
to command and the innate propensity to obey, what Tocqueville calls the
"aristocratic elements" of society have little to do with aristocracy per se:
these elements are in effect equally amenable to post-aristocratic modern
France and to a society with no aristocratic precedents such as American
democracy.

Taming Democracy?

Aristocracy then refers to more – and much else – than just aristocratic
rule. The plurality of meanings Tocqueville assigns to such an essential

---

44 DIA Introduction, 8.
45 Guizot, *Histoire de la civilization en Europe*, "Fourth Lesson" (Paris: Didier, 1857),
    96–97.

notion can explain but also helps clarify ongoing debates over the potential utility he may have accorded to aristocracy in taming modern democracy. On this disputed matter Tocqueville appears to me, throughout his
writings, quite unambiguous. His thoughts can be summed up as follows:
although no viable aristocracy and no aristocratic habits of heart and
mind can emerge in democratic society, aristocratic inclinations, aspirations, and ambitions are nonetheless congruous with the democratic
condition even among people where equality attained its most complete
development — for these penchants are engraved in the human heart.

Aristocracy, whatever its definition, has indeed no viable prospect
either in a pure democracy such as America or in a "democracy in
the making" such as France.[46] People may conquer territories and subject other nations, yet from conquest, aristocracy will never again arise
because it will never acquire the benevolent and hereditary consent it
had enjoyed in the distant past. But should that certitude apply when a
democracy vanquishes a foreign country where society is still in its political infancy? Could, for instance, the French conquest of Algeria in 1830
eventually generate some kind of aristocratic "social state"? Nowhere in
the pages he devotes to the Algerian question does Tocqueville postulate
such a course. True, he was writing in the immediate years following
the conquest, where the prospect of voluntary consent to French rule, let
alone to the settlement of French colonial communities, appeared simply
unthinkable. True also, he yields for a while – a very short while – to
the delusion of "molding as French [*franciser*] the country around us";
he even allows that "a people as strong and civilized as ours may exert
by the very fact of its enlightenment an almost invincible influence on
the small peoples more or less barbarous; and that in order to coerce
their incorporation into us it has only to establish lasting relationships
with them."[47] Such hopefulness will be soon toned down, even though
Tocqueville continues to believe both in the necessity of settling a European population in Algeria – "the centerpiece of our power in Africa" –
and in the promises of a peaceful cohabitation there between French and
Arabs. Yet all the arguments he garners in favor of that purpose foreclose,
explicitly or indirectly, any form of aristocratic blueprint.

For one thing, the different tribes and communities that make up Algerian society embody one single people "endowed with the same origin,
the same memories, the same opinion, the same mores" and cemented,

[46] DIA I.2.x, 383.
[47] OC 3:1, 145–146, 148, 153, my translation.

what is more, by the same religion. And although the Algerians enjoy neither political institutions nor political liberty, writes Tocqueville, they are led by a "religious and military aristocracy" of a sort.[48] In short, these populations "who place [their] liberty above all pleasures" have little in common with those "vegetative" classes of earlier centuries, prone to succumb eventually to aristocratic predominance.

There is still another reason why aristocracy could never arise on Algerian soil. The primary condition for the establishment of aristocratic rule is an extensive ownership of landed property. Here, such a perspective is both inconceivable and impractical. When conquering Algeria, asserts Tocqueville in a lengthy report to French Parliament, "we did not pretend, as the Barbarians who had invaded the Roman Empire, to take possession of the vanquished lands. Our sole objective was to seize government."[49]

Thus, if no allusion to setting up an aristocracy ever haunts Tocqueville's reflections on Algeria, it is simply because such a prospect would have appeared to him neither achievable nor desirable. On the contrary, all his recommendations advocate simultaneously the reinforcement of French political rule, the acceleration of European colonization, and ... the preservation of Arab material and cultural autonomy: the French should guarantee the indigenous peoples' property, help them restore their schools, multiply their educators, and help train among them legislators and religious ministers "with whom Muslim civilization, no more than ours, can do away."[50] Not the best recipe for establishing a lasting aristocracy.

As for democratic societies, none of the conditions conducive to aristocratic rule (or to aristocratic social eminence for that matter) can prevail in their midst, least of all the possession of an extended and hereditary landed property that yields hereditary power. Aristocracy, explains Tocqueville, "is rooted in the land. It attaches to the soil and leans on it. It is not established by privileges alone, or constituted by birth; it is landed property transmitted by heredity." Thus, wherever fortunes are not territorial, there can be no aristocracy. Yet from the outset the American soil "absolutely repelled territorial aristocracy."[51] And what repelled aristocracy even more, in America and later in France, were the laws of

[48] OC 3:1, 134, 143; see 221 ff.
[49] "Rapport fait par M. de Tocqueville sur le projet de loi relatif aux credits extraordianires demandés pour l'Algérie", OC 3:1, 326, my translation [WES, 143].
[50] OC 3:1, 276–277, 325, my translation [WES 112–113, 142–143].
[51] DIA I.1.ii, 30.

succession. For when the law of inheritance permits (as in America) or when it ordains (as in France under the Revolution) the equal partition of land, property is bound to be fragmented continuously into smaller portions. Hence, the power to command it had conferred upon its owner, and the spirit, the virtues, and the habits attached to that power disintegrated accordingly. Under the law of equal partition, then, no aristocracy can either emerge or survive. The very notion of heredity, the bond between one generation and another, and the sense of continuity and of common fate lose their purpose and eventually their vitality.[52]

Furthermore, the aristocratic vision of society as fixed and immobile is simply not viable under the relentless bout of the democratic process, the inexhaustible promise of human perfectibility, and the boundless opportunities offered to men's individual ambitions. Aristocratic peoples, Tocqueville observes elsewhere, "[. . .] like to persuade themselves that they have attained nearly the degree of greatness and knowledge that our imperfect nature permits; and as nothing around them is moving, they willingly fancy that everything is in its place." Such a notion is literally unconceivable in the democratic centuries where men are "mixed tumultuously," where usages, customs, and laws vary, where new truths are constantly brought to light, "old opinions disappear and others take their place," where "the image of an ideal and always fugitive perfection is presented to the human mind."[53] Moreover, in such a vibrant and agitated society, no time can be spared on acquiring the luxurious science of refined manners, the epitome of aristocratic rule, and even when acquired, it by no means necessarily procures social prestige let alone lasting authority.[54]

Tocqueville concludes *Democracy in America* on an unequivocal note. It would not be reasonable, he advises, "to demand of men of our time the particular virtues that flowed from the social state of their ancestors, since the social state itself has fallen and has confusedly carried away in its fall all the goods and all the evils it brought with it."[55]

Nevertheless, although democratic man may lack the natural instincts, habits, and prejudices of both aristocracies considered by Tocqueville, he is by no means immune to aristocratic ambitions. Hailing the Federalists and their struggle against the indefinite extension of popular power, Tocqueville suggests that this crucial issue – narrowing or expanding public

[52] DIA I.1.ii, 46–49.
[53] DIA II.1.viii, 427.
[54] DIA I.1.iii, 51.
[55] DIA II.4.viii, 675.

power – pertained to two contrasting passions: one democratic, the other aristocratic:

I do not say that American parties always have as their ostensible goal – or even as a hidden goal – to make aristocracy or democracy prevail in the country; I am saying that aristocratic or democratic passions are readily found at the foundation of all parties; and that although they may escape one's notice, they form, as it were, their sensitive spot and soul.[56]

This is quite an extraordinary pronouncement. It suggests that although aristocracy remains foreign to the social state of U.S. society, the polarity between aristocracy and democracy is the founding feature of political life – in short, that aristocratic passions are not extinguished but rather revived by the democratic process.[57] In a letter written a few months before his death, Tocqueville confides:

The ultra-democratic system has so much triumphed in America that it is impossible to push it further, and it enjoys a majority so overwhelming and supported by legislation that struggling against it would be a folly. There are infinitely more partisans of aristocracy, even of monarchy, in the United States than people imagine. I think that most of the wealthy incline towards this opinion. But the struggle being absolutely impossible, they resign and keep silent. Often they even add their acclamations to those of the crowd.[58]

Vivid as these passions may appear in the secrecy of men's souls, they cannot be publicly avowed; they remain a covert sin, a denied aspiration, sometimes even self-denied. Hence they yield no social import and produce no lasting cultural bearings and no enduring traditions; they have in fact nothing really aristocratic to them either in form or substance.

Likewise, it is just as easy to demonstrate the fundamentally democratic nature of the so-called aristocratic elements cited by Tocqueville to tame democracy.[59] Voluntary associations? Those "plain citizens" who, by gathering together "can constitute very opulent, very influential, very strong beings" are labeled "aristocratic persons" essentially for the sake of economy of language.[60] The industrialists? When claiming that industry "could well lead men back to aristocracy," Tocqueville merely refers to the sharp "division of labor" between the master who commands and

[56] DIA I.2.ii, 170.
[57] See Manent, *Tocqueville et la nature de la démocratie*, 31–32.
[58] OC 6:3, 305, September 5, 1858 (my translation).
[59] On the permanent aristocratic elements in democratic society and, more generally, on Tocqueville's view of aristocracy, see Alan S. Kahan, "Aristocracy in Tocqueville," *The Tocqueville Review* 27 (2006), 323–348, esp. 340–345.
[60] DIA II.4.vii, 668.

the worker who obeys and to the width of distance – in wealth, culture, mentality – that separates these two social figures who eventually grow less and less alike. The one is characterized by his soaring strength, opulence, and a knowledge embracing an ever-wider range of things; the other by his increasing dependence, shrinking resources, and constricted intelligence gradually confined to the prosaic scope of his daily tasks. "The one resembles more and more the administrator of a vast empire, the other a brute." But this "manufacturing aristocracy," Tocqueville hastens to qualify, is not only "an exception, a monster, in the entire social state;" it by no means "resemble[s] those that have preceded it."[61] In effect it possesses none of the latter's distinctive attributes: it does not form a coherent body – let alone a political ruling class – united by a genuine bond, but an aggregation of individuals whose authority comes and goes with their fortune; it generates no "reciprocal benevolence" between masters and workers whose relations remain purely contractual, mostly impersonal, and by definition impermanent – an aristocracy as it were that has nothing aristocratic about it. Lawyers, on the contrary, do form a permanent distinctive class; they are distinguished by a specific body of knowledge; an established authority; shared cultural affinities, habits, and inclinations; a taste for order, and a natural distrust of change – all aristocratic traits that fail nonetheless to meet the three elementary features of a living aristocracy – the natural calling to govern, the inborn power to command, and the hereditary character of both.

Voluntary associations, the press, industrialists, and the legal profession are deemed aristocratic only in that they derive their legitimacy – and their power – not from any constitutional arrangement but from the self-perception, or the particular station, of their members. They may offer useful correctives to democracy, but they bring it about by purely democratic means. Heredity, among these groups, even when tangible, is identified with no immutable right and no timeless tradition.

We should therefore take Tocqueville at his word when he writes the following words in an unpublished fragment: "Use democracy to moderate democracy. That is the sole path of salvation open to us."[62]

[61] DIA II.2.xx, 530–532.
[62] DIA (Nolla) [II.4.viii], 1279 note b.

CHAPTER 3

Tocqueville's Burke, or Story as History

Ralph Lerner

The brooding presence of Edmund Burke can hardly be overlooked in the first volume of Alexis de Tocqueville's *Ancien Régime and the Revolution*. His opinions, judgments, and very words serve as bookends to the first part of that work and to the volume as a whole. It is clear that Tocqueville found great value in a witness who was, so to speak, present at the creation. And such a witness he was! A man of long experience, with powers of close observation, and distant enough from the scenes of action not to be entangled in the factional maneuverings that beset the French both before and during the dismantling of their state. Tocqueville would expect Burke's understanding of contemporary events to be as discerning as one might hope for – comparable in value, albeit for different reasons, to the firsthand observations of Arthur Young. It is no less clear, however, that Burke served Tocqueville as an exemplary case of contemporary ignorance and bewilderment about the Revolution.

Burke, whose loathing for the Revolution radiated through his mind from its birth, even he for a few moments was uncertain when it happened. His first prophecy was that France would be weakened and virtually destroyed by it. "We may assume," he said, "that France's military capacity has for a long time been removed, maybe forever, and that men of the following generation will be able to echo the words of this ancient writer: *Gallos quoque in bellis floruisse audivimus.* (We have heard that the Gauls, too, once excelled in war)."

Judgments of an historical event from close to are no better than those coming well after it.[1]

[1] Alexis de Tocqueville, *The Ancien Régime and the French Revolution* [sic], trans. Gerald Bevan (London: Penguin Books, 2008), 1.1, 18. References to the text of the one volume of this projected work that was published in Tocqueville's lifetime are hereafter cited in

One might even say that any reader whose understanding of Burke's views on France relied solely on Tocqueville's reportage of those views would put the book down with some skewed notions indeed. The more Burke saw, the less he understood. His astonishment was misdirected. He mistook accidental features of the French Revolution for fundamental causes. His magnificent fulminations made for great reading, but they would not bring you closer to understanding the peculiar character and vehemence of that revolution. For that deeper understanding, you the reader have to have waited for Tocqueville. So Tocqueville would have you conclude.

Recent researches, and most especially the meticulous detective work of Robert Gannett in the Tocqueville archives, have brought to light how intensely Tocqueville labored before settling on his artful use of Burke as a foil in his book.[2] On the face of it, the Frenchman ought to have found much to admire in the Briton. Consider that the latter's great broadside, *Reflections on the Revolution in France*, had been written when the Revolution was still in its early stages – only some lynchings and mob actions, nothing like the steady parade of tumbrels rattling through the streets bringing the daily ration of victims for the guillotine's yawning maw. If only for his quick-sightedness, Burke deserved to be treated with regard, even respect. Yet, strange to say, Tocqueville's stance toward Burke falls just short of being derisive. For all that Burke saw and foresaw, he just did not get it. Consider this brief passage in which Tocqueville displayed both his own astonishment and Burke's as well, and yet ended up disparaging the latter:

I am astonished at the surprising ease with which the Constituent Assembly was able to destroy at a stroke all the former French provinces, several of which were more ancient than the monarchy and then to divide methodically the kingdom into eighty-three distinct districts as if it was dealing with the virgin soil of the New World. Nothing surprised and even terrified the rest of Europe more, since it was not prepared for such a sight. "It is the first time," said Burke, "that we have seen men tear their country into shreds in such a barbarous fashion." In fact [Tocqueville adds], while they seemed to be dismembering living bodies, they were only butchering dead flesh.[3]

this translation as AR, giving Tocqueville's part and chapter numbers, followed by the page number of this edition.

[2] Robert T. Gannett, Jr., *Tocqueville Unveiled: The Historian and His Sources for "The Old Regime and the Revolution"* (Chicago: University of Chicago Press, 2003), 60–65, 70–77.

[3] AR 2.7, 83.

By Tocqueville's account, Burke mistook the French, he mistook what he imagined to be the enduring "ancient common law of Europe," and he even mistook the effectual truth about his own British regime.[4]

Commingling Praise, Blame, and More

Here, then, is my point of departure. Why was it not enough for Tocqueville to document with care and precision whatever it was that Burke had grasped and, correspondingly, what he had failed to see? He does indeed do that. But pressing further, he leaves a reader with the sense that he and Burke are engaged in a kind of winner-takes-all contest. Whatever points can be made against Burke's account redound to Tocqueville's advantage. This is, to say the least, puzzling. What political or rhetorical necessity might dictate such a stance? Given that so much of Tocqueville's narrative testifies to the ignorance, blindness, and folly of the historical actors involved, why single out Burke? It is still more puzzling that Tocqueville, after praising Burke for his acumen in seeing so much while events were still unfolding, insists on blaming Burke for not perceiving what now comes to sight only after the dust has settled. His assessment is that Burke's account is "filled with true touches, but very false on the whole."[5] One might be inclined to excuse this behavior – without, of course, admiring it. It calls to mind a nineteenth-century professor, persuaded of the decisive advantage he enjoys as an investigator thanks to his coming later and knowing what was to follow, confidently beginning, "Wir wissen heute," and taking it from there. His temporal distance from the events he studies permits him to penetrate the fog and obfuscations generated by the passions of partisans.

There is more than a little of this in Tocqueville's book. His first chapter concludes with these assurances:

The time for investigation and judgment seems to have arrived. Today we are positioned at *that exact moment* when we can best decipher and assess this important event. We are far enough from the Revolution to experience only a pale version of the enthusiasms which disturbed the sight of those who led it, yet near enough to be able to empathize with the spirit which guided it and to understand it. Soon it will be difficult to do such a thing, since those great revolutions which are a success conceal the causes which have inspired them

---

[4] AR 1.5, 35.
[5] Cited in Gannett, *Tocqueville Unveiled*, 61–62, and 188 n. 41.

and thus they run beyond our capacity to understand because they were so successful.[6]

Tocqueville's point is not only that the moment is right for seeing better. Our author goes on to stake a further claim: *we* know today what contemporaries could not have known because *I*, Tocqueville, have studied the unmediated true confessions of that time. Thanks to my archival researches in Tours, thanks to my examination of contemporary letters and reports written in confidence, thanks to my assiduous collection and collation and comparisons, I can present you at long last with a true understanding of the beast itself. Mark that well: I did it.

It is no surprise that Tocqueville should put himself at center stage. Even in *Democracy in America* (and not only in the famous author's preface to the twelfth edition), he makes readers cognizant of his actions, tenets, feelings, and so forth. He is no Flaubert hiding behind his story while displaying his omniscience. Rather, Tocqueville means for readers to accompany him as he makes his discoveries, be they of a new world or a newly uncovered past. This makes for engrossing reading and enables him to get away with offering readers a single example while assuring them that he could offer a thousand more. This relentless insertion of the author into the consciousness of the reader is especially marked in *The Ancien Régime and the Revolution*. Gannett's researches in the Tocqueville archives show how studied Tocqueville was in crafting his ethos as an author. His candor with us entitles him to enjoy our trust that he has in fact seen further and understood better than all his predecessors.

All the more reason, then, to wonder at the anger and edginess bordering on scorn that creep into Tocqueville's dismissal of Burke. A gentleman would not descend to that; still less should a nobleman. And when one goes on to reflect on the many points of congruence between Burke and Tocqueville, this tone seems both unbecoming and unwarranted. Both authors deplore the religious fervor that pervaded the Revolution. They both disdain the abstract certainties of the fashionable men of letters, those *Luftmenschen* whom Burke dismissed at the end of his *Reflections* as "the aëronauts of France."[7] Both of them lament the loss and destruction of intermediate bodies that would have offered the various strata of French society the opportunity to come to know one another, to hear and

---

[6] AR 1.1, 20 (emphasis added).
[7] Edmund Burke, *Reflections on the Revolution in France*, ed. J. C. D. Clark (Stanford: Stanford University Press, 2001), 414.

to be heard. Both cherish institutions and habits that reinforce a sense of liberty and the personal dignity that accompanies it. There was, in short, much in Burke's moral taste that would have appealed to Tocqueville's humane liberalism. Yet, for all that, Burke will not do. As Tocqueville put it in his reading notes on *Reflections on the Revolution in France*:

> In sum, this is the work of a mind in itself powerful, and provided with those notions of practical wisdom which are acquired, so-to-speak without thinking about it, in a free country. We see in him, to a supreme degree, the superiority which the practice of [freedom] gives for judging the significance of institutions and their short-term effect. This same effect makes a farmer of good sense like [Arthur] Young so superior, in this regard, to an inexperienced man of genius like Mirabeau. Thus Burke is admirable when he judges the details of new institutions, their immediate effects, the countless errors arising from the new reformers' philosophical presumption and inexperience. He foresees several of the great dangers of the future. But the general character, the universality, the final significance of the Revolution which is beginning, completely escape him. He remains seemingly buried in the old world and the English part of that world, and does not understand the new and universal thing which is happening. He does not yet see in the Revolution anything but a French accident; he does not perceive anything but the strengths the Revolution is taking away from France, and does not see the strengths it will give her. In this work his already furious hatred for our innovators (for he senses that it is his old world that is being attacked, without yet seeing that it is going to fall) is mingled with a supreme contempt, not merely for their villainy, but for their foolishness, their ignorance, their impotence. Later this hatred, stronger and stronger, is mingled with terror and with the kind of respect that one has for great abilities used for doing evil. "These are rogues," he says in 1792, "but the most terrible rogues the world has ever known."[8]

As Tocqueville would have it, Burke was drunk on his vision – really an imagination – of an England resting on solid establishments. What Burke took to be bedrock in Britain had in fact been undergoing the same decay of a feudal and aristocratic order that had afflicted France and the rest of Europe for the past ten generations. Burke's seeming blindness prompts Tocqueville to vent his spleen: "You see this destruction of all individual influence and you seek the causes of the Revolution in accidents! You who see a great aristocracy live before your eyes, do not perceive that the aristocracy here is not just sick but dead before one touches it!"[9] Only a gross phantasm could have prompted Burke to urge upon the

---

[8] OR II, 480. The translation has been slightly altered in light of the French text printed by André Jardin in his edition of *L'ancien régime et la révolution: Fragments et notes inédites sur la révolution* (Paris: Gallimard, 1953), 340–341. This volume corresponds to OC 2:2.

[9] Cited in Gannett, *Tocqueville Unveiled*, 64.

French the fatuous project of trying to reform a corrupt, moribund state. "I must think such a government well deserved to have its excellencies heightened; its faults corrected; and its capacities improved into a British constitution."[10] Tocqueville can hardly contain himself in the face of such advice.

It is surprising that what today appears so easy to see remained as tangled and hidden as it was even to the most farsighted observers.

"You wished to correct the abuses of your government," said Burke himself to the French, "but why stir up novelty? Why did you not adhere to your old traditions? Why not limit yourselves to recovering your old freedoms? Or, if you found it impossible to recover the obliterated character of the constitutions of your ancestors, why did you not cast a glance in our direction where you would have found the ancient common law of Europe?" Burke did not perceive what lay beneath his gaze, namely that the Revolution itself must abolish this ancient common law of Europe. He did not spot that this and nothing else was what it was about.[11]

Even more narrowly, there were no such materials, Tocqueville insisted, whereby the French might have soberly attempted to emulate their neighbors across the Channel. They had been systematically stripped of the institutions and practices by which men who exercised power could be held accountable. Reaching for a grand generalization, he said that anyone who had closely studied the condition of France on the eve of the deluge should have readily foreseen (even without the prophetic gift) that now all desperate actions would be possible – however reckless, however violent. Given Tocqueville's silence about anyone who did comprehend the void at the heart of France, one is tempted to mumble that hindsight is always 20/20. But what about Burke? He was no casual observer.

"What," cried Burke in one of his eloquent pamphlets, "is there not one single man who can reply on behalf of the smallest district? In addition, I do not see anyone who can speak on behalf of anyone else. Each man is arrested without resistance in his own home whether it is for royalism, moderantism or anything else." Burke did not realize in what conditions this monarchy he regretted had left us to our new masters. The administration of the Ancien Régime had in advance removed from the French both the possibility of and the desire for mutual support. When the Revolution took place you would have searched in vain throughout the greater part of France for ten men who might have possessed the habit of acting in tandem on a well-organized basis or of looking after their own defence. The central government was supposed to take charge of these matters. The result was

[10] Burke, *Reflections*, 299; and see 185–189.
[11] AR 1.5, 34–35.

that the central power, having fallen from the hands of the king's administration into those of a sovereign and irresponsible assembly, from being good-natured to being terrible, saw nothing which could stop its progress nor even slow it down even briefly. The cause which so easily brought the monarchy low had made everything possible after its downfall.[12]

Burke ought not to have been astonished at the Frenchmen's inability to act in defense of their own liberties. Strictly speaking, France had long since lost a public capable of being so roused. The old-world order was a house of cards although its inhabitants – even its most farsighted ones – had hardly an inkling of that fact.

Different Moments, Different Urgencies

I confess to having much trouble accepting a reading of Burke that discounts his acumen so heavily. I say this not as a partisan of his politics (which I am not) but as an admirer of his demonstrated conscientious discernment in so many of the great political contests of his day. Burke was congenitally incapable of shooting from the hip, but when he did shoot, you could be confident that he had taken careful aim. Here is a suggestion I offer with much tentativeness. Is it possible that Tocqueville, in turn, mistook his man? Or, worse, is it just possible that Tocqueville chose to mischaracterize one of his most valuable contemporary informants for reasons sufficient to himself? I would not need to be so cautious and tentative today if I asked whether Burke chose for reasons sufficient to himself to mischaracterize features of both France and Britain in his *Reflections on the Revolution in France.* Any half-awake reader can sense that the author of that book is driving with a fully open throttle. Hyperbole abounds; irony, outrage, a cultivated moral imagination, cutting humor, and more are all enlisted in the service of a master of English prose. But to what end? Young Monsieur Charles-Jean-François Depont, the ostensible addressee, was in no position to act on Burke's counsel and criticisms, even had he been so inclined. The fairly common understanding today is that Burke's primary audience was the British public itself, especially those members of the political elite who, enthralled that the French had at long last cashiered a corrupt and repressive government, could imagine following suit and likewise poise themselves to enter into a brighter and happier era. Burke aimed to destroy and besmirch every vestige of that seductive tale lest Britons come to believe it and choose to follow the latest Paris fashion. With that in view, he felt free, perhaps even

[12] AR 3.8, 201–202.

compelled, to present his concerns in the most vivid language. Readers of Burke's writings and speeches on America, Ireland, India, economical reform, religious toleration, and representation know that exaggeration is a tried and tested modus operandi for him. Burke was undoubtedly a master of telling detail, but his powers of persuasion relied less on the exactness of details than on the emotive truth of the whole ensemble. Thus in telling his story to the British, Burke elided the radical and bloody discontinuities that marked so much of their own national history. I like a characterization I once heard of the account Burke gave of the events that led to the replacement of James II by William and Mary: "This is Burke rowing with muffled oars through the Glorious Revolution." Precisely. Burke praised the Convention Parliament of 1689 for throwing "a politic, well-wrought veil" over proceedings that might otherwise constitute a dangerous precedent. He did not want to trivialize (and thereby encourage) extreme acts by domesticating them.[13]

So it strikes me as odd indeed that Tocqueville – himself no stranger to the uses of rhetorical devices – should have given no sign in the text of *The Ancien Régime and the Revolution* that Edmund Burke was not acting as a rapporteur of public sentiment at the time of the outbreak of the Revolution but rather as a dedicated, hyperactive shaper of that public sentiment. Had he chosen to read Burke's flamboyant prose in that way (yes, Burke, like his hapless Dr. Richard Price, was capable of going off the deep end), Tocqueville might have been tempted to extend toward Burke the same kind of slack that I am about to extend toward Tocqueville.

There is no call for me to rehearse here the evidence and grounds for my conviction that the text of *The Ancien Régime and the Revolution* can be read as an example of political defensive theology – the type of argument that the medieval Arabs called by the name *kalām*.[14] In Tocqueville's case, this aggressive defense was mounted not in the name of what had been but for the sake of what might yet be. To show that this was not just another piece of utopian fantasizing, Tocqueville was compelled to identify prefigurations in French history and in French national character, reaching back if need be to ancient portrayals of the early Gauls. He had to show that France, his France, the country presently lulled into stupefaction by the Nephew, still had a useable past. This

---

[13] Burke, *Reflections*, 166.
[14] Ralph Lerner, *Revolutions Revisited: Two Faces of the Politics of Enlightenment* (Chapel Hill: University of North Carolina Press, 1994), 57–66, 122–134.

was by no means the first time he resorted to this tactic. A notable earlier instance can be found in his bravura speech of September 12, 1848, opposing a proposed constitutional guarantee of a right to work. Tocqueville made repeated references there to the goals of the French Revolution, identifying them with the "proud" beliefs and even dreams of that revolution's "immortal assembly – the Constituent Assembly" of 1789. He conjured his contemporaries: "Recall the French Revolution, gentlemen. Return to the terrible and glorious origin of our modern history." There, in those opinions and actions of the men of 1789, later generations would find a standard and a corrective to which they should repair.[15] I cannot improve on Robert Gannett's words: "Revisiting the Revolution of 1789 in these ways, Tocqueville extolled rupture in an earlier era as part of a strategy to resist it in his own."[16] Buried in the detritus of the Revolution were episodes worthy of a difficult but potentially great people. Tocqueville meant to unearth and salvage those possibly redeeming moments, casting them not as a history but as a story. In telling that story, he had to reject Burke's story.

Tocqueville's situation differed from Burke's. There were aspects of the old-world order whose passing this son of an ancient noble family might genuinely have regretted. He might have sought politically acceptable institutions and practices as surrogates for what could no longer be.[17] For Tocqueville, however, unlike Burke, that old world was irretrievably gone. The Revolution had only ratified that fact. Burke, for his part, might have known as much in his bones, but he would never let on. He accepted the new understanding of political economy, with a clear-eyed recognition of the terrible human costs it exacted. To the extent that he would not concede the fight, Burke could not serve Tocqueville's purposes. Tocqueville aimed to redirect and awaken his people's pride. He told a story of what he presented as France's finest hour, that all-too-brief moment when love of liberty inspired a people to rouse itself. His story is a call to remember that not so long ago Frenchmen had believed in themselves. He took care to mute or suppress the fact that those

---

[15] Alexis de Tocqueville, "Speech on the Right to Work," in *Tocqueville and Beaumont on Social Reform*, ed. Seymour Drescher (New York: Harper Torchbooks, 1968), 183, 185, 191.

[16] Robert T. Gannett, Jr., "Tocqueville as Politician: Revisiting the Revolution of 1789," in *Enlightening Revolutions*, ed. Svetozar Minkov (Lanham, MD: Lexington Books, 2006), 235–236.

[17] Consider his treatment of the legal profession and jury trials as surrogates for the aristocratic institutions that a young democracy had never known, DIA I.2.viii.

brave, somewhat mad Frenchmen of 1789 were products of a world now utterly vanished. That silence of his is perhaps the most telling part of his story.

To recapitulate, Burke and Tocqueville each engaged all their art in retelling their nation's history with a view to reshaping prevailing perceptions. For all their overlapping beliefs, the more significant fact is that they confronted different urgencies and differed in their stance toward past, present, and future. Tocqueville was delighted to have become aware of so perceptive a foreign observer of the tumultuous events that formed the stuff of his work in progress. He could not, however, accept Burke's program of trying to salvage the past and, hence, could not accept the way in which that program colored Burke's observations and interpretations. For Tocqueville, Burke's was a lost cause over which the Frenchman would shed nary a tear. He would, instead, focus his own mind and that of his readers on the conditions under which France and the French might yet recover a commitment to political liberty. Achieving that would entail a revolution of another kind, a psychic self-transformation rivaling the events of 1789. The servitude of his countrymen had stretched from the reign of the Sun King down to his own days. Tocqueville needed to offer a rival story, a different perspective by which to take in both the old order and its successor. Were he to succeed, a moment in 1789 might come to be accepted as proof that the French were not forever fated to lead such diminished lives.

The Historian's Slippery Slope

As friends of liberty and human dignity we can only cheer on Tocqueville's efforts on behalf of his people. Whatever they might recover or achieve by dint of his labors would be a net gain for mankind, at least by way of inspiring example, and would entail no loss to ourselves as non-Frenchmen. Yet our admiration is tinged by a shadow or misgiving. As readers of histories (without presuming to speak for the historians among us), we have to wonder whether his admixture of edifying intent does not in fact dilute and corrupt the value of what he presents as a sober and true account. Does not the Muse of History demand more of him, and are we not obliged to insist on his honoring and fulfilling that duty?

Granted that in the very first sentence of his preface Tocqueville disclaims any intention of writing a history of the French Revolution. That has already been done; he means only to present a "study" of that revolution. Adjusting our expectations accordingly, we need not look within

the covers of his book for a large cast of characters or a narrative of mem-
orable episodes. We are, from the outset, pointed in another direction.
The drumbeat of his chapter headings is on "how," in effect announcing
in the table of contents that this is a summary report of findings. The
heavy work of collecting evidence and evaluating its import has been
done behind the scenes. To the extent that concrete details are adduced
at all in the book, they are offered only as exemplary. The reader thus is
spared the messy business of sifting through dusty documents – for which
the reader might well be grateful. At the same time, however, the very
neatness of Tocqueville's account effectively purges or camouflages the
uncertainties, false starts, and surprises that dogged his long efforts to
give his research a shape and resolution. The air of finality that suffuses
the work and the highly rhetorical interjection of its author in the text
combine to rouse suspicions even while attempting to quiet them. This
study emerges as an extended essay in persuasion in pursuit of a political
objective.

In a skeptical age, such a conclusion might be dismissed as bordering on the banal. It would be asked, what work of historical writing
is not political in its intent and formulation? In some cases, the author
openly shows his colors without hesitation or apology. Thus, for example, Winston Churchill nailed to the prow of his multivolume account
of the Second World War (as seen from his high office) both a moral
of the work as a whole ("In War: Resolution / In Defeat: Defiance / In
Victory: Magnanimity / In Peace: Good Will") and the theme of its first
volume ("How the English-speaking peoples through their unwisdom,
carelessness, and good nature allowed the wicked to rearm"). No reader
is to miss those lessons – lessons drawn from the past but intended to be
absorbed and acted on by the coming generations.[18]

Other authors might tread more lightly, muting their didactic and
political intent under cover of setting the historical record straight. A
striking case in point is the way Abraham Lincoln enlisted his skills as a
historical researcher to buttress his moral argument against the Kansas-
Nebraska Act of 1854.

To demonstrate that documentary evidence supported his claim that the Founders
had been ashamed of slavery and had worked within practical limits to prevent
its extension required specific citation of a large number of events, dates, and
documents. His intention was to create a valid alternative to what seemed to him
the false history of legal and public opinion about slavery circulated by those
favorably or indifferently disposed to it.

---

[18] Winston S. Churchill, *The Gathering Storm* (Boston: Houghton Mifflin, 1948).

[His] was, he recognized, an optimistic reading, an alternative vision that took its force from his increasing commitment to the power of narrative to create the truth that comes from belief in the narrative itself.

As an historian, he looked to the past to support the views he desired to promote in the present. The effort was a prodigious one precisely because he recognized that human experience provided powerful oppositional arguments. Slavery and slaveholding were an indisputable historical reality.[19]

As was the case with Tocqueville's retelling of his people's revolution, so too with Lincoln's: we might well cheer on his effort to recall his fellow citizens to the better angels of their nature. Patriotic feeling was to be enlisted in behalf of a country in which one could rightly take pride. If Lincoln pressed Jefferson's principle further than its author had the inclination (or courage) to venture on his own in his own time, it was for the sake of the same cause – liberty and self-governance. Yet the nagging doubt recurs: does this degree of partiality not detract from the claim that an account is indeed the unvarnished truth, the genuine history of an event or place?

In this respect such histories and historians fall short of the highest standards pronounced by Pierre Bayle in the name of the "Lawgiver of the Historians": that legislator's commands are, first, that historians not dare to say anything that is false and, second, that they have the boldness to speak the whole truth. It is fair to say that Bayle devoted the larger part of his life and energies to detecting and exposing others' violations of those commands. Yet even he acknowledged that to act on the second command was well-nigh suicidal, given the ways of the world and the passions of the wicked. And even he acknowledged that a judicious historian would trim his sails, so to speak, by avoiding current events and still-living rulers as subjects of his research lest he expose himself to the resentments of the powerful. Still, this acknowledgment was not a warrant for passing off an untruth as a truth. While allowing a historian to give less than a full account for present purposes, it left room for his successors to fill in the story in calmer times. Given Bayle's concession to an individual historian's concern for his own preservation, might not comparable slack be cut for a historian intent on helping to preserve an entire form of government or even an entire civilization?[20]

---

[19] Fred Kaplan, *Lincoln: The Biography of a Writer* (New York: HarperCollins Publishers, 2008), 248–250.

[20] For an overview of Bayle's counsel to historians and readers of histories, see Ralph Lerner, *Playing the Fool: Subversive Laughter in Troubled Times* (Chicago: University of Chicago Press, 2009), 63–86.

It must be confessed that with such considerations in mind we have ventured forth onto a dangerously slippery slope. At the bottom of that incline lie the preposterous overstatements of "identity museums," the effrontery of myths and other human inventions parading as verifiable facts, and the tendentious accounts that help a people feel doubly resentful of its history of having suffered the malevolence of oppressors or supremely indifferent to its own role in abusing vulnerable others. Psychic satisfaction is not cost free. Yet any aggregation of human beings conscious of itself as linked in some significant way – all the more in cases where it conceives of itself as a people – needs and wants to hear its story told and retold. And, having to take its bearings in a changing world, that people needs a story reaffirming its worth by helping it distinguish whatever is substantial and enduring in its sense of peoplehood from the accidental and transient events that fill its everyday horizon and distort its vision of itself. Rare indeed have been those historians and storytellers whose conscientiousness and self-control enabled them to tell all the truth their times could bear hearing without slipping into fawning, flattery, and lying. They remain, in our age no less than in the age of Tacitus or Bayle, an endangered species.

PART TWO

DEMOCRATIZATION IN A NON-WESTERN CONTEXT

CHAPTER 4

Tocqueville and Religion: Beyond the Frontier of Christendom

Alan Kahan

Alongside each religion is found a political opinion that is joined to it by affinity.

– Alexis de Tocqueville[1]

Tocqueville's Point of Departure

Tocqueville's understanding of religion has been the subject of, to say the least, considerable commentary.[2] Outside the question of his personal faith, where letters are the chief evidence, the literature has focused primarily on *Democracy in America* and to a lesser extent on *The Old Regime and the Revolution*. This focus is justified by the considerable attention Tocqueville devoted to religion in these works, particularly in *Democracy*. Their subject matter naturally led Tocqueville to focus his discussion of religion on Christianity because America and France were predominantly Christian nations. Although *Democracy* contains a notable chapter on pantheism and brief comments on Islam and on the Hindu/Buddhist doctrine of metempsychosis, commentary that relies on

---

[1] DIA (Nolla) [I.2.ix], 467.
[2] Among many others, see Agnès Antoine, *L'Impensé de la démocratie. Tocqueville, la citoyenneté, et la religion* (Paris: Fayard, 2003); Doris Goldstein, *Trial of Faith: Religion and Politics in Tocqueville's Thought* (New York: Elsevier, 1975); Joshua Mitchell, *The Fragility of Freedom: Tocqueville on Religion, Democracy and the American Future* (Chicago: University of Chicago Press, 1999); Barbara Allen, *Tocqueville, Covenant and the Democratic Revolution: Harmonizing Earth with Heaven* (Lanham, MD: Lexington Books, 2005); and Ralph Hancock, "The Uses and Hazards of Christianity in Tocqueville's Attempt to Save Democratic Souls" in Ken Masugi (ed.), *Interpreting Tocqueville's "Democracy in America"* (Savage: Rowman and Littlefield, 1991), 348–393.

89

Tocqueville's chief works for his views on religion is largely limited to discussing his view of Christianity or of religion in general.

In certain respects, however, the context of *Democracy* and *The Old Regime* hinders the understanding of Tocqueville's thought about religion, even with regard to Christianity. The discussion of religion in these books is strongly influenced by their intended readership and in particular his French readers. Tocqueville wanted to persuade French liberals that the Catholic church was not necessarily the enemy of freedom and French Catholics that democracy was not necessarily the enemy of the Catholic church. The needs and prejudices of his readers combined with Tocqueville's own concerns to shape his discussion of religion in these two books. If we step beyond them, beyond the bounds of Tocqueville's discussion of Christianity, we can find new perspectives from which to examine his views. His comments on Islam and Hinduism were filtered through his perennial concern with the relationship between religion and democracy. They were still shaped by the readers Tocqueville had in mind, but they refract Tocqueville's views from different angles and, to some extent, escape the influences that shaped the discussion of religion in *Democracy* and *The Old Regime*. By examining Tocqueville's views of Islam and Hinduism we can see better how Tocqueville understood the relationship between religion, democratic society, and freedom.

It is testimony to the importance Tocqueville gave religion that he read and annotated both the Koran and the Laws of Manu.[3] His knowledge of both Islam and Hinduism nevertheless remained relatively superficial, although to describe his accounts of them as "almost scandalously stereotyping" is anachronistic and unfair.[4] It is true that he knew nothing of Shi'a Islam or of the vast traditions of Islamic law and commentary. Nor are the Laws of Manu the only or the final word in Hindu religious practice. There are far better ways of learning about Islam or Hinduism than reading Tocqueville. Nevertheless, Tocqueville did devote significant study to them. The impulse behind his study was not abstract curiosity, nor was it merely theoretical – such motives rarely moved Tocqueville. His study of Islam was provoked by his political involvement with France's colonization of Algeria and his study of Hinduism by a contemplated book on the English conquest of India, intended with France and Algeria

---

[3] The so-called Laws of Manu are the title given to translations of the "Manava-dharma-Shastra," a work compiled in the first or second century AD, incorporating earlier materials, which serves as a basic guide to Hindu thought and practice. Tocqueville read the French translation of 1833.

[4] Allen, *Tocqueville, Covenant, and the Democratic Revolution*, 279.

in mind, and later by the Great Mutiny of 1857. However, his notes and comments on Islam and Hinduism were not solely directed at these limited contexts. In his reading of the Koran and of Hindu literature, as in his discussion of Christianity and religion in general, Tocqueville sought to understand the political ramifications of different forms of spirituality. It is for this reason that these writings merit a more extended discussion than they have previously received.

Certain aspects of Tocqueville's general approach to religion need to be stressed to understand his approach to Islam and Hinduism. For Tocqueville, religious belief of some kind is an essential bulwark of freedom. Happily, indeed providentially, religion is not an accident.[5] Human beings are naturally religious in the same way that they have a natural desire for freedom. Tocqueville did not think religion was destined to disappear with economic and educational progress.[6] However, while Tocqueville's analysis did not lead to a prediction that religion would necessarily disappear (yet another instance where Tocqueville was wiser than Marx), the existence of democratic society does not necessarily imply the persistence of religion either. Even if some sort of spiritual faculty is present in human souls at birth, just as with the desire for freedom, it is capable of being extinguished by stronger passions, for example, materialism. Although "the instinct and the taste of humanity uphold this doctrine [spiritualism/religion],"[7] Tocqueville feared that religion might disappear. Therefore:

... no matter which religion has put down deep roots within a democracy, be careful about weakening it; but instead protect it carefully as the most precious heritage of aristocratic centuries; do not try to tear men away from their ancient religious opinions in order to substitute new ones, for fear that, during the transition from one faith to another, when the soul finds itself for the moment devoid of beliefs, love of material enjoyments comes to spread and fill the soul entirely.[8]

Tocqueville is desperate for democratic societies to retain their religion. Any religion is better than none. However, religion is subject to

---

[5] DIA (Nolla) [II.2.xv], 959–960.
[6] DIA (Nolla) [I.2.ix], 473; [II.2.xv], 960 note j.
[7] DIA (Nolla) [II.2.xv], 959.
[8] DIA (Nolla) [II.2.xv], 958. See also the following discussion, 958–959. Viewing religion as an inheritance from aristocratic society is inevitable, because society was historically both aristocratic and religious. However, it is paradoxical with regard to Christianity and Islam. Christianity, in Tocqueville's view, is "of all religious doctrines ... the one most favorable to equality," DIA (Nolla) [I.2.ix], 469. Islam is nevertheless in some respects even more egalitarian, according to Tocqueville, because of the absence of a priestly class.

pressures that may cause it to disappear – to the greater profit of despotism. This fundamentally pro-religious perspective needs to be borne in mind whenever Tocqueville criticizes particular religious beliefs or practices.

Three of the reasons Tocqueville thought religion so necessary to democratic societies are particularly relevant to his discussion of Islam and Hinduism: the relationship between religion and materialism in democracies, already alluded to; the psychological relationship between religious belief and freedom; and finally the relationship between religion and the state. These reasons make up a kind of rubric according to which particular religions can be judged.

The relationship between religion and materialism is, like most of the relationships Tocqueville draws, situational rather than constant. In an aristocratic society, people are too inclined to ignore their material interests, and Tocqueville would have tried to make them less interested in the other world and more interested in material needs. "But today, I feel indulgent towards all the follies that spiritualism can suggest. The great enemy is materialism, not only because it is in itself a detestable doctrine, but also because it is unfortunately in accord with the social tendency." Tocqueville argued that "there is no religion that does not place the object of the desires of men above and beyond the good things of the earth, and that does not naturally elevate his soul toward realms very superior to those of the senses." This is true even of "the most false and dangerous religions," whose name is left carefully unspecified, so that readers may fill in the name of whatever denomination displeases them most. Religion thus plays, with regard to materialism, the role of a counterbalance: " . . . religious peoples are naturally strong precisely in the places where democratic peoples are weak; this makes very clear how important it is for men to keep their religion while becoming equal."[9]

Tocqueville wrestled with the issue of balance between the spiritual and the material. This becomes clear in his letters and in some of the rejected passages for the *Democracy*. Thus a rejected passage reads:

To be concerned only with the needs of the body and to forget about the soul. That is the final outcome to which materialism leads.

To flee into the deserts, to inflict sufferings and privations on yourself in order to live the life of the soul. That is the final outcome of spiritualism. I notice at the one end of this tendency Heliogabalus and at the other St. Jerome.

I would very much want us to be able to find between these two paths a road that would not be a route toward the one or toward the other. For if each of these

[9] DIA (Nolla) [II.1.v], 745–746; [II.2.xv], 956 and 962 note n.

two opposite roads can be suitable for some men, this middle road is the only one that can be suitable for humanity.[10]

The image of Heliogabalus and St. Jerome is also found in a letter by Tocqueville to his friend Louis de Kergorlay where, after carefully stating that he will now come to what he thinks himself, Tocqueville states that because human beings have both bodies and souls, they are a mixture of the angel and the beast and that any philosophy or religion that tries to ignore one or the other will produce some extraordinary individuals but will not have much impact on humanity at large.[11] Tocqueville therefore has struggled to discover "a middle path to which humanity can keep and which leads to neither Heliogabalus nor St. Jerome." Thus, Tocqueville writes, he is not so shocked by "honest materialism" as Kergorlay. He despises it, "but I look at it practically, and I ask myself if something if not similar then at least analogous is not still the best that one can ask not of a given individual, but of our poor species in general." Tocqueville prefers spiritualism ("I adore the angel, and I would like to see it predominate at any price"), but he will settle for a balance because that is all that it is possible to achieve with the crooked timber of humanity.[12]

Spiritual balance is not only necessary to humanity in a moral sense or in response to the democratic tendency to materialism; it also plays a directly political role. Tocqueville's views on this subject are complex, but to state them as simply as possible, in a democratic society religion is not a necessary precondition for freedom, because he never says that it must come first, but it is a necessary accompaniment of a durable freedom: "For me, I doubt that man can ever bear complete religious

---

[10] DIA (Nolla) [II.2.xv], 960k. Heliogabalus was a particularly dissolute Roman Emperor of the third century AD.

[11] The image of human nature being a combination of the angel and the beast/animal comes from Pascal's *Pensées*, where it is used at several points. The closest to Tocqueville's use is in #358 in the des Granges edition. Usually translated something like "Man is neither angel nor beast; and the misfortune is that he who would act the angel acts the beast"; a more literal translation comes closer to Tocqueville's meaning: ". . . he who would make the angel makes the beast." The French is "le malheur veut qui veut faire l'ange fait la bête." As so often, however, Tocqueville here accepts Pascal's psychology without drawing a Pascalian, i.e., Christian, conclusion from it.

[12] Tocqueville to Louis de Kergorlay, August 5, 1836, OC 13:1, 389. On the theme of balance between spiritual and secular concerns, see his letter to Kergorlay of August 4, 1857, in which he writes: "I confess I have always [in my heart], considered a book like *The Imitation of Jesus Christ*, for example, when considered other than as instruction intended for the monastic life, supremely immoral. It is not *healthy* to detach oneself from the earth. . . . A certain concern with religious truths which does not go to the point of absorbing thought in the other world has therefore always seemed to me the state which conforms best to human morality in all its forms," SLPS, 357.

independence and full political liberty at the same time; and I am led to think that, if he does not have faith, he must serve, and, if he is free, he must believe." This passage is more complex than it first appears. Individual religious faith, arrived at independently, is not enough to preserve political freedom, for such an independent faith would suggest the complete religious independence that Tocqueville said is incompatible with political liberty. Rather, one must belong to an organized religion; one must have subordinated one's individual judgment in religious matters if one is to preserve the open psychological space necessary for freedom. This reading is confirmed by what Tocqueville says of religion elsewhere: "A religion is an association in which you give up your liberty in a permanent way. Associations of this type are necessary." Why? Because if democratic human beings follow their democratic instinct to decide all questions themselves, there will simply be too many questions to decide, and in despair they are likely to accept the first despotic authority that will take this terrible burden away from them. "Men cannot do without dogmatic beliefs... among all dogmatic beliefs, the most desirable seem to me to be dogmatic beliefs in the matter of religion." To preserve their ability to choose in some areas, human beings must surrender it in others. Tocqueville evidently (if tacitly) thought it more important that everyone be politically independent than religiously independent.[13]

Nevertheless, Tocqueville strongly rejected the idea of a state religion imposed on all citizens to spare them the burden of religious freedom. Tocqueville's Rousseauianism never extended this far. Free democratic human beings need to have a religion, in Tocqueville's view, but they do not all need to have the same religion and in no circumstances whatsoever should this be a religion imposed by the state. Tocqueville's reasoning on this point was as much political as it was religious. In *The Old Regime* he argued that "it was much less as a religious doctrine than as a political institution that Christianity aroused... furious hatreds." As soon as it becomes associated with the government, religion risks becoming discredited whenever governments fall into discredit. Tocqueville's remarks about the relationship between church and state in *The Old Regime* echo the thoughts he had expressed in general terms in *Democracy*:

... as for State religions, I have always thought that if sometimes they could temporarily serve the interests of political power, they always sooner or later become fatal to the Church.

[13] DIA (Nolla) [II.1.ii], 714; [II.1.5], 743, 745.

Nor am I one of those who judge that in order to raise religion in the eyes of the people, and to honor the spiritualism that religion professes, it is good to grant indirectly to its ministers a political influence that the law refuses to them.

I feel so convinced of the nearly inevitable dangers that beliefs run when their interpreters mingle in public affairs, and I am so persuaded that Christianity must at all cost be maintained within the new democracies, that I would prefer to chain priests within the sanctuaries than allow them out of it.[14]

Tocqueville rarely advocated chaining anyone, even metaphorically. That he would chain priests in their sanctuaries rather than see them involved in politics shows the depth of his hostility to either a state religion or a political clergy.

These aspects of Tocqueville's thought about the role of religion in democratic society, the relationship between religion and materialism, the psychology of religion and freedom, and the relationship of religion to the state are particularly important to understanding Tocqueville's judgment of Islam and Hinduism. Of the two, Islam attracted more of Tocqueville's attention because of his involvement with Algeria.

Tocqueville on Islam

We do not know when Islam first came to Tocqueville's attention, or how. Certainly he was familiar at an early date with Montesquieu's discussion of Islam in the *Persian Letters* and *Spirit of the Laws* and probably with other references to Islam in eighteenth-century French literature. This is all that is necessary to explain the first brief reference to Islam in volume one of *Democracy*, published in 1835. When Tocqueville states there that religion, rather than fear, can take the place of patriotism under despotism, he gives the example of the Turks who identified their sultan with Islam. Fear, by contrast, was the sole principle of despotic government according to Montesquieu, and Tocqueville, as often in *Democracy*, was taking the opportunity to contradict his teacher.[15]

However, by the time he made his second reference to Islam in volume two of the *Democracy*, published in 1840, Tocqueville had read and annotated a considerable portion of the Koran.[16] He wrote two articles about Algeria during his unsuccessful parliamentary campaign in 1837, and Algeria would preoccupy him from his election to parliament in 1839 until the end of the July Monarchy in 1848. To understand Algeria, it was

[14] DIA (Nolla) [II.2.xv], 961–962.
[15] DIA (Nolla) [I.1.v], 158–159 note y.
[16] He read the Koran in March 1838.

only natural that someone with Tocqueville's views of the political and social importance of religion should try to understand Islam, the religion of its inhabitants. Tocqueville's first impressions of Islam were mixed, but he became more hostile over time, although it is possible by reading Tocqueville somewhat against the grain to make out a more favorable Tocquevillean view of Islam.

Tocqueville went to considerable trouble to try to find a good French translation of the Koran and the Hadith, the traditions of Mohammed's life and actions. His informants told him there were none and directed him to what they considered the best available French translation of the Koran. In March 1838 Tocqueville wrote to his friends Francisque de Corcelle and Louis de Kergorlay that he was reading the Koran in his spare time. He told Corcelle that he was not seduced by Mohammed but that Mohammed was "an able man amid all his divagations. It is difficult to strike a more able bargain between spiritualism and materialism, the angel and the beast. The Koran is nothing but this." This is, in a certain respect, the highest praise Tocqueville could give a religion because he thought that any religion that sought to affect humanity at large had to recognize that human beings were a mixture of "the angel and the beast," and he himself sought constantly to find a middle path between the two. The letter to Corcelle implies that the Koran might be such a path. However, in the same month as his letter to Corcelle, he wrote in a very different tone to Kergorlay. Although he again stated that the Koran was "a pretty able compromise between materialism and spiritualism," he also found it vastly inferior to the Gospels and said he could not conceive how a mutual acquaintance had found it superior to them. He described the compromise between materialism and spiritualism made by Mohammed in negative terms and complained that "the *violent* and *sensual* tendencies of the Koran are so striking that I don't see how they can escape a man of good sense" (emphasis original). Tocqueville was disturbed that "the first of all religious duties is to blindly obey the prophet" and that "holy war is the first of all good works."[17] Tocqueville went on to say that the Koran represented progress over polytheism in that it contained "clearer and truer ideas of God" and "embraces certain general duties of humanity with a more extended and clearer vision. But it arouses passions, and in this respect I do not know if it has not done more harm to men than polytheism." "Mohammed has," wrote

---

[17]   Tocqueville is translating, or rather citing the translation of, the ambiguous term "jihad" as holy war. This may be dubious but is certainly a common translation of the word.

Tocqueville, "exercised an immense power over the human species that I think, all in all, has been more harmful than salutary."[18]

Moving from Tocqueville's letters to his notes on the Koran, we find the same mixed but on balance negative appraisal. He writes that the Koran contains "almost all the general principles of morality that all religions contain," and he approves of its special emphasis on charity. However, he remarks on Mohammed's violence, particularly toward idolaters and Jews, the injunction to Jihad, and the killing or conversion of infidels by force. In almost all the Koran, Tocqueville writes, "Mohammed is much more concerned with making people believe than with giving rules of morality. And he employs terror more than any other motivation." Lest one think the Koran is unique in this, however, Tocqueville compares Mohammed in this respect to Moses, and he states that "one recognizes Moses all the time. It [the Koran] hardly goes beyond the Ten Commandments."[19]

Thus, although Tocqueville gave possible grounds for an apology for Islam – that is, that it is the sort of able compromise between the material and spiritual that is needed in a religion in a democratic society – he himself did not take this view of Islam, and he preferred Christianity as an antidote to materialism. A similar argument could be made in regard to Islam as "submission" (the meaning of the word "Islam") to the will of God. Given that Tocqueville argued that religion is a kind of association in which human beings must surrender their liberty, as long as they are part of the association, and that such associations are necessary, especially in democracies, then the fideistic aspect of Islam (as of other religions) would seem to meet with Tocqueville's approval.

However, in practice, Tocqueville thought that Islam's affinity was with despotism rather than freedom (even if it is possible to use some of his ideas to make the opposite case). The reasons Tocqueville thought so are often misunderstood, and in this context it is well to dismiss two possible objections to Islam that Tocqueville might plausibly be supposed to have held but that he did not. The first of these is the problem of predestination. Like Calvinists, Muslims believe that the question of individual salvation is predetermined. Tocqueville, as is well known, rejected all theories, whether secular or religious, that claimed that the future of humanity or of individual human beings was predetermined. Indeed, he

---

[18] Letter to Corcelle, March 19, 1838, SLPS, 98; Letter to Kergorlay, March 21, 1838, OC 13:2, 28–29.
[19] *Notes sur le Coran*, in OC 3:1, 154, 156, 158–160.

wrote in *Democracy* that the "doctrine of fatality" is particularly attrac-
tive to people in democratic times and that if it took hold, "it would
soon paralyze the movement of new societies and reduce Christians to
Turks." French republican anticlericals would later attack Catholicism
for encouraging fatalism (was Tocqueville projecting a potential critique
of Christianity onto Islam?).[20] However, Tocqueville was well aware
that the Puritans, whose contribution to American freedom he thought
crucial, were Calvinists who believed in predestination. There is a distinction to be made between the theological doctrine of predestination
and the human practice of fatalism. It is only the latter that Tocqueville
condemned. Tocqueville ascribed the stagnation of Islamic societies to
reasons other than the doctrine of predestination.

Secondly, in *The Old Regime* Tocqueville compared the revolutionaries with Islam because, like Islam, the Revolution "flooded the earth
with its soldiers, apostles and martyrs."[21] This would be a rejection of
Islam only if it was a rejection of the Revolution. Certainly, Tocqueville
criticized both the French Revolution and Islam for tendencies to excessive violence. Nevertheless, Tocqueville was by no means an opponent of
the Revolution (at least of what he considered its "good parts"), and the
same could be said, in this respect at least, of Islam. Proselytism, whether
religious or political, is in Tocqueville's view a necessary consequence of
the idea of equality.

Nevertheless, Tocqueville's overall judgment of Islam was negative
(and it became more so over time) despite the positive elements he saw
in it. The main reason for his disapproval of Islam had less to do with
any particular disposition of the Koran than with its larger context. What
led Tocqueville in the final analysis to strongly reject Islam was its relationship to political freedom. Islam has a natural affinity with despotism,
according to Tocqueville, not because of predestination or even fatalism
and not because of violence but rather because of the absence of any separation between church and state. The reason Tocqueville gives for the
lack of separation of church and state in Islam is at first glance paradoxical: it is the absence of a priesthood, an absence that Tocqueville thinks
is in principal good.

In preparation for his first voyage to Algeria in May and June 1841,
Tocqueville read and annotated a variety of material about Algeria and
its population. At some point in this period, he wrote a piece titled "Why

---

[20] DIA (Nolla) [II.1.xx], 858.
[21] OR I, 101.

There is no Priesthood (*sacerdoce*) Among the Muslims." Unlike most of his Algerian notes, according to the editor, these pages "are written without crossing-out and in an exceptionally legible manner, which allows one to suppose that Tocqueville, intending to preserve this note, carefully recopied it."[22]

Tocqueville thought the absence of a priesthood in Islam a striking fact, a fact "which in itself seems at first glance very unusual, because all religions, and above all those which have strongly influenced the human imagination, have acquired or preserved their influence with the aid of a priestly corps very separate from the rest of the nation and very strongly constituted." This absence was "a good amidst all the evils to which the Muslim religion has given birth. For a priestly body is in itself the source of much social malaise, and when a religion can be powerful without the aid of such a means, one must praise it for that."[23] In this passage Tocqueville, freed from the constraints of a Catholic audience, allowed a Protestant side of his thought to be glimpsed. The democratic "priesthood of all believers," as Martin Luther put it, was to be preferred to the aristocratic if not hereditary position of the Catholic clergy. In this regard, Islam was even more egalitarian than Protestantism.

Tocqueville gave two reasons why Islam had no priests. Early Islam was organized for war, and as a result, there was little ritual, and what there was was simple, without any need of a priest to perform it. But much more important, according to Tocqueville, was that "Islam is the religion which has the most completely combined and intermixed the two powers [civil and religious]." Because there was no separation of church and state, there was no need, and for that matter no means, of distinguishing the clergy from other educated people. Tocqueville's chief complaint about Islam is that the separation between church and state, so laboriously acquired in Europe, never happened in Islam. Tocqueville recognized that this separation did not come about in Europe with the church's consent, but what mattered was that it never came about at all in Islam. "Religion and justice have always been combined in Muslim countries, like the ecclesiastical courts tried to do in Christian Europe."[24]

The fundamental problem was that the Koran simultaneously regulated the general moral and religious duties of humanity and provided detailed rules of civil and political law. This combination led to two

[22] OC 3:1, 173, 173 note 1.
[23] OC 3:1, 174.
[24] OC 3:1, 173–174, 181.

serious problems from Tocqueville's perspective – one of political organization and one of social organization – which together had disastrous
results for Muslim countries. The political problem was that Islam had
combined civil and religious authority "in such a way that the high priest
is necessarily the ruler, and the ruler the high priest, and that all the
acts of civil and political life are more or less regulated according to
religious law." Thus, the politico-religious institution of the caliphate,
which combined supreme civil and religious authority in one individual, was anathema in Tocqueville's eyes. Socially, "since the Koran is
the common source from which issue religious law, civil law and even
in part secular science, the same education is given those who want to
become religious ministers, doctors of law, judges and even scholars. The
sovereign takes indiscriminately among this educated class the ministers
of religion or imams [Tocqueville does not consider imams a priestly
body], the doctors of law or muftis and the judges or Cadis." Thus, the
secular and the sacred were constantly intermixed. Although Tocqueville
did not say if this was detrimental from a religious point of view, it was
catastrophic from a secular perspective: "This concentration and confusion established by Mohammed between the two powers has on the one
hand produced this particular good [the absence of a priesthood], and on
the other hand it has been *the first cause of the despotism and above all
of the social immobility which has almost always been characteristic of
Muslim nations, and which finally made them all fall before the nations
which have embraced the opposite system.*"[25]

This is the reasoning behind Tocqueville's negative judgment of Islam
found in volume two of *Democracy* (1840), a judgment both more knowl-
edgeable and more hostile than that found in volume one:

Mohammed made not only religious doctrines, but also political maxims, civil
and criminal laws, and scientific theories descend from heaven and placed them
in the Koran. The Gospel, in contrast, speaks only of the general relations of men
with God and each other. . . . That alone, among a thousand other reasons, is
enough to show that the first of these two religions cannot long dominate during
times of enlightenment and democracy, whereas the second is destined to reign
during these centuries as in all others.[26]

Two things worth noting about this passage are, firstly, the tone of false
confidence that Tocqueville adopts with regard to the domination of
Christianity. He was by no means confident that the democratic religious

---

[25] OC 3:1, 174, emphasis added.
[26] DIA (Nolla) [II.1.v], 746–747.

future would be Christian rather than pantheist or frankly material-ist. This passage was probably written to help convince devout French Catholic readers of his bona fides. Was he sincere in his praise of Chris-tianity? Doubtless he was, at least of his ideal of Christianity. Historical reality, as Tocqueville knew, was another matter. However, to convince French readers of the need to reconcile religion and freedom, it made more sense to appeal to the ideal than to the real.

With regard to Islam, however, Tocqueville had no need to develop an ideal different from what he perceived to be the reality, and he did not. His reasoning of 1840 is repeated in an 1844 letter to Richard Monckton Milnes. Milnes had made a trip to the Middle East and returned, in Tocqueville's view, "a little more Muslim than is suitable." As far as Tocqueville was concerned:

As I got to know this religion better, I better understood that from it above all comes the decadence that before our eyes more and more affects the Muslim world. Had Mohammed committed only the mistake of intimately joining a body of civil and political institutions to a religious belief in a way to impose on the first the immobility that is in the nature of the second, that would have been enough to doom his followers in a given time first to inferiority and then to inevitable ruin. The grandeur and holiness of Christianity is in contrast to have tried to reign only in the natural sphere of religions, abandoning all the rest to the free movement of the human mind.[27]

Regardless of the accuracy of Tocqueville's statement about Chris-tianity (when he attempted to make a similar remark in *Democracy*, his brother and father criticized it, and he left it out),[28] the fundamental source of his rejection of Islam seems clear. Islam presented many advan-tages from a Tocquevillean perspective: a stance midway between mate-rialism and spiritualism, a proper dogmatism in matters of faith, a strong emphasis on charity (very important to Tocqueville), and the absence of a priesthood. Nevertheless, none of this could compensate for its histori-cal failure, by comparison with Christianity, to establish and maintain a strong separation – political, civil, and educational – between church and state, the religious, and the secular realms. Tocqueville's views on Islam

---

[27] Letter to Milnes (Lord Houghton), May 29, 1844, cited in DIA (Nolla) [II.1.v], 747 note e. He said much the same thing in a letter to Gobineau, who had also been much taken with Islam, in a letter of October 22, 1843, OC 9, 68–69, in which he also suggested that Islam on the whole was a regress in comparison with polytheism. Given his other remarks on the subject, this letter was probably meant merely to counter Gobineau's enthusiasm, rather than representing Tocqueville's settled conviction.

[28] See DIA (Nolla) [I.12.ix], 468 note a.

and his reading of the Koran underline the importance he placed on this separation.

The problem lies less in the difference between the Koran and the Gospels, however much Tocqueville preferred the latter, than in the historical developments that led to a separation of church and state in Christendom and not in the Islamic world. Even in this regard the reader of Tocqueville's *Old Regime* is made very aware of the intermingling of the Catholic church and the state in old regime France, just as his nineteenth-century reader, and Tocqueville himself, was very aware of the close alliance between throne and altar in much of Europe. By Tocqueville's own account, the historical versions of Christianity do not live up to Tocqueville's ideal Christianity. Naturally, the history of Islam is even further removed from it.

Is the solution for the Islamic world, then, conversion to Christianity? Absolutely not, in Tocqueville's view. This is in accord with the statement made in *Democracy* that it is wrong to try to persuade a democratic nation to change its religion. This attitude (as well as the rest of his views of Islam) was only confirmed by his visits to Algeria. Thus in his 1847 report on Algeria, written after his second trip to Algeria in November and December 1846, Tocqueville wrote that it was wrong to try to discourage Islamic education in Algeria and that on the contrary Islamic religious education ought to be encouraged for fear that otherwise ignorant and fanatical leaders would take the place of a more educated and presumably more moderate class. This is not to say that Tocqueville was sanguine about Islam's fate. How could he be, when he was not confident in the fate of Christianity? Thus, he wrote that Islam too was faced with the danger of materialism, and indeed that Islamic faith, while still very lively, was daily losing ground in Algeria to "the interests of this world," as shown by the fact that many Muslim Algerians were willing to take service in the French army.[29] However, neither Tocqueville's parliamentary reports on Algeria nor his notes on his travels say very much about Islam directly besides lamenting the lack of a good translation of the Koran and wishing the French government would finance one.[30] We can only infer from this that they did not change Tocqueville's views.

[29] "Report on Algeria," OC 3:1, 326; "Second Letter on Algeria," August 22, 1837, OC 3:1, 151–152. Elsewhere he complains about insufficient salaries being paid to Muslim clerics. See OC 3:1, 421–422.
[30] See OC 5:2, 207.

Thus, Islam neither could nor should be replaced by Christianity. Rather, it should be preserved. Were Tocqueville a Muslim, we might imagine him encouraging elements in Islam that could lead to a separation of mosque and state. Islam does, from a Tocquevillean perspective, potentially meet many of the needs of democratic society. Historically, the egalitarian traits of Islam had led only to democratic despotism under a sultan or caliph, all equal beneath the master. In the future, a reformed Islam might be the foundation of democratic freedom. However, Tocqueville was not a Muslim. His interest in Islam was an outgrowth of his interest in Algeria, and his interest in Algeria was from a purely French perspective. Tocqueville had enough to do trying to put French colonization in order without concerning himself with the reform of Islam – a reform he would doubtless have judged difficult for an outsider to influence and perhaps dangerous for French domination. But Islam, because like Christianity it is a fundamentally democratic religion in Tocqueville's view, has the latent potential to become, like Christianity, freedom's friend. Freedom needs the support of religion because to endure it needs people whose character mingles the "angel and the beast" rather than sinking into materialism and individualism. The Koran provides this. If the Koran does not provide the means for separating mosque and state, then we should remember that in Tocqueville's view, it was not the Gospel verses about "render unto Caesar" that performed this separation in the West but the course of medieval history. If the affinity of Christian dogma with freedom is superior in Tocqueville's eyes, that superiority is not in itself sufficient to make Christianity freedom's friend. Conversely, if the affinity of the Koran with freedom is less than that of the New Testament, this inferiority, given the other potential contributions to freedom found in the Koran, is not sufficient to prevent Islam from becoming freedom's friend – once that potential is liberated by the separation of mosque and state. The liberation of the Muslim world and the end of its long decadence depend on that separation.

Hinduism, on the other hand, lacks this potential – it cannot become a bulwark of freedom. There are some continuities in Tocqueville's analysis of Islam and Hinduism, but the differences far outnumber them. The chief continuity is a criticism – the view that Hinduism, like Islam, contributed to social immobility and stagnation. However, beyond this Tocqueville's view of Hinduism is very different than his view of Islam and much less favorable. Whereas Islam is a religion that at least in some respects may be adequate to the needs of modern democratic society, Hinduism, in Tocqueville's view, is an aristocratic or pseudo-aristocratic religion that for centuries has been completely inadequate to the needs of Indian civilization.[31]

Tocqueville on Hinduism

Tocqueville took some time to arrive at this conclusion. He did not discuss Hinduism at all in volume one of *Democracy*. He briefly mentioned the doctrine of metempsychosis (the transmigration of souls) in volume two. He did not like it and thought the idea that a formerly human soul might one day inhabit an insect an affront to human dignity and an act of *lèse humanité*. Nevertheless, it was better than materialism. It gave people some incentive to despise the body and some elevation to their ideas. Thus, it possessed at least some merit.[32]

However, Tocqueville only began to study India and Hinduism seriously in 1841 to 1843 after *Democracy* was completed. He then considered writing one or two articles and even a book about the British conquest of India, with Algeria in mind. The project was abandoned, but not before Tocqueville had done a considerable amount of reading and taken many notes that naturally devoted considerable attention to Hinduism. In particular Tocqueville read the French translation of the "Manava-dharma-Shastra," the Laws of Manu, and annotated them. The Laws of Manu, thought to have been written circa 100 to 200 AD but containing earlier material, embody a relatively conservative vision of Hinduism.

Tocqueville's discussion of Hinduism is sharply distinct from his discussion of Islam. Islam, Christianity, and most other religions share a more or less common set of moral principles, in Tocqueville's view – but not Hinduism. Tocqueville found the morality of the Laws of Manu offensive. He was appalled at the fact that ritual errors, such as defecating incorrectly, could be mortal sins and that both ritual and real sins could be washed away by the performance of rites without any demand for repentance. According to Tocqueville, the Laws of Manu ordain that if a Brahmin kills a Sudra, he need only say a certain prayer 100 times to wipe out the sin. Meanwhile, any Brahmin who cooks a meal for a Sudra will go to hell, where he will be plunged in boiling oil. Even worse, certain prayers of absolution are only known to certain castes or can

---

[31] "Ebauches d'un ouvrage sur l'Inde," OC 3:1, 446.
[32] DIA (Nolla) [II.2.xv], 958–959.

only be performed by certain castes, and thus prayer becomes "the privilege of certain men only. One could not combine two more abominable principles."33

Tocqueville blamed some of this immorality on the doctrine of metempsychosis, "from which the Indians conclude that morally there is as much evil in stepping on an ant as in committing a homicide." Tocqueville finally concluded:

What a school of practical morality is such a religion! And amidst these abominable maxims, one finds the statement that to practice virtue in order to receive a reward is good, but that to practice virtue without regard for any recompense is perfection, and leads directly to paradise. What a chaos of ideas superior to those of most pagan religions and dogmas more coarse than any other! Almost all religions have proceeded by purifying and improving themselves. This one seems to present a source of light which grows continually darker.34

Hinduism's failings derived, in Tocqueville's view, from one fatal flaw – the caste system. Tocqueville had no sympathy for caste whatsoever. And there was no escape from it because in Hinduism (as in Islam), "religion is mixed into everything . . . everything is a religious act among the Hindus," and thus everything was a matter of caste. Those without caste were as imprisoned by it as anyone else. Rejecting the claim of a French commentator who held that the untouchable classes were all thieves and that this proved that the caste system was a social necessity in India, Tocqueville wrote: "He does not see that on the contrary this is because of the caste system. The pariahs are contemptible and lawless because opinion despises them and makes them outlaws." The fact that most Indians belong to lower castes that are hereditary and from which there is no escape led, in Tocqueville's view, to complete political indifference on the part of the mass of the population.35

Hinduism did have at least one good trait lacking in both Islam and Christianity: "Brahmanism is . . . the most tolerant of religions." However, even this virtue becomes a fault in Tocqueville's eyes – Brahminism cannot produce religious intolerance as a form of ersatz patriotism. According to Tocqueville, there is only one duty that is not part of the Hindu religion: "to die for the country." This too is a result of the caste system. In India, "there are a multitude of castes, there is no nation, or

---

33 "Ebauches," OC 3:1, 544–545.
34 OC 3:1, 548.
35 OC 3:1, 480 marginal note (b), 537.

rather each of these castes forms a little nation apart, which has its separate spirit, customs, laws, government. The national spirit of the Hindus is confined to the caste." Tocqueville went on to generalize that "in a country of castes, the idea of the fatherland, of the nationality, disappears in some sense. There is nothing but the caste and it is too weak to resist. The caste spirit when it becomes all-powerful strongly favors conquest."[36]

It may appear ironic to see Tocqueville, who favored the maintenance of French power in Algeria, chastise Hinduism for not inspiring greater resistance to the British. However, Tocqueville never condemned either Algerians or Indians for resisting European conquest; rather, he condemned Hinduism for its complicity. This led Tocqueville to pronounce a further anathema against Hinduism:

The religion which has introduced among them so many vicious institutions and harmful principles has thus not produced this single good which one has a right to expect from even the worst religions. It has never inspired in them that pious fervor which has led so many peoples to oppose conquest when the conqueror professes another faith than their own and which has led them to save their nationality in wishing to honor their religion.[37]

Besides tolerance, the other advantage Tocqueville found in Hinduism was also a mixed blessing. Hindus, according to Tocqueville (although later in his notes he questioned this), neither convert nor persecute because they do not believe all human beings are equal: "it is the idea of the common origin of the human species, of the similarity of men . . . which introduced proselytizing and persecution into the world. Both have always been unknown in India." Hindus, far from wanting to convert other people, even have an aristocratic reluctance to tell others about their religion. Proselytism is fundamentally a democratic idea, according to Tocqueville; it can only come "after that of the equality of men and above all that of the unity of the human race."[38] Hinduism is an aristocratic religion in an aristocratic society. As such, it reinforces its society's flaws rather than moderating them.[39]

Hinduism's aristocratic nature, or rather its perversion of aristocracy into caste, was its fundamental failing in Tocqueville's eyes. Its lack of

[36] OC 3:1, 447–448, 537.
[37] OC 3:1, 449.
[38] Those who question whether Tocqueville really preferred democracy to aristocracy should take his rejection of aristocratic Hinduism into account.
[39] OC 3:1, 448, 507, 542.

either patriotism or intolerance was "explained very well if one pays attention to the fact that it is a religion of privileges. The necessary limits of its devotees are those of the race. One belongs to it by right of birth: there is no means of entering it if one is not born in its bosom." Hinduism is an aristocratic religion of the worst kind. It is a religion of caste from which there is no escape, a sort of humanly enforced social determinism that Tocqueville abhorred even more in practice than in theory. Tocqueville's attacks on the French nobility of the old regime as a caste likely derived some of their vigor from the picture of caste Tocqueville first painted on an Indian background. Indeed, it is only by seeing how violently Tocqueville rejected the caste system in India that the accusation that the French nobility had become a caste, rather than an aristocracy, takes on its full force in Tocqueville's eyes.[40]

Hinduism's failings caused Tocqueville to question the argument of *Democracy* that any religion is better than none. Even though Hindu sannyasis ("ascetics") did help maintain, according to Tocqueville, the necessary ascendancy of the spiritual over the material, and the Hindu religion was the "sole link which holds together all these different nations that we call castes," this did nothing to soften Tocqueville's judgment that Hinduism was, in the end, "a demoralizing religion," indeed "an abominable religion, perhaps the only one which is worth less than none."[41]

In Tocqueville's view, it was impossible to fundamentally improve the condition of India without completely destroying the caste system and all the institutions and mores associated with it. However, Tocqueville did not think it possible to make a "*table rase*," as he put it. "Will the Hindus adopt our civilization and our religion?" he asked. The answer was that "nothing yet announces this. Christianity is in decline in India." Precisely because Hinduism was involved in every aspect of daily life, every aspect of daily life would have to be changed at once for Hinduism to be replaced. Whether or not India would benefit, Hinduism was therefore unlikely to be replaced in the near future, although there were "signs of a society in the course of dissolution in Hindu society. Mixing of castes, their members working outside their respective attributions, incredulity amidst superstition. But all this is weak, this work will have to take a long time."[42]

---

[40] OC 3:1, 448.
[41] OC 3:1, 480 marginal note (b), 546, 549.
[42] OC 3:1, 480, 480b, 540, 544.

It is possible to imagine an Islam of which Tocqueville would approve. It is much more difficult to imagine this for Hinduism. Does this mean Tocqueville despaired of the future of India, or of the formation of an Indian nation? Not at all. Rather, "the English will end up by putting the Hindus into a condition to resist them" – a paradoxical consequence of English success in their *mission civilisatrice* in India – "but this time is very far away." In a peculiar foreshadowing of Gandhian methods, Tocqueville then cited an incident that took place in a village near Varanasi, when the whole population went on a hunger strike until a new tax was removed. Tocqueville concluded from this incident that this was "a unique example which simultaneously proves the gentleness of this people, but at the same time its faculty of association and the energy it can put into its political associations." High praise indeed from Tocqueville. In the long run, therefore, Tocqueville was not entirely a pessimist in the Indian case.[43]

However, Tocqueville's optimism about India is not optimism about Hinduism. He was not explicitly optimistic about Islam either (indeed, he was implicitly pessimistic about Catholicism at times, especially later in his life). Unlike in the case of Islam (or Catholicism), however, there is no prospect for the reform of Hinduism, no imaginable path such a reform might take, and no way for Hinduism to become freedom's friend. If English conquest has introduced the seeds of democratic society into India and thus sown resistance in a time to come, neither democracy nor resistance will owe anything to Hinduism. Rather the decline of the caste system Tocqueville noted was implicitly a decline in Hinduism. When in 1857 the Great Mutiny occurred in India, Tocqueville did not attribute it to Hinduism, incapable, in his view, of stimulating patriotism. Rather it was "the revolt of barbarism against pride," the pride being the Englishman's own sense of caste and racial superiority, too freely expressed by English officers to native soldiers.[44] Tocqueville may well have been wrong to disassociate Hinduism from the Mutiny. However, even if we associate Hinduism with the caste pride the English affronted, Hinduism in Tocqueville's perspective then becomes no more than a sort of "collective individualism" of the sort Tocqueville castigated in France in *The Old Regime*.[45] It may spark a revolt; it cannot serve as the foundation for freedom.

---

[43] OC 3:1, 481.
[44] Letter to Henry Reeve, 30 January 1858, SLPS, 363–364.
[45] OR I, 163.

Tocqueville, Religion, and Freedom

Understanding Tocqueville's views of Islam and Hinduism does not result in a great upheaval in our understanding of Tocqueville's thought. His concerns about the social and political functions of religion remain the same, as do his analytical methods. Nevertheless, this examination permits us to understand his attitude to religion in new ways. Because neither Christianity nor the Christian/Catholic prejudices of a broad readership were engaged – there was no readership for his notes, only one reader at a time for his letters, and his official reports on Algeria gave very little consideration to Islam – Tocqueville could more freely express some of his attitudes. Thus, for example, we see him develop a Protestant view of the priesthood and present a largely instrumental view of religion. If some aspects of his analysis of religion in *Democracy* are repeated – for example, the role of religion in combating materialism – other sides to this story are now given greater emphasis, as in the crucial importance Tocqueville placed on the separation of church/mosque and state, or else given new expression, for example, the need for religions to balance materialism and spiritualism.

Tocqueville's discussion of Islam and Hinduism thus allows us to make a more general statement, at least in some respects, of his view of the relationship between religion and freedom, one that is not limited by the historical circumstances of old regime France or poly-Christian America. In his view, religion needs to withdraw from the public sphere to make room for freedom to exist, yet it must remain present there for freedom to endure. The separation of religion and the state is an essential element of a free society. At the same time, however, religion must continue to influence the conduct of people in both the public and the private spheres because otherwise freedom in democratic society will be very fragile. Freedom in democratic society will be vulnerable without support from religion because individuals will be more vulnerable to materialism and to psychological disorientation, both of which encourage them to prefer an orderly despotism to a disorderly freedom, and both of which are tempered by religion. Religions (except perhaps Hinduism), regardless of whether they consciously support or oppose freedom, will indeed serve this purpose, at least to some degree. However, if a religion opposes freedom, and especially if it fails to recognize the necessity for its withdrawal from the state, freedom will suffer, society will suffer (e.g., the decline of the Muslim world vis-à-vis Europe), and in the long run religion itself will suffer. This long-run consequence is perhaps the most deadly because in a democratic society, Tocqueville thinks, it is very hard for a new religion to become established, and widespread materialism and psychological disorientation are the most likely result of a religion's decline, rather than its replacement by a new religion.

Above all, however, we learn from Tocqueville's discussion of Islam and Hinduism that for him the relationship between religion and democratic society, religion and freedom, is not simply a concern of the West. For Tocqueville, democracy is a global phenomenon, and the relationship between democracy and religion is not just a story about Christianity or Western religions. Whether he was examining Christianity or Islam or Hinduism, what concerned Tocqueville was the relationship that religion might have with democracy and with freedom. That relationship, like all the social relationships Tocqueville discussed, was a complex one, mingling causality and affinity, historical accident and philosophical logic. It took different shapes in different times and places. However, when it comes to religion, Tocqueville is always consistent on one point: however aristocratic his thought may be in certain respects, the fundamental moral equality of all human beings and all human souls, wherever and whenever they might be, is central to his way of thinking. When it comes to religion, Tocqueville is without reservation a democrat.

CHAPTER 5

Deliberating Democratization with Tocqueville: The Case of East Asia

Cheryl B. Welch

Introduction

In the millennial issue of the *Journal of Democracy*, public intellectuals from around the globe addressed issues affecting the future of democracy through the texts of Alexis de Tocqueville. The editors commented: "One may say with little exaggeration: We are all Tocquevilleans now."[1] This characterization is particularly true of scholars who study the emerging democratic politics of East Asia for two reasons. First, the theoretical *point de départ* of many of these scholars is eminently Tocquevillean. Just as Tocqueville combated the view of conservatives that France's aristocratic history and hierarchical religion rendered the French unfit for self-government, many theorists of democracy in East Asia struggle against the premise that patterns of paternalistic authority and popular dependency in Confucian societies prevent true democratization. However, just as Tocqueville also doubted that socioeconomic development would eventually bring freedom in its wake, directing attention instead to the uncertain political trajectory of transitional societies, many contemporary observers of Asian economic tigers argue that the fate of democracy in the region is unclear. Consolidating democracy, they argue, depends on contingent connections among modernization, political cultures, state structures, and political will. They are speaking Tocquevillean prose without knowing it. A second reason for Tocqueville's salience in this context arises from a different sort of *conjoncture*. Unlike other nineteenth-century theorists of the European democratic transition, who tend to reject both the form

[1] *Journal of Democracy* 11, no. 1 (2000), 9.

and dynamics of traditional cultures, Tocqueville's normative and rhetorical concerns align him in a particular way with a group of East Asian intellectuals who draw on the ghosts of the past to reorient the present. A consideration of Tocqueville's attempt to go beyond nostalgia and avoid self-delusion, I argue, may be instructive for East Asian theorists who share this hope.

The plan of the paper is as follows. After recalling the main themes of Tocqueville's discussion of the transition to democracy in Europe, I explore an alignment of concerns between Tocqueville and some of those engaged in debates over the cultural patterns that infuse state/society relations in contemporary Asia. I then turn to certain similarities of rhetoric that arise from the effort to transpose vanished values into a different – democratic – register. Before proceeding, however, I must make two disclaimers. Most important, I am not a scholar of comparative politics or of East Asia. Selective rather than systematic, my discussion of themes in the literature is very much an outsider's impressionistic foray into the field.[2] A second disclaimer concerns Tocqueville himself. I shall not analyze his own scattered references to East Asian culture and Confucianism, which reflect the European prejudices of his time. Rather, I read him for his insights into the social psychology and group dynamics of a modernizing society and for his intuitions about the challenge of motivating political elites living in a rapidly disappearing traditional order to establish a "free way of life."

Tocqueville's *idées mères* – Aristocracy, Democracy, Freedom, and Despotism

Structuring Tocqueville's understanding of Europe's democratic transition are several recurring polarities: his *idées mères*. The most important of these are the contrasts between aristocracy and democracy and between freedom and despotism. In *Democracy in America*, he attempted both to evoke what was passing away – an aristocratic society in which status inequalities were thought to be fixed in the cosmic order – and to bring into sharper focus what was emerging – a dynamic society of social equals.

---

[2] My references are primarily to works on China and Korea, with some attention to the general literature on East Asia. I am indebted to Meg Rithmire for making my discussion less selective and impressionistic than it would have been without her expert guidance. I also thank my friend and former colleague Seong-Ho Lim, professor at Kyung Hee University, who invited me to attend the World Congress of Korean Studies in Busan in 2007 to speak about Tocqueville and sparked my interest in this topic.

In feudal aristocratic Europe, "all generations are ... in a sense contemporaneous. A man almost always knows and respects his forbears. In his mind's eye he can already see his great-grandsons, and he loves them."[3] Moreover, members of different classes – although separated by rank – were intertwined in customary local webs of dependence and cooperation. Aristocracy linked all citizens together "in a long chain from peasant to king"; democracy "breaks the chain and severs the links."[4] Freed from collective temporal and spatial constraints, democratic individuals face one another as existential equals in economy, society, and polity.

The notion of an inevitable movement from aristocracy to democracy was not unique to Tocqueville, but he was unusual in arguing that if social democratization was irreversible, its political significance had yet to be determined. A free way of life (citizens with a vital local civic culture who ruled themselves successfully through representative national institutions) and an unfree existence (passive individuals dominated by new forms of bureaucratic, Caesaristic, or quasi-military rule) were both inherent possibilities of the modern age. To achieve the former and avoid the latter depended on decoding certain signs that revealed the ways in which the new social state constrained politics.

These indicators were not auspicious. In Tocqueville's account, several tendencies inherent to democracy combine to make self-government precarious. With the emergence of social equality comes a passion for equality: "ardent, insatiable, eternal, invincible."[5] This passion imbues society with a restless competitiveness that directs energies into economic rather than political pursuits and renders inequalities of any sort increasingly intolerable. Although equality also brings with it a desire for independent action – a taste for freedom – that taste may easily be overpowered by the stronger love of equality. The phenomenon Tocqueville calls *individualisme* reinforces the tendency toward withdrawal from political life. If the aristocratic ethos is group oriented, the democratic ethos is centered on discrete individual families. As distinguished from selfishness or egoism, individualism is "a reflective and tranquil sentiment that disposes each citizen to cut himself off from the mass of his fellow men and withdraw into the circle of family and friends, so that, having created a little society for his own use, he gladly leaves the larger society to take care of

---

3 DIA (G) II.2.ii, 585.
4 DIA (G) II.2.ii, 586.
5 DIA (G) II.2. v, 594.

itself."[6] The democratic social state, then, undermines aristocratic webs of connection without providing obvious replacements, creating an associational void that is rapidly filled by the ever-expanding reach of central authorities. The default destination of modern societies – that which happens without careful political effort – is not self-government through representative institutions but rather administrative rule by a centralized state.

Democracy in America, however, is not a book of despair but of qualified optimism: filled with examples of how Tocqueville's exemplary Americans successfully avoid, reverse, check, or neutralize the slide toward despotism. Among the causal factors that allowed Americans to become free – circumstances, laws, and moeurs – moeurs were the most important. Tocqueville uses *moeurs* to refer not only to "what one might call habits of the heart, but also to the various notions that men possess, to the diverse opinions that are current among them, and to the whole range of ideas that shape habits of mind."[7] A capacious term, it is sometimes rendered by the phrase "social instincts." In a useful formulation, Arthur Goldhammer has parsed Tocqueville's conception of such instincts as "quasi-durable and unreflective dispositions to act in certain ways, yet subject to modification by a range of notions, opinions, and ideas."[8]

In Tocqueville's account of American political development, lawmakers and citizens shape social instincts in two ways. In some cases they nurture inherited institutions and constitutional structures to dam the democratic floodwaters. In others they unleash democracy's power: "it is sometimes the case that extreme freedom corrects the abuses of freedom and extreme democracy guards against the dangers of democracy."[9] Two of these counterintuitive arguments about going with democracy's flow have dominated recent appropriations of Tocqueville in political science. The democratic tendency to form associations to further selfish interests, Tocqueville argues, does not impede the emergence of the general good but is essential to it. And the religious impulses and organizations characteristic of a democratic society – if church and state are strictly separated – do not threaten but rather energize and stabilize free politics.

[6] DIA (G) II.2.ii, 585.
[7] DIA (G) I.2.ix, 331.
[8] "Translating Tocqueville: The Constraints of Classicism," in Cheryl B. Welch (ed.), *The Cambridge Companion to Tocqueville* (Cambridge: Cambridge University Press, 2006), 158–159.
[9] DIA (G) I.2.iv, 222.

Tocqueville believed that Americans of the early nineteenth century had tamed self-interest, practicing what he first termed *égoisme intelligent* and then called *intérêt bien-entendu.*[10] Central to this redirection of interest was the use they made of groups or "factions." Tocqueville's judgment was very different from the still predominant view in democratic theory that factions must corrupt public life. Associations (civil groups formed voluntarily by citizens as well as permanent local political associations such as townships, cities, and counties) could substitute for traditional orders and groups that had previously both kept the king in check and fostered the trust required for any joint action. Although democratic individuals formed associations or participated in local governing groups to further their interests, iterative cooperation gave them a larger view and transformed their habitual behavior. Moreover, associational activities in the civil and political spheres were mutually reinforcing in complicated ways.[11] Finally, associations in America indirectly countered the drag of individualism, forcing people to establish social ties in which "feelings and ideas are renewed, the heart expands, and the human spirit develops."[12] Tocqueville concluded that if associations were allowed to form freely and in public and if government action facilitated rather than co-opted these groups, the patterns they promoted would become instinctual and internalized, eventually forming new moeurs.[13]

Tocqueville depicted American religious beliefs and practices as another powerful means by which Americans enlisted the natural inclinations of democracy to produce a form of society at once free and disciplined. He offered several arguments on behalf of the connection between religion and free democratic mores, including a surprising insistence on the alleged resurgence of Catholicism.[14] The Church of Rome's emphasis on the equality of all souls and on equal subordination to central authority, Tocqueville noted, resonated strongly in any democratic society. Moreover, if it were severed from state sponsorship and purged of the symbolic baggage carried over from its alliance with aristocracy, Catholicism's dogmatic and hierarchical structure could provide unexpected resources for democratic freedom. A minimum of dogma, authoritatively dispensed, would keep democratic individuals from becoming lost in doubt, would tether democratic imaginations, and would counter

[10] DIA (G) II.2.viii, 611.
[11] See, for example, DIA (G) I.2.v, 246; I.2.vi, 279; I.2.ix, 329, 352.
[12] DIA (G) II.2.v, 598.
[13] DIA (G) II.2.iv, 594.
[14] DIA (G) II.2.vi, 511.

the restless instability of democratic life. On this view, religion can reinforce self-government not because it is congruent with existing patterns
of social and economic life but rather because it satisfies psychological and spiritual yearnings that otherwise go unmet or find dangerous
outlets.

Tocqueville's America, then, offered a laboratory in which to study
new social and cultural moeurs that appeared to make democratic freedom possible. This portrait was constructed to answer the questions and
to counter the fears of a European audience much taken up with a different example: an apparently dysfunctional French democratic culture that
vacillated between dictatorship and revolution. Although this counter
example was never far from Tocqueville's mind or text in *Democracy in
America,* he explicitly shifted his focus to France in his final published
work, *The Old Regime and the Revolution.* Canvassing archival records,
amassing statistics, reconstructing the social psychology at work in a
society undergoing rapid change, and enlisting the aid of the comparative
method, Tocqueville set out to study the transformation of social instincts
in a democratizing society.

Perhaps the most important thing to note about this study is that it was
less an analysis of how traditional values and social instincts were "semi-
durable" in France than a revelation of how notions, opinions, ideas, and
new circumstances had modified them beyond recognition. During the
eighteenth century, Tocqueville argued, a centralizing state and an egalitarian society emerged in tandem, in the process transforming France's
political culture. The "ancien régime" of his title was not feudal aristocracy but rather a democratic authoritarian state, partially veiled by
the persistence of defunct feudal forms and lingering aristocratic mores.
In this complex work, Tocqueville focuses on the paradoxical and unin-
tended consequences of the interaction between state and society in this
new hybrid: how caste barriers hardened even as individuals became more
alike; how the peasantry was progressively alienated from other classes
even as it became emancipated; how interest was improperly understood
even as state officials trumpeted their dedication to public goods; how
kings and ministers eliminated the very partners they would later need
to implement salutary reforms that could have saved the monarchy; and
how group life divided rather than connected individuals. Tocqueville's
subtle analysis of this French version of democracy should serve as an
antidote to any reading that attributes to him a naïve faith in associations. France before the Revolution was in many ways a model portrait
of an intense associational culture within a strong state infrastructure

that both deliberately and inadvertently thwarted political cooperation and promoted political immobility.

A Similar *point de départ*

Let me turn now to the ways in which Tocqueville's discussion of the dilemmas of Western democratization resonates in the East. Characterized by debates over both the role of political culture and the coercive capacity of strong, deeply rooted states, the literature on democracy in Asia presents immediate parallels with Tocqueville. Perhaps the deepest affinity is the common focus on understanding and reconstructing the political role of moeurs. Indeed, Tocqueville's understanding of moeurs has been compared directly to the Confucian view that the habits of daily life are engrained and unreflective dispositions that become a kind of second human nature.[15]

A sensitivity to how moeurs change, persist, or resurface in new guises, and especially to how they relate to the changing role of the state in different societies, runs through the study of politics in East Asia. One might take one's initial bearing from William de Bary, who argues that what is most important in ascertaining the possibility of democracy in Asia is to explore the historical record in these societies, to identify and understand reinforcing or complementary loops of action that have formed cultural patterns, particularly in relation to the imperial state in East Asia.[16] Social scientists and historians of China in particular have scrutinized associational culture in eighteenth- and nineteenth-century China with the hope of identifying patterns with implications for contemporary politics.[17] Consider, for example, Prasenjit Duara's study of culture, power, and the state in late-nineteenth-century North China, which focuses on "how the most vital areas of village life become deeply enmeshed in the ordering efforts of an intrusive state."[18] With a comparative eye on the model of state making in Europe, Duara – like Tocqueville – calls attention to

---

[15] See Hahm Chaihark, "Constitutionalism, Confucian Civic Virtue, and Ritual Propriety," in Daniel A. Bell and Hahm Chaibong (eds.), *Confucianism for the Modern World* (Cambridge: Cambridge University Press, 2003), 47.

[16] "Introduction" to *Confucianism and Human Rights*, eds. Wm. Theodore de Bary and Tu Weiming (New York: Columbia University Press, 1998), 10–11.

[17] For a review of this literature, see Frederic Wakeman, Jr., "The Civil Society and Public Sphere Debate: Western Reflections on Chinese Political Culture," *Modern China* 19 (1993), 108–138.

[18] Prasenjit Duara, *Culture, Power, and the State: Rural North China, 1900–1942* (Stanford: Stanford University Press, 1988), 9.

the reinforcing loops of action between the realms of culture, society, and state and to the ways in which the same process can have integrating and isolating effects, "paradoxical tendencies that are not necessarily predictable."[19]

How does one chart the changing nature and significance of such complementary loops of action? Tocqueville sometimes used linguistic transformations as pregnant markers, for example, in his famous contrast in the *Old Regime* between the word *gentleman* and *gentilhomme*. Implicit in the use of the English word in the nineteenth century was the historical collapse of the nobility into an amorphous aristocracy of education and wealth, a transformation that indirectly facilitated political cooperation between elites and people. French usage, in contrast, retained the original antithesis between *gentilhomme* (nobleman) and *roturier* ("plebeian") until the Revolution, when both words dropped out of common use altogether.[20] The lack of a French word to bridge social caste differences helps to explain the class animosities that later emerged in the Revolution, as well as to suggest that France would need to develop new politically inflected forms of civic identity.

Tracking the evolution of political moeurs in East Asia prompts analogous attention to the importance of language and its implications. For example, two Chinese theorists have argued that the Chinese have no word for a society that fuses civic awareness with claims of individual rights. The Chinese word for "mass society" (*qunzhong shehui*) in both its traditional and contemporary usage, on this view, connotes subordination to rulers and thus serves as a measure of the weakness of civic awareness in China and of the great challenge faced by those who wish to institutionalize new forms of governance.[21] Another example comes from Korea. Kyung Moon Hwang argues that late-nineteenth-century Confucian reformers used *kukka*, the Korean word for state, to mean a "people-centered political order, if not popular sovereignty itself."[22] This usage drew on ideas embedded in earlier Confucian reform movements. Only later, during the Japanese occupation, did an increasing number

---

[19] Duara, *Culture, Power, and the State*, 265.
[20] OR I, 153–154.
[21] Liu Zhiguang and Wang Suli, "Cong qunzhong shehui zouxiang gongmin shehui," ["From mass society to civil society"], *Zhengzhixue yanjui (Political Research)* 5 (1988); cited by Shu-Yun Ma, "The Chinese Discourse on Civil Society," *The China Quarterly* 137 (1994), 184.
[22] Kyung Moon Hwang, "Country or State? Reconceptualizing *Kukka* in the Korean Enlightenment Period, 1896–1910," *Korean Studies* 24 (2000), 19.

of intellectuals adopt a statist formulation imported from the West that equated the term *kukka* with the ruling authority or the state. In contrast to the Chinese example, this exploration of the etymology of the Korean word for state induces a certain optimism about Korean democratization. The implication is that there may be latent moeurs favoring political democracy that can be mobilized in Korean reform efforts.

Entangled in these examples, and sometimes difficult to separate, are two debates about the character of the political moeurs that connect social and political institutions in East Asia. First, there is the question of whether certain generally observed patterns (deference to authority, popular dependence, moralistic and hierarchical values among political elites, a general appreciation of collective over individual values) are continuous with deeply rooted ancient cultures or whether they are better considered as linked to more recent economic and political developments. Second is the question of whether these moeurs – whether understood as continuous or discontinuous – should be thought of as potential resources for a civil society that can facilitate the emergence of robust political democracy or as semipermanent obstacles to democratization. Tocqueville is germane to both of these debates, although those who occasionally invoke his authority sometimes obscure his true significance.

Lucien Pye is the most prominent example of the view that paternalistic conceptions of power in Asia – with the partial exception of Japan – are distinctive and deeply rooted in traditional ways of thought that predate the modern era.[23] Pye's book is more subtle and nuanced than this categorization suggests, but nevertheless it is fair to say that he holds that democratization is unlikely to occur in anything like the Western sense because the process depends on distinctive cultural and religious values absent in Asia. The view is echoed in the work of David Steinberg, who traces Korean notions of the need for political purity – and the consequent belief in the pollution of ideological heterodoxy – to the grip of its Confucian traditions. "Conformity, the adherence to social norms of behavior, and its intellectual corollary orthodoxy, have been major social forces in Korean history, perhaps more so than in many other nations."[24] This view about the distinctive historicity of Asian moeurs is often, although not always, combined with arguments that these traditions are hostile to

[23] Lucian Pye, *Asian Power and Politics: The Cultural Dimensions of Authority* (Cambridge, MA: Harvard University Press, 1985).
[24] David Steinberg, "Civil Society and Human Rights in Korea: On Contemporary and Classical Orthodoxy and Ideology," *Korea Journal* 37 (1997), 150.

democracy, and it was famously exploited by authoritarian Asian leaders in the so-called Asian values debate of the 1990s.[25]

Unlike those who stress continuity in Asian political culture, many historians and theorists emphasize definitive ruptures, although they draw very different conclusions about the significance of such breaks. In Joseph Levenson's portrait of the decay of the Confucian social order in China, traditional culture survives into the twentieth century only in detached fragments, as in a museum exhibition of cultural fossils.[26] Levenson argues that traditional culture was irreversibly replaced with a communist ideology that retained only the pride and will to power associated with older conceptions of Chinese identity. To overcome the humiliation of dependence on the West, leaders purged Chinese political identity of both the traditional past and the Western-polluted present. Whatever else it is, contemporary China, on this view, is definitively "post-Confucian." If Levenson, writing in the early 1960s, emphasized that a rupture with the past had produced a distinctively new monopoly of rule and expression, scholars like Edward Friedman later use the discontinuity perspective to bolster the notion that a definitive break with both the traditional past and the authoritarian present is possible and that political cultures in Asia have changed and are changing radically in response to political choices and the human will.[27]

Tocqueville is sometimes mistakenly put in the company of scholars like Pye and Steinberg who believe that authoritarian rule arises from inherited norms about power and legitimacy.[28] I would argue, however, that he fits squarely into the opposing category – those more struck by historical discontinuities – and that he helps us see the power of this position. Indeed, Tocqueville's deepest insight about Europe is that what may look like legacies from aristocracy or inexplicable revolutionary innovations are really patterns compounded from the decay of traditional

[25] On this debate, see the articles by Margaret Ng, Bilahari Kausikan, Joseph Chan, and Theodore de Bary in Larry Diamond and Marc F. Plattner (eds.), *Democracy in East Asia* (Baltimore: The Johns Hopkins University Press, 1998), 3–57.

[26] Joseph R. Levenson, *Confucian China and Its Modern Fate: A Trilogy* (Berkeley, CA: University of California Press, 1958, 1964, 1965), Vol. 3: *The Problem of Historical Significance*, 120.

[27] *The Politics of Democratization: Generalizing East Asian Experiences*, ed. Edward Friedman (Boulder, CO: Westview Press, 1994). All the contributors oppose the view that East Asia has an ancient predisposition for political authoritarianism.

[28] Edward Friedman himself attributes to Tocqueville the view that France was inherently undemocratic by history and habit in "Democratization: Generalizing the East Asian Experience," in *The Politics of Democratization*, 50.

society and the false flourishing of centralized power. Like Levenson, his focus is on post-aristocratic societies; like Friedman, he argues that new authoritarian patterns are themselves malleable.[29]

If we can clearly place Tocqueville on one side of the first debate over the salience of culture, he cannot so easily be located in the second: do Asian political cultures contain potential resources for political democratization or present peculiar obstacles to it? How civic or civil is political culture in Asia? Thrust into public consciousness by the East European democratic transitions and now ubiquitous in the theoretical literature, the concept of civil society also pervades discussions of democratization in East Asia.[30] Like the concept itself, these discussions are both murky and difficult to parse. Here I merely wish to call attention to a persistent division in the way this term is employed in the Asian context. Some use it to refer to associational cultures (civil societies) favoring democratization that are alleged to exist or to be emerging in East Asia. Others, however, claim either that it is a mistake to describe Asian societies as civil or a mistake to see them as pro-democratic.

Those who deploy the concept of civil society to link associational life in Asian countries to the emergence of political democracy come in various stripes. Some point to the ways in which economic modernization fosters forms of Western-style organizations that demand (or will eventually demand) participation and civilian political activity.[31] One example of this type would be Han Sang-Jin's argument that a combination of socioeconomic modernization and university-centered popular movements in Korea have led to counter publics, a "new backbone of

---

[29] Levenson, then, writes a Chinese version of the *Old Regime and the Revolution*. For an explicit attempt to use Tocqueville's *Old Regime* as a model for developments in Asia, see Hiroshi Watanabe, "The Old Regime and the Meiji Revolution," unpublished paper delivered at the Colloque international commémorative du Bicentennaire de la naissance d'Alexis de Tocqueville, Tokyo, Japan, June 2005. Robert T. Gannett Jr. begins his "Village-by-Village: What Seeds for Freedom" in *Tocqueville on China: A Project of the American Enterprise Institute* (April 2009) by asking whether China's new local village governments will end up as schools for freedom or, as in the *Old Regime*, props for the central government.

[30] Among the general works on this topic, see *Civil Society and Political Change in Asia: Expanding and Contracting Democratic Space*, ed. Muthiah Alagappa (Stanford: Stanford University Press, 2004); *The State of Civil Society in Japan*, ed. Susan Pharr and Frank J. Schwartz (Cambridge: Cambridge University Press, 2003); *Between States and Markets: The Voluntary Sphere in Comparative Perspective*, ed. Robert Wuthnow (Princeton: Princeton University Press, 1991).

[31] See Tony Saich, "The Search for Civil Society and Democracy in China," *Current History* 93 (1994), 260–264, and David Stand, "Protest in Beijing: a Civil Society and the Public Sphere in China," *Problems of Communism* 39 (1990), 1–19.

civil society" that he calls the "middling grassroots."[32] Some find in Asian associational practices more indigenous forms of civil society. It has been explicitly argued for the case of Taiwan that strong group consciousness – even if these groups are hierarchical – can contribute to a democratic transition.[33] In Korea some scholars have argued that distinctive networks based on blood, school, or region are innovative webs of connection that may provide the kind of flexibility and support needed to sustain further economic and political development.[34]

On the other side of the opinion divide about the role of civil society are those who argue that the Asian case demonstrates not the capacity of new or evolving associations to support independent political action but rather the ease with which the state can manipulate such groups. As did Tocqueville in the *Old Regime*, these writers depict a political culture with a fatal attraction to centralized autocracy. Some of these studies of culture and democratic governance in Asia deny the usefulness of the term *civil society* altogether.[35] Others employ the term only to note that the character of civil society can make democratization less rather than more likely. The literature is replete with references to the unwillingness of the middle classes in East Asia to sacrifice for the public good and their readiness to be mobilized into new nationalist ideologies.[36] Frequently the term *Bonapartist* surfaces, referring to strong leaders who use a hollow traditionalist rhetoric to dominate materialistic apolitical urban elites.[37] Helen Hardacre argues that Japan – the most developed Asian

---

[32] Han Sang-Jin, "The Public Sphere and Democracy in Korea: A Debate on Civil Society," *Korea Journal* 37 (1997), 95.

[33] John Fuh-Sheng Hsieh, "East Asian Culture and Democratic Transitions, With Special Reference to the Case of Taiwan," *Journal of Asia and African Studies* 35 (2002), 29–42.

[34] Lew Seok-Choon, Chang Mi-Hye, and Kim Tae-Eun, "Affective Networks and Modernity: The Case of Korea," in Bell and Chaibong (eds.), *Confucianism for the Modern World*, 201–35.

[35] William Callahan, "Comparing the Discourse of Popular Politics in Korea and China: From Civil Society to Social Movements," *Korea Journal* 38 (1998), 279–315. See also Adrian Chan, "In Search of Civil Society in China," *Journal of Contemporary Asia* 27 (1997), 242–251, and X. L. Ding, "Institutional Amphibiousness and the Transition from Communism: The Case of China." *British Journal of Political Science* 24 (1994), 293–318.

[36] Lucien Pye, *Asian Power and Politics*, 338; David Martin Jones, "Democratization, Civil Society, and Illiberal Middle Class Culture in Pacific Asia," *Comparative Politics* 30 (1998), 147–169.

[37] For the case of Korea, see Bruce Cumings, "The Abortive Abertura: South Korea in the Light of Latin American Experience," *New Left Review* 173 (January–February 1989), 12; for the case of Indonesia, see Richard Robison, "Indonesia: Tensions in State and Regime," in Kevin Hewison, Richard Robison, and Garry Rodan (eds.), *Southeast Asia in the 1990s* (Sydney: Allen & Unwin, 1993), 41.

democracy – has only a limited public sphere, with discourse about the public good dominated by a collusion of economic corporations with the state.[38] Many scholars also focus on Asian political practices that appear to frustrate democratic consolidation. Consider Jongryn Mo's study of legislative gridlock in the Korean legislature in the period of democratization. Even while denying that Asian values are inherently authoritarian, he explores what we might call dysfunctional path dependencies between cultural elements and political stalemate, arguing that the public's penchant for strong leadership, combined with the tendency of legislators to distrust out-groups and to adhere to rigid positions in intergroup negotiations, contributed to policy gridlock over economic reform and thus to the economic crisis of the late 1990s.[39]

Again, those theorists of Asian democratization who explicitly invoke Tocqueville in the context of debates over civil society often miss his true legacy. Taking their bearings from theoretical discussions of social capital in the West, they use *Tocquevillean* or *neo-Tocquevillean* as a simplistic shorthand for the optimistic view that private civil associations are learning grounds for democracy and that such groups automatically socialize citizens in such a way as to promote political efficacy.[40] I would argue, however, that Tocqueville – and thus the Tocquevillean perspective – encourages us to bracket such preconceptions and to explore empirically the space linking state, society, and culture – a space that may be filled by unexpected and counterintuitive social instincts. Indeed, the discussions of civil society in East Asia that betray the strongest Tocquevillean bent are those that alert us to all the political uses and effects of associational life – not just those that are congruent with individualistic values but also those that compensate for democratic deficits and those that may compound those deficits. Here one might place the empirical research of Lily Tsai, who locates alternate forms of political accountability in the particular ways in which temple associations, lineage groups, and other traditional solidary groups in contemporary rural China hold

[38] Helen Hardacre, "Japan: The Public Sphere in a Non-Western Setting," in Wuthnow (ed.), *Between States and Markets*, 219.

[39] Johngryn Mo, "Political Culture and Legislative Gridlock: Politics of Economic Reform in Precrisis Korea," *Comparative Political Studies* 34 (2001), 467–489.

[40] Muthiah Alagappa, for example, sees a difference between Tocqueville and so-called neo-Tocquevilleans but believes that both conceptualize civil society only in relation to political democracy. "Civil Society and Political Change: An Analytical Framework," in *Civil Society and Political Change in Asia*, 40–46. I would argue, however, that Tocqueville – like Alagappa – recognized quite well that the space linking state, society, and culture may contain both democratic and nondemocratic effects.

village leaders responsible for their decisions. Her purpose, however, is less to trumpet the emergence of civil society or to lament the inexorable undertow of the state than to suggest that we always need to "pay more attention to important interaction effects between social structures and state structures."[41] Or we might look to Hagen Koo's nuanced study of how a strong state and a contentious society have developed side by side in Korea, locked into distinctive patterns that can be grasped only by careful attention to historical contingencies and the discontinuous, uneven, paradoxical, and conflict-ridden process of recent Korean history.[42]

A Convergence of Political Rhetoric

So far I have argued that Tocqueville's attempts to understand how political moeurs inflect democratization can help us recognize and navigate the continuing tensions in the literature on transitions to democracy in East Asia and that some of the most insightful attempts to negotiate these tensions have an unacknowledged Tocquevillean pedigree. I now turn to a different sort of coincidence: the shared aims and strategies between Tocqueville and those who wish to chart a third democratic way in Asia that both acknowledges and transcends its past.

In the words of French scholar Laurence Guellec, the aim of *Democracy in America* was to "[forge] a style capable of combining thought and action, of imparting knowledge while simultaneously shaping the world."[43] The same impulse to use scholarship to open up a particular universe of possibilities and to inspire policy makers to act on them characterizes some contemporary theorists of Asian democracy. Indeed, these writers adopt strategies remarkably similar to those Tocqueville employed to destabilize conventional assumptions that he thought were paralyzing political life in France. I want to consider three of those strategies here: finding human exemplars that contradict settled beliefs, narrating "just so" counter histories that bolster the political will, and reducing anxiety about change by valorizing the role of the family.

[41] Lily L. Tsai, "Solidary Groups, Informal Accountability, and Local Public Goods Provision in Rural China," *American Political Science Review* 101 (2007), 370.

[42] Hagen Koo, "Strong State and Contentious Society," in Hagen Koo (ed.), *State and Society in Contemporary Korea* (Ithaca, NY: Cornell University Press, 1993).

[43] Laurence Guellec, "The Writer Engagé: Tocqueville and Political Rhetoric," in Welch (ed.), *Cambridge Companion to Tocqueville*, 169.

Living Contradictions

In *Democracy in America* Tocqueville told a somewhat improbable story about the increasing role of Catholicism in democratic America to encourage his readers to consider a different role for religion in politics. French republicans were hostile to religion as a whole, Tocqueville thought, because they misread Catholicism's historical association with aristocracy and absolutism as necessary rather than contingent. The Right, on the other hand, opposed democratization partly because they thought it entailed secularization. Again they mistook accident for necessity. An obvious move, then, was to find sincere Catholics who were also democrats – hence, the authentically democratic priests who populate Tocqueville's discussion of religion in the United States and elsewhere: figures who contest the beliefs of his readers by their very existence.

A similar impulse underlies some reconsiderations of the social role of Confucianism. In the words of Daniel Bell and Hahm Chaibong, editors of a volume of essays on *Confucianism in the Modern World*, the scholars represented in the book share a common purpose: "to articulate some Confucian values and practices that could shape modern political, economic, and legal institutions in desirable ways, mitigating some of their more obvious excesses."[44] Among these is the scholar Wang Juntao, who wishes to counter the widespread – and, he thinks, misguided – assumption that the Confucian heritage is inimical to the transition to liberal democracy in China. He canvasses the historical record to find political actors who embraced both Confucianism and democracy, thus challenging conventional opinion by attempting to demonstrate that Confucianism "is capable of embracing the idea of democracy and that it can be developed for this purpose."[45] These scholars assume that the historical fusion of Confucianism and political centralization was in some ways a betrayal of more authentic Confucian traditions. As De Bary puts the point, central Confucian values were both "historically embedded in, but at the same time restive with, repressive institutions."[46] This was precisely Tocqueville's attitude toward Catholicism, embedded in aristocracy and early modern European absolutism, but restive within those social forms because of its values of universal equality and personal accountability.

---

[44] Bell and Chaibong, "Introduction" to *Confucianism for the Modern World*, 28.
[45] Wang Juntao, "Confucian Democrats in Chinese History," in Bell and Chaibong (eds.), *Confucianism for the Modern World*, 69.
[46] De Bary, *Confucianism and Human Rights*, 6.

French and Korean Just So Stories

Another way to persuade one's audience that political democracy of a certain kind is feasible is to discover a viable historical prototype, as Tocqueville did in his appendix to the *Old Regime* on the province of Languedoc. Languedoc had the same history as the rest of France save that it had retained the traditional local assembly of estates, which had a measure of taxing power and control over public works. These assemblies, Tocqueville argued, provided a mediating space in which nobles, bourgeois, clergy, and monarchs could cooperate for the public good, and they did so. Languedoc reveals what the French provinces "could all easily have become."[47]

The lesson of Languedoc was not so much that older patterns of deference, or even old institutions, could have survived but rather that a new democratic spirit – manifest in the economic development of the province and in the political dominance of the bourgeois majority – appropriated and worked its will by creatively transforming existing institutions. This new power was both restrained by other groups and able to work in creative partnership with a strong centralizing state. Whatever the truth of Tocqueville's account, it was this path on which he hoped to push his contemporaries. The example of Languedoc was a road-not-followed elsewhere in France only because of the lack of "perseverance and effort" on the part of political elites.[48] A pep talk in the guise of a scholarly appendix, Languedoc provided a fictitious history that, in the words of Tocqueville scholars Mélonio and Furet, "gave flesh to the dreams of those who did not possess the reality of freedom."[49]

Perhaps the best illustration of this impulse to use Asian history to incarnate democratic freedoms is the scholarly focus on certain social and political practices of the Chosŏn dynasty in Korea.[50] Chang Yun-Shik, for example, offers an historical investigation of the reinforcing patterns that allegedly once existed between webs of social connection and the tempering of state authority. Explicitly recognizing a parallel between Tocqueville's conception of administrative despotism and the emergence of strong executive power and centralization in Korea, his aim

---

[47] OR I, 249–256.
[48] OR I, 256.
[49] OR I, Mélonio and Furet, "Introduction," 74.
[50] For a review of the issue, see John Duncan, "The Problematic Modernity of Confucianism: the Question of 'Civil Society' in Chosŏn Dynasty Korea," in Charles K Armstrong (ed.), *Korean Society: Civil Society, Democracy, and the State* (London: Routledge, 2002), 36–56.

is to discover what cultural elements existed to counter this phenomenon and under what conditions cultural elements "cease to be antagonistic to [the] new political ideal and system [liberal democracy]."[51] He argues that the ethic of mutual help, a neighborhood or communal ethic in premodern Korea, might yet develop into a more generic network ethic – transferable to urban settings and capable of fueling opposition democratic movements through the creation of study circles formed by "mutual consultation, persuasion, encouragement, and criticism within a circle of close friends."[52] Here personalist associations – often decried for their contribution to corruption, crony capitalism, and unaccountable rule – have a different history and a hopeful trajectory.

Even more frequent are historical studies focused on local neo-Confucian elites steeped in moral education who are portrayed as having brokered relations between family and state and who represent not centralization but rather the enduring ideals of localism and community power. Hein Cho, for example, calls attention to backwoods literati who "stayed in the wilderness as notables to lead the rank and file of society" and sees them as an elaborate form of checks and balances that maintained communicative networks and constrained monarchical power.[53] Finally, Jongryn Mo looks at agencies designed to censor the monarch within the bureaucracy of the Chosŏn dynasty itself. He argues that two of these agencies – together known as the Censorate – meet modern standards for effective horizontal accountability, especially during the height of their influence in the late fifteenth century.[54] This historical prototype validates the notion that independent accounting agencies may play an important role in contemporary democratization if there are safeguards against the subversion of such entities by the state. The goal is to motivate contemporaries to consider such measures as alternatives to the "standard set of solutions" promoted by the "Washington Consensus."[55]

Doubts about the utility of focusing on living contradictions or counter histories center on the lack of demonstrable connections with the present

---

[51] Chang Yun-Shik, "Mutual Help and Democracy in Korea," in Bell and Chaibong (eds.), *Confucianism for the Modern World*, 91, 105.

[52] Chang Yun-Shik, "Mutual Help," 110.

[53] Hein Cho, "The Historical Origin of Civil Society in Korea," *Korea Journal* 37 (1997), 31–32. See also Gilbert Rozman, "Center-Local Relations: Can Confucianism Boost Decentralization and Regionalism," in Bell and Chaibong (eds.), *Confucianism for the Modern World*, 181–200.

[54] Jongryn Mo, "The Challenge of Accountability: Implications of the Censorate," in Bell and Chaibong (eds.), *Confucianism for the Modern World*, 57.

[55] Jongryn Mo, "The Challenge of Accountability," 55.

or the difficulty of proving counterfactuals. When De Bary says that a community orientation in Confucianism – although not strong enough in the past to stand up against state forces – nevertheless was and is a worthy ideal, and in Korea "perhaps more than a memory," critics want concrete evidence of what it means to be more than a memory.[56] In one sense, however, such criticisms are misplaced. The point of finding exemplars or conjuring up paths-not-taken is not to set the record straight but to identify heroic action, to find indigenous forbears who resisted the allegedly traitorous slide of their own traditions toward despotism. The lesson is that contemporaries possess the same capacity for discernment and decisive action and that to choose a democratic future is not to side with a foreign devil.

Family Values

I have been arguing that a school of writers on democracy in East Asia share Tocqueville's implicit aim of unsettling current opinions through the transvaluation of historical norms and practices. These strategies are meant to bolster the resolve to find a different route forward, to create something new under the sun. Nevertheless, this turn to the past runs the continual risk of being seduced by a yearning for the irrecoverable. Tocqueville once said that he chose the democratic future over the aristocratic past because he did not wish to live his life among the dead. But attentive readers know that he did not always avoid this temptation, prompted by anxieties about the democratic future that he could not fully repress.

Fears of social dissolution and frightening premonitions of market societies deprived of any moral compass are especially keen in East Asia, with its lightening rates of economic modernization and legacy of strong collective values. It is not surprising, then, that writers should be attracted to Tocqueville's expression of similar anxieties. Hahm Chaibong, for example, locates the Asian values debate in a long Western controversy over the individualistic implications of liberal democracy and the free market, a controversy now moving into an "intercultural and intercivilizational" register.[57] Chaibong uses Tocqueville to explore the question of whether the social and existential problems of individualism that Tocqueville outlined are the inevitable price that must be paid for democracy or whether

---

[56] De Bary, "Why Confucius Now?" in Bell and Chaibong (eds.), *Confucianism for the Modern World*, 367.

[57] Hahm Chaibong, "The Cultural Challenge to Individualism," *Journal of Democracy* 1 (2000), 134.

they may yet be avoided. Like others, he also follows Tocqueville in his hope that family values may play a major part in such avoidance.

Tocqueville kept his own fears about the isolating effects of democracy in check – and assured his audience that democratic challenges were not too great for them to master – in part by romanticizing the role of women and the family. In democracies, he argued, the family both anchored and disciplined male citizens and offered them a respite from the unpredictability and competitiveness of economic and political life. Rather than becoming competitors, women would assume the role of empowering and consoling silent partners. Educated to negotiate the freedoms of an individualistic society and equal in intellectual and moral capacity to men, they voluntarily retreated upon marriage into a democratic "cloister."[58]

This analysis is one of the least convincing parts of *Democracy in America* because it rests on an implausible account of democratic women's abdication of any unmediated political role or voice. Tocqueville alternately projects onto democratic women the vanished values of aristocratic self-sacrifice and quiet acceptance of outside authority; they appear as altruistic saviors of democracy or as victims of majority opinion coerced for the public good. Although Tocqueville construes family life in the United States as yet another case (like the tendency to form associations and to cleave to religion) in which Americans exploited the tendencies of democracy itself, he fails to explain how and why women escape the psychological transformations wrought by equality, with its affinities for self-assertion and its resentment of perceived inequalities. And the subsequent revolution in the lives of women, in their roles as citizens, and in conceptions of how gender intersects with the polity have in fact belied his account that stable political democracy demands the sequestering of women.

In contemporary East Asia, there is a similar yearning to recast the traditional family as a bulwark against the materialism of the market and the encroachments of the state.[59] It is true that in Asia the family has a different relation to conceptions of public and private than in the West. Never consigned to the private or natural realm, the traditional family has long been the locus of moral socialization for both men and

---

58　DIA (G) II.3.x, 695.

59　The issue has aroused both considerable anxiety and has become an important theme for social scientists. See, for example, *Confucianism and the Family*, eds. Walter H. Slote and George A. De Vos (New York: State University of New York Press, 1998), especially Kwang Kyu Lee's article, "Confucian Tradition in the Contemporary Korean Family," 249–261.

women. In his study of neo-Confucian attempts to reconstruct a ritual-ized family sphere as a counterweight to empire, Chaibong offers one of the most sophisticated discussions of the differences between how West-ern and Eastern understandings of the family have been embedded in the larger social and political universe.[60] His aim, however, is to vali-date the project of these neo-Confucian intellectuals, who deliberately sought to construct an intermediary body between individual and state that allegedly created what some hope to achieve in civil society – that is, a moral space with a telos of its own. There is no reason why the institution of the family, Chaibong argues, cannot be "rethought, rearticulated so that it can be privileged above and beyond society or perhaps even the state."[61] However, this view of the Asian family as a mediating institution, like Tocqueville's characterization of ordered family life as the necessary substratum of a well-functioning democratic polity, equally depends on constraining women's lives and choices. Chaibong himself recognizes that "there is no easy way out of the dilemma" posed by the reality that the Confucian family ethic is "hierarchical, authoritarian, and gender biased."[62]

Although some have advocated pushing Asian political practice toward a "care-oriented" Confucianism that elevates the mother's role within tra-ditional familism, it is unclear how far women themselves have endorsed such an aim.[63] In an essay specifically focused on the resources of Confucianism for Asian feminism, Chan Sin Yee concludes that the project has definite limits.[64] It is perhaps evidence of the difficulty of re-traditionalizing the role of the family in a way that maintains democ-racy as a universal aspiration that few Asian feminists have framed their demands for justice and equality in traditional language; rather, they adopt a version of what is sometimes called the normative language of globalization – that is, the language of human rights and democracy.[65]

---

[60] Chaibong, "Family versus the Individual: The Politics of Marriage Laws in Korea," in Bell and Chaibong (eds.), *Confucianism for the Modern World*, 334–359.
[61] Chaibong, "Family versus the Individual," 358.
[62] Ibid.
[63] See Geir Helgesen, "The Case for Moral Education," 161–180, and Seok-Choon, Mi-Hye, and Tae-Eun, "Affective Networks," 201–217 in Bell and Chaibong (eds.), *Confucianism for the Modern World*.
[64] Chan Sin Yee, "The Confucian Conception of Gender in the Twenty-First Century," in Bell and Chaibong (eds.), *Confucianism for the Modern World*, 312–333.
[65] Seung-sook Moon argues that the rise of a policy sensitive to women's rights in South Korea has been motivated more by global discourse on gender equality, non-discrimination, and human rights than by traditional conceptions. See "Overcome by Globalization: the Rise of a Women's Policy in South Korea," in *Korea's Globalization,*

I have suggested that Tocqueville and East Asian scholars promoting their own version of democracy recast and reclaim historical practices to contest conventional views and to jolt their readers into imagining new political arrangements. Enlisting the family to repress anxieties about rapid and disorienting change, however, more often appears to bow to convention and to shutter the imagination. Maintaining a sacrosanct family sphere becomes the last defense against the menace of atomism. To borrow an analogy much favored by nineteenth-century writers on democracy, including Tocqueville, these writers see themselves as piloting a democratic ship in uncharted waters. Evoking examples of intrepid ancient mariners, they hope to rally the crew to sail safely into ports unknown. One of the most tenacious of sailing superstitions, however, is the fear of women on board – and neither Tocqueville nor East Asian fellow travelers entirely escape the temptation to give in to it.

Conclusion

Throughout this essay I have argued that Alexis de Tocqueville's acute observations about the coming of democracy in Europe can help us to see what is at stake in discussions of democratization in East Asia because both his methodological and normative concerns are alive in the literature. Tocqueville reminds us of the essential malleability of political cultures as well as the semi-durable social instincts that arise from the collision of changing social structures and expanding state power in periods that are post-traditional but not yet self-governing. He also alerts us to common patterns of argument among scholars who wish to vindicate the possibilities of a world "totally new" by excavating ideas and practices buried in the old.[66] Here Tocqueville's example is in part an admonition because following this path means treading a fine line between appropriating the past and being taken in by it. A recurring blindness to the ways in which women's autonomy may be forfeit to a new traditionalism warns us that reclaiming tradition may slip into unthinking and faint-hearted reliance on conventional wisdom.

---

ed. Samuel S. Kim (Cambridge: Cambridge University Press, 2000), 126–146. Similarly, Katharine Moon notes that other traditionally marginalized groups (such as foreign workers in South Korea) have also tended to frame their demands in the normative language of human rights and democracy. See her "Strangers in the Midst of Globalization: Migrant Workers and Korean Nationalism," in Kim (ed.), *Korea's Globalization*, 147–169.

[66] The phrase is Tocqueville's, DIA Introduction, 7.

If I end on a cautionary note, it is still a Tocquevillean one. Tocqueville himself notes that the thing we should most dread in democratic times is the loss of free thought and free will; we need to embrace the "trouble of thinking and the difficulty of living."[67] To deliberate democratization with Tocqueville is precisely to welcome this double embrace.

---

[67] DIA (G) II.4.vi, 818.

CHAPTER 6

Tocquevillean Thoughts on Higher Education in the Middle East

Joshua Mitchell

Anyone who has read *Democracy in America* will have noted its rather bold claim that the movement toward equality is something "fated" and that this movement amounts to the supplanting of one human type, namely "aristocratic man," with another type, namely "democratic man."[1] At times Tocqueville writes that this movement pertains to the Christian lands, at times to the civilized world, and at times to the entire world.[2] And although he did write about other places,[3] his focus was the transformation taking place in Europe and in America – that land to the west where Europeans could in some measure see the two sorts of equality – equality in freedom, or equality in servitude – that might await them in the future.[4]

Tocqueville scholarship has, accordingly, focused largely on his writings about Europe and America. During the Cold War, Tocqueville's work was brought to bear on the question of American exceptionalism, a term that nowadays is often taken to mean American uniqueness but that at the time meant something else: whether the lack of class relations

---

[1] DIA (L) Introduction, 12; II.4.viii, 704.

[2] Consider Tocqueville's assessment of Islam: "Mohammed brought down from heaven and put into the Koran not religious doctrines only, but political maxims, criminal and civil laws, and scientific theories. The Gospels, on the other hand, deal only with general relations between man and God and between man and man. Beyond that, they teach nothing and do not oblige people to believe anything. That alone, among a thousand reasons, is enough to show that Islam will not hold its power long in ages of enlightenment and democracy, while Christianity is destined to reign in such ages, as in all others," DIA (L) II.1.v, 445.

[3] See Alexis de Tocqueville, *WES*.

[4] DIA (L) I.1.iii, 57.

in the United States of the kind that predominated in Europe meant that the claim about the historical inevitability of communism might not apply in the American case.[5] With the fall of the Berlin Wall, another wave of Tocqueville scholarship attended to the question of whether the mediating civic institutions about which he wrote might be able to be instantiated in lands now without political compass.[6] Among political theorists, on the other hand, Tocqueville's writings have largely been seen through the lens of the field's central question, viz, what is the origin, nature of, and prospect for "modernity"[7] – a word Tocqueville never uses but that notion lurks in all that he writes.

Might Tocqueville's analysis shed light on other lands beyond Europe and America? I suspect the question would not have occurred to me had I not spent the past five years teaching and holding senior administrative positions in American-style universities in the Middle East. Before I arrived in Doha, Qatar, in 2005, I was prepared to believe that Tocqueville had little to offer in the way of analysis outside of Europe and the United States. By the time I left Sulaimani, Iraq, in 2010, I was convinced that much but not all of his theoretical frame could shed light on the current developments in the Middle East. That conviction came not, strictly speaking, through my role as a political scientist but rather through my role as a teacher and senior administrator. In those twin capacities I was able to assess the "sum of ideas that shape [the] mental habits,"[8] as Tocqueville calls them, of my students and local colleagues. In them I found much that Tocqueville would have recognized and much that can help us understand the deep apprehensions about modernity that prevail in the Middle East. There, as in the Europe of Tocqueville's time, the outcome of the battle may have already been decided in favor of one or another form of equality, but the obstacles are many. My remarks here will be broken into two sections: the first will pertain to my role as teacher; the second will pertain to my role as a senior administrator.

---

[5] See Louis Hartz, *The Liberal Tradition in America* (New York: Harcourt Brace & Co., 1955), Ch. 1, 6: "The hidden origin of socialist thought everywhere in the West is to be found in the feudal ethos. The *ancien régime* inspires Rousseau; both inspire Marx."

[6] See Robert Putnam, *Making Democracy Work* (Princeton: Princeton University Press, 1993). Putnam's book quickly became a touchstone for work on the beneficent effect of civic associations for democracy.

[7] See, for example, Harvey Mansfield and Delba Wintrop, DIA "Editors Introduction," xvii–lxxxvi.

[8] DIA (L) I.2.ix, 287.

Teaching Tocqueville

Most students in the Middle East do not understand the United States, although many think they do. In the Gulf, many of them are disposed to be suspicious when they are introduced to a book titled *Democracy in America*. There, the United States is often seen as the preeminent force of Westernization and, so, is understood to threaten a social fabric that is already strained by rates of development that are nowhere else seen on the planet. To this, add U.S. support for Israel, which inflames the imagination in the Gulf even though in private many will admit animosity toward the Palestinians they purportedly support. In the Kurdish region of Northern Iraq, on the other hand, the U.S. imposition of the No-Fly-Zone after the first Gulf War (in late 1992) helped to produce sympathy toward the United States of the sort that is found nowhere else in the Middle East. In that respect, the contrast between the two regions could not be greater. The U.S. failure to maintain peace after the deposition of the Saddam regime in 2003 certainly dampened pro-American sentiment there but not enough to stop Kurds from having a generally favorable view of the United States. A nation of some 40 million without a state of their own, sentiment toward Israel among the Kurds is surprisingly strong as well, although it is seldom stated publically.[9] The crush of the surrounding civilizations – Anatolian, Persian, and Babylonian – would make independent statehood unlikely even if the U.S./Turkish alliance did not already do so. Israel for the Kurds is less an ally than a marker for their own national aspirations.

These differing political judgments about U.S. foreign policy are not the final word, however, about Gulf and Iraqi students' understanding of the United States. What equally troubles them is the "delinked" condition that Tocqueville claims characterizes the new democratic age of equality. "Aristocracy links everybody, from peasant to king, in one long chain. Democracy breaks the chain and frees each link," he writes.[10] By this Tocqueville meant to suggest that the old, organic ties that bound each person to the next through loyalty (although seldom affection) have been

---

[9] The March 16, 1988, chemical gassing of Halabja, the destruction of some 4,000 Kurdish villages in the North, as well as the forced introduction of Arabs from the South into Kirkuk – all authorized by Saddam Hussein – have given a powerful recent impetus to Kurdish nationalism. This impetus has been favorably greeted by the U.S. State Department, in large measure, I fear, because of its fixation on identity politics as a desideratum for U.S. foreign policy.

[10] DIA (L) II.2.ii, 508.

undone and cannot be put back together again, try though we may. Each person increasingly stands alone, sees the world from the vantage point of individual self-interest, and feels no compunction to be bound by the ascribed authority of another.

The questions that most concerned Tocqueville were how far that delinking would proceed and how the delinked person would respond to that condition. Most students throughout the Middle East understand this movement well – either because of the astounding pace of modernization in the Gulf or because of what the Baath Party was able to dismantle over the course of four decades in Iraq. In both cases the consensus among students there is that they are far more delinked than were their parents or grandparents. They are haunted by this fact and see in the United States the specter of the complete delinkage they fear, quite irrespective of whether they detest U.S. foreign policy or embrace it.

To begin to get a sense of the depth of apprehension students have about this delinked condition, consider the term *Westernization* and its close relative, *modernization*. In the Gulf, as I mentioned earlier, the term of choice is modernization. Both Westernization and modernization are understood to be processes by which the wealth of nations is increased. Westernization, however, is taken to mean that process by which wealth is increased, although with the delinked individual being both the cause and consequence of that increase. Modernization, on the other hand, is taken to mean that process whereby wealth is increased, while the current social arrangements are left largely intact.

If we take a look at commercial arrangements, we can see how this plays out. In the Gulf and in much of the rest of the Middle East, a fully delinked commercial man does not yet exist. This is not to say that wealth, avarice, and greed do not exist. They do, just like everywhere else. It is important to note, however, that the way wealth is generated in the Middle East has little to do with the arrangements of commerce as Tocqueville and most Americans understand them. In the United States, commerce is inconceivable, for example, without delinked man freely moving about in search of the best price for his labor – hence, the common term *labor market*. Not so in much of the Middle East. There, states are largely patronage networks; corporations are generally cross-border joint ventures through which prominent families receive tribute from foreign companies intent on entering local markets; and rather than there being a free market for labor, workers are often contracted through elaborate sponsorship schemas, which tend to the overpayment for much needed ex-pat expertise and to the gross underpayment of laborers and servants.

Most students in Qatar are familiar with these arrangements. Some of them even benefit from them. All of them, I think, wonder whether those arrangements can or will be maintained.

Most students, then, say they want modernization but not Westernization. The latter term is a proxy for the delinkage they think prevails in the United States. The former term is meant to suggest an alternative path, still unspecified, by which the improvements that commerce brings may be secured without the delinkage, perceived or real, that historically has accompanied such improvements in Europe and in the United States. Said otherwise, modernization purports to be a path to prosperity that allows many if not all of the current social arrangements to remain intact. I doubt that is going to be able to happen. To some extent in the Gulf, and to a much greater extent in much of the rest of the Middle East, a deep apprehension about delinked man still fills the imagination of peoples neither quite able to embrace nor repudiate the world that is now upon them.

In Iraq, commerce, as Americans understand it, is largely unrecognizable as well. Businesses of even modest size operate because of their political party affiliations. In return, the political parties receive a portion of the revenue that businesses generate. These corporatist arrangements preclude the development of a robust private sector and tend to make political parties dissociate from the people they purport to represent because the source of their revenue lies elsewhere. Labor in Iraq is not organized around the consignment system that prevails in the Gulf because the revenue of the relatively well-developed petrochemical industry has yet to be directed toward building a vast commercial infrastructure with foreign labor. That may change if an export compromise can be reached between the regional Iraqi factions; however, for now the Iraqi labor force is both protected and hobbled by an arrangement in which workers can rarely be fired but in which they also cannot leave their place of employment unless "released" by their employer. In practice this means that good companies cannot search for the best employees because they are unlikely to receive permission to hire them away from their current jobs.

Students in the Gulf and in Iraq see the constraints under which labor operates. Most realize that such constraints produce an arrangement in which there are permanent winners and permanent losers. Yet the idea of a labor market, where people compete openly for jobs – and can be fired for incompetence – makes them uncomfortable. They do not quite see themselves as individual workers who might have to search for work rather than be directed toward a job by the government or invited into one because of family lineage or political affiliation. In short, although they generally want commerce to thrive, they are not prepared to live as the more delinked individual they would probably have to be in order for that to happen. That is why they want modernization but not Westernization.

Tocqueville's writings can be seen, of course, as announcing the advent of Westernization, although with some important caveats. That is, Tocqueville's writings suggest that the delinked individual is, indeed, the sort of individual who will prevail in the future. Students neither wish this to occur nor are eager to be subject to the sort of market failure Tocqueville thought would be necessary for commerce to thrive. They read Adam Smith's *Wealth of Nations*[11] and attend to his arguments – but look at the delinked social relations he presumes through the eyes of Marx: "The bourgeoisie, wherever it has got the upper hand, has put an end to all feudal, patriarchal, idyllic relations. It has pitilessly torn asunder the motley feudal ties that bound man to his 'natural superiors,' and left remaining no other nexus between man and man than naked self-interest, than callous 'cash payment.'"[12] When students in the Middle East read Marx, they do not have medieval Europe in mind. Instead they have merely to look around at their own societies to see the sort of relationships that are purportedly ripped apart by "capitalism" – a term that Smith himself never uses. In the Middle East, as in medieval Europe, labor does not move about freely. That is because the ties of family bind much more firmly and extensively there than they do in contemporary Europe or in North America.[13] More to the point, consanguineous marriage – a union between a man and a woman who are genetically related to a common ancestor – is in many places the norm rather than the exception. Europe and North America have, by contrast, extremely low

---

[11] Adam Smith, *Wealth of Nations*, ed. Edwin Cannan. (Chicago: University of Chicago Press, 1976).

[12] Karl Marx and Friedrich Engels, "Manifesto of the Communist Party," in *The Marx-Engels Reader*, ed. Robert Tucker (New York: Norton, 1978), 475.

[13] An underestimated contributor to the breakdown of the extended bloodline family is the Christian notion of marriage, the service of which has changed over time, notwithstanding its ancient roots. Although it is seldom considered these days, the format, "do you, X, take Y to be your lawful wife," etc., supposes that the pertinent name is not the family name but rather the first – or what, until recently, was called the Christian – name. This is not without significance. Marriage, on this account is not a unification of families but rather a new union based on the spiritual transformation that the taking of a Christian spouse supposes. If the Christian marriage service involved a unification of families, the format would more likely be something like, "do you, X, son of...," etc.

consanguinity rates.[14] With the exception of Oman, consanguinity rates on the Arabian Peninsula exceed 50 percent. The rates are similar in Pakistan. In Iraq, Sudan, and Yemen, the figure is 40 percent. In Egypt and the rest of the Levant, the figure is less than 20 percent.[15] Consanguineous marriage relations tend to produce strong intra-familial loyalties and, by extension, distrust of those outside the family orbit. Anyone who has taught in the Middle East will have noted that students – especially the girls[16] – often spend evenings and weekends involved in family events that routinely include first and second cousins. This often has deleterious consequences for their studies, although in vain does the teacher implore them always to think first about their obligations to their school work. Many students do not think of themselves first and foremost as individuals; they think of themselves, first, as bearers of a family name. Tocqueville noted that marriage in the aristocratic age united families, whereas in the democratic age it united hearts. That change has not yet really happened in much of the Middle East, although I suspect it is underway.

The binding ties of family in the Middle East, then, makes labor much less mobile. It is safe to say, in fact, that there is so little mobility of labor that what we usually think of as a labor "market" does not exist. To this, add the fact that wages for large sectors of the economy are established by governmental decree. (I will return to this matter in the next section.) The result is that it is well-nigh impossible to establish the real market price of labor in vast stretches of the Middle East. And because the price of labor is one of the component costs of natural price, it is therefore nearly impossible to establish what the natural price of any good or service there really is.

A business in an unimpeded market does not succeed or fail because of the market price it can get for its goods or services; it succeeds or fails if the market price it can secure exceeds or falls below the natural price of the good or service that it sells. In much of the Middle East it is impossible

---

[14] Why this has occurred – why, in fact, Europe and North America are much more individualistic – is one of the vexing questions historians face. Marx, as I indicated, argues that the internal contradiction within feudalism led to capitalism and the individualist ethic found there and that the contradiction within feudalism that brought this about was the expansion of global trade that followed the age of discovery.

[15] See http://www.consang.net. The map is a based on research documented in the tables that the Web site also provides. It should be noted that the data is very uneven and that some of the surveys identified are recent, whereas others date to the 1950s.

[16] Calling girls "women" in the Middle East often presumes that they have had conjugal relations, so our policy in Qatar and, to a lesser extent in Iraq, was to publically refer to them as girls.

to determine whether a business would be a success or a failure on its own because of the extensive market distortions governments there bring to bear. Subsidies, crony-socialism, and the lingering vestiges of family privilege make any talk of market commerce in much of the Middle East quite out of place. Under these circumstances it is nearly impossible to establish whether or not capital is being put to good use. Commerce there may be but not market commerce of the sort Smith imagined – where natural price can be established, where profit and loss can be calculated, and where capital is able to flow in profitable directions.

The first confirmation, then, that my students want modernization rather than Westernization is that they object to the notion of a "free" labor market. Tight and extended family relations largely preclude the development of an individuated person, unencumbered and free to move about in search of the best price for his labor. The second objection students have, as I mentioned earlier, pertains to the necessary winnowing out of businesses that must occur when the market price falls below the natural price.

In talking with students about this, I have come to realize that the issue is, at its root, a cultural one. Notwithstanding the immense cultural variance in the Middle East, the one common feature is the centrality of honor. In the United States, on the other hand, there is what could be called a failure culture. Honor cultures, to press the point, are face-saving cultures. What this means for commerce is that it is much less likely that market failures – or other institutional failures of competence – are going to be called out. Indeed, much of what, through Western eyes, looks to be corruption is, through Middle Eastern eyes, face-saving. Tocqueville wrote that in the aristocratic age, money was much less important than it is in the democratic age because of the nonpecuniary ties that held each person in his place, immobile even if thereby secure.[17] The same sort of thing still exists in parts of the Middle East – which is to say that it is aristocratic, in Tocqueville's sense of the word.

I do not wish to suggest that money is unimportant there, however, for it surely is. But the Middle East today can, I think, best be said to be in a transitional phase: on the one hand, face-saving and honor are still strong enough to assure that patronage arrangements of the sort that Tocqueville wrote about remain intact; on the other hand, the social dislocations that in Tocqueville's estimation make it necessary to rely increasingly on

---

[17] DIA (L) II.3.xvii, 615: "In aristocratic nations money is the key to the satisfaction of but a few of the vast array of possible desires; in democracies it is the key to them all."

money have also taken hold. The result has been a sometimes monstrous hybrid in which a permanent patronage class of winners receives all the money. Not really any longer aristocratic but not yet democratic either, the Middle East seems to occupy a place between the two nodal points about which Tocqueville wrote. The revolutionary movements that swept through the Middle East in the mid-twentieth century were, of course, attempts to eliminate that permanent patronage class. That those political revolutions have simply replaced one patronage class with another, far more despised, suggests that the problem is deeper than politics.

I do not think it will be possible to move beyond this nether location so long as a face-saving, honor culture perdures there. Political revolution may destroy one group of patrons, but only a failure culture can get rid of a permanent patron class altogether. That is because a failure culture cares not a jot about your social standing, your name, or the power you currently have.[18] Members of a failure culture necessarily look inward and ask the question, "How am I at fault for the failure that is now upon me?"[19] Members of an honor culture look outward when failure occurs and ask the question, "How is face-saving possible in light of what is now upon me?" Failure cultures are concerned first and foremost with competence, merit, and personal responsibility – not so with honor cultures.

When students in the United States are presented with the notion that markets work because price signals drive success and failure, they are generally not alarmed. When a business fails, the owner must liquidate his assets and start over.[20] They do not comment on this because they

---

[18] See Immanuel Kant, "Perpetual Peace," in *On History*, trans. Lewis White Beck (New York: Macmillan Publishing Co., 1963), Section II, n. 2, 95: "But with respect to the right of equality of all citizens as subjects, the question of whether a hereditary nobility may be tolerated turns upon the answer to the question as to whether the pre-eminent rank granted by the state ought to precede merit or follow it." Family name, in Kant's thinking, is a heteronomy, which cannot form the basis of rational citizenship.

[19] See Augustine, *City of God*, trans. Henry Bettenson (New York: Penguin Books, 1984), Bk. I, Ch, 8: "Though the sufferings [endured by the good and by the wicked] are the same, the sufferers remain different. Virtue and vice are not the same, even if they undergo the same torment. The fire that makes the gold shine makes the chaff smoke." Augustine argues that the Christian must always look inward when suffering occurs, with a view to faith, hope, and love.

[20] The matter is made more complicated when the interests of stake holders must be taken into consideration, as they often are in Western Europe. This suggests, for better or worse, that although both the United States and Europe are "failure cultures," the U.S. version is starker. When politics is in a great measure a matter of rapprochement between the various estates in society, as it is in Europe, rather than a matter of the representation and mediation of interests, as it is in the United States, a failure culture is likely to be somewhat attenuated.

are not members of an honor culture. Students in the Middle East, on the other hand, know that there are other reasons why commercial ventures succeed or fail, the most important of which is whether it is a part of a patronage network of the sort that honor cultures construct. In short, they want commerce; however, they cannot imagine it within the context of failure Smith and Tocqueville thought inevitable and necessary.[21] Although it might sound odd, the orienting lecture I gave to students in Iraq was titled, "In Praise of Failure." It never occurred to me to offer such a lecture in the United States; it was not necessary there – or so I thought until recently.[22] Not only is commerce impossible without failure; so, too, is a liberal arts education – a point I will develop shortly.

Commerce is not the only domain that reveals my Middle Eastern students' apprehensions about the delinked modern condition. Politics does as well. Discussions with Iraqi students in class revealed that they had little understanding of civic associations. Civic associations presuppose an already individuated person who then voluntarily joins a group, the purpose of which is limited, and whose duration is fixed. Tocqueville understood that this entirely new mode of being "gathered together" would be necessary in the democratic age.[23] Once democratic man became delinked, he would have to be voluntarily relinked.

Students there, however, are not yet entirely delinked; they are bound together by family ties, as I have mentioned. However, they are also bound together in political parties that have insinuated themselves into nearly every aspect of their lives outside of their family. As a consequence, most students cannot conceive of volunteering for an activity independent of the political party of which they are a member. The saying "everything is political" is used loosely in the United States, but it does not yet apply here; in Iraq and in other parts of the Middle East where socialism

---

[21] Tocqueville, for example, notes that Americans have very high rates of bankruptcies (DIA (L) I.2.v, 224) but takes for granted that such failures will occur.

[22] The matter is not quite this simple. In the democratic age, Tocqueville noted, delinked man will want to be treated equally in all respects. One of the consequences of this development is that the notion that no one should fail slips easily into the democratic imagination. The conditions of equality may, then, undermine the market commerce that has produced the improvements that attenuate the middle class anxiety that becomes prevalent in the democratic age. See DIA (L) II.2.xiii, 535–538.

[23] See Joshua Mitchell, "It is Not Good for Man to Be Alone," in *Friendship and Politics: Essays in Political Thought*, eds. John von Heyking and Richard Avramenko (Notre Dame, IN: University of Notre Dame Press, 2008), 268–284.

destroyed the old order and where the individuated person is not yet an accomplished fact, everything is indeed political. Civic associations consequently cannot yet exist. There is more to say about this, but I will do so in the context of my responsibilities as a senior administrator.

Administration in the Shadow of Tocqueville

Shortly after I arrived in Iraq to take up my duties at The American University of Iraq – Sulaimani (AUI-S), the academic students asked for a meeting. Rather demure and deferential, they asked if I would authorize the formation of student government. Cognizant that under Saddam Hussein's reign citizens had scant political rights and mindful of Locke's claims in the *Second Treatise* that man did not need the authorization of a sovereign to form government, I told them that they did not need my permission to do so.[24]

I quickly learned that students did not live in the near innocence of a Lockean state of nature. On the contrary, their intention was not to form a student government but rather to bring into the university one or another of the existing political parties, with a view to making AUI-S an apparatus of those parties – something that had occurred in every other university in the Kurdistan region and, I suspect, in other parts of Iraq to the south as well. When I discovered what was happening, I banned both student government and student newspapers because such newspapers were also beholden to the political parties at issue.[25] It was a sobering lesson: students were not Lockean individuals at all; their political affiliations had already been formed, and AUI-S was going to be the venue for the rehearsal of well-orchestrated positions at which their political parties had arrived long ago. Not so, I told them; instead we would work together learning about civic associations for a year or two. Perhaps after that we would reopen the question of student government. The first pre-political lesson, I told them, was that politics need not assume the winner-take-all form that it now takes in Iraq, which entails that political parties penetrate into every conceivable space, lest by not doing so a different political party would step into the breach. Instead we would

---

[24] See John Locke, "An Essay Concerning the True Original, Extent, and End of Civil Government," in *Two Treatises of Government*, ed. Peter Laslett (Cambridge: Cambridge University Press, 1960), Ch. VIII, ¶104, 336.
[25] Thanks to the fortuitous arrival of Jackie Spinner (former *Washington Post* Baghdad chief) at AUI-S in early 2010, we were able to move forward with the student newspaper long before we anticipated we would. See http://www.auisvoice.org.

start with something more modest, namely, civic associations. There, our students would learn to voluntarily perform a community task in which politics played no overt part; there they would learn to gather together and then disband as tasks emerged that needed doing and then were completed.[26]

The idea that individuals rather than permanently ensconced political parties should animate society is a foreign idea in Iraq and in much of the Middle East. One reading of Tocqueville is, as I have mentioned, that much of the Middle East remains in the aristocratic age: the individual not yet having emerged into the light of day, men and women understand themselves in terms of their affiliations. Tocqueville's aristocratic age, however, did not have political parties of this sort in it; the affiliations he had in mind were the more or less inherited ones that pertained to family name and rank order in a society. There are still echoes of that in Iraq and much of the Middle East; however, the mid-twentieth century socialist revolutions that occurred throughout the region (with the obvious exception of the Gulf) dismantled much of that old order, but without firmly establishing the individuated person in its place. In this liminal space between the two ages about which Tocqueville wrote, the manner of being gathered together in Iraq involves political parties that have none of the decorous understanding of social balance and conciliation found in the aristocratic age nor any sense, as yet, that an individual's political affiliations are one among many partially overlapping affiliations, which characterizes Tocqueville's democratic age. Conjoin these political observations with what I have said earlier about economic corporatism in Iraq, and it can easily be seen that Iraq and much of the Middle East is still a long way from the condition Tocqueville thought would characterize the democratic age. So fixed in place does this intermediate arrangement seem to be that there is reason to wonder if Tocqueville's "democratic man" will ever really fully emerge in the Middle East.

The matter is made more complicated by developments on the ground, so to speak, among the younger generation. This cannot be the place to consider what a generation raised on MTV, Facebook, cell phones, and text messaging thinks of itself. What can be mentioned here, however, is that educators around the Middle East recognize that the older methods of education are not sustainable. In Iraq, for example, all high school students must take a national test, the scores from which more or less determine what professional course they will follow for the rest of their

---

[26] To that end, our Student Services department established a program through which our students could volunteer to teach English to young children at the local orphanage.

lives and what several schools they may apply to. Still a command economy, notwithstanding what has happened since the fall of Baghdad on
April 9, 2003, officials in Baghdad annually decide how many doctors,
pharmacists, engineers, and other professionals Iraq will need in the coming years and allocate college slots based on those projections.[27] The
Iraqi model of higher education may have had its roots in a noble, early-
twentieth century model of British higher education, but the Baathists
corrupted it beyond recognition – so much so that in Iraq every course syl-
labus and textbook is determined or authorized by the Minister of Higher
Education in Baghdad and every faculty member and senior administrator is hired or fired by that same Ministry[28] – no Baghdad, no higher
education.

Almost everyone knows that these arrangements are not sustainable,
not only for the future of Iraq but also because the younger generation of
students increasingly finds their classroom environments to be antithetical
to the way they understand themselves. From their earliest days in school
until their last days at the university level, students are graded on how well
they repeat, often verbatim, what their professors have taught them. And
by *teach*, I mean lecture, often with notes that have not been updated
for decades. Absent a guild system of tenure and once appointed by a
government ministry to teach, professors have no incentive to update
lecture notes for class.[29] Students dutifully do what they are instructed

---

[27] Many of the young students with whom I spoke wanted to be pharmacists. The reason,
I was told, was that Iraqi citizens are able to set up an independent practice within two
years of completing their studies, which would allow them to supplement the meager
wages paid by the government for those in that position.

[28] The arrangement in Kurdistan is, for the moment, less certain. The Federal compromise
enshrined in the new constitution has emboldened the Kurds to develop a full complement of ministries through which they intend to have as many administrative decisions
about the Kurdistan region be made in the Kurdistan region itself. The Ministry of
Higher Education in particular, under the able, forward-thinking leadership of Dlawer
Alaadin, has taken a number of important steps aimed at reforming a nearly broken
system of higher education there.

[29] After long discussions with education professionals in Iraq and with State Department
officials posted there, I have become convinced that the single most important thing
the U.S. government can do to help restart higher education in Iraq is to take the
innocuous step of making sure that the journals for all the disciplines and professions
are available to educators there, online if possible. The availability of these will help
foster the redevelopment of the disciplines and wrest control of tenure decisions from
the politically appointed administrators whose interest seldom coincides with that of
disciplinary integrity and the advancement of knowledge. There are, of course, reasons
to worry that the intellectual fashions found in every discipline will produce its own
set of distortions. However, the alternative – academic tenure determined by politically
motivated administrators of one sort or another – is worse.

to do, and some get through without being too scarred by the entire enterprise. They know, however – as do those government officials who are intent on building a vibrant Iraq – that the system of higher education must be rethought, at its foundations.[30]

One other point needs mentioning by way of introduction to higher education in the Middle East. The liberal arts model does not exist.[31] In the 1950s, as many septuagenarians reminded me, Baghdad was the home of a Jesuit high school, Baghdad College, which was based on the liberal arts and which produced some of Iraq's brightest lights. Baghdad College, however, was the exception. Higher education throughout Iraq is a highly specialized affair: students enter the university knowing what their profession will be for the rest of their lives. This fixity of professional trajectory is a stark contrast to the self-understanding of the Middle East's younger generation, which is by disposition inured against thinking that anything whatsoever in its world can be fixed and firm.

Against this background, AUI-S was deliberately set up as a liberal arts university. Our view was that if Iraq was really going to thrive, it would need a younger generation that was able to think and write for itself. I doubt those who enrolled really understood what was in store for them. In class they were asked what they thought about this or that idea – something no teacher in their primary and secondary school had ever asked them. For their homework they were asked to write what they thought about this or that author's ideas – something no teacher in their primary or secondary school had ever requested of them.

In Tocquevillean terms, the liberal arts lead to that most precious of achievements, the development of an authorial voice – a voice constituted not by imprint from without but rather by internal reflection.[32] Of

---

[30] I note in passing that the mantra now repeated by administrators across the Middle East is "student-centered learning." This is counter-poised against the old model, presumably something like "faculty-centered education," which administrators are trying to replace. The deep and, I suspect, fatal flaw of this effort at reform is that it is being driven forward by a new breed of U.S. educators who believe in educational outcomes that can be numerically measured. This is a developing morass in U.S. higher education; however, it has not yet completely taken hold. In the Middle East there are few bulwarks against it, which has left university officials there lost in this new labyrinth and concerned largely with how to assess what students learn rather than with what should be taught.

[31] This is true even in Israel, although the Shalem Center is well underway in its effort to set up Shalem College, which will be Israel's first liberal arts college.

[32] See DIA (L) II.1.i, 429. Tocqueville's reflections on what he calls "the American philosophical method" haunt the entirety of Vol. II and culminate in his worries, in Part IV, that the delinked, independent citizen will succumb to a new form of tyranny, still without a name.

necessity this enterprise has some of the marks of what has been called a "hermeneutic of suspicion" because questioning is one weapon in the arsenal needed to produce liberal-minded citizens. At its best, however, the enterprise also relies on what I will here call a "hermeneutic of deference." For absent a sense of reverence in the encounter with great works of philosophy and literature, questioning itself is hollow and apt to produce not thoughtful citizens but rather nihilistic subjects and not equality in freedom but rather equality in servitude.

Can a liberal arts education produce a thoughtful citizen who is able to think both critically and deferentially? Tocqueville does not, of course, think that most of what passes for education should be directed toward the liberal arts.[33] In the age of democracy, men will be concerned with well-being, and their education must accordingly be directed toward that end.[34] Tocqueville, however, could presume in his analysis of democracy in America a much more delinked soul than now exists throughout the Middle East. The development of an authorial voice is, I suggest, perhaps the single most important thing higher education in the Middle East can aspire to. In the gentle safety of the classroom, students find their way to ideas that they can finally call their own in communion with authors who give them reason to believe that the solitude of the democratic age is not the final word. They learn what Tocqueville thought we all had to learn in the democratic age, viz, that while we are delinked, we need not be alone. That lesson must finally be learned outside the classroom, of course, but that in the Middle East it may be learned in the classroom at all is a breathtaking promise. By virtue of the unschooled independence of mind that is already there in the minds of millions of Middle Eastern students – brought about as it has been by MTV, Facebook, cell phones, and text messaging – liberal arts education is peculiarly well suited for a generation in search of a voice it cannot yet find.

There were less lofty, but no less important, reasons for building a liberal arts university in Iraq. A lock-step system of higher education can

---

[33] DIA (L) II.1.xv, 476: "An obstinate determination to teach nothing by the classics in a society always struggling to acquire or keep wealth would produce very well-educated but dangerous citizens. For the state of politics and society would always make them want things which their education had not taught them how to earn, and they would perturb the state, in the name of the Greeks and the Romans, instead of enriching it with industry."

[34] See DIA (L) I.1.iii, 55–56.

survive within a command economy; however, in a free market economy it cannot. In a rapidly changing world of the sort that a free market economy supposes, no university can assure its incoming students that the specific "skills" that are taught there will serve them well for the rest of their lives. In that light, the task of higher education in the Middle East must shift in some measure away from teaching a specific body of information to teaching students how to learn. A liberal arts education during the first few years of college followed by immersion into specific fields singularly facilitates that goal. Our view was that the seeming antinomy between a liberal arts education and an education unto a specific specialization need not occur. Indeed, our view was that to produce the best specialists, an early immersion in the liberal arts was necessary.

Notwithstanding the promise that liberal arts education offers for Iraq and for the whole of the Middle East, there are a number of reasons it is likely to be opposed: first, until a free market economy takes hold, there is no real incentive to have universities produce more supple-minded citizens who are really able to think for themselves; second, a liberal arts university supposes already the existence of a decentralized system of education, with little political intervention; and third, it is not clear that university professors in Iraq or elsewhere have the interest or ability to shift to a liberal arts model. Each of these obstacles is significant in itself; conjoined, they are formidable. On the other side of the ledger are several bald facts: the current system is broken and cannot be repaired, and it does not accord with what, earlier, I called the unschooled independence of mind that the younger generation has.

Just how extensive and how rapid the transformation of Middle Eastern higher education will be remains to be seen. The good news, I suggest, is that no matter how fierce the opposition to U.S. foreign policy in the region may be, there is near-universal good will toward the U.S. system of higher education, which students and administrators alike see as a much-needed corrective to the system currently in place. Unfortunately, neither USAID nor the State Department seems to understand the important role it can play in this transformation. The State Department in particular, under Secretary Hillary Clinton, has become enamored of the purportedly revolutionary role social media can play among the young people of the region. It is fanciful, however, to think that this initiative ought to be the centerpiece of its efforts. That said, social media has emerged because it comports with the habits of a younger generation accustomed to fewer palpable connections to their friends, families, and neighbors. As such, it confirms what Tocqueville long ago suggested, namely, that with each passing generation in the democratic age, the linkages between citizens would become more tenuous – even as the sympathies citizens felt for others they do not even know in other parts of the world increased.[35]

Conclusion

Tocqueville's thinking about the delinked condition is helpful, I think, in understanding the changes now underway in the Middle East. I have suggested, however, that with respect to commerce and politics, much of the Middle East is caught between the two nodal points of aristocracy and democracy, leaving a large swath of the globe seemingly fixed and without either the certainties and securities of the premodern, nor the liberties of the modern, world. The recent protests and uprisings across North Africa, the Levant, the Gulf, and Mesopotamia have not, however, surprised me. The seemingly stable equilibrium between the two has shown signs of unraveling to anyone who has had extensive dealings with a younger generation that is, in some ways, as delinked as is the younger generation in the United States. So compared, the changes underway would seem to point to the emergence of a long-deferred abstract freedom that both easily understand.

Against this optimistic prospect should be set Tocqueville's intimation that absent the "laws, ideas customs and mores [that are] needed to make [a democratic] revolution profitable," the likely result will be failure that unwittingly ushers in re-enchantment movements not unlike those witnessed in Europe during the twentieth century.[36] Writing in the aftermath of the French Revolution, he noted to his fellow Europeans: "We have destroyed an aristocratic society, and settling down complacently amidst the ruins of the old building, we seem to want to stay there like that forever."[37] In his view, there was no going back to a world that had been destroyed. Indeed, *Democracy in America* can be read as Tocqueville's attempt to show what the way forward might look like. The enchanted past was over; the attempt to re-enchant it could not work. A century later, in Europe, the specter of delinked man led Fascists and National Socialists to form a polity based on purported organic models of community drawn from Europe's pagan past and led communists everywhere to

---

[35] See DIA (L) II.2.ii, 507: "In democratic ages . . . the duties of each to all are much clearer but devoted service to any individual much rarer. The bonds of human affections are wider but more relaxed."

[36] DIA (L) Introduction, 13.

[37] DIA (L) Introduction, 16.

posit a remedy to the delinked condition in a post-revolutionary future. I suspect Tocqueville would have been distraught of these developments. He would not, however, have been surprised.

Were Tocqueville alive today, his apprehension about the twenty-first century, I submit, would be that Middle Eastern societies were increasingly becoming delinked and, like his nineteenth-century Europe, are without a way to turn that condition to their profit. As a consequence, re-enchantment movements are likely to occur. Christianity could not provide what was needed for Europeans of the nineteenth century because it does not offer a comprehensive "way of life." That is why European re-enchantment movements turned to pagan themes instead. With considerable caution, it is worth noting that a postcolonial version of Islam does, in fact, purport to offer a remedy to delinked man in the Middle East in the twenty-first century. Moreover, it is important to note that such a movement will come to the fore not in spite of the revolutionary calls for freedom echoing across the Middle East at the moment but because of them.

However, if Tocqueville is correct, these re-enchantment movements will not be the final word, for nothing is more certain in the modern age than that any effort to relink man organically, under the aegis of a comprehensive way of life, cannot but fail.

PART THREE

CHALLENGES OF GLOBALIZATION:
DEMOCRACY, MARKETS, AND NATIONHOOD

CHAPTER 7

Tocqueville and the Unsettled Global Village

Susan McWilliams

This is no outer dark
But a small province haunted by the good,
Where something may be understood
And where, within the sun's coronal arc,
We keep our proper range,
Aspiring, with this lesser globe of sight,
To gather tokens of the light . . .

              – Richard Wilbur[1]

Alexis de Tocqueville worked well within boundaries, particularly within the boundaries of the nation-state. In most of his writing, he grounds his theoretical claims in the analysis of a particular country: England, France, the United States. Yet even as his writing seems to rely on the existence of borders between states in that way, in other ways Tocqueville draws attention to the impermanence and even impotence of political borders in the modern world. He says he bears witness to a time in which "the barriers that separate nations within humanity and citizens within the interior of each people tend to disappear."[2] The "frightening spectacle" that Tocqueville professes to behold in *Democracy in America* is in large part the spectacle of a world where long-standing political borders, especially at the international level, are being crossed and compromised at a furious rate.[3] Democratization seems to him the great political development of the modern age in part because it transcends

---

[1] Richard Wilbur, "Icarium Mare," in *Collected Poems, 1943–2004* (San Diego: Harcourt, 2004), 94–95.

[2] DIA II.I.v, 421.

[3] DIA, Introduction, 7.

and often obliterates what have long seemed to be the settled political markers and lines of the globe.

As Barbara Allen mentions, this sense of things led Tocqueville to anticipate and contemplate questions about politics in an age of what we now call globalization.[4] In particular, he considers what the experience of "living globally," to use a contemporary phrase, might be like at the individual and community levels. Tocqueville thinks seriously about what it is like to live in conditions of global scale, conditions in which political borders are few and far between, and in which even those borders are readily permeable. Or, as Sheldon Wolin puts it, he wonders what happens when "certain bonds of identity slacken" in the face of universalizing political claims and movements.[5] Although Tocqueville never speaks about "global governance" or "global justice" in the contemporary sense of those terms, he speaks a great deal about the psychological and social dynamics that attend a world in which such concepts are viable and in which there exists what Charles Beitz has called a "nascent global capacity to act" – the world, in short, of the early twenty-first century.[6] We can thus read his work, in those terms, as contributing to contemporary conversations about what it means to live in an age of global realities and temporalities.

In considering such dynamics, the note that Tocqueville strikes is not exactly bleak, but it does carry an unmistakable tone of warning. Sensing the rise of global political forces that "cannot be stopped," he argues that there are great political dangers in a globalized or globalizing world, and those dangers stem from a sense of disconnection at the internal or emotional level. According to him, it is critical to understand the extent to which the broadening and weakening of political boundaries may be disorienting to human beings, even when such developments unearth and make possible more fluid identity practices and signal an apparent expansion of freedom and choice. In Tocqueville's telling, as one scholar puts it, "individuals experience a kind of vertigo" when political borders are understood to be permeable and unstable, a vertigo that stems from feelings of loneliness and disorganization. Those feelings may even reach the point at which "all decisions become a source of even more anxiety

[4] Barbara Allen, *Tocqueville, Covenant, and the Democratic Revolution: Harmonizing Earth with Heaven* (Lanham, MD: Lexington Books, 2005), 261–262.
[5] Sheldon S. Wolin, *Tocqueville Between Two Worlds: The Making of a Political and Theoretical Life* (Princeton: Princeton University Press, 2003), 566.
[6] Charles Beitz, "Cosmopolitanism and Global Justice," *Journal of Ethics* 9 (2005), 11.

because there is no foundational ground for choosing."[7] Because those feelings of anxiety are awful if not unbearable, people in conditions of relative borderlessness will yearn for some orienting principle or authority in their lives. That yearning for order, Tocqueville thinks, is inevitable in situations where ancestral and particular sovereignties are losing or have lost their grip. But that inevitable yearning is also a constant threat to political liberty because it tempts people to "give themselves a master" – to facilitate their own political repression in both direct and indirect ways.[8]

To be sure, as Tocqueville knew, this is a phenomenon that emerges first within the modern nation-state itself. After all, the emergence of modern states is accompanied by what Reinhard Bendix describes as "the decline of estate-society with its hierarchy of ranks and hence by the social isolation of the individual citizen." Except for the "paroxysms of fraternal enthusiasm" that often accompany its founding, the modern nation-state tends to be associated with a certain level of individual alienation, as Tocqueville makes clear.[9] The scale of the modern nation-state is large and expansive, dwarfing individuals and disorienting them even as it includes them in a broad category of membership. In Tocqueville's telling, though, things do not stop there. The modern nation-state almost inevitably falls in thrall to universalizing and internationalizing political movements, movements that enervate even the thin political linkages that accompany modern statehood. This enervation only aggravates the individual's experience of political disconnection and the accompanying threat of a turn to tyranny.

Given, then, conditions in which people rightly perceive an increase in border crossings and a decrease in settled political boundaries – given, in other words, what we usually call globalization – Tocqueville suggests that the challenge facing political scholars and statesmen is to find ways to counter the disoriented anxiety that can stymie or undermine political liberty. To do that, they must work to support those forms of bounded authority that provide individuals with a sense of order but that do not, at the same time, undermine political freedoms. If political

[7] Corey Robin, "Why Do Opposites Attract? Fear and Freedom in the Modern Political Imagination," in *Fear Itself: Enemies Real and Imagined in American Culture*, ed. Nancy Lusignan Schultz (West Lafayette, IN: Purdue University Press, 1999), 10.
[8] DIA II.i.v, 418.
[9] Reinhard Bendix, *Embattled Reason: Essays on Social Knowledge*, Vol. 1 (New Brunswick, NJ: Transaction Publishers, 1988), 213.

life is to be both global and free, Tocqueville argues, it is necessary to strengthen such forms of particular, extra-political authority. The alternative is an almost inevitable global turn toward authoritarianism or even totalitarianism. We can thus regard Tocqueville's famous announcement that "a new science of politics is needed for a world altogether new" as pointed precisely at those ends, toward the challenge of preserving political liberty in a world of increasingly evident global scale.[10] This project, "to help people comprehend a changing world" in a way that supports liberty, depends on the efforts of political thinkers and theorists – those "men of imagination and vision" who are audacious and creative enough to see politics in terms beyond its most narrow and evident horizons.[11]

In his 54 years as a French citizen, Tocqueville lived under five constitutions and seven regimes.[12] So perhaps it is not surprising that the concepts of political uncertainty and transformation exist at the fore of his work or that he focuses on the modern world in terms of its "sudden and momentous" changes – in particular, changes that unsettle conceits of political sovereignty and stability. He begins the 1848 introduction to *Democracy in America* with "a solemn warning that society changes its forms, humanity its condition, and that new destinies are impending" and with the image of being "placed in the middle of a rapid river."[13] In his *Recollections*, he describes mid-nineteenth-century France as going through not merely the changing of details on a political horizon but the changing of the political horizon altogether.[14] The language of great change is also sprinkled throughout *The Old Regime and the Revolution*.[15] Even in his writings on Algeria, as Jennifer Pitts observes, Tocqueville makes clear that he is writing in response to what he understands to be the "revolutionary developments in Europe's relations with the non-European world" taking place around him.[16] All of Tocqueville's

---

[10] DIA Introduction 7.
[11] Susan Dunn, *Sister Revolutions: French Lightning, American Light* (New York: Faber and Faber, 1999), 32.
[12] Seymour Drescher, introduction to *Tocqueville and the French*, ed. Françoise Mélonio, (Charlottesville: University of Virginia Press, 1998), xi.
[13] Alexis de Tocqueville, *Democracy in America*, ed. Henry Reeve as translated by Francis Bowen and Phillips Bradley (New York, Vintage Books, 1990), I, xix; I, 7.
[14] R, 22.
[15] OR I, 23ff.
[16] Jennifer Pitts, Preface to WES, xi.

work, as Saguiv Hadari observes, is concerned with the "macrophenomena of rapid change" in modern political life.[17]

In particular, as those references begin to make clear, Tocqueville draws a picture of a modern world wracked by changes of a decidedly internationalizing or globalizing sort. Much of his attention is focused on democratization, of course, but it is noteworthy that he describes democratization in terms of its power to steamroll over borders and continue "advancing today amid the ruins it has made."[18] Tocqueville grasps the universalizing nature of democratic thought itself, its natural assumption of "an international character" and tendency toward making cross-cultural political claims.[19] Even the spectacle of mass human movement across the Atlantic Ocean and then across the North American continent seems in Tocqueville's work to embody the boundary-crossing (and boundary-disrespecting) nature of democratization. "It fells the forests and drains the marshes; lakes as large as seas and huge rivers resist its triumphant march in vain," he writes. "This incredible destruction" and "this even more surprising growth," in his telling, bode the obliteration of long-standing political constructions.[20] Elsewhere, Tocqueville writes about how colonial entanglements both create and complicate cross-border politics, and given that he sees such entanglements as to a certain degree inevitable, his work is imbued with the idea that all the nations of the modern age must be understood in a "global context."[21] As Wolin explains, Tocqueville understands his own task in terms of opening political wisdom to a newly "cross-cultural politics."[22]

Throughout his writings on America in particular, Tocqueville builds an exhaustive case that modern democratization both links previously unlinked peoples and confounds traditional notions about the nature of political communities and boundaries; "it has destroyed or modified relations that formerly existed, and established new ones" in a way that reshapes "no less than the visage of the political world."[23] He describes, for instance, his own shock at learning that Americans did not primarily

---

[17] Saguiv A. Hadari, *Theory in Practice: Tocqueville's New Science of Politics* (Stanford: Stanford University Press, 1989), 26.
[18] DIA Introduction, 6.
[19] André Jardin, *Tocqueville: A Biography* (New York: Farrar, Strauss, and Giroux, 1988), 498.
[20] "A Fortnight in the Wilds," JA, 351.
[21] Pitts, "Introduction" to WES, xii.
[22] Wolin, *Tocqueville Between Two Worlds*, 117.
[23] DIA Notice, 399.

identify themselves (and were not identifiable) in terms of their various ancestral backgrounds. "In America," he writes, "even more than in Europe, there is one society only." Tocqueville had expected to see more evidence of political multiplicity in the United States on numerous counts: "I supposed," he says, that America "ought to show all conditions of existence and provide a picture of society in all its ages." Yet he quickly learned that "nothing is true in this picture." Tocqueville notes that differences in religion or ancestry or education that would signal major political differences in Europe did not signal the same in the United States. And within the United States, people who were separated by hundreds of miles – a geographical distance that, Tocqueville imagined, must bode political variation – were relatively indistinguishable. When his ship docked in Detroit, for instance, Tocqueville says he expected to find a very different city from those he had seen on the East Coast, but he found the merchants there as well stocked as those in New York. Moreover, the inhabitants of Michigan, although they might live in cabins that seemed "the asylum of all wretchedness," spoke "the language of towns" and talked about politics in the same way the inhabitants of New York talked about politics.[24] He says he was astonished that the bank notes of the United States "are accepted at the frontier of the wilderness for the same value as in Philadelphia." Americans have "long since broken the bonds that attached them to native soil," Tocqueville writes, and no longer judged particulars of land or ancestry to be markers imbued with political meaning.[25] Although Tocqueville notes and appreciates certain variations in American political life, he returns again and again to the overwhelming similarity of political culture across its vast expanse.

Moreover, Tocqueville writes that his experiences in the United States, particularly in terms of its political uniformity, undermined his belief that physical geography determines political culture and attuned him to the sheer magnitude and force of modern democratization.[26] On the frontier, he writes, "the institutions, ideas, customs, and efforts of the settlers appeared to overcome the effects of the environment." The seeming indomitability of the American settlers made it clear – "the facts are as certain as if they had already occurred" – that American and

[24] JA, 355; 358; 356–357.
[25] DIA I.2.x, 373; I.2.ix, 270.
[26] James T. Schleifer, *The Making of Tocqueville's "Democracy in America"* (Chapel Hill: The University of North Carolina Press, 1980), 46.

democratic expansionism would continue. "In but a few years these impenetrable forests will have fallen," and "the noise of civilization and of industry will break the silence."[27] Just as the ancient forests tumbled down in the face of the American onslaught, so, too, Tocqueville intimates, will the ancient ways of approaching the world; all the old and particular things will fall in the face of a globalizing and universalizing political culture.

When Tocqueville announces that "in America I saw more than America," then, one of the things he means is that in America he saw a land where the old political distinctions and loyalties were ceasing to matter and where societies that had been previously distinct were becoming interconnected if not indistinct. He sees a world in which the old ways are not just being put aside but are also being destroyed, and at a furious rate. His own experiences convinced Tocqueville that the entirety of the modern world moves toward a political convergence; the world moves toward becoming something of a "global village" in present-day parlance:

Variety is disappearing from within the human species; the same manner of acting, thinking, and feeling is found in all corners of the world. That comes not only from the fact that all peoples deal with each other more and copy each other more faithfully, but from the fact that in each country, men diverge further and further from the particular ideas and sentiments of a cast, a profession, or a family and simultaneously arrive at what depends more nearly on the constitution of man, which is everywhere the same. They thus become more alike even though they have not imitated each other.

For Tocqueville, nineteenth-century America presaged a world in which the old political identities and borders were going to apply less and less, where sharing attachments to particular ancestries or memories or landscapes would no longer be considered legitimate as the building blocks of political community. Moderns are like "travelers dispersed in a great forest," he says, moving around and crossing paths and in doing so ultimately reshaping everything with which they come into contact – including each other.[28] Tocqueville's grand narrative is very much a story about a world in which the old measures and markers of political connectivity are ceasing to matter in the ways they once did. What Tocqueville describes as the boundless quality of American existence prefigures a more boundless world.

[27] JA, 399.
[28] DIA II.3.xvii, 588.

As his image of moderns-as-travelers suggests, it is not just democracy but also mobility that grounds Tocqueville's depiction of modernity in this regard. His own travels across the vast distances of the globe convinced him how readily a political border might be crossed and, in a relatively short time, rendered all but irrelevant. His own mobility drew his attention to the way in which mobility is a central feature of modern political life, helping to eliminate old hierarchies and weaken traditional authorities. Increasing mobility intensifies the democratic inclination toward boundlessness because it helps to unsettle almost every provincial association and establishment. The two forces feed off of and reinforce each other. For Tocqueville, "the future global system will look 'Americanized'" not just because of growing democratic commitments but also because of increased mobility.[29] As Harvey Mitchell says, Tocqueville foresaw that in modern times, mobility would be "a permanent feature of Western society" if not global society, undermining the classical idea that there are "boundaries across which there could or should not be movement."[30] Increasing mobility works hand in hand with democracy to increase the scale of modern political life, unsettling individuals and communities in both the literal and figurative senses.

This increase in scale and speed, Tocqueville notes, is reflected in a general expansion and speeding up of economic exchange that itself portends a further breaking down of borders. "Money," he writes in *The Old Regime*, "has acquired an astonishing mobility, ceaselessly changing hands" in the modern world.[31] This change in the rate of economic interaction hastens and deepens the sense of increased scale and boundlessness that modern people experience. Along those lines, even though Tocqueville probably did not anticipate the full global scope and driving power of modern industry, he did see its infancy and identify the predominant modern trend toward ever-greater speeds and scales of production; a signal feature of the modern world, he observes, is its tendency to increase the scale of agricultural production, with large estates "growing larger every day at the expense of the small," and the "habit of cultivation on a large scale" becoming more widespread.[32] In the very tangible and immediate realm of economic exchange, Tocqueville sees even further reason

[29] Thomas Bender, *Rethinking American History in a Global Age* (Berkeley: University of California Press, 2002), 359.
[30] Harvey Mitchell, *America After Tocqueville: Democracy Against Difference* (Cambridge: Cambridge University Press, 2002), 51.
[31] OR I, 87.
[32] JEI, 242.

to suspect that the modern world will be one dominated by ever greater sizes and scales – scales that dwarf traditional communities and render them ever more unstable and powerless.

In Tocqueville's telling, all of these changes, too, have a kind of kinship with and indebtedness to Enlightenment philosophy, which itself encourages an internationalizing and universalizing approach to politics. As he portrays it in *The Old Regime*, sounding something like Edmund Burke, the Enlightenment encouraged political thought that is highly generalized – an "abstract and literary politics," he calls it – as opposed to an approach to politics that is rooted in an awareness of particular attachments and loyalties.[33] That sort of generalized thinking has a certain affinity with democratic thinking, due to the fact that democratic commitments have an abstract theoretical character, and Tocqueville seems constantly aware of the resemblance between the boundlessness of democratic doctrine and the boundlessness of highly abstracted thinking. It also is at home in a world where increasing mobility seems to justify a more broad-scale and generalized view of the world. His analysis turns back repeatedly, as Wolin observes, to the "increasingly abstract character of the political" in the modern age.[34]

And at least in some measure, Tocqueville himself saw the attraction of such abstract political thinking, as his assertion that the "constitution of man" is "everywhere the same" indicates. While writing *Democracy in America*, for instance, he noted his own inclination to root political thinking in the "realm of the abstract" rather than in the tangible dimensions of the world.[35] And in his speeches about Algeria, Tocqueville dismisses the importance of understanding that country – or even the continent of Africa – in its details and insists that only the most abstract and general precepts of "good government" are required for political planning there.[36] Although, as I will argue, Tocqueville was ultimately quite wary of a political world that is overly dependent on what he called "general ideas," his own work at times reflects the spirit of the age he discusses

---

[33] OR I, 195. See also Robert A. Schneider, "Self-Censorship and Men of Letters: Tocqueville's Critique of the Enlightenment in Historical Perspective," in *Tocqueville and Beyond: Essays on the Old Regime in Honor of David D. Bien*, ed. Robert M. Schwartz and Robert A. Schneider (Cranbury, NJ: Rosemount Publishing, 2003), 192–225.

[34] Wolin, *Tocqueville Between Two Worlds*, 281.

[35] See Laurence Guellec, "The Writer Engagé: Tocqueville and Political Rhetoric," trans. Arthur Goldhammer, in *The Cambridge Companion to Tocqueville*, ed. Cheryl B. Welch (Cambridge: Cambridge University Press: 2006), 171.

[36] WES, 121.

(and of which he is a part).[37] Part of the reason that Tocqueville is so attuned to the tendency toward universalism and abstraction in the modern age may be that he felt the pull of that tendency so strongly himself.

In any case, the big picture Tocqueville draws, throughout his writing, is of a world in which many, if not all, the traditional political boundaries – boundaries in the literal as well as in the imaginative sense – seem increasingly unguarded and in which the scale of political life expands all the time. It is a world that appears demarcated not by borders but by the very absence of borders. It is a world in which institutions and ideas seem constantly to extend their size and scope, enfeebling traditional loyalties, ranks, and forms of rule. And because, in Henry Steele Commager's words, Tocqueville understands that "size is not just a phenomenon or area of population, but of economy and culture," not to mention power, his writing points our attention to what all that change in scale and size means for political life.[38] He draws our attention, that is, to what it means to live in a truly global world, a world like our own in which living globally seems to be a dominant concept or mode.

For the most part, Tocqueville draws attention to the political dynamics of globalization through an analysis of how globalization is experienced emotionally or internally – that is, he "performs consciously as a kind of psychologist" on the individual and collective levels, exploring what kind of internal effects might be brought about by increasing scales and weakening borders.[39] He looks, as one scholar puts it, at the way the "external forces" of a globalizing world act upon or interact with the "internal designs" of the human animal.[40] And from that approach, Tocqueville quickly identifies one major theme: a primary consequence of living in conditions of relative boundlessness is an increase in feelings of anxiety at the individual and social levels.

[37] Kathleen S. Sullivan provides a nice gloss on Tocqueville's apprehension of "general ideas" in her essay "Toward a Generalized Theory of Equality," in *Feminist Interpretations of Alexis de Tocqueville*, ed. Jill Locke and Eileen Hunt Botting (University Park: The Pennsylvania State University Press, 2009), 205.
[38] Henry Steele Commager, *Commager on Tocqueville* (Columbia: University of Missouri Press, 1993), 53.
[39] Laura Janara, *Democracy Growing Up: Authority, Autonomy, and Passion in Tocqueville's "Democracy in America"* (Albany: State University of New York Press, 2002), 33.
[40] Michael A. Nicholas, *America Uncensored: A Nation in Search of Its Soul* (Victoria, BC: Trafford Publishing, 2004), 121.

Throughout his work, Tocqueville emphasizes that a globalizing or interconnecting world is one in which "traditional ties, supports and restrictions have been left behind along with their assurances about a person's self-worth and identity."[41] The "anxiety that to Tocqueville seems the earmark of democratic man" is an anxiety that comes from the perception of boundarilessness, from the decline of particular authorities and ancestral rules; anxiety is the flip side of the processes that we tend to call globalization.[42] That anxiety, in turn, works to shape human action in the world, over time coming to dominate political dynamics and reshape political institutions.

Tocqueville begins this story, and first draws this connection, in *Democracy in America*, when he describes how the decline in relevance of the old borders – the central process of globalization – had already created in the United States an amount of basic identity uncertainty where there had been little to none before. It is a concern that dominates the book; in fact, one writer has said that "one of the first things that jumps out at the cultural analyst reading de Tocqueville's work is the meaning and identity vacuum that faced members of the emerging American society."[43] Indeed, Tocqueville introduces this theme early on in his description of the lives of the first Anglo-American settlers. In his discussion of them, he focuses on the constant breakdown of political boundaries that they cause and experience. "As they go forward, the barriers which imprisoned society and behind which they were born are lowered; old opinions, which for centuries had been controlling the world, vanish; a course almost without limits, a field without horizon, is revealed," he writes. "The human spirit rushes forward and traverses them in every direction." The breakdown of old political borders, as he describes it, was in some way a liberation for the early Americans; it enlarged and excited them. Yet that sense of enlargement and excitement had its limits. The early settlers, it seems, were only able to embrace conditions of relative political boundlessness because they had the sense of a very bounded and ordered spiritual world. "When it arrives at the limits of the political world," Tocqueville explains, the human mind "halts, trembling."[44] He then goes on to describe that

[41] Robert Shulman, *Social Criticism and Nineteenth-Century American Fictions* (Columbia: University of Missouri Press, 1987), 29.
[42] Marvin Zetterbaum, *Tocqueville and the Problem of Democracy* (Stanford: Stanford University Press, 1967), 79.
[43] Stephen W. Twing, *Myths, Modes, and U.S. Foreign Policy* (Boulder: Lynner Reinner Publishers, 1998), 17.
[44] DIA I.1.ii, 43.

for the early Puritan settlers, the "spirit of liberty," marked by a lack of
boundaries and restrictions in the political world, depended on the presence of a certain kind of ethereal counterweight, the "spirit of religion."
The early settlers' religious beliefs reassured them of ultimate borders
and boundaries, a reassurance that allowed them to thrive in conditions
where the political world did not seem as fixed.

Although many scholars have set upon Tocqueville's idea of a symbi-
otic balance between the spirit of religion and the spirit of liberty in the
lives of the early Anglo-American settlers, few emphasize the underlying
psychological story that Tocqueville is telling about the experience of
living where traditional sovereignties and borders no longer apply. The
early settlers rely on their religious order not just to prevent "the society
from falling into chaos" in institutional or tangible terms, as many people have said, but more fundamentally to help manage their fears about
living in a world where inherited political boundaries have fallen away.[45]
The experience of living in a world where borders are being crossed and
collapsed is frightening, even as it liberates.

Tocqueville tells and retells this story, with many variations, throughout his writings on the United States. He relates, for instance, his own
formative experience of traveling past the border of the western American frontier. He and his friend Gustave de Beaumont were thrilled by
the idea of going beyond civilization's boundaries, but on the way to
meet their guides in the forest, the young men got separated. Screaming
for his friend, Tocqueville was terrified to hear nothing in return. "My
voice long re-echoed in the surrounding solitudes. But I got no answer,"
he writes. "I shouted again and listened again. The same silence of the
dead reigned in the forest." When the two find each other a few minutes
later, they embrace and promise never to be apart again. The experience
convinced him that although the dream of unfettered liberty is always
alluring to humans, the practice of living in conditions of unfettered liberty is terrifying and makes one yearn for a signpost or some social order.
The experience of living without borders – or just with the perception
that borders are disappearing – is, in practice, disorienting and anxiety
producing. Tocqueville says he saw proof of this fact again and again. He
saw it in Saginaw, Michigan, where the residents of that frontier town cast
only looks of "suspicion on one another," living in a state of generalized

---

[45] Robert Booth Fowler, et al., *Religion and Politics in America: Faith, Culture* (Oxford:
Westview Press, 2004), 304.

anxiety and distrust.[46] He saw it in New York, in the frantic behavior of the city's elite.[47] He saw it in the ways Americans wrestle with "the cares that torment them" at every turn.[48] Even Tocqueville's famous idea that Americans are a people of "perpetual restlessness" depicts, as Raymond Aron observes, a society anxious in an atmosphere where so much seems "never certain."[49] Where we feel boundless, we feel nervous.

This connection appears again and again throughout Tocqueville's corpus. In *The Old Regime*, he elaborates on the idea that the more that it seems "nothing is fixed," the more people are "constantly tormented" by fears: fears of losing the ability to distinguish themselves from others, fears of falling, fears of becoming irrelevant, and so on.[50] And in his writings on Ireland, he notes that living in conditions where borders and fences are not certain means living in "too great and continual a state of agitation."[51] As Joshua Mitchell points out, Tocqueville is consistent in following Montesquieu's teaching about the interplay between motion and boundaries: "for Montesquieu, as for Tocqueville, boundaries (or fences) enclose space, order it, and render it possible to establish the speed and direction of the motions most felicitous to the preservation of that space." Boundaries corral motion and establish a sense of order and moderation. In the absence of boundaries, people are troubled by a sense of overwhelming disorder. They experience terror at "a world that unrelentingly 'comes at one'" without any intercession.[52]

Tocqueville stresses that "men are soon frightened" in conditions that are "limitless," and he talks about how "the perpetual agitation of all things . . . fatigues" people subject to such fluidity.[53] For Tocqueville, the problem of "fear before this unlimited liberty," as Pierre Manent writes, is endemic to conditions of relative political boundlessness and, thus, a permanent problem not just of democratization but also of the processes

---

[46] JA, 378, 395.
[47] Hugh Brogan, *Alexis de Tocqueville: A Life* (New Haven: Yale University Press, 2006), 151.
[48] DIA II.3.xv , 583.
[49] Raymond Aron, *Main Currents in Sociological Thought: Montesquieu, Comte, Marx, Tocqueville* (New Brunswick, NJ: Transaction Publishers, 1999), 284.
[50] OR I, 87.
[51] JEI, 119.
[52] Joshua Mitchell, *The Fragility of Freedom: Tocqueville on Religion, Democracy, and the American Future* (Chicago: University of Chicago Press, 1999), 29–31.
[53] DIA II.1.v, 418.

associated with internationalization and globalization.[54] The universalism and border-breaking qualities of those processes "occasion social dislocation and uncertainty," which themselves cause "extreme forms of anxiety."[55] The "fear of freedom" that Tocqueville contemplates is a fear of rootlessness, a fear of living without limits, and a fear of the flux and uncertainty generated by political change that extends beyond borders.[56] In Tocqueville's writing, anxiety is the "key word" that explains the psychological condition of people in a world where the old borders no longer seem fixed; the individual becomes "uncertain" and "does not know how to orient his life."[57]

Underlying Tocqueville's argument here is the premise that people find it difficult to embrace uncertainty and fluidity at all levels of their lives. Fundamental uncertainties are tolerable to most people only in small doses. Tocqueville argues that feeling "almost always surrounded by uncertainties" is a condition fit only for philosophers – and even then he does not posit the philosophical life as a happy one.[58] For Tocqueville, too much exposure to the contingency of the human condition "produces an anxious and restless misery which, if unmoderated, becomes unendurable."[59] Put another way, he believes that "the human condition... must not ordinarily appear to the mind as problematic as it is."[60] So for modern citizens to thrive in a world where political identity is evidently fluid and unsettled, they need to have access to feelings of security and boundedness in some other part of their existence. In Tocqueville's thinking, "there must always be boundaries; where they do not exist in the material world, they must exist in the mind."[61] Without some fixed pole star in their sky, people will be overcome with insecurities – "such a state cannot fail to enervate souls; it slackens the springs of the will" – and become

54 Pierre Manent, "Christianity and Democracy: Some Remarks on the Political History of Religion, or, on the Religious History of Modern Politics," in *Modern Liberty and Its Discontents*, ed. and trans. Daniel J. Mahoney and Paul Seaton (Lanham, MD: Rowman & Littlefield Publishers, 1998), 105.
55 Corey Robin, "Why Do Opposites Attract?" 10.
56 John Stone and Stephen Mennel, "Introduction" to *Alexis de Tocqueville on Democracy, Revolution, and Society* (Chicago: University of Chicago Press, 1980), 38.
57 Pierre Manent, *Tocqueville and the Nature of Democracy*, trans. John Waggoner (Lanham, MD: Rowman & Littlefield, 1996), 59.
58 DIA II.1.v, 417.
59 Peter Augustine Lawler, *The Restless Mind: Alexis de Tocqueville on the Origin and Perpetuation of Human Liberty* (Lanham, MD: Rowman & Littlefield, 1993), 7.
60 Eduardo Nolla, *Liberty, Equality, Democracy* (New York: NYU Press, 1996), 6.
61 Joshua Mitchell, *The Fragility of Freedom*, 31.

paralyzed with inaction.[62] Such paralysis is at odds with political liberty; the existence of the former almost guarantees the latter's demise.

Put simply, people cannot live contentedly when they are deeply anxious. And so whenever there is a breakdown of borders in the political world, Tocqueville argues, there is not only a generalized sense of anxiety but also a concomitant "yearning for the securities of structured social order."[63] It is inevitable that in such times people will feel unsettled and instinctively seek relief from the anxiety of political uncertainty. Yet it is in this natural yearning to relieve the anxiety of political boundlessness that a grand danger lies. The simplest way to counteract anxiety about disorder is to pursue order, perhaps even to excess; the simplest way to counteract anxiety about borderlessness is to create borders that are stronger than ever before. To relieve anxiety about unboundedness, people are inclined to create new political boundaries and authorities. In other words, in conditions of globalization, people become tempted to facilitate their own political repression in all sorts of ways. In such times "fear," Tocqueville writes, extracts more "than was formerly given out of respect and love," and people do not live as truly free men and women.[64]

Notably, in Tocqueville's writing, both the tyranny of the majority and individualism – his nominees for the two great threats to liberty in democratic life – are trends that emanate from the individual's desire to free himself from the anxieties associated with unbounded political life. The former is a kind of relinquishing of individual agency to the mass, born of an anxious desire not to feel like "a stranger" in the world.[65] As Joshua Mitchell says, "The great irony, for Tocqueville, was that the very boundlessness of America (an ever-expansive land without fences)," would create "inhabitants who would 'enclose thought within a formidable fence,'" and so make free thinking difficult."[66] In Tocqueville's account individualism, too, stems from the desire to escape the anxiety of boundlessness; it is a process in which one attempts to "isolate himself from the mass of those like him" and "withdraw to one side with his family and friends" – quite literally, to form a little bounded domestic kingdom apart from the vagaries and uncertainties of a political existence that feels borderless.[67] In

---

[62] DIA II.1.v, 418.
[63] Janara, *Democracy Growing Up*, 181.
[64] DIA Introduction, 9.
[65] DIA II.4.vi, 663.
[66] Joshua Mitchell, *The Fragility of Freedom*, 30.
[67] DIA II.2.ii, 482.

Peter Lawler's words, individualism "seems almost inevitably to generate a soft or gentle form of despotism, where the individual surrenders control of the details of his life to some provident, impersonal authority."[68] In the manifestations of both individualism and tyranny of the majority, the natural inclination to relieve the anxiety of life where old ranks and borders have been broken down leads to conditions that are essentially despotic – conditions that are antithetical to political liberty.

The anxiety attendant on a loosely bounded political life may also catalyze a dangerous culture of materialism, a culture that itself is hostile to the preservation of political liberty. In conditions where "neither laws nor customs retain any person in his place" – in a society, that is, where political identity is not fixed – people have a natural inclination to try to fix themselves in the world through material objects. In such conditions, "the soul clings" to material objects, Tocqueville says, and tries to "hide" from the rest of the world.[69] Materialism in all its guises tempts anxious people because it offers a kind of tangible comfort; it culminates in the "materialism of science," which, as Lawler says, "claims to show them that their anxious loneliness is an illusion."[70] In the end, though, Tocqueville knows that materialism is only a distraction from the anxieties of unboundedness and an unsatisfying distraction at that. For one thing, materialism does not in fact relieve that anxiety and may even exacerbate it. The pursuit of worldly welfare through material, says Tocqueville, causes new waves of "troubles, fears, and regrets" and keeps the mind "in a sort of unceasing trepidation."[71] If anything, as Patrick Deneen says, materialism "leads to a rushing from thing to thing, from sensation to sensation, and results in a loss of any sense of true human permanence, exacerbating, instead, the feeling of impermanence."[72] Rather than relieving the anxiety of political unboundedness, materialism exacerbates the feeling of unboundedness – a fact that Tocqueville underscores in his description of Americans as "so restless in the midst of their prosperity." Moreover, materialism can pave the path to tyranny; it is a most

---

[68] Peter Augustine Lawler, "End of History 2000," in *Faith, Reason, and Political Life Today*, ed. Peter Augustine Lawler and Dale McConkey (Lanham, MD: Lexington Books, 2001), 102.

[69] DIA II.2.xi, 509.

[70] Peter Augustine Lawler, "*Lost in the Cosmos*: Walker Percy's Analysis of American Restlessness," in *Poets, Princes, and Private Citizens: Literary Alternatives to Postmodernism*, eds. Joseph M. Knippenberg and Peter Augustine Lawler (Lanham, MD: Rowman & Littlefield, 1996), 182.

[71] DIA II.2.xiii, 512.

[72] Patrick Deneen, *Democratic Faith* (Princeton: Princeton University Press, 2005), 221.

dangerous truth, Tocqueville writes, that men who "believe they are following the doctrine of interest" by tending to "what they call their affairs" may in fact "neglect the principal one, which is to remain masters of themselves." Moreover, men who pursue such "little enjoyments" are so anxious that the "fear of anarchy holds them constantly in suspense," and they become willing to give up their own political liberty to preserve their material possessions.[73]

As one writer says, "Tocqueville turned people's attention inward, to the quotidian betrayals of liberty inside their anxious psyches." The problem of that anxiety is significant, and it is inherent in the atmosphere that prevails during periods of globalization. In light of that, Tocqueville devotes a great deal of his energy to identifying and articulating ways to help channel or relieve that anxiety, without threatening political liberty. Tocqueville thinks that in such times "the self would have to be shored up by creating firm structures of authority," which have a function that is "less political than psychological and integrative."[74] In other words, he thinks that people require a place of order and certainty in their lives outside politics if they are to be able to tolerate relative boundlessness and uncertainty within politics. When people "find themselves so close that at each instant all can come to be intermingled in a common mass," it is desirable for "a multitude of artificial and arbitrary classifications" to spring up, allowing each individual "to set himself apart, out of fear of being carried away into the crowd despite himself."[75] Yet the task of cultivating and supporting those artificial distinctions is not easy, requiring attention to elements of human life that do not appear to be political at first glance. What Tocqueville seeks are means that exert an indirect influence on political life. The challenge is to find and cultivate oases of certainty to which people can attach themselves, but oases where there are no claims of certainty made directly about political matters (which would promote restrictions on political freedom).

As his account of the early Anglo-American settlers makes clear, Tocqueville thinks that in some cases religion can serve the purpose of giving people some sense of boundaries and alleviating their anxiety about an uncertain political world. He indicates, says Aristide Tessitore, that

---

[73] DIA II.2.xiv, 515–516.
[74] Corey Robin, *Fear: The History of a Political Idea* (Oxford: Oxford University Press, 2004), 87.
[75] DIA II.3.xiii, 578.

the Americans had benefitted from founders who, having a "fixed horizon for moral and religious truths in place," then felt comfortable to "open the human world of politics to radical and bold innovation."[76] The example of the founders helps illustrate a more general case. On the whole, having "fixed ideas about God and human nature," Tocqueville thinks, can provide the ballast for living in a relatively boundless political circumstance. Thus, in Tocqueville's well-known formulation, the spirit of religion works to support the spirit of liberty. Tocqueville says that he is even inclined to believe that political freedom depends on religious belief. Without some sense of spiritual certainty, he argues, people who live in conditions of political uncertainty are even more likely to "allow their freedom to be taken away" or even "give it over."[77] In Joshua Mitchell's words:

> Laws may allow, even encourage, the full development of a world ever in motion and without boundaries; yet this unremitting movement must be countered by a stasis of the imagination if the American soul (or any other) is not to fall into terror or tyranny. Religion, which channels the mind down certain paths so that the unrelenting terror of the unbounded imagination may be averted, singularly accomplishes this.[78]

Religious belief, Tocqueville thinks, gives people a sense of order and authority – a longed-for sense of firmness and stability in the universe, a sense that better equips them to deal with the fluctuations and uncertainties of a world without tight and fixed political boundaries.[79] He emphasizes, as one writer says, the "indirect influence that religion exercises in grounding the whole order of liberty."[80]

Tocqueville also issues his well-known brief for the importance of civic associations in terms of the sense of boundedness that they offer to people. He describes them as "particular little societies," or bounded entities that help people to navigate in an era of mass politics.[81] For Tocqueville, "situating the self in civic associations" provides a "bulwark

[76] Aristide Tessitore, "Alexis de Tocqueville on the Incommensurability of America's Founding Principles," in *Democracy and Its Friendly Critics: Tocqueville and Political Life Today*, ed. Peter Augustine Lawler (Lanham, MD: Lexington Books, 2004), 67.
[77] DIA II.1.v, 418.
[78] Joshua Mitchell, *The Fragility of Freedom*, 31.
[79] DIA II.1.v, 418.
[80] David Walsh, *The Growth of the Liberal Soul* (Columbia: University of Missouri Press, 1997), 191.
[81] DIA II.3.xiii, 577.

against an anxiety threatening to introduce the worst forms of tyranny seen yet."[82] Tocqueville posits civic associational life as helping to bolster the self-perception of people who otherwise feel themselves to be "independent and weak," devoid of particular attachments and a sense of place. Because the influences that fix people together are "almost nonexistent in a democratic country," they must be "artificially created" – and civic associations do that work. In Tocqueville's telling, civic associations are valuable not just because they teach a practical "art of associating" – although they certainly do that – but further because they provide a kind of ordered and delimited communal experience.[83] Civic associations help to "construct, within each locality, a coherent and powerful moral and spiritual community."[84] Psychologically speaking, they serve much the same role as religion in providing individuals with a sense that some part of their lives operates within demarcated limits. As a "relatively bounded" form of organization, civic associations serve "as the basis of social solidarity" in a political world where such solidarity is not always easy to find.[85] They provide a means by which individuals may develop a sense of social order and cohesion that does not impinge on political freedom.

And yet Tocqueville does not present either religion or civil association as a panacea; he recognizes that neither wholly cures the threats that stalk liberty in a globalizing age. He argues, for instance, that not all religions are as salutary as the Puritan religion in terms of their ability to help individuals freely negotiate political life. In particular, he stresses that religions only function to support the spirit of liberty when they limit their pronouncements to the sphere of the soul, and do not seek "to extend their power further than religious matters."[86] For obvious reasons, a religious organization that seeks its own political power or dominance does not fulfill what Tocqueville deemed to be the healthy, indirect relationship between religious belief and political liberty. And religions that include specific political dictates, Tocqueville says, evidently are incompatible with political liberty. It is key, in his analysis, for religion to be restricted to and exist mostly as a source of psychological certainty if it is going to

---

[82] Robin, *Fear: The History of a Political Idea*, 87.
[83] DIA II.2.v, 490–491; II.2.vii, 497.
[84] Robert K. Fullinwider, *Civil Society, Democracy, and Civic Renewal* (Lanham, MD: Rowman & Littlefield, 1999), 94.
[85] John Field, "Social Capital," in *Handbook of Economics and Ethics*, ed. Jan Peil and Irene van Staveren (Northampton, MA: Edward Elgar Publishing, 2009), 510.
[86] DIA II.1.v, 419.

promote political freedom – and he is well aware that not all religions operate only at that level.

Tocqueville knows that the salutary power of civic association is limited as well. The "spirit of association," he writes, may at times be "intimately combined" with a "spirit of exclusion."[87] In terms of political liberty, that is not usually a problem: a knitting club is going to exclude people who cannot or do not want to knit things, but that bounded circle of knitters is not likely, on the basis of their social association, to work actively to undermine the political liberty of non-knitters. Still, there are cases in which there may be an "exclusion problem," as Keith Whittington terms it – cases in which people who participate in bounded civic associations develop the habit of excluding certain outsiders and then extend their exclusions beyond the social and into the political sphere.[88] When that happens – when people attempt to impose the exclusions of social life onto political life – political liberties may well be undermined. Like religions, civic associations may try to become too directly political. They may allow people to overcome the anxieties attendant to political life in globalizing times but at the cost of political freedom. In such instances they are only tools for tyranny.

It is revealing that Tocqueville recognized that neither religion nor civic association could altogether solve the problem of political anxiety in an interconnected age, and yet he continued to speak up for the value of each. This outspokenness makes clear how serious he is about the idea that anxiety can undermine liberty in ages in which political borders do not seem fixed. That he is willing to risk a certain amount of social exclusion and religious fanaticism in the pursuit of encouraging bounded experiences suggests how likely he thinks it is that a soft despotism will emerge in conditions in which people feel unbounded. It is difficult to advocate a certain amount of social exclusion in the abstract, but it is much easier to do so when the alternative is global tyranny. In other words, Tocqueville's support of religion and civic association, despite their defects, makes clear exactly how weak he deems political liberty in globalizing conditions. Tocqueville "*knows* that the modern world can travel the road either to

[87] JEI, 88.

[88] Keith Whittington, "Revisiting Tocqueville's America: Society, Politics, and Association in the Nineteenth Century," in *Beyond Tocqueville: Civil Society and the Social Capital Debate in Comparative Perspective*, ed. Bob Edwards, Michael W. Foley, and Mario Diani (Hanover, NH: University Press of New England, 2001), 26.

despotism or to the republic," and the risk of the former is great.[89] His idea that "*social* condition could bring servitude or freedom," as Allen writes, reveals an acute awareness of the "vulnerabilities" that attend not only democratic transitions but also globalization.[90] By themselves, political rules and institutions cannot be counted on in such times to preserve liberty.

Moreover, his analysis of religion and civic association reveals the degree to which Tocqueville believes that the quality of politics, particularly in a globalizing world, depends on what may seem at first to be extra-political or even nonpolitical factors. Even the most obvious political solution to the anxiety attendant on globalization – ensuring the existence of relatively independent local governments – only works, he says, when a certain kind of extra-political social culture is in place. When Tocqueville discusses New England townships, he is careful to note that their municipal governance is sustained by "a spirit of the township." To the extent that local governance provides some anchorage in a boundless political world – "it acts, it is true, in a circle that it cannot leave" – it depends on a spirit that is extra-institutional. He makes clear that New England's township governance cannot be replicated by rules alone because although "there are townships and township life in each state," township governance is not equally important across all states. For instance, "As one descends toward the south, one perceives that township life becomes less active."[91] It is not enough, in Tocqueville's telling, for the formal forms of township governance to exist. The relatively intangible spirit of the town, sustained by social forces like religion and civic association, is what provides the fire and the force to local governance. If strong local governments help give people some sense of order and boundaries and in so doing orient them in a disorienting world, that only reinforces the importance of social forces like religion and civic association. Strong local governments cannot exist without them.

Tocqueville's call for a new science of politics itself underscores the extent to which he thinks the health of politics in global age depends on what might seem to be extra-political factors. The call for a new science is a call to intellectuals – a call to re-engage with political thought.

---

[89] Harvey Mitchell, *Individual Choice and the Structures of History: Alexis de Tocqueville as Historian Reappraised* (Cambridge: Cambridge University Press, 1996), 140.

[90] Allen, *Tocqueville, Covenant, and the Democratic Revolution*, xv.

[91] DIA I.1.v, 63; I.1.v, 76.

In particular, James Ceaser argues, Tocqueville hopes that by directing intellectuals to think about the psychological and cultural foundations of politics, he might cultivate a class of people who understand the
importance of bounded and particular experiences, especially in a loosely
bounded political age. Those intellectuals might then be positioned to
help shape political thought by setting the tone for a more general respect
for such spiritual and social groups. His "indirect strategy" of taming
political excess – and providing "people with the means and will to
maintain their freedom" – depends in some measure on cultivating a
new kind of political thought that itself will help to sustain the social
and cultural factors that can in turn sustain political liberty.[92] In critical
ways, Tocqueville believes that a general class of intellectuals, who have
a complex and multilayered understanding of the relationship between
culture and politics, may hold the fate of political liberty around the
globe in their hands – at least in the same measure as, and perhaps more
than, do political officials. They may help instill a sense of boundaries
in an anxiety-producing, loosely bounded world. Certainly, Tocqueville
believes that if intellectuals begin to disdain religion and civic associations and the broader social boundedness that they represent, they will
help speed the course of global despotism; he associates overly abstracted
and rationalized thinking in a culture with the magnification of political
power.[93] Believing that societies may collapse when intellectuals cease
to understand the grand dynamics of their own time and place – he
attributes the decline of long-standing Chinese dynasties to that cause –
Tocqueville addresses his book predominately to intellectuals who might
help shape the tenor of a quickly globalizing culture.[94] To the extent that
intellectuals may help shape that cultural tenor, they may help or hin-
der political liberty. Tocqueville believes that intellectuals must become
committed to seeking out and supporting those elements of culture that
provide psychological boundaries without eviscerating political liberty.

In general, Tocqueville's vision of a healthy global politics depends
on the cultivation and maintenance of social diversity. A respect for
diversity is implicit in Tocqueville's respect for religion and civic associations because a world in which religions and civic associations provide

[92] James Ceaser, "Alexis de Tocqueville on Political Science, Political Culture, and the Role
of the Intellectual," *American Political Science Review* 79 (1985), 663, 671.
[93] Robert A. Nisbet, *The Sociological Tradition* (New Brunswick, NJ: Transaction
Publishers, 1993), 129.
[94] DIA II.1.x, 438-439.

experiences of spiritual and social boundedness is a world that is spiritually and socially diverse. A globe in which people have access to particular bounded experiences is one in which there are different spiritual and social options. Thus, we might say that for Tocqueville, in a globalized age, political liberty depends on spiritual and social diversity. He describes the "particular little societies" of religious and civic association in contrast to an image of a "coarse and tyrannical" world in which all people are compelled "to lead a common existence."[95] Indeed, "diversity, for Tocqueville," is "the precious source of the unexpected richness of life" and "constitutive of freedom."[96] He "insisted that only political freedom could remedy the ills to which equality of conditions give rise," and he saw political freedom as somehow connected with repeated exposure to varieties of experience.[97] Modern peoples need to attune themselves to particularities and social diversity. "Any perpetuation of political life" in the modern age, as Lawler has put it, "requires the world's continued incoherence" or variety; exposure to variety can reveal "the inner freedom of the human soul, its ability to resist theoretical determination."[98] The intellectual leader's great task is to "produce and defend diversity within a mass culture" to lessen the dangers of mass despotism by providing some source of boundedness within the lives of individual people.[99]

When Tocqueville invokes "the new state of societies" in the world, he can be said to draw attention to the particular threats to liberty that exist in conditions of globalization – threats that emerge from the unsettling of political identity and the anxiety such unsettling provokes.[100] Roger Boesche's description of Tocqueville as a scholar of "anxiety in an age of transition" gets to the heart of things.[101] In an era of globalization, there is an endemic anxiety problem. That anxiety can lead people to engage in behaviors – deference to the majority, retreat into individual fortresses,

[95] DIA II.3.xiii, 577.
[96] Harvey Mitchell, *Individual Choice and the Structures of History*, 144.
[97] Harvey C. Mansfield and Delba Winthrop, Editor's Introduction to DIA, xxvii, xxxv, lxxxvi.
[98] Lawler, *The Restless Mind*, 173.
[99] Alain Touraine, *What Is Democracy?*, trans. David Macey (Boulder, CO: Westview Press, 1997), 12.
[100] DIA II.4.viii, 675.
[101] Roger Boesche, *The Strange Liberalism of Alexis de Tocqueville* (Ithaca, NY: Cornell University Press, 1987), 27.

incessant pursuit of material goods – that undermine political liberty. The grand threat is a creeping global despotism without counterweight. In light of that threat, it is critical to cultivate a kind of "balance of power within society" by helping to maintain and cultivate spiritual and social spheres where individuals may find the solace of bounded experience.[102] Bounded spiritual and social experiences, rather than undermining political liberty, will actually help people to feel freer – and less afraid – in a fluid, global context.

A striking aspect of Tocqueville's analysis is that he sees globalization – the breakdown of barriers between previously sovereign states – as inevitable and to a certain extent desirable. He not only talks about the changes he sees in the world as having a providential quality, but he also indicates that providence points in the direction of justice.[103] When he talks about his travels across the Atlantic, Tocqueville admires the restlessness of the Americans he meets and sees because he believes that restlessness is a manifestation of their political liberty. "To live in freedom one must grow used to a life full of agitation, change, and danger," he writes, "to keep alert the whole time with a restless eye on everything around: that is the price of freedom."[104] He sees in the early American republic the possibility of a world made new for political freedom, and he certainly admires the aspiration toward a more global or universal political liberty.[105]

Even if Tocqueville sees majestic possibilities in the aspiration to global or universal political liberty, though, he is also wary about extending his enthusiasm too far or embracing it too uncritically. He seeks the "dark aspects" that go along with such ambitions: the disorientations and anxieties within the individual that can lead down the path to despotism. In Tocqueville's writing, "it is not only foolish to long for world community, but also dangerous." The social communities that actually support global political liberty are based on "narrower fraternal loyalties" – those small private circles – which, by limiting people spiritually and socially,

[102] B. A. Haddock, *A History of Political Thought: 1789 to the Present* (Malden, MA: Polity Press, 2005), 78.
[103] DIA Introduction, 12.
[104] JEI, 116.
[105] As Roger Boesche notes, even Tocqueville's support of imperialism owes – in perhaps a misguided way – to this belief. For instance, he called again and again for training, in Algeria and India, "in local government and establishing the mores for self-rule." See *Tocqueville's Road Map: Methodology, Liberalism, Revolution, and Despotism* (Lanham, MD: Lexington Books, 2006), 116.

help, almost paradoxically, to free them politically.[106] The preservation of political liberty in a globalizing age depends on the existence of social and spiritual forces that help stabilize people outside politics – to provide them with spaces in which they can cultivate a bordered and bounded identity – so that they can flourish in a political world where boundaries are perpetually contestable and uncertain.

---

[106] Cheryl B. Welch, "Tocqueville on Fraternity and Fratricide," in *The Cambridge Companion to Alexis de Tocqueville*, ed. Cheryl B. Welch (Cambridge: Cambridge University Press, 2006), 306–307.

CHAPTER 8

Nationhood – Democracy's Final Frontier?

Ewa Atanassow

Tocqueville's first and most celebrated work heralds the irresistible rise of democracy throughout the world. Alongside its striking forecast and prophetic tone, much of the work's originality consists in redefining the nature of democracy. More than a type of political order, in Tocqueville's analytical vocabulary, democracy comes to mean something "altogether new." It identifies a dynamic state of society that remolds every aspect of communal life along egalitarian lines: not just political institutions and the relationship between rulers and ruled but also social practices, opinions, and values, down to the prevailing mentality and the "manner of thinking and feeling." Democracy for Tocqueville is at once a comprehensive social condition and a way of understanding the world that shapes a novel human type: a democratic humanity.[1]

Just as Tocqueville expands a time-honored political notion – democracy – to encompass the entire way of life of a society and a new form of mankind, so, too, he transforms a geographical category – the frontier – into a historical thesis. In the "Introduction" to the first volume of *Democracy in America*, speaking for the perspicacious observers of his day, he proclaims that "the gradual and progressive development of equality is at the same time the past and the future of history." It is in the New World, moreover, that this progressive development has reached

---

[1] DIA Notice, 399; II.4.viii, 676. As Robert Pippin states in this volume, Tocqueville's contribution to the Western intellectual tradition is to announce the new and inevitable dawn of a democratic form of life and elaborate a comprehensive understanding of this new form. For a thorough analysis of this understanding, see Pierre Manent, *Tocqueville and the Nature of Democracy* (Lanham: Rowman & Littlefield, 1996).

its "extreme limits." In Tocqueville's account, not only a geopolitical notion, North America comes to signify a historical frontier as well. The New World exemplifies "the new state of the world" – a more advanced historical experience that reveals the character and meaning of the modern age.[2] What defines this new world in the sense of the modern world is equality not simply as established principle but as a "generative fact" – a continuous transformation and ongoing process of equalization of conditions. Brought into broad daylight in the "Christian universe," this unrelenting democratizing process is not restricted to the Christian West. From its opening pages, Tocqueville's *Democracy in America* announces the impending global democratic revolution.[3]

Tocqueville points to the advent of democracy – the worldwide spread of a comprehensively egalitarian form of life – as the distinguishing feature of the modern age and of what we today call globalization. And yet, while representing modernity as a single historical trajectory, he does not view it as a uniform movement. As I shall argue in this chapter, in Tocqueville's account, the democratic movement operates in two seemingly opposite directions simultaneously: on the one hand, it tends toward universality and growing interdependence between various parts of the world that lay bare "for the first time" one unified humanity[4]; on the other, the coming together of diverse cultures and forms of life leads to affirmation of local specificity and resurgence of particularism. I hope to show that for Tocqueville the current of modernity not only issues from the confrontation of cultural and political alternatives but in a sense reinforces these alternatives. Likewise, although set in motion by European expansionism and triggered by the often violent meeting of civilizations, this global democratizing process is not synonymous with imposing European ways.

Tocqueville, in other words, understands the providential unfolding of modern equality to be at root a dialectical phenomenon that simultaneously effaces and accentuates social and cultural particularity. In this chapter, I aim to explicate Tocqueville's view of the dynamics of modernity. Drawing on both his analytical works and his political and parliamentary writings, I will seek to elicit Tocqueville's vision of the global significance and long-term prospects of democratization.

[2] DIA Introduction, 3, 7; Notice, 400.
[3] DIA Introduction, 3, 5–6, 317. DIA (Lawrence), xiii; OC 5:1, 377, 384. See also Capdevila's and Mitchell's essays in this volume.
[4] DIA II.1.xvii, 461.

Honor, Nationhood, Democracy

In *Democracy in America* Tocqueville calls for a "new political science" to account for the new democratic condition of the world. The point of departure for this new science of politics is the pivotal distinction between aristocracy and democracy that articulates the entire human history and reveals the meaning of the modern age. Explored throughout *Democracy*, the dichotomy finds a systematic recapitulation in the chapter "On Honor in the United States and in Democratic Societies." Elaborating a *sui generis* genealogy of morals, the honor chapter illumines the origins and rationale of aristocratic and democratic value systems. It thus offers a summary statement of Tocqueville's conceptualization of society and the transition from the old world of aristocracy to the new democratic condition.[5]

Tocqueville defines honor as the ethical system, in light of which each community considers human action and distributes praise and blame. In his account, communal life necessitates a moral compass – that is, shared principles and moral standards that regulate public conduct and orient life's effort toward particular ends. Apart from "the simple notions of the just and the unjust" common to all human collectivities, each society is characterized by conventions and valuations specific to itself that distinguish its way of life and reflect its self-understanding. Tocqueville calls these "honor."[6] Every society, then – be it aristocratic or democratic – obeys a code of honor that constitutes its cultural and moral outlook. Although the phenomenon of honor is universal, pertaining to society as such, its concrete manifestations differ vastly across time and place. In the body of the chapter Tocqueville labors to show that, far from arbitrary, society's morals are grounded in particular needs and evolve in complex interrelation with the physical environment, economic and material conditions, and political institutions.

---

[5] DIA Introduction, 7; II.3.xviii. See Jonathan B. Hand, "Tocqueville's 'New Political Science': A Critical Assessment of Montesquieu's Vision of a Liberal Modernity" (PhD diss., University of Chicago, 2002), 86.

[6] DIA II.3.xviii, 589–591, 596–58; also II.1.ii. Tocqueville's definition thus deliberately broadens the understanding of honor operative in feudal society, and in the work of its leading theorist Montesquieu. As a draft note states: "Montesquieu spoke about our honor and not about honor," DIA (Nolla) [II.3.xviii], note v, 1110. Compare with Montesquieu, *The Spirit of the Laws*, Book III, Ch. 7 and 8. See also Ran Halévi, "La pensée politique de l'honneur," in *Penser et vivre l'honneur à l'époque modern*, eds. Hervé Drévillon and Diego Venturino (Rennes: Presses universitaires de rennes, 2011).

Honor, in brief, is inherent in communal life. It is the ethos and moral bond, or what we might call cultural identity, that holds society together and justifies its distinctness from – and superiority to – other societies. Toward the end of the honor chapter, summarizing its argument, Tocqueville highlights the "tight and necessary relation" between honor and the inequality of conditions. Honor stands in a twofold relation to inequality. As the criterion that distinguishes public virtue and vice, it is the source of moral cleavages within the community. At the same time, lying at the core of cultural particularity, honor discriminates between societies or social groups. It marks the frontiers between classes and nations. Tocqueville concludes the honor chapter by outlining the effects of democratization on these frontiers: "Ranks are mixed, privileges abolished . . . and all the *singular notions* that each *caste* called honor are seen to vanish successively; honor flows from nothing more than the particular needs of the *nation* itself; it represents its *individuality* among peoples."[7]

Tocqueville portrays aristocratic society as divided into numerous classes or castes, each characterized by "singular notions" of honor, or a particular ethical perspective. As he explains elsewhere, what unites these "prodigiously unalike" social bodies is strict division of labor and social hierarchy, as well as a shared opinion about the essential inequality of human beings and groups, and their fixed, indeed fated, station in the universal order.[8] Against this vision of society, articulated into a plurality of superimposed social strata and diverse manners of life, Tocqueville depicts democratization as a twin process.

On the one hand, the gradual equalization of conditions levels classes and assimilates moral outlooks. As class distinctions are erased or rendered inconsequential, the corresponding "singular notions" of honor weaken or disappear. The nation becomes the primary source of honor – that is, of the moral valuations that shape the citizens' self-conception and orient their way of life. So democratization for Tocqueville is the process of society's gradually coming together in moral agreement. This agreement manifests itself in supplanting class consciousness with national consciousness.[9]

---

[7] DIA II.3.xviii, 598–599, emphasis added.
[8] DIA II.3.xvii, 587; also Introduction 8; I.2.x, 394–395, II.1.iii–iv, II.2.ii; II.3.i,v.
[9] Or, to twist the title of Eugen Weber's classic study, in making peasants – and also bourgeois, clergy, and nobles – into Frenchmen. Arguably, to facilitate this transformation is among the chief pedagogical aims of Tocqueville's oeuvre in general and of his foray

On the other hand, as the moral and political hold of class distinctions slackens, the principal differences that remain, hence the chief source of particularity and diversity, are those between societies or nations. Henceforth national, rather than family or class belonging, appears as the main distinguishing characteristic and relevant category for self-understanding. The nation, in other words, comes to epitomize society's moral and political order and "represents its individuality among peoples."[10]

The rise of democracy thus issues in two seemingly opposed phenomena: as the frontiers between classes blur, those between nations crystallize. Along with the gradual erosion of class differences, democratic transition brings about the consolidation of nation-states and the surfacing of national differences as the principal resource for political and cultural self-definition. For Tocqueville, then, as for many a modern historian, modernization and nationalism are the two sides of the same democratizing coin.[11]

Tocqueville's account of democratization can be usefully compared with that hugely influential vision of the modern age outlined in the *Communist Manifesto*. Like Tocqueville, Marx and Engels consider modernity as an inevitable process of global transformation, critically driven by international trade and the dynamism of the British Empire.

---

into French history in particular. See Ralph Lerner's essay in this volume, as well as his *Revolutions Revisited: Two Faces of the Politics of the Enlightenment* (Chapel Hill: University of North Carolina Press, 1994), ch. 7; Eugen Weber, *Peasants into Frenchmen: The Modernization of Rural France, 1870–1914* (Stanford: Stanford University Press, 1976). Jay M. Smith's *Nobility Reimagined: The Patriotic Nation in Eighteenth-Century France* (Ithaca, NY: Cornell University Press, 2005) offers a comprehensive account of the conceptual and historical change that contributed to forging French national consciousness.

10 DIA II.3.xviii, 599. Stéphane Dion, "La conciliation du libéralisme et du nationalisme chez Tocqueville," *La Revue Tocqueville/The Tocqueville Review* 16 (1995), 222.

11 See, e.g., Ernest Gellner's seminal work *Nations and Nationalism* (Ithaca, NY: Cornell University Press, 1983). As Gellner argues, the formation of modern nations presupposes the creation of a literate mass culture that dissolves the stratifications of preliterate agrarian societies, and issues in a rise of nationalist ideologies. In a similar vein, Rogers Brubaker's Tocqueville-informed study shows how and why democratization and the "development of national citizenship represents a displacement of personal boundaries – that is boundaries between personal statuses – from within to between nations." Brubaker thus seeks to account for the processes that transformed the initially cosmopolitan spirit of the French Revolution into "the xenophobic nationalism of its radical phase," *Citizenship and Nationhood in France and Germany* (Cambridge: Harvard University Press, 1992), ch. 2, esp. 44–45. Also Pierre Nora's "Nation," in *A Critical Dictionary of the French Revolution*, eds. François Furet and Mona Ozouf, trans. Arthur Goldhammer (Cambridge: Harvard University Press, 1989), 742–753.

They anticipate, however, that global capitalism will break national and cultural bonds and reduce the multiplicity of political units to the antagonism between bourgeois and proletarians. National and religious differences progressively dissolve into more fundamental economic differences, so that the final struggle will be that between the haves and have-nots of the world.[12]

Noting the interaction between material and moral causes, Tocqueville grants relative priority to moeurs – that is, to the ethical dimension.[13] In his view, what above all defines the social system is not – as for Marx – what people have nor how they produce it but what they esteem and hold dear, or what Tocqueville refers to as their "honor." So, whereas for Marx and Engels modernization inexorably leads to planetary struggle over the distribution of material goods, for Tocqueville the fundamental fault lines are cultural and moral: group divisions are first and foremost ethical divisions, less over what we have than over who we are, and how deserving.

In short, although both *Democracy in America* and the *Communist Manifesto* sketch modernity as a process of increasing homogenization, the two analyses significantly differ. Marx and Engels view globalization primarily as the effect of commercial expansionism that dissolves nations or political units and consolidates classes, paving the way for an ultimate showdown between proletariat and bourgeoisie. Tocqueville, by contrast, claims that the spread of equality leads to the erosion of class differences and accentuation of national ones: class honor gives way to national honor and to the attendant mobilization of national consciousness and passions. Nationhood thus emerges as the last obstacle to the universalization of equality. At the same time, Tocqueville acknowledges that far from stopping at national borders, democratization presses against them: universalist ideals as well as globalizing processes intensify patterns of interdependence and level differences between societies.[14]

---

[12] Karl Marx and Friedrich Engels, "Manifesto of the Communist Party" in *The Marx-Engels Reader*, ed. Robert C. Tucker (New York: W. W. Norton & Co., 1978), esp. 474–477 and note 8, 488–489. See also "On the Jewish Question," Marx's most virulent repudiation of national and religious particularity, 26–52 in the same volume.
[13] DIA I.2.ix, esp. 292–293.
[14] DIA I.2.x, 395; II.1.xvii, 461; II.3.xvii, 588; II.4.v, 652; II.4.viii, 674–675; also OC 5:1, 190–191. Cheryl B. Welch, "Tocqueville on Fraternity and Fratricide," in *The Cambridge Companion to Tocqueville*, ed. Cheryl B. Welch (Cambridge: Cambridge University Press, 2006), 305–310. See also Susan McWilliams' chapter in this volume.

Tocqueville's analysis of the dynamics of equality thus points to the realm of international relations as the ultimate theater in the battle for democracy and to the nation as its final frontier. Can democracy cross this frontier? And what, in Tocqueville's view, are the long-term prospects of the struggle for equality?

Races

Democracy in America has relatively little to say about international relations. Nor does it forecast the outcome of democracy's final battle. Although on multiple occasions Tocqueville notes the weakening of national differences and augurs the global revolution that gives rise to "one vast democracy of which each citizen is a people," his political vision seems locked within the horizon of a multinational system. This has led Pierre Manent to suggest that Tocqueville "did not seriously envisage the substantial transformation, much less the disappearance of the national form." Nevertheless, the closing paragraphs of the honor chapter signal that, as a hypothesis at least, the possibility of "democracy without nations" was not altogether outside Tocqueville's purview.[15]

One place in the work where Tocqueville seems to reflect on a global democratic future is the concluding chapter of volume one, titled "Some Considerations of the Present State and the Probable Future of the Three Races that Inhabit the Territory of the United States." As commentators have observed, although said to consider subjects particular to America rather than universally democratic, Tocqueville's discussion has broader implications. This broader relevance is indicated by the chapter's focus on race: a term that for Tocqueville signifies cultural and moral rather than natural differences and carries a range of meanings from class and people to humanity as a whole.[16]

As in the title so too in the body of the chapter, Tocqueville takes care to distinguish the three races from the territorial and political unit that sets

---

[15] DIA II.3.xviii, 599 and II.1.xvii, 461. See Pierre Manent, *La raison des nations* (Paris: Gallimard, 2006), 26, translated into English as *Democracy without Nations?* (Wilmington: ISI Books, 2007).

[16] DIA I.2.x, 303. Eduardo Nolla notes that, in revising the race chapter, Tocqueville substituted "Anglo-American" for the original "European." It seems as if he Americanized the chapter only as an afterthought, DIA (Nolla) [I.2.x], 526 note n. In Ralph Lerner's words, more than American, the chapter offers "some large generalizations about the world rivalry among colonial powers and its possible outcome," *The Thinking Revolutionary. Principle and Practice in the New Republic* (Ithaca, NY: Cornell University Press, 1988), 175. Also see Nestor Capdevila, *Tocqueville et les frontières de la Démocratie* (Paris: Presses universitaires de France, 2007), 67.

up the context for their entanglement. The chapter's first two sections discuss the condition of the Indians and the blacks, whereas the subsequent three analyze the future of the American Union, the longevity of republican institutions, and the source of its commercial might. Although, as this arrangement indicates, African and Native Americans effectively take no part in the U.S. Constitution, the chapter suggests that the political future of the Union will largely depend on the possibility of their inclusion; a possibility Tocqueville regards with profound skepticism. Put otherwise, Tocqueville's account of the prospects for the United States – the democratic society par excellence – points to crossing racial and civilizational frontiers as the decisive factor and greatest challenge to democracy's future.[17] In this fashion the story Tocqueville tells, although peculiarly American, seems to exemplify the universally democratic problem of the mingling of cultures and civilizations. It epitomizes the worldwide effects of Europe's encounter with non-Europeans.[18]

Canvassing in poignant detail the tragic consequences of this encounter, the image Tocqueville paints is that of the "European race" reigning victorious and "tyrannical" over all others. This victory is secured above all by breaking up the moral bonds of family, language, and religion that hold other nations together and perpetuate their way of life – that is, by dissolving peoples and cultures that cannot make or defend their claim to equality.[19] Ralph Lerner points out that, in Tocqueville's telling, the collision of the three races is not unlike that of the American North and South or of the French and Spanish with the Anglo-Americans. These fateful confrontations are but "variations on the same theme." Along with the irresistible ascent of the democratic way of life best exemplified by the Puritans' descendants, the theme Tocqueville explores, as his footnote states it, is "the destructive influence that very civilized peoples exert on those who are less so."[20]

Especially striking in Tocqueville's account is that, in the North American context, this "destructive influence" is not necessarily the result of military conquest or physical violence. It appears, rather, as a spontaneous effect of the clash of moral outlooks and the coming "face to

---

[17] See Tocqueville's extensive analysis of the social and political consequences of slavery and the dangers it poses to the future of the American Union in DIA I.2.x, 348–379. For a similar assessment of the French prospects in Algeria, see OC 3:1, 329; WES, 146.

[18] Jennifer Pitts, *A Turn to Empire: The Rise of Imperial Liberalism in Britain and France* (Princeton: Princeton University Press, 2006), 197.

[19] DIA I.2.x, 304–305, 310, 320–325; also SLPS, 68–73.

[20] DIA I.2.x, 317–319 and notes; also 391–396. Lerner, *The Thinking Revolutionary*, 185–186.

face" of human alternatives.[21] Tocqueville goes on to assert that, for all its atrocities, the Spanish *conquista* had been less successful in destroying cultures and wiping out local populations. In contrast to the violent incorporation of the Spanish colonies, the story of the three American races puts on dramatic display how peoples can be subdued or annihilated through legal and commercial dealings, perfectly "respectful of the laws of humanity."[22]

For Tocqueville, then, the West was won less by conquest than through commerce. Engaged in a contest "with the most civilized and, I shall add, the greediest people on the globe," the Indians as well as the blacks (and to some extent southerners, French and Spaniards) succumb to a "fatal competition." The story of the three races thus calls into question the distinction, so dear to Montesquieu and to the eighteenth- and nineteenth-century liberal thought, between commerce and conquest. Not unlike Marx, Tocqueville seems to suggest that, in the realm of international and intercultural relations, the former could be just as, and perhaps more, devastating than the latter.[23] In sum, if Lerner and others are right to insist that – more than American – the race chapter contains a universalizable message, the message seems to be universally bleak: the coming together of civilizations that attends the advent of democracy is likely to lead

---

[21] Tocqueville first studies this clash in *Fortnight in the Wilderness*, a posthumously published record of his travels to the American frontier. As I argue elsewhere, the travelogue is also Tocqueville's earliest exploration of the meaning of civilization and democracy's ultimate limits, OC 5:1, 342–387; Ewa Atanassow, "Fortnight in the Wilderness: Tocqueville on Nature and Civilization," *Perspectives on Political Science* 35 (2006), 22–30.

[22] DIA I.2.x, 325. In Tocqueville's words, the Indian nations residing on the territory of the United States were being destroyed "tranquilly, legally, philanthropically, without spilling blood, without violating a single one of the great principles of morality." The African population too had been imported on American soil as a result of a legal trade that flourished for centuries under the auspices of European powers (DIA I.2.x, 326, I.1.ii, 31 and note 4). Only at the beginning of the nineteenth century did Britain undertake to police and gradually abolish, even by force, the so-called "Trade." For an account of the epic dimensions of this struggle, see Charles H. Fairbanks Jr., "The British Campaign Against the Slave Trade: An Example of a Successful Human Rights Policy," in *Human Rights and American Foreign Policy*, ed. Fred E. Baumann (Gambier, OH: Public Affairs Conference Center, Kenyon College, 1982). For Montesquieu's contrasting assessment of the effects of Spanish and British imperialism, see Spector's chapter in this volume.

[23] DIA I.2.x, 317–318. Tocqueville's account of the American polity, the middle class society par excellence, seems to concur with Marx's and Engel's appreciation of the "most revolutionary" role of the bourgeoisie, *Communist Manifesto*, 474–479, esp. 475. Cf. DIA I.1.2, 30 and I.1.3; also DIA (Nolla) [II.1.ix], 767 note f.

either to destruction or enslavement or if to amalgamation, then only after massive bloodshed.[24]

If the Western frontier looks grim, so does the Eastern. In a foreign policy speech, occasioned by the 1840 crisis in the Near East, Tocqueville paints in similar colors the effects of European expansionism:

Do you know what is happening in the Orient? An entire world is being transformed; from the banks of the Indus to the Black Sea, in all that immense space societies are crumbling, religions are being weakened, nationalities are disappearing, all the lights are going out, the old Asiatic world is vanishing; and in its place the European world is rising.[25]

Alongside other passages from Tocqueville's oratory, this pronouncement seems to identify globalization as in effect "westernization." Spurred by commercial necessities and political competition, European powers undertake colonial ventures and create overseas dependencies, disrupting or destroying in the process whole societies, religions, and nationalities. The "great European chain already encircling the world" brings about a new global order, in which humanity finds itself united under the harsh philanthropy of the white race.[26] And yet, already in the account of the three American races there are indications that triumphalism may be out of place. With its premonitions of racial war and civil conflict, the first *Democracy*'s final chapter intimates the precariousness of European victory. Far from a final battle, Tocqueville's stylized portrayal of the encounter of the three races appears to be merely the opening act of a longer and broader process, whose momentous consequences are still to follow.

Algeria

Rife with symbolic significance, the chapter on the three races is factually limited.[27] Taking a bird's eye view of the problem of race and the

---

[24] Tocqueville's "account encourages us to draw parallels between the whites' triumph and the democrats' triumph ... In each case, the triumph is accompanied by a tragic fate from which even victors are not exempt." Lerner, *The Thinking Revolutionary*, 186.

[25] OC 3:2, 290. For a commentary on this speech and its broader context, see Seymour Drescher, *Tocqueville and England* (Cambridge: Harvard University Press, 1964), 156–164.

[26] JA 365 and OC 5:1, 377; OC 3:2, 270–271, 279–280, 282, 284; see also OC 6:1, 58; OC 9, 243–244; OC 11, 116.

[27] Barbara Allen offers a well-documented correction to Tocqueville's analysis of American slavery. Although prescient about the challenges, Tocqueville, Allen judges, was

melding of civilizations, it is a suggestive tableau more than an analytical argument. As Jennifer Pitts has proposed, to properly view its implications, one has to look beyond it to Tocqueville's political practice, especially to his over a decade-long involvement with one instantiation of what I have termed democracy's "final frontier": Algeria.[28]

Tocqueville considered France's engagement in Algeria as the issue of the greatest moment for his country. It was also a central aspect of his political career that culminated in a brief tenure as a foreign minister and whose main (although not exclusive) focus was France's foreign policy and standing in the world. As the most salient of his political causes, Tocqueville's commitment to the Algerian affair throws into stark relief his vision of international politics and the emerging global order.[29] While in a sense exemplary of his statesmanship, Tocqueville's investment in France's attempt to establish modern society in Algeria epitomizes his life-long theoretical interest in the problem of colonization.[30] Alongside his comprehensive study of the North American settlements, parliamentary and journalistic reports on the French and British colonies in the Caribbean and an unpublished study of British India, Algeria is the colonial society that Tocqueville observed most closely and where he could analyze in depth and detail the effects of European expansionism. I suggest that, taken as a whole, the Algerian writings reveal Tocqueville's most considered view of the cultural and civilizational frontiers of democracy. As such they merit a careful look.

unduly pessimistic about American democracy's ability to integrate race differences, "Racial Equality and Social Equality," in *Conversations with Tocqueville*, ed. Aurelian Craiutu and Sheldon Gellar (Lexington Books, 2009). For an account of one Indian nation's successful coping with civilizational crisis, see Jonathan Lear's *Radical Hope: Ethics in the Face of Cultural Devastation* (Cambridge, MA: Harvard University Press, 2006).

[28] Jennifer Pitts, preface to WES, xiii, xv.

[29] OC 3:1, 298, 254, 271, 300, 305, 355. Tocqueville was a foreign minister from June to October 1849. Dion, "La conciliation du libéralisme et du nationalisme chez Tocqueville," 220; Françoise Mélonio, "Nations et Nationalismes," *La Revue Tocqueville/The Tocqueville Review* 18 (1997), 61.

[30] Colonization goes to the heart of Tocqueville's view of societal formation as the mutual grafting of cultures and populations, DIA (Nolla) [I.1.ii], 46–48 and note d. Owing much to Guizot's civilizational vision, Tocqueville's understanding of society as an amalgamation of various cultural and ethnic "elements" contrasts with the purist and racial views advocated by Gobineau and later racial theorists. Compare OC 16, 472–477 and François Guizot, *General History of Civilization in Europe*, ed. George Wells Knight (New York: D Appleton and Co., 1896), esp. Lecture I and II with Arthur de Gobineau, *The Inequality of Human Races* (New York: Howard Fertig, 1999), ch. IV and XVI.

To briefly recall the situation, France's occupation of Algeria began in 1830 with a punitive expedition targeting what one historian calls the "most intractable of the Barbary states" that for centuries harbored piracy and the slave trade in the Mediterranean. Prompted by the Restoration government's domestic concerns, the invasion was at once an opportunistic attempt and a long-contemplated act – indeed, the culmination of a cross-European *cause célèbre* that spanned over half a century and was championed by Enlightenment luminaries such as Abbé Raynal and Thomas Paine. Armed with prerevolutionary arguments and relying on a military strategy developed by Napoleon, the Algerian campaign was a striking example, not without its ironies, of the sturdy thread of continuity in French political history. Although the 1830 invasion seems to have been aimed not at permanent occupation but at political reconfiguration that would turn the region toward agriculture and trade, the vigorous public debate in the decade following the surrender of Algiers was eventually settled in favor of colonization.[31]

Dating from 1837, Tocqueville's earliest writings on the colony – the two *Letters on Algeria* – echo the stakes of this debate. They also single out as an interlocutor Amédée Desjobert, one of the most vocal opponents of French colonial settlement. Judging by Desjobert's anti-colonial pamphlets, however, even this opposition was in favor of exerting French influence in Northern Africa. Without too much of a simplification, therefore, one can say that the debate surrounding *la question d'Afrique* was less about the *whether* than about the *how* of maintaining France's presence in the region.[32]

---

[31] For a critical survey of the disputed beginnings of the conquest, see Ann Thomson, "Arguments for the Conquest of Algiers in the Late Eighteenth and Early Nineteenth Centuries," *The Maghreb Review* 14 (1989). Also see Herbert Lüthy, *France Against Herself*, trans. Eric Mosbacher (New York: Meridian Books, 1968), part III; Benjamin Stora, *Algeria 1830–2000. A Short History*, trans. Jane Marie Todd (Ithaca, NY: Cornell University Press, 2001), 3–5; Vincent Confer, *France and Algeria* (New York: Syracuse University Press, 1966), ch. 1; and Jean Meyer, *Histoire de la France coloniale: des origines à 1914* (Paris: Armand Colin, 1991), 327–334. Under presidents Jefferson and Madison, the new republic had its own series of disputes with the North African beyliks in what came to be known as the Barbary Wars. Frank Lambert, *The Barbary Wars* (New York: Hill and Wang, 2005), ch. 7; also Michael Oren, "Early American Encounters in the Middle East" in *Power, Faith, and Fantasy* (New York: Norton, 2007).

[32] In a book-length statement of his views on Algeria, Desjobert insists that national interest alone should guide foreign policy and advocates "maritime occupation without colonization," *L'Algérie en 1846* (Paris: Guillaumin, 1846), ch. VI, X, esp. 112; Cf. Pitts, *Turn to Empire*, 187 and note 99. Tocqueville's 1841 "Essay on Algeria" argues that unless Algeria is settled and made to flourish on its own, France's occupation of the African coast would be "ruinous for the treasury, destructive of our influence in the world, and above all precarious." WES, 92 and 61–62.

Tocqueville's official engagement with the colony begins nearly a decade after the capture of Algiers, at a point when the occupation was a fait accompli and a political consensus in favor of colonization was crystallizing. Notable at first sight in the colonial works is the change of rhetoric. Where the chapter on the three races is by turns elegiac and debunking, exposing as much as lamenting the human toll of civilizational clash, the Algerian writings strike a more conciliatory note. Geared to the practical objective of France's settling the North African territories, Tocqueville's language is for the most part cool headed and pragmatic – calibrated less to raising moral questions than to envisioning and promoting political solutions. This difference in genre notwithstanding, to suggest that in entering political life Tocqueville sets aside his "sociological and ethical awareness" and becomes and enthusiast of colonization is to vastly overstate the case.[33]

From the outset of his involvement with the colony, Tocqueville's stance is as critical as his analysis is sobering. Although expressing support for the colonizing effort, his parliamentary oratory and even the official reports are replete with indictments of the way in which this effort is conducted and the government to which it gives rise. Indeed, Tocqueville's censure is so comprehensive, and his criticism so unsparing, that the opponents of French colonial rule need not look further than his published works to find evidence for their arguments.[34] If Tocqueville's

---

[33] Melvin Richter, "Tocqueville on Algeria," *Review of Politics* 25 (1963), 363. The compatibility of Tocqueville's political practice with his democratic theory has been the subject of a vibrant scholarly debate. On one side of it are those who, like Richter, regard Tocqueville's endorsement of French colonization as a betrayal of his liberal principles, e.g., Roger Boesche, "The Dark Side of Tocqueville: On War and Empire," *Review of Politics* 67 (2005), 737–752; Cheryl B. Welch, "Colonial Violence and the Rhetoric of Evasion," *Political Theory* 31 (2003), 235–264; also Pitts, *Turn to Empire*, 175, 185, 200, 205. On the other are interpretations that stress the continuity between Tocqueville's colonial and analytical writings: Richard Boyd, "Tocqueville's Algeria," *Society* 66 (2001), 65–70; Jean-Louis Benoît, "Relectures de Tocqueville," *Le Banquet*, no. 16 (2001); Stéphane Dion, "Durham et Tocqueville sur la colonisation libérale," *Journal of Canadian Studies* 25 (1990), 60–77; Françoise Mélonio, "L'idée de nation et idée de démocratie chez Tocqueville," *Littérature et nation* 7 (1991), 5–24; and Tzvetan Todorov, *On Human Diversity*, trans. Catherine Porter (Cambridge: Harvard University Press, 1993), 191–207. Neither camp seems to have sufficiently appreciated Tocqueville's view of the inseparability of domestic and foreign affairs in the emerging global order. A closer look at Tocqueville's foreign policy may reveal the rationale, thus help reconcile, his simultaneous reservations about and guarded support for the French colonization of Algeria. See in this connection David Clinton's essay in this volume.

[34] E.g., OC 3:1, 139–144, 292–307, 419–428, 436–440. Tocqueville's Algerian writings include two official reports compiled on behalf of a parliamentary commission reviewing the 1848 budget for the colony. With no surviving record from the proceedings,

public pronouncements voice misgivings about France's colonial vocation, his private notes and correspondence are all the more outspoken. To adduce two early examples, in the fall of 1840 in preparation for his first voyage to Algeria, Tocqueville studied the records documenting the initial decade of the French occupation. "Perusing these reports," he writes,

leaves a painful impression. It is inconceivable that in our times, and coming from a nation that calls itself liberal, near France and in the name of France, a government is established that is so disorderly, tyrannical, officious [*tracassier*], so profoundly illiberal *even in the portion where it could safely afford not to be such*, so estranged from the elementary notions of a *good colonial regime* . . . one sees generals and administrators, who after having suffered at home the yoke of public opinion, the application of the principles of liberty, and the rule of law [*l'empire des regles*], seize with delight the occasion to act freely at last, and to satisfy *passions and tastes* spurred by the restraints, in a country whose exceptional situation serves them as pretext.[35]

Around the same time he states in a letter to Corcelle, his parliamentary colleague and friend: "I think that we shall never do in Algeria all the great things of which we delude ourselves and that, all in all, we have there a rather sorry possession [*une assez triste possession*]."[36]

What Tocqueville contemplates in these early notes and letters and will reiterate in public later on is that the French presence in Algeria, rather than imparting orderly ways to a new society, provides an occasion to indulge motives and behavior normally repressed at home. Instead of the metropolis civilizing the colony, the colony brings out the worst of the mother country – both in the kind of people it attracts and in the conduct of those people in the peculiar circumstances of colonial life.[37] Nor was this criticism only ex post facto. An 1833 sketch significantly titled "Some Ideas About What Prevents The French from Having Good Colonies" states Tocqueville's doubts about the capacity of the French

Tocqueville's contribution cannot be ascertained. As the editor notes, however, Tocqueville was pressured to tone down the language of the reports, OC 3:1, 322 n 3.

[35] OC 3:1, 197, translation and emphasis mine. For similar points, see the *Essai*, OC 3:1, 205, 261–262, 275.

[36] OC 3:1, 151, translation mine.

[37] OC 3:1, 197, 323, 421–422; OC 5:2, 216–217; OC 5:1, 56–57. Noting the shady motives that drive the colonial project, Tocqueville points to the possibility of a "good colonial regime" with pronounced (if limited) liberal features and to the superiority of the English colonies. Tocqueville's later study of what he took as the model of liberal colonization shows a far more critical attitude toward the British mission in India, OC 3:1, 441–535; also OC 6:1, 252–255; OC 7, 281–282. See also Alan S. Kahan, *Alexis de Tocqueville* (London: Continuum, 2010), ch. 5.

to establish prosperous settlements on account of nothing less than their national character and political culture.[38]

If Tocqueville is skeptical about the French government's capacity to discipline its own nationals, his reservations are only magnified when he turns to consider the task of governing the indigenous people. In the 1841 "Essay on Algeria" – the first sustained exposition of his colonial policy – Tocqueville states: "I am under no illusion about the nature and the value of the domination France can found over the Arabs. I know that *even if we handle it in the best possible way*, we shall *never* create anything but an often troubled and habitually onerous government there." Among the chief reasons Tocqueville pinpoints is "the social organization of this people, about which *for a very long time, perhaps forever*, we won't be able to do anything."[39]

If Tocqueville's judgment may be questioned, its pessimism is indisputable: there is little France can do about the social and economic condition of the native population. Its tribal and nomadic way of life makes establishing a regular government as difficult as its effects would be precarious. So long as this mode of societal organization persists, there is no hope of initiating political and economic development in Algeria by co-opting local powers. And changing that organization would entail a social revolution whose effects are likely to be very slow and will surely be "very painful."[40] This is why from the beginning of his involvement with the colony Tocqueville insists on settling the African territory in the ancient Roman or modern American way – that is, by attracting agricultural colonists from Europe who would commit their destiny and fortune to developing the land.[41] This, however, as he well knew from the American case, would only multiply the difficulties. Colonists require land. The threat of dispossession makes a warlike population take up arms with all the greater energy, which in turn entails the "lamentable necessities" (*nécessités fâcheuses*) of a struggle for pacification. What is

[38] OC 3.1, 40; also OC 3:2, 271; OC 14, 146. By the time Tocqueville writes the *Old Regime*, Algeria has come to epitomize ancien régime politics and spirit of government, OR I, 273, 281, 342; OR II, 282, 310, 362, 482.

[39] WES 62, 65; OC 3:1, 218, 221, my emphasis.

[40] OC 3:1, 218, 221, 293–294; OC 5:2, 211–217; LC 562. During his 1846 trip to Algeria, Tocqueville writes to Corcelle: "whatever happens one can be sure that our vicinity will bring about among the Arabs a social revolution whose work will be very painful." OC 15:1, 224.

[41] OC 3:1, 149–149, 217, 254. As Céline Spector argues in this volume, Tocqueville's colonial writings inscribe themselves in a century-long controversy over the advantages and disadvantages of colonization for France.

more, introducing European settlers creates the intractable problem of integrating on the same territory and under the same government two – or as in the Algerian case three – very different and soon enough mutually hostile modes of life.[42]

Tocqueville's first colonial writings, the anonymously printed *Letters on Algeria*, express unexampled optimism about cultural intermixing that is absent both from the chapter on the three races and from his later pronouncements on the North African colony. How to account for this momentary change of heart is a worthy matter for scholarly debate. Might their publication in the context of Tocqueville's first electoral campaign help explain the *Letters'* relatively sanguine tone and hopeful proposals?[43] Whatever the case, by 1841 Tocqueville harbors no more illusions about the possibility of integration. At least since his first trip to Algeria, he is well aware that the hatreds born of the iniquities of conquest and aggravated by profound discrepancies in customs and ways of life raise enormous barriers between colonists and natives. Not only is a gradual fusion of Christian and Muslim societies an unlikely prospect, but there also seem to be insuperable challenges to peaceful coexistence. As Tocqueville has already observed in America, the asymmetry of power and ways of life, or what he terms "civilization," is extremely difficult to overcome. Moreover any attempt, however well intentioned, at bridging this asymmetry is inevitably tainted with violence:

The indigenous population has the greatest need of tutelage at the moment when it comes to mix with our civilian population and finds itself, partly or completely, subjected to our officials and our laws. It is not only violent behavior that it has to fear... the same rules of administration and justice that seem to the European to be guarantees of liberty and property, appear to the barbarian as intolerable oppression... the forms that we call tutelary, they name tyrannical, and they

---

[42] OC 3:1, 218, 227, 298. In the "Essay" Tocqueville notes: "I have come to believe that if France renounced colonization even now, we would have less trouble making our domination accepted. But such domination would always be *unproductive* and *precarious*," WES, 62; OC 3:1, 217, emphasis in the original. See also André Martel, "Tocqueville et les problèmes coloniaux de la Monarchie de Juillet," *Revue d'Histoire Economique et Sociale* XXXII, no. 4 (1954), 369–376.

[43] In his American account, Tocqueville notes the "secret affinity" in character between the French and the Indians and their frequent intermixing (OC 5:1, 378; DIA I.2.x, 316 note 17, contrast with 342). His initial optimism about Algeria may have issued from related expectations: the 1837 *Letters* describe the Arabs as an aristocratic people, enamored of courage and military glory and comment on the "unreflective enthusiasm" they inspired in the French. After visiting the colony, however, Tocqueville declares all hopes of peaceful amalgamation "chimerical." Compare OC 3.1, 151–153 with 275, 293–294; LCS, 565–556.

would rather withdraw than submit to them. This is how, without drawing the sword, the Europeans of North America ended by pushing the Indians off of their territory.[44]

This passage from the 1847 parliamentary "Report on Algeria," for which Tocqueville was the official rapporteur, spotlights the central contradiction of colonial rule: the insistence on legal equality means instituting moral tyranny, whereas recognizing moral differences results in legal and social inequality that cannot fail in time to radicalize the subject population.[45] Nowhere does Tocqueville articulate this colonial dilemma more poignantly than in a letter to Henry Reeve, his English friend and first translator of *Democracy in America*. Tocqueville writes the letter in response to Reeve's article on India, published in the aftermath of the 1857 Sepoy uprising. Begun as a mutiny within the army of the British East India Company, the uprising escalated into civilian conflict so considerable that it has been dubbed India's First War of Independence.

Commenting on Reeve's article, Tocqueville grants its central claim: that Britain "cannot retain India without the consent, at least tacit, of the Hindus." Yet, bringing up the insurrection as a stark example, he explains why colonization puts this consent out of reach. Tocqueville blames the insurgence of the Hindu army not on poverty or oppression but on the lack of camaraderie between soldiers and captains. The "real or pretended superiority" of the Europeans mortifies the pride and self-respect of the native inhabitants, and "the resulting anger is much greater than any political oppression can produce." Differences in civilization and race, and the exceptional pride of the English – haughtiness, he adds, that is the very source of their great qualities – introduce insurmountable

---

44 WES, 144; OC 3:1, 327–328; LCS, 565–566. Compare with OP 1, 774–775; DIA I.2.x, 321–323. In DIA Tocqueville lists the exceptional mode of colonization among the crucial factors that contributed to the success of American democracy. That same model, however, resulted in a highly decentralized government that was too weak to protect the native and African populations. This is one reason why Tocqueville's Algerian writings call for a strong central power with extensive administrative competences. DIA I.1.ii, 36–37; I.2.x, 321–323, 442 and note 381.

45 Louis Napoleon's effort to extend civil and political rights to Algeria's native inhabitants is a case in point. Proclaiming himself "as much the Emperor of the Arabs as of the French" (thus alienating the Berbers), he offered full citizenship rights to all who would renounce their religious status. Between 1865 and 1875, only 371 individuals volunteered. As Vincent Confer observes, "the offer of citizenship came to nothing as most Moslems would not relinquish their Koranic law," *France and Algeria*, ch. 1; Stora, *Algeria*, 5; also Pierre Laffont, *Histoire de la France en Algérie* (Paris: Plon, 1980), ch. xx.

distance between colonizers and natives and daily remind them of their inequality.[46]

Here it might be helpful to recall that pride [*orgueil*], which Tocqueville defines as the sentiment of one's superior worth, is a paradigmatic inegalitarian passion and a key element of his anthropology. The psychological seat of individuality – and of each person's or group's self-conception as singular and unique – pride for Tocqueville is the shared root of virtue and vice. His analysis of America highlights the sentiment of pride as an indispensable (if also problematic) precondition for self-government.[47]

Rendering the colonial question in psychological terms, Tocqueville's letter to Reeve seems to conclude that colonialism is unsustainable in the long run less because it violates right than because it offends against pride and the sense of dignity and distinctness – or in contemporary terms, identity – of the subject peoples. Far from obliterating that identity, intensified contact between cultures reawakens it and makes it more defiant. In another letter of the same year, Tocqueville states with characteristic sweep that the Sepoy rebellion is more than a rebellion. It reveals "a new and general *fact*: a universal reaction against the European race . . . [which] is occurring everywhere and is the common cause of a thousand different effects." While too weak at present, it is only a matter of time before this universal reaction seeks to dismantle Europe's domination.[48]

Tocqueville undeniably stakes a great deal of his political career on supporting the French colonial empire. Nevertheless, throughout his official involvement in Algeria he remains deeply skeptical of its immediate success, as well as long-term prospects. The salient point for our present

---

[46] OC 6:1, 252–255; SLPS, 360–365 and DIA I.2.x, 316 n17, 342; Jean Alphonse Bernard, *Tocqueville in India* (Paris: Les Editions d'En Face, 2006), xvii, 247. For a similar analysis, see Karl Marx's article "The Indian Revolt" in the *New-York Daily Tribune*, September 16, 1857.

[47] Cf. DIA II.3.xv, 582; also II.3.iii, 543–544, II.3.xiii, 578; II.3.xix, 604 and II.4.vi, 663–664. In the race chapter, the respective fates of Indians, Negroes, and the whites are analyzed in terms of their pride, DIA I.2.x, 306, 359; also OC 3:1, 136. For a thematic discussion of the problem of pride in Tocqueville, see my "Tocqueville and the Question of the Nation" (PhD diss., University of Chicago, 2007), ch. 5; also Peter Augustine Lawler, *The Restless Mind, Alexis de Tocqueville on the Origin and Perpetuation of Human Liberty* (Lanham: Rowman & Littlefield, 1993), esp. ch. 4; and Joshua Mitchell, *Fragility of Freedom. Tocqueville on Religion, Democracy, and the American Future* (Chicago: University of Chicago Press, 1999), ch. 2.

[48] Letter to Adolphe de Circourt, OC 18, 486, my translation and emphasis; also OC 9, 243–244.

concern, moreover, is that for Tocqueville, the difficulty of planting a successful colony in Northern Africa is due not merely to the condition of the native peoples or the incapacity of the French but to the nature of the colonial enterprise itself. Whereas France's efforts in Algeria may be especially vexed by the peculiarities of French national character, Tocqueville's analysis suggests that the decisive challenges inhere in the very structure of colonial rule:

> There is no government so wise, so benevolent, and so just that it can suddenly bring together and intimately unite populations whose history, religion, laws, and practices are so profoundly divided... We believe it would be imprudent to think that we can manage easily and in so little time to destroy in the heart of the indigenous populations the blind hatred created and sustained by foreign domination. It is therefore necessary, whatever our conduct, to remain strong.[49]

As this recommendation implies and Tocqueville's colonial writings showcase, Europe's attempted dominion over the world recalls the characteristics of aristocratic rule. Ultimately, both have their origin in force. Force is the inevitable outcome of the confrontation of moral differences just as tyranny and exploitation are the likely effects of the asymmetries of power and civilization.[50] Yet, as Tocqueville's account of feudal society makes clear, although established by force and to some extent maintained by it, the aristocratic polity succeeded with time in gaining stability and enlisting the tacit consent of its subjects. By enduring for centuries, thus becoming a habitual circumstance and accepted reality, aristocratic society replaced physical coercion with the authority of law and opinion – that is, the shared opinion of the inequality of persons and groups and of their divinely ordained hierarchical order.[51]

In light of Tocqueville's own analysis, however, no such prospect was open to Europe's colonial efforts of the nineteenth and twentieth centuries, not least because of the very principles that animated those efforts. In an 1843 article calling for the abolition of slavery in the old colonies, Tocqueville proclaims that sooner or later European powers as a whole, and France in particular, will have to make good on their liberal and egalitarian commitments. For "nations cannot, with impunity, show indifference to the ideas and sentiments that have long characterized them and that they have used to rouse the world. They cannot abandon them

---

[49] OC 3.1, 328; also 153.
[50] OC 3:1, 80, 117, 313, 309, 221, 217; OC 15, 22; DIA Introduction, 4, 10; I.2.x, 384.
[51] DIA I.2.x, 383–384. See note 8 in this chapter and Ran Halevi's essay in this volume.

without quickly sinking in the public esteem and entering into decline."
Tocqueville's sermon continues:

These notions of freedom and equality that are weakening or destroying servitude
everywhere: who spread them throughout the world? This sentiment, disinterested
and yet impassioned with the love of men, which all at once made Europe hear
the cry of slaves – who propagated it, directed it, illuminated it? We were the
ones. Let us not deny it. It was not only our glory but our strength . . . Thanks to
us these ideas have become the symbol of the new politics.[52]

Here and elsewhere, Tocqueville points to the "new politics" grounded
in the notions of freedom and equality as essential to the world-historical
ascendancy of Europe – for its "glory" as well as its "strength."[53] At the
same time, he suggests that the very success of this new politics cannot but
undermine European domination. For Tocqueville, I propose, Europe's
attempt to create a global society that would unite and hold together
vastly different cultures and modes of life was bound to be short lived.
For to be lasting, European imperialism would require the reinstitution of
permanent hierarchies that runs against the spirit of the age and against
the principles and practices of modern nations. On the other hand, in the
context of colonial society, for coercion to be superseded by the rule of
law and the government of opinion, by moral equality and persuasion,
a considerable assimilation of fundamental ideas and ways of life would
have to take place. However, precisely that, which makes assimilation
necessary, is also what stands in its way: the sense of national distinctness
and prideful attachment – of both colonizers and colonized – to their
particular manner of life and its ethical perspective, or to what Tocqueville
calls honor. As long as these cultural divisions subsist, there can be neither
moral justification for colonial rule in the eyes of those subjected to it nor
the possibility of an all-encompassing community of ideas and practices.
While Tocqueville's public pronouncements often imply that achieving
such a community is a question of time and the habit of coexistence, his
analytical writings and private reflections indicate that this period may
be very long indeed and altogether longer than the empire of Europe can
afford.[54]

---

[52] WES, 206–207, see also 225. Cf. DIA I.2.x, 353–354. As Tocqueville argues in DIA,
"there are certain great social principles that a people makes pervasive everywhere or
allows to subsist nowhere," II.3.viii, 559.
[53] See also Tocqueville's foreign policy speeches OC 3:2, esp. 291, 326, 426; R, 240 and
note.
[54] Throughout his engagement with the colony, Tocqueville calls for diversifying the legislation to accommodate moral differences. As in DIA, so too in the Algerian writings, he

Democracy's Final Frontier?

The chapter on honor concludes with the following reflection:

> If it were finally permissible to suppose that all races should intermingle and all the peoples of the world should come to the point of having the same interests and the same needs, and of no longer distinguishing themselves from one another by any characteristic feature, one would cease entirely to attribute conventional value to human actions; all would view them in the same light.
>
> It is the dissimilarities and inequalities of man that have created honor; it is weakened insofar as these differences are effaced, and it should disappear with them.[55]

Did Tocqueville expect the dissimilarities and inequalities of man eventually to vanish and humanity to come together in "one equal civilization" in which all would view human life in the same light? Or did he believe, as he states elsewhere, that it is our permanent condition, indeed the "wretchedness of our nature," to be divided by language and country and confounded by a plurality of incompatible moral views?[56] If the colonial writings are any indication, Tocqueville's thinking on this weighty question seems pointed in two opposite directions.

The first is what we today call globalization, of which Europe's colonizing project writes a seminal chapter. The global ascendancy of Europe is the point of departure of Tocqueville's account of the modern world. This ascendancy is the undisclosed mover, if not the "first cause," of the providential rise of equality to which his theoretical work bears witness. However, neither in Europe itself nor anywhere else has democracy "sprung full-grown and fully armed from the midst of the old society," like Athena from the head of Zeus.[57] Rather, equality is born in the throes of prolonged, violent, social, and political struggles, spearheaded by the unrelenting dynamism of the British Empire and its former colonies or,

<hr>

points to fundamental similarity in civilization and mores as a *sine qua non* of egalitarian society, OC 3:1, 142, 149, 275, 293–295, 322–324, 329; DIA I.1.viii, 159–161; I.2.ix, 289–290; I.2.x, 341 and note, 369–370; François Furet, "The Conceptual System of 'Democracy in America'" in *The Workshop of History*, trans. Jonathan Mandelbaum (Chicago: University of Chicago Press, 1984), ch. 10, 180.

[55] DIA II.3.xviii, 599.
[56] These formulations come from *Fortnight in the Wilderness*, OC 5:1, 347, 354, 381. Also, OR II, 262.
[57] DIA I.1.ii, 36. Although Tocqueville asserts America's exception in this respect, he does so by self-consciously abstracting from the fate of Native and African Americans. Cf. II.2.iii, 484; II.3.xxi, 606.

as the conclusion to the first volume of *Democracy* has it, by the "Anglo-American race."[58] Just as on the national, so too on the international level Tocqueville takes this process, its irresistibility as well as its providential goodness, largely for granted. A historical and geopolitical given, Europe's global expansion, and the democratic movement to which it gives impetus, is not something that can be arrested or steered otherwise than by partaking in it. This is why, I suggest, despite many and profound reservations, Tocqueville cautiously embraces his country's colonial vocation and advocates France's playing an active role in "the great affair of the century." A matter of necessity more than of choice, participation in the "movement of the century" is the only reasonable and, Tocqueville argues, honorable course of action that would counterbalance Anglo-American predominance and safeguard France's say in the affairs of the world.[59] In short, Tocqueville views European imperialism as an instrument of the movement toward equalization and a vehicle for spreading the new liberal-democratic politics that defines the modern age. While deploring this movement's cultural and humanitarian losses, he also appreciates the civilizational and moral gain: the rising ideal of universal fellowship that "puts the shape of the human race in broad daylight for the first time," thus pointing to a "more just" human order.[60]

On the other hand, the Algerian writings offer a sober account of the inveteracy of cultural and moral divides, whose deep roots – in our pride and sense of honor – seem to constitute psychological and anthropological givens. As the preceding remarks demonstrate, Tocqueville balanced his support for the colonial project with a clear-sighted assessment of its future prospects. His assessment suggests that he did not expect Europe's global domination to long endure. Whereas in cases of extreme asymmetry, this domination might result in cultural extinction or assimilation, the meeting face-to-face of civilizations is no less likely to equalize the opponents and revitalize differences by bolstering national and cultural self-conceptions. So, rather than crush the peoples over whom they rule,

---

[58] DIA I.2.x, 391; OC 6:1, 273–275. Cf. *Communist Manifesto*, 474–475 and note.

[59] OC 3:2, 271, 289–301, 345, 430; Barbara Allen, *Tocqueville, Covenant and the Democratic Revolution* (Lanham, MD: Lexington Books, 2005), 239–240; Boesche, "The Dark Side of Tocqueville," 743–745. For a sustained discussion of Tocqueville's foreign policy, see David Clinton's *Tocqueville, Lieber, and Bagehot. Liberalism Confronts the World* (Palgrave Macmillan, 2003), ch. 1.

[60] DIA II.1.xvii, 461; II.4.viii, 674–675. Tracy B. Strong, "Seeing Differently and Seeing Further: Rousseau and Tocqueville," in *Friends and Citizens*, ed. Peter Denis Bathory and Nancy L. Schwartz (Lanham: Rowman & Littlefield, 2001), 104–105.

Tocqueville expects European powers to mobilize their pride and hand them the means of successful resistance. Already in the 1830s he highlights the chief among those means: political centralization and nation building. Tocqueville's account of Abd-el-Kader's leadership – the fiercest opposition the French encountered in Algeria before the Front de Libération Nationale, which ended their rule – points to the rise of Arab nationalism that exploits religious passions to build moral unity and to consolidate political power over a territory divided by centuries-old ethnic and tribal hatreds. Availing themselves of "the ideas and arts" of Europe, local elites fight to overturn traditional social structures and to centralize authority, so as to make a compelling claim to self-determination. Likewise in his notes on India, Tocqueville anticipates that sooner or later "the English will end up putting the Hindus in a position to resist them."[61] Although in the Algerian writings, as in *Democracy in America*, Tocqueville studiously avoids making long-term predictions, taken as a whole his colonial works signal that the most likely result of European expansionism is neither global assimilation nor servitude but wars of decolonization and the making of new nations.[62] The final frontier seems to replicate itself.

To recapitulate, in Tocqueville's account, the confrontation of ethical outlooks and civilizational alternatives ends up stimulating human diversity no less than thwarting it. The coming together of cultures and ways of life does not simply assimilate nations but prompts them to strive for a more robust cultural and political self-definition, whereby to assert their "individuality among peoples." For Tocqueville, I suggest, just as individual faculties and self-understanding are developed through active participation in civic life, so too cultural particularity and self-conception is enhanced not in tranquil isolation but in the "rough school" of political practice and international engagement.[63]

Tocqueville, then, understands the modern world to be moving in a dialectical fashion. In his view, democracy's future, like its past, manifests itself in the movement of equality, fueled and propelled by the clash of moral alternatives. However, this movement is not only produced by the struggle of particulars; it is also productive of that struggle. Although seemingly antagonistic moments, the simultaneous bridging and corroborating of cultural and moral differences, of universalization and

[61] OC 3:1, 132–133, 145, 151, 219–223, 481; OC 6:1, 230, 236; Bernard, *Tocqueville in India*, 25–28. See also Alan Kahan's essay in this volume.
[62] Jean-Louis Benoît, *Comprendre Tocqueville* (Paris: Armand Colin, 2004), 140.
[63] DIA II.2.ii–iv, I.1.ii, 29.

individuation, could be seen as representing what I have called the dialectical dynamic of democratization. A kind of self-perpetuating motion, its meaning comes to the fore, once again, in contrast to the Marxian vision. Whereas both Tocqueville and Marx view history as spurred by conflict and the struggle of contradictions, for Marx these contradictions can and will be overcome and "the riddle of history solved" in the beatific state of fully achieved communism.[64] For Tocqueville, I suggest, the human condition is marked or marred by a permanent tension between the abiding passion for universality and equality and the just as abiding desire for individuality and distinction whose paradigmatic symptom is pride – or to borrow Kant's formulation, by "unsocial sociability." Although, as Susan McWilliams argues in this volume, Tocqueville claims the current of modernity to be "something entirely new in the world" – tending toward faster motion and larger scales, hence toward ever-greater groups and unprecedented conflicts – as long as these anthropological givens endure, history's riddle appears insoluble. Democracy, in Nestor Capdevila's words, is "an end without an end."[65]

---

[64] "Economic and Philosophical Manuscripts of 1844" in *The Marx-Engels Reader*, 84; also 34–35, 52, 193–200 in the same volume. Following Kolakowski, Eric Hobsbawm notes that Marx's claim of the inevitable overthrow of bourgeois society and humanity's emancipation from its contradictions "represents a hope, read into his analysis of capitalism, but not a conclusion necessarily imposed by that analysis." Hobsbawm, "Introduction" to Karl Marx, Friedrich Engels, *The Communist Manifesto: A Modern Edition* (London: Verso, 1998), 25. Leszek Kolakowski, *Main Currents of Marxism* (Oxford: Oxford University Press, 1978), vol. 1, 130.

[65] Immanuel Kant, "Idea for a Universal History with a Cosmopolitan Purpose," in *Political Writings* (Cambridge: Cambridge University Press, 1991), Fourth Proposition, 44–45. See also McWilliams' and Capdevila's essays in this volume.

CHAPTER 9

Commerce, Glory, and Empire: Montesquieu's Legacy

Céline Spector
Translated by Patrick Camiller

"This book is not precisely in anyone's camp."[1] Should we take at face value this statement at the end of the introduction to volume one of *Democracy in America*? Or should we see it, more subtly, as an echo of the quotation from Ovid with which Montesquieu prefaced *The Spirit of the Laws*: *prolem sine matre creatum*, a work created without a mother? For Tocqueville, as for Montesquieu, the point is by no means to forgo the inspiration of past sources but rather to announce a new method – the "new political science for a world altogether new," which he evokes in keeping with the science of society for which *The Spirit of the Laws* laid the groundwork.[2] From the first volume of *Democracy in America* – weaving together geographical causes, laws, and customs – to *The Ancien Regime and the Revolution*, which redeploys the method of *Considerations on the Causes of the Greatness of the Romans and Their Decline*, Tocqueville pursues Montesquieu's project: to determine the causes of institutions (laws, customs) and assess their effects in a comparative light,

---

[1] "Ce livre ne se met précisément à la suite de personne." OP 2, 18; DIA Introduction, 15. Montesquieu, *The Spirit of the Laws* (Cambridge: Cambridge University Press, 1989), henceforth SL, cited by volume, chapter, and/or page numbers.

[2] DIA Introduction, 7. Raymond Aron, *Les Étapes de la pensée sociologique* (Paris: Gallimard, 1967), 226–227, 237; Melvin Richter, "The Uses of Theory: Tocqueville's Adaptation of Montesquieu," in Melvin Richter, ed., *Essays in Theory and History: An Approach to the Social Sciences* (Cambridge: Harvard University Press, 1970), 74–102, here 101. See also Richter's "Comparative Political Analysis in Montesquieu and Tocqueville," *Comparative Politics* 1 (1969), 129–160; David Carrithers, "Montesquieu and Tocqueville as Philosophical Historians: Liberty, Determinism, and the Prospects for Freedom," in Rebecca Kingston, ed., *Montesquieu and His Legacy* (Albany: State University of New York Press, 2009), 149–177.

to theorize the adaptation of legislation to the "genius" of the people it is meant to govern, and to explain the deep causes of radical historical breaks, without denying any leeway to the human will.[3]

Nevertheless, it is not sufficient to quote Tocqueville's famous phrase about his three "fetish authors": Montesquieu, Rousseau, and Pascal.[4] Beyond the parallels, we need to revisit an affinity that his contemporaries recognized but that has since been lost from view.[5] Like the American Framers such as Madison and Hamilton, Tocqueville knew his debt to the "rarest political writer" of all time. In his eyes, however, Montesquieu was never a politician and would doubtless not have known how to be one.[6] It is therefore necessary to separate theory and practice. As a political theorist, Tocqueville drew on analyses of England as a free, trade-oriented nation, and he suggested that the French should study the "American model," to see liberty "as if in a mirror" and judge how free were their own institutions.[7] As a politician, Tocqueville gradually distanced himself from the author of *The Spirit of the Laws*. His role in the debate on the colonization of Algeria led him to reject the conception of commercial colonization that Montesquieu had defended in relation to the England of his time. The purpose of this chapter, then, is to identify the breaking points in Tocqueville's exploration of the new frontier between democratic society and the unprecedented rise of imperial rivalries.

---

[3] DIA I.2.ix, 323, 326. This first volume is more inspired by Montesquieu than the second, which in many respects owes more to Rousseau or Pascal; Agnès Antoine, *L'Impensé de la démocratie. Tocqueville, la citoyenneté, la religion* (Paris: Fayard, 2003), 9.

[4] "There are three men with whom I spend time every day, Pascal, Montesquieu, and Rousseau." Letter to Louis de Kergolay, November 10, 1836, OC 13:1, 418. Unless otherwise noted, all translations from the French are by Patrick Camiller.

[5] Molé, for example, noted: "You have not limited yourself to doing for America what Montesquieu did for the Romans: that is, to elucidate its origins, to explain its development and to foresee what it might still achieve or the causes that might bring on its decline. You present it as having outstripped old Europe and reached before it the goal towards which it pointed the way." OC 16, 278.

[6] "I have sometimes heard it regretted that Montesquieu lived in an age when he could not experiment with politics, even though he did so much to advance it as a science. I have always found much poor judgement in such regrets; perhaps his somewhat rarefied shrewdness of mind would have often made him miss the precise moment when the success of a matter is decided; it may well be that, instead of becoming the rarest of political writers, he would have been only a rather bad minister, and not very rare at all." OC16, 231.

[7] SL XI:6, 156–157. See Paul Rahe, *Soft Despotism. Democracy's Drift* (New Haven: Yale University Press, 2009); also Annelien de Dijn, *French Political Thought from Montesquieu to Tocqueville* (Cambridge: Cambridge University Press, 2008), which emphasizes the notion of "aristocratic liberalism."

Commerce, Freedom, and Empire in *The Spirit of the Laws*

Spirit of Conquest and Spirit of Commerce

Montesquieu's critique of territorial empire is well known.[8] Whereas the *Considerations on the Causes of the Greatness of the Romans and Their Decline* show that the expansion of empire can only lead to its decline, the *Reflections on Universal Monarchy* provides a lesson for the use of modern politics: no stable hegemony such as that of the Romans is possible any longer in Europe.[9] The theme reappears in *The Spirit of the Laws*: universal monarchy is now meaningless, and if the project of Louis XIV had succeeded, "nothing would have been more fatal to Europe."[10] To increase absolute greatness at the expense of relative greatness is absurd – territorial expansion makes a prince more vulnerable, not more powerful.[11] Modern conquests testify to the failure of such enterprises. On the pretext of civilizing and converting other peoples, Spain and Portugal were more fearsome than Rome in their cruelty and barbarity.[12] France should not follow the example of Spain, which "in order to hold America... did what despotism itself does not do": enslave or destroy the conquered peoples.[13] In this respect, the failure of the Hispanic model expresses the law of every conquering empire: there are natural limits to the expansion of republics and monarchies, beyond which their power declines. If empires are too large, they can guarantee neither external nor internal security. Unless one man can hold a vast territory at every

---

[8] See the various contributions in Céline Spector, ed., "Montesquieu et l'empire," special issue of *Revue Montesquieu*, no. 8 (2005–2006).

[9] Catherine Larrère, "Introduction" to the *Réflexions sur la Monarchie universelle*, in Patrick Andrivet and Catherine Volpilhac-Auger, eds., *Oeuvres completes*, vol. 2 (Oxford: Voltaire Foundation, 2000).

[10] SL IX:7, 136.

[11] SL IV:2, IX:6–9, and *Pensées*, No. 271, with the deleted footnote "mis cela dans les *Romains*." Book VIII of *The Spirit of the Laws* raises the question of maintaining the monarchical principle in such a way as to exclude the link between monarchy's ethos and the spirit of conquest (VIII:17–18). If monarchies agree to conquer only so much that they remain within the "natural limits" of their government, they are rewarded with national homogeneity and prosperity (X:9).

[12] Montesquieu, *Persian Letters*, C. J. Betts, trans. (London: Penguin, 1973), henceforth PL, Letter 121, 216–219; *Pensées*, No. 1268. On Spain, see Barrera, "Espagne," in *Dictionnaire Montesquieu*, Catherine Volpilhac-Auger and C. Larrère, eds. (2008), available at http://Dictionnaire-Montesquieu.ens-lsh.fr.

[13] SL VIII:18, X:3–4. Montesquieu severs the usual associations between monarchy and colonialism and honor and heroism. Even if "the spirit of monarchy is war and expansion" (IX:2), he no longer considers its wellspring to be exploits of conquest. As regards honor, the reader may like to refer to chapter one of my *Montesquieu. Pouvoirs, richesses et societies* (Paris: P.U.F., 2004; repr. Hermann, 2011).

moment (as was the case, exceptionally, with Alexander the Great or Charlemagne), any earthly empire runs the dual risk of invasion and insurrection. It is doomed to dissolution or despotism: "the quick establishment of unlimited power is the remedy which can prevent dissolution: a new misfortune after that of expansion!"[14]

Yet Montesquieu also conceived of an empire that served the good of men, respecting their liberty and beneficial to their reason. In the famous example of Alexander, an empire does not merely preserve the diversity of laws, customs, and mores but enables the progress of enlightenment and the destruction of "barbarous" superstitions.[15] Similarly, instead of "infinite woes," might the Spanish not have brought real goods such as the abolition of destructive prejudices and an improvement in the lot of conquered peoples? Such a line of thinking is doubtless not without its risks – and we seem to see here the glimmerings of an apologia for enlightened despotism, so remote from Montesquieu and his critique of the "tyranny of opinion."[16] However, *The Spirit of the Laws* upholds a certain figure of reason in history: the philosopher's judgment bears not so much on intentions (building an empire "for the sake of the good," albeit at the price of violence and war) as on the beneficial or harmful effects of institutions. Thus, while underlining the "immense debt" that conquerors incur, Montesquieu also speaks of certain "advantages" for a "vanquished people," either because the conquest frees it of tyrannical rule, because it allays its oppression and poverty, or because it brings civilizing effects in its train: "a conquest can destroy harmful prejudices, and, *if I dare speak in this way*, can put a nation under a better presiding genius."[17]

This tension appears more than once, and an evolution might be traced from Montesquieu's early ideas about the laws "fittest to make a republic or colony prosper."[18] Decisive in this context are the chapters on the colonies that he finally withdrew from the printed edition of *The Spirit*

---

[14] SL VIII:17.

[15] See Pierre Briant, "Montesquieu, Mably et Alexandre le Grand: aux sources de l'histoire hellénistique," *Revue Montesquieu* 8 (2005–2006), 151–185.

[16] SL XIX:3. See Catherine Larrère, "L'empire, entre fédération et république," *Revue Montesquieu* 8 (2005–2006), 111–136.

[17] SL X:4. See Michael Mosher, "Montesquieu on Conquest: Three Cartesian Heroes and Five Good Enough Empires," *Revue Montesquieu* 8 (2005–2006), 81–110.

[18] *Pensées*, 185 (written in 1731?). The evolution of Montesquieu's thinking on the right of conquest is brought out in Jean Terrel, "A propos de la conquête: droit et politique chez Montesquieu," *Revue Montesquieu* 8 (2005–2006), 137–150.

of the Laws.[19] He notes of these: "Here is a piece on the colonies, part of which will go into my second book on commerce, part at the end of the book on the number of inhabitants, and part into Book 11 on conquests. We shall see where is best."[20] The planned book on the colonies never saw the light of day, and its content – which Montesquieu contemplates distributing among Books XXI, XXIII, and X, was not published in its entirety.[21] In the piece in question, using a typological approach, Montesquieu makes it clear that settler colonies are only suitable for "republican" (not absolute-monarchical or despotic) states; only republics benefit from their capacity to relieve overpopulated states of the "burden of poor citizens."[22] On certain conditions, the implantations may represent a gain in power:

The colonies should keep the form of government of their mother country: this creates an alliance and a natural amity that is often stronger than one based on covenants. So it is that the various colonies of America have various governments in keeping with the one of the peoples that established them. They should keep the religion, customs and manners of the mother country.[23]

Settler colonies may be beneficial, so long as they contrive "wise" laws (intermarriages, trade legislation, religious community, balance between home, country, and colonies); they may be useful, insofar as they are not "under the domination" of a central power but "united" with it in upholding its interests "in principle."[24] The demographic danger is then under control: "We have seen, in their settlements founded in the two Indies, that the English and Dutch have established themselves in Asia and America without being weakened in Europe, and that they have shed

---

[19] According to Catherine Volpilhac-Auger, these chapters (in the writing of secretary H.) were composed between 1741 and 1742 and discarded during the revision of 1743–1744, but it is not impossible – given the remarks of secretary O., who was active between 1745 and 1747 – that Montesquieu intended to put some fragments back into *The Spirit of the Laws*. See C. Volpilhac-Auger, ed., *Montesquieu. Manuscrits inédits de La Brède* (Naples: Liguori, 2002), 43–67, and the updated version in her introduction to *De l'esprit des loix (manuscrits), Oeuvres complètes de Montesquieu* (Oxford: Voltaire Foundation, 2008), vol. 4, 766–767.

[20] *De l'esprit des loix (manuscrits)*, 766.

[21] Marginal notes in the hand of secretary L. ("I think this is good for bk. eleven"; "taken from bk. on the colonies, moved to bk. 11") indicate that this would have been Book XI. Some chapters on confederations would also have been meant for this Book.

[22] *De l'esprit des loix (manuscrits)*, 775–776.

[23] *De l'esprit des loix (manuscrits)*, 779.

[24] This is the case when the settlers are granted citizenship rights, *De l'esprit des loix (manuscrits)*, 775.

only what was too much for them."[25] On the other hand, the colonies of (absolute) monarchical or despotic states only depopulate and weaken them and inordinately extend the body politic, as was the case with the Spanish and Portuguese, who did not increase but divided their power. To the question of whether "it is advantageous for France to have colonies," Montesquieu therefore gives a negative reply. Was it out of prudence that he refrained from publishing such a verdict at a time when the French colonial empire was expanding?[26] No doubt. For modern monarchies, the conquering empire was from now on destined for tragedy, if not for myth.

Land Empire and Sea Empire

However, Montesquieu did not dwell on this vigorous opposition to France's imperial ambitions. Far from any sweeping condemnation, *The Spirit of the Laws* draws a distinction between land empire and sea empire, in which the former leads to poverty and servitude, the latter to power and liberty. In Anthony Pagden's fine eulogy, *The Spirit of the Laws* offered the eighteenth century's most lucid analysis of the conquering empire and the trading empire, the transition from war to commerce being the only possible solution for Europe's imperial future.[27] Let us look at this more closely.

In Book XXI, Montesquieu develops his distinction between land empires and maritime empires. The sea gives rise to a dynamic of communication among peoples, which Montesquieu constantly counterposes to the dynamic of separation that characterizes conquering empires: "the history of commerce is that of communication among peoples."[28] It is a polemical statement: the mercantilism of Colbert and Montchrétien deemed colonization necessary to unburden the kingdom of its surplus population, to work for the glory of God, to spread civilization among savage peoples, and to acquire endless riches from the supply of raw materials.[29] Colbert wanted to extend the project of universal monarchy

[25] *De l'esprit des loix (manuscrits)*, 776.
[26] It never went beyond a note in the original manuscript.
[27] Anthony Pagden, *Lords of all the World* (New Haven: Yale University Press, 1995), 115–123. See also his *Peoples and Empires* (New York: The Modern Library, 2001), ch. 7.
[28] SL XXI:5.
[29] See Antoine de Montchrétien, *Traicté de l'oeconomie politique*, ed. Th. Funck-Brentano (Paris: Plon, 1889), 315–329.

to Canada and the Caribbean through a state unified by language, customs, religion, laws, and blood – in short, an empire of cultural unity.[30] In his *Treatise on Political Economy*, Montchrétien supported this conception: France is "the glory of the world, to which not only all lands but all seas owe obedience."[31] To be sure, like many of his contemporaries, he invoked the model of the Roman Empire, but he thought the Spanish model of territorial aggrandizement through navigation to be a mark of the superiority of the moderns over the ancients.[32]

Now, whereas this model involves applying the art of war to commerce, Montesquieu turns it around and sees commercial colonization as essentially peaceful and indicative of the greater "refinement" of the moderns. Some modern nations have known how to change "objects of conquest" into "objects of trade," delegating sovereignty to the trading companies to ensure the blossoming of commerce:

Many peoples acted so wisely that they granted empire to trading companies who, governing these distant states only for trade, made a great secondary power without encumbering the principal state. The colonies formed there are in a kind of dependence of which there are very few examples among the ancient colonies, because those of today belong either to the state itself or to some commercial company established in that state. The purpose of these colonies is to engage in commerce under better conditions than one has with neighbouring peoples with whom all advantages are reciprocal. It has been established that only the mother country can trade with the colony, and this was done with very good reason, for the goal of the establishment was to extend commerce, not to found a town or a new empire.[33]

Far from it being the case that land empire is confined to the ancients and sea empire to the moderns, both the one and the other are horizons of modernity.[34] Whereas colonies of conquest are subject to control or settlement by people from the metropolis, colonies of commerce are mere trading posts administered by the East and West Indies companies. In his *Essai politique sur le commerce*, Melon already drew this distinction and attacked the Spanish model that led to depopulation and extermination

---

[30] After 1663, when the Compagnie des Indes Occidentales established itself in Canada, the Antilles, and so on, French settlers were encouraged to marry native people. This Gallicization of the savages was intended to increase the population in the colonies, and thereby the forces available against the English. See "Mémoire à Jean Talon," April 6, 1607, cited in Pagden, *Lords of all the World*, 149–150.

[31] Montchrétien, *Traicté de l'oeconomie politique*, 279.

[32] Montchrétien, *Traicté de l'oeconomie politique*, 282.

[33] SL XXI:21.

[34] See Carl Schmitt, *Land and Sea* (Washington: Plutarch Press, 1977).

of the Amerindians.[35] With this in mind, Montesquieu argued that the dividing line in the modern world ran between the Spanish empire (in the ancient mold of the Romans) and the empire of "peoples more refined than they," who knew how to use colonial expeditions only for economic growth, so that external trade fueled the development of their internal trade.[36]

In this regard, Montesquieu's history of commerce in Book XXI castigates the mercantilist vision of empire. Whereas Père Huet dedicated his *Histoire du commerce et de la navigation des anciens* to Colbert, seeking to show the superiority of the Roman model as an inspiration for the French,[37] the author of *The Spirit of the Laws* identified wholeheartedly with the Athenian model, which he distinguished from the Roman, and pointed to England as its modern representative. In his view, then, the dividing line ran between two types of empire in antiquity itself: the Greek empire, unlike the Roman, was a sea empire, and its sway was proportional to the number of nations that it managed to form. Greece was at the heart of an economic world open to the outside, endowed with secondary zones and a periphery. The colonial domination attained by the Greek cities (Athens, Corinth, Rhodes, and Orchomenus), quite contrary to that of the Romans, symbolized the solid and beneficial foundation of prosperity.[38] Greece treated other peoples as subjects but did so without subjugating them. Its settler colonies were organized not for destruction but for conservation and prosperity, in keeping with the true spirit of conquest. Whereas the Romans established inequality between citizens and vanquished, resorting to tyranny and pillage, the Greeks carried the independent spirit characteristic of republican government to Italy, Spain, Asia Minor, and Gaul; "these Greek settlements brought with them a spirit of freedom which they had acquired in their own delightful country."[39]

---

[35] Jean François Melon, "Essai politique sur le commerce," in Eugène Daire, ed., *Economistes et financiers du XVIIIᵉ siècle* (Geneva: Slatkine Reprints, 1971), ch. IV, 677–678.

[36] SL XXI:21.

[37] Père Huet, *Histoire du commerce et de la navigation des anciens* (Paris: Fournier, 1716), the work was written at an earlier date. See C. Larrère, "L'histoire du commerce dans *L'Esprit des lois*," in Michel Porret and Catherine Volpilhac-Auger, eds., *Le Temps de Montesquieu* (Geneva: Droz, 2002), 319–336; and Céline Spector, *Montesquieu et l'émergence de l'économie politique* (Paris: Honoré Champion, 2006), ch. 8.

[38] SL XXI:7, also X:3, XXI:12. See the *Considerations on the Romans*, ch. VI.

[39] PL, Letter 131, 235. Adam Smith takes the distinction further in Edwin Cannan, ed., *The Wealth of Nations* (Chicago: University of Chicago Press, 1976), Book Four, ch. 7 and 8.

The English paradigm, which went outside the original typology of regimes, therefore needed to be reappraised.[40] In the *Persian Letters*, Montesquieu describes England as "mistress of the seas (a thing without precedent), combining trade with empire."[41] Like Athens, Carthage, and Holland, England embodies the maritime figure of empire, destined for commerce, not domination:

> If this nation inhabited an island, it would not be a conquering nation, because overseas conquests would weaken it. It would be even less a conqueror if the terrain of this island were good, because it would not need war to enrich it. . . . This nation, made comfortable by peace and liberty, would be inclined to become commercial. If it had some one of the primary commodities used to make things that owe their high price to the hand of the worker, it could set up establishments apt to procure for itself the full enjoyment of this gift of heaven.[42]

Athens, enamored of glory, did not take things very far in terms of trade; it was "more attentive to extending its maritime empire than to using it."[43] However, England knew how to create a productive and cooperative community that led to prosperity and freedom. Should we see in this an embodiment of *le doux commerce*? Montesquieu certainly cannot be accused of naïve irenicism: England practices sea warfare and has the natural pride of those who possess a maritime empire. Driven by commercial jealousies, the British believe that, while their power is limited internally, it is externally "as boundless as the ocean."

> The dominant nation, inhabiting a big island and being in possession of a great commerce, would have all sorts of facilities for forces upon the seas; and as the preservation of its liberty would require it to have neither strongholds, nor fortresses, nor land armies, it would need an army on the sea to protect itself from invasions; and its navy would be superior to that of all other powers, which,

---

[40] That England is a "nation where the republic hides under the form of monarchy" is a later formulation (SL V:19).

[41] PL, Letter 136, 242. On the question of whether the England described by Montesquieu is an example of his favored "trading imperialism," see the debate between J. Shklar (who thinks it is) and S. Mason: Judith Shklar, *Montesquieu* (Oxford: Oxford University Press, 1987), 65–66; and Sheila Mason, "Montesquieu, Europe and the Imperatives of Commerce," *Journal for Eighteenth Century Studies* 17 (1994), 65–72.

[42] SL XIX:27. Concerning the *Constitution of Athens*, Montesquieu comments: "You might say that Xenophon intended to speak of England" (SL XXI:7). According to Bernard Manin, the concept of the sea empire comes from a work titled *The Constitution of Athens*, which is not by Xenophon (as was believed in the eighteenth century) but by an author now known as pseudo-Xenophon, "Montesquieu, la république et le commerce," *Archives européennes de sociologie* XLII (2001), 573–602.

[43] SL XXI:7. In these lines, Manin also hears an echo of Thucydides and his *History of the Peloponnesian War*.

needing to employ their finances for a land war, would no longer have enough for a sea war. A naval empire has always given the peoples who have possessed it a natural pride, because, feeling themselves able to insult others everywhere, they believe that their power is as boundless as the ocean.[44]

Far from abandoning empire, England aims to expand its power together with its liberty. In the case of the United States, the mother country communicates its political regime to its distant colonies: "as one likes to establish elsewhere what is established at home, it could give the form of its own government to the people of its colonies; and as this government would carry prosperity with it, one would see the formation of great peoples, even in the forests to which it had sent inhabitants."[45] This judgment, on which Montesquieu himself casts doubt, will be challenged in later years, insofar as commercial rivalries among European nations turned into armed confrontation.[46]

Commerce, Honor, and Empire in Tocqueville's Work

To what extent did Tocqueville inherit this conception of the benefits of maritime trading empires? To what extent did he break with the distinction between spirit of conquest and spirit of commerce that Benjamin Constant, for one, took over from *The Spirit of the Laws*?[47]

Liberty and Empire

As his work and political career progressed, Tocqueville gradually distanced himself from Montesquieu's critique of territorial empire.[48] In a page in the first volume of *Democracy in America* in which Montesquieu's

---

[44] SL XIX:27.

[45] SL XIX:27.

[46] Marco Platania, "Dynamiques des empires et dynamiques du commerce: inflexions de la pensée de Montesquieu (1734–1802)," *Revue Montesquieu* 8 (2005–2006), 43–66. The relationship of friendship can degenerate into hatred and a struggle for independence, as Montesquieu prophesied for the English colonies in America. See his "Notes on England" (http://ouclf.iuscomp.org/articles/montesquieu.shtml#notesone): "I don't know what will be the result of sending so many of Europe's and Africa's inhabitants to the West Indies, but I think that, if any nation is abandoned by its colonies, that will begin with the English." On the concept of commercial jealousy, see Istvan Hont, *Jealousy of Trade* (Cambridge: Harvard University Press, 2005).

[47] Benjamin Constant, "The Spirit of Conquest and Usurpation," in Biancamaria Fontana, ed., *Political Writings* (Cambridge: Cambridge University Press, 1988), Part One, ch. 2, 52–54.

[48] On the chronology of this distancing process, see Melvin Richter, "Tocqueville on Algeria," *Review of Politics* 25 (1963), 362–398.

inspiration is especially strong, Tocqueville praised the advantages of small republics, the "cradles of political freedom," in which there is no reason for self-glory. And he lucidly observed: "It has happened that most of them have lost that freedom by becoming larger."[49] The passions that are fatal to a republic increase with the size of its territory: "It is therefore permissible to say in a general manner that nothing is so contrary to the general well-being and freedom of men as great empires."[50] Following the example of Montesquieu and the Federalists (Hamilton, Madison), Tocqueville advocates the federal model on the grounds that it combined the advantages of large and small states.[51]

The famous chapter on the "Three Races that Live on the Territory of the United States" offers another glimpse of Montesquieu's legacy. On the one hand, Tocqueville seems more convinced than his predecessor that it is impossible to civilize a people by conquest: indeed, barbarian peoples rise to civilization or absorb enlightenment from other nations only when they dominate them militarily.[52] On the other, the author of *Democracy in America* blurs the distinction between colonies of conquest and colonies of commerce: North American Indians cannot integrate with dignity into the colonizing nation, not even commercially, because the relationship of material and intellectual forces is unfavorable to them. The effects of "competition" are "fatal," driving them into poverty and servitude.[53] Aware, like Montesquieu, of the tyranny of government and the greed of the settlers, Tocqueville further denounces the imposition of free institutions on the Amerindians without their consent, which impels them toward savagery, not civilization.[54] In contrast to *The Spirit of the Laws*, the first volume of *Democracy in America* no longer uses Spanish-style colonization simply as a negative foil to the more refined colonization stemming from free republican institutions. On the contrary, Tocqueville suggests that the Indian population in Latin America, which escaped massacre, "in the end mixes with those who have defeated it and adopts their religion and mores," whereas the legalism of the

[49] DIA I.1.viii, 150.
[50] DIA I.1.viii, 151.
[51] DIA I.1.viii, 152; cf. SL IX:1.
[52] DIA I.2.x, 316–317. Montesquieu had a favorable view of the Jesuit reductions in Paraguay (SL IV:6).
[53] DIA I.2.x, 318–319.
[54] DIA I.2.x, 318, 322–324.

North Americans led to a still more pernicious policy of deportation and extinction:

The Spanish, with the help of unexampled monstrous deeds, covering themselves with an indelible shame, could not succeed in exterminating the Indian race, nor even prevent it from sharing their rights; the Americans of the United States have attained this double result with marvellous facility – tranquilly, legally, philanthropically, without spilling blood, without violating a single one of the great principles of morality in the eyes of the world. One cannot destroy men while being more respectful of the laws of humanity.[55]

Once he became a politician, however, Tocqueville went back on this outright condemnation of colonization and "race war."[56] With India no longer just a trading post but a territorial conquest, he drew all the consequences implied for the rivalry between England and France. However, Algeria gave him the opportunity for a defense of empire. Unless one colonizes a country, one's domination will always be unproductive and precarious: "It has often been said that the French should limit themselves to dominating Algeria without trying to colonize it, and some people still think so. Studying the question has given me an entirely contrary position."[57] The distance from Montesquieu is evident here: Book XXI, chapter 8, of *The Spirit of the Laws* answered negatively to the question: "must one conquer a country in order to trade with it?"[58] Tocqueville in turn answers positively to the question: Must a country be conquered in order to dominate it? Neglecting the modern theory of prudence that he had developed as a philosopher, the politician now argues that military victory is the prerequisite for economic domination and, above all, political power.

Of course, one should not minimize the hesitations that some pernicious effects of colonization aroused in Tocqueville. After a moment of enthusiasm for the idea of cultural fusion between colonizers and colonized, his first trip to Algeria, in 1841, made him aware of the insurmountable obstacles to the harmonious blending of peoples. The danger was not only that military high-handedness and administrative despotism would feed the settlers' hatred. The conquered seminomadic, tribal people would never become reconciled to colonial domination, which would

[55] DIA I.2.x, 325.
[56] See Nestor Capdevila, *Tocqueville et les frontières de la démocratie* (Paris: P.U.F., 2007).
[57] "Essay on Algeria (October 1841)," WES, 61.
[58] SL XXI:8, 365.

tend to kindle a sense of national unity that had not previously existed.[59] No government, however just or well meaning, can immediately unite peoples so different in their history, religion, laws, and practices. For all that, Tocqueville does end up justifying what his chapter on the three races tended to exclude: the need to use "all means to ruin the tribes," including trading ban; pillaging and crop destruction; military raids; and seizure of old people, women, and children. Although he disapproves of gratuitous violence, the politician is concerned to quiet the shouts heard in France against such practices. He even invokes an ad hoc "right of war," which Montesquieu, following Locke, vigorously dismissed.[60]

The Softening of Mores: A New Curse?

One reason for his parting ways with Montesquieu is doubtless Tocqueville's unease over the mediocrity of democratic passions. In *Democracy in America*, he deflects Montesquieu's reflections on *le doux commerce* – that is, the beneficial effects of trade for peace and liberty.[61] In a chapter in the second volume titled "Why Great Revolutions Will Become Rare," he points out that commerce leads to greater liberty and keeps revolutions at a distance:

I know of nothing more opposed to revolutionary mores than commercial mores. Commerce is naturally the enemy of all violent passions. It likes even tempers, is pleased by compromise, very carefully flees anger. It is patient, supple, insinuating, and has recourse to extreme means only when absolute necessity obliges it. Commerce renders men independent of one another; it gives them a high idea of their individual worth; it brings them to want to handle their own affairs and teaches them to succeed at them; it therefore disposes them to freedom but moves them away from revolutions.[62]

Could commerce replace honor in giving people a high idea of their worth and preserving their liberty against the threat of despotism? Montesquieu had held that trade and finance, being independent of their international circuits, could contribute to political liberty.[63] While considering the rule-abiding and fanciful realm of honor to be incompatible with the

---

[59] See Ewa Atanassow's essay in this volume.

[60] WES, 70.

[61] See Albert. O. Hirschman, *The Passions and the Interests* (Princeton: Princeton University Press, 1977); C. Spector, *Montesquieu et l'émergence de l'économie politique*, ch. 4.

[62] DIA II.3.xxi, 609.

[63] "What makes traders more independent is the fact that sovereigns are less able to get their hands on their goods," *Pensées*, No. 776. See C. Spector, *Montesquieu et l'émergence de l'économie politique*, ch. 4 and 5.

conditions that underpin despotism, in *The Spirit of the Laws* he places the main emphasis on the realm of commerce: "Commerce, sometimes destroyed by conquerors, sometimes hampered by monarchs, wanders across the earth, flees from where it is oppressed, and remains where it is left to breathe: it reigns today where one used to see only deserted places, seas, and rocks; there where it used to reign are now only deserted places."[64] Thanks to the deterritorialization of wealth and the mobility of credit, the violent acts of princes (persecution, confiscation) are now condemned to impotence.[65]

Noting the decline of honor in democratic societies, Tocqueville faces up to a new political fact: the real danger is no longer princely power but revolution and popular revolt. And from this point of view, the growing importance of movable property is a factor weighing against revolutionary violence.[66] In this particular set of circumstances, the movable property that Montesquieu saw as a guarantee against despotism becomes its trump card because this form of property makes it possible for the state to appropriate and control private wealth. At the moment when the Industrial Revolution is taking off, the ever-expanding "industrial class," which is gaining the upper hand over the merchant class, "carries despotism within its ranks, and that despotism naturally spreads as the class grows."[67]

Tocqueville, then, takes Montesquieu's analysis in a new direction: on the one hand, he too asserts that commercial institutions produce a real taste for liberty; on the other, he draws out the consequences of the Industrial Revolution and the redefinition of democratic despotism.[68] As to the new physiognomy of servitude, associated not with violence and cruelty but with the weakness of political passions and the softening of mores, there is a move away from the vision of *The Spirit of the Laws*: a softening of mores is not only the trump card of modernity, but it is also a risk against which the democratic centuries have to be on their guard. The evolution of mores dictates a profound shift. Montesquieu saw only the beginnings of a tendency in which the heroic love of glory gives way to

---

[64] SL XXI:5, 356 and III:5.
[65] SL XXI:20, XXII:13.
[66] DIA II.3.xxi, 609.
[67] DIA II.4.v, 656–657.
[68] Alexis de Tocqueville, *Sur la démocratie en Amérique, Fragments inédits* (Paris: Crété, 1959), 8. "Commercial institutions produce not only skill in making use of liberty, but also a real taste for it. Without commerce, such a taste for political liberty amount to no more than childish desires or youthful fears."

the lure of gain, ostentation to utility, and prestige to profit.[69] Tocqueville, faced with the continuing decline of honor and civic associations, fears that the enslaving love of well-being will tame heroic political passions.[70]

Tocqueville's different vision of modernity opens the way for the restoration of greatness by means of empire. It is expressed in a disagreement with his friend and correspondent, John Stuart Mill, in March 1841:

> I do not have to tell you, my dear Mill, that the greatest malady that threatens a people organized as we are is the gradual softening of mores, the abasement of the mind, the mediocrity of tastes (. . .) one cannot let this nation take up easily the habit of sacrificing what it believes to be its grandeur to its repose, great matters to petty ones; it is not healthy to allow such a nation to believe that its place in the world is smaller, that it is fallen from the level on which its ancestors had put it, but that it must console itself by building railroads and by making the well-being of each private individual prosper amidst peace, under whatever condition the peace is obtained. It is necessary that those who march at the head of such a nation would always keep a proud attitude, if they do not wish to allow the level of national mores to fall very low.[71]

A Resurgence of Honor?

Beyond any factors related to the immediate situation, Tocqueville's ambivalence toward Montesquieu's legacy could be understood as follows. Faced with the fait accompli of French colonization following a long period of Ottoman rule, the politician thought he saw an opportunity for France to regain its glorious reputation. Whereas his speech supporting the abolition of slavery presented this as a question of honor for democratic France as the bearer of human rights, his letters and speeches on Algeria adopt a different tone.[72] Beginning in 1841, he is

---

[69] "It is the commercial spirit that prevails today" (*Pensées*, No. 810); "what used to be called *glory, laurels, trophies, triumphs, crowns*, is today ready cash" (*Pensées*, No. 1602). See also *Pensées*, Nos. 575, 760, and 761.

[70] DIA II.3.xviii. Tocqueville, *The Ancien Regime* (London: J. M. Dent, 1988), ch. 20, 168.

[71] Letter of March 18, 1841, SLPS, 151; translation modified by Jennifer Pitts, *A Turn to Empire: The Rise of Imperial Liberalism in Britain and France* (Princeton: Princeton University Press, 2006), 195. According to Pitts "Mill responded to Tocqueville's confidence with a scolding. He agreed reluctantly "that the feeling of orgueil national is the only feeling of a public-spirited and elevating kind which remains and that it ought not therefore be permitted to go down." But French politicians – and Mill did not exclude Tocqueville – had offered the French public only "low and grovelling" ideas of what "constitutes national glory and national importance"; they had "sacrificed good government and solid achievement for boisterous self-importance."

[72] Intervention in the debate on the law governing slaves in the colonies, May 30, 1845, OC 3:1, 124.

mainly concerned with a strategic, even tactical, question: how to prevail militarily at the least cost and how to administer in the most effective (that is, decentralized) manner. In line with Marshal Bugeaud or General Lamorcière, he approved of the war to defeat Abd-el-Kader and Arab "fanaticism" while at the same time attaching importance to the settlement of French civilians in the newly conquered colony.[73] However, he began to develop a justification beyond immediate interest, arguing that France's honor was at stake in the rivalry with Britain.

How should we interpret this appeal to honor? Again, the distance from *Democracy in America* (which nevertheless was published around the same time) needs to be emphasized. In the second volume, the lesson Tocqueville drew from Montesquieu was transposed to the new context that he saw as inevitably transforming honor in the democratic centuries.[74] Inspired by Saint-Lambert's article "Honneur" in the *Encyclopédie*, by notes from Tocqueville père and by private conversations with Kergolay, the famous chapter on honor is impregnated with the analyses of *The Spirit of the Laws*.[75] However, feudal honor, which he considers to have been "extraordinary," is now explained in terms of the very special needs of an aristocratic caste. Democratic societies cannot but renounce the ethos of distinction and promote a morality of likeness and resemblance. The rules for the allocation of praise and blame are no longer bizarrely particular, subject to peer assessment of one's reputation, but are internalized and generalized; the disappearance of nations

---

[73] Richter, "The Uses of Theory," 377. Richter mentions Tocqueville's silence in 1846 when it was discovered that hundreds of Arabs had been smoked to death during raids that he had described as humane – a policy that Lamartine, for instance, fervently opposed (389–390).

[74] Here I would disagree with Paul Rahe, who argues that Montesquieu had predicted the decline of the "ridiculous" prejudice of honor in the age of Enlightenment, and that Tocqueville was merely following him on this point (*Soft Despotism*, 170).

[75] In January 1838, during a four-day visit to Baugy, Louis de Kergolay probably helped Tocqueville in the drafting of this chapter. On January 18, Tocqueville wrote to Gustave de Beaumont: "Louis has just spent four days here; I was *bricked up* in a system of ideas and unable to break free. It was a real intellectual cul de sac, which he got me out of in just a few hours," OC 8:1, 279. Tocqueville had previously asked his father to consult the librarian at the Institut Royal de France for information about the feudal code of honor. However, M. Feuillet had done no more than refer him to the relevant article in the *Encyclopédie* and to Books III, IV and XXVIII of *The Spirit of the Laws*. Hervé de Tocqueville then compiled some notes of his own and sent them to his son on January 17, 1838 (OP, 1150–1153). This thoughtful chapter on honor should not be underestimated. In his "Discours de rentrée des tribunaux sur le duel," which he delivered in November 1828 before the judges at the Versailles law courts, Tocqueville had argued that "a state perishes if it [honour] does not reign where virtue is no longer," OC 16, 63. The speech should be read in its entirety.

will lead to the disappearance of national honor itself. The particularist ethic of the aristocratic centuries is being supplanted by a universalistic morality of conscience.[76]

In his writings on Algeria, however, Tocqueville is a long way from looking beyond the nation-state and endorsing the peaceful industrial future of honor, as he did in the second volume of *Democracy in America*.[77] The Algerian question is now an opportunity to impart new vigor to the national honor.[78] From 1837 on, honor helps to justify the direct domination of civilian populations: "Independent of the tribes over whom it is in our interest to attempt to exercise no more than an indirect influence at present, there is a considerable enough part of the country that our security as much as our honour obliges us to keep under our immediate power and to govern without intermediaries."[79] As reporter of the parliamentary commission on Algeria, Tocqueville preferred to argue in terms of honor rather than financial, agricultural, or commercial interest (acquiring the treasury of the Dey of Algiers, fertile lands and manufacturing markets, control over the Mediterranean). He scarcely ever used the much-heard rhetoric about France's "civilizing mission" to free the Christian slaves and oppressed peoples of the Ottoman Empire, to dispel fanaticism and spread enlightenment.[80] For Tocqueville, the cardinal issue is that France must preserve its great power status on the international stage: "I do not think France can think seriously of leaving Algeria. In the eyes of the world, such an abandonment would be the clear indication of our decline. It would be far less disturbing to see our conquest taken from us by a rival nation."[81] In the aftermath of the

[76] DIA II.3.xviii, 597–599.

[77] DIA II.3.x–xii.

[78] As Pitts writes, "Tocqueville turned to the conquest of Algeria as a facet of his political efforts to generate in France the national pride and public virtue he believed the nation required," *A Turn to Empire*, 196. Some rejoice in the newly virile politics outlined by Tocqueville, Harvey C. Mansfield and Delba Winthrop, "Tocqueville's New Political Science," in Cheryl B. Welch, ed., *The Cambridge Companion to Tocqueville* (Cambridge: Cambridge University Press, 2006), 81–107.

[79] "Second Letter on Algeria," WES, 23.

[80] These two arguments are already found in abbé Raynal's *Histoire philosophique et politique des établissements et du commerce des Européens dans les Deux Indes* (Paris, 1770), vol. IV, 113–116. See Ann Thomson, "Arguments for the Conquest in the Late Eighteenth and Early Nineteenth Centuries," *The Maghreb Review* 14 (1989), 108–118.

[81] "Essay on Algeria," WES, 59. On this, see Cheryl Welch, "Colonial Violence and the Rhetoric of Evasion: Tocqueville on Algeria," *Political Theory* 31 (2003), 235–254; and Richard Boyd, "Imperial Fathers and Favorite Sons. J. S. Mill, Alexis de Tocqueville, and Nineteenth Century Visions of Empire," in J. Locke and E. Hunt Botting, eds., *Feminist Interpretations of Alexis de Tocqueville* (University Park: Pennsylvania State University Press, 1992), 225–252.

Anglo-French crisis of 1840, he was hostile to Guizot's policy of appeasement overseas:

If France shrank from such an enterprise in which she found nothing but the natural difficulties of the terrain and the opposition of little barbarous tribes, she would seem in the eyes of the world to be yielding to her own impotence and succumbing to her own lack of courage. Any people that easily gives up what it has taken and chooses to retire peacefully to its original borders proclaims that its age of greatness is over. It visibly enters the period of its decline. If France ever abandons Algeria, it is clear that she could do it only at a moment when she is seen to be doing great things in Europe, and not at a time such as our own, when she appears to be falling to the second rank and seems resigned to let the control of European affairs pass into other hands.[82]

Not only would this invite France's rivals to step in and take over, but the loss of Algiers would be damaging to the nation's honor: "Our action in the world will be suspended, and it is as though the arms of France were paralysed – a state of affairs that we must quickly bring to an end, for our security as much as for our honour."[83] Tocqueville's attitude not only differs from that of a left critic of the colonial adventure in Algeria, who would see honor being manipulated by those with an economic interest in the conquest.[84] It also diverges from the principles of another great liberal inheritor of Montesquieu: Benjamin Constant, who was much more suspicious of the illusions of grandeur and honor present in colonial policy.[85]

Without being justified, Tocqueville's turn on the question of empire is understandable in light of his role as a politician directly embroiled in the tragedies of history. Montesquieu considered that territorial conquest threatened to lead to the worst genocide and, ultimately, to the decline of the conquering nation; he criticized France's expansionist urges and held up Britain as an example of modern commercial colonization, more refined than that of countries which imitated the Roman model. Faced with a shift in Britain's colonial policy, Tocqueville too sought to take it

[82] "Essay on Algeria," WES, 59.
[83] "Essay on Algeria," WES, 61.
[84] On the opposition of Amédée Desjobert, see Pitts, *A Turn to Empire*, 185–189.
[85] Constant died in December 1830, shortly after the conquest of Algeria. We therefore have only one text by him on the question: "Alger et les élections" (*Le Temps*, June 20, 1930), in which he describes it as a matter of honor between the Dey of Algiers and Charles X but remains alert to the dangers of political manipulation and increased oppression, Pitts, *A Turn to Empire*, 184.

as his principal model while remaining as aware as his predecessor of the peculiarities of the French national character – more capable of dazzling feats than of lasting conquests.[86] However, the British model was now carrying all before it, as we can see from Tocqueville's preparatory work on the colonization of India: "India. A great position, from which England dominates all Asia. A glory which revives the entire English nation. What a sense of grandeur and power this possession creates in every part of that people! The value of a conquest ought not to be calculated only in terms of financial and commercial considerations."[87] In relation to colonization more than in internal affairs, Tocqueville's aristocratic liberalism only sorrowfully accepted the individualism and honest materialism of the democratic centuries.

The difference between Tocqueville and Montesquieu is therefore not only because of the change in historical circumstances. It also has to do with Tocqueville's loyalty to certain aristocratic values, even as he defended the new spirit of democracy. This loyalty, which is also a loyalty to Montesquieu, sometimes sets Tocqueville at odds with himself. Can one preserve a form of honor in a society that has replaced honor with clear-sighted self-interest as the dominant passion? Nothing is less evident. Compare, for example, a letter to Corcelle from 1840, in which Tocqueville excludes any option other than abandonment or complete domination, with one written to the same correspondent six years later: "How can we manage to create in Africa a French population with our laws, our mores, our civilization, while still preserving vis-à-vis the indigenous people all the considerations that justice, humanity, our interest well understood, and, as you have said, our honour strictly oblige us to preserve?"[88] Honor has changed sides: its weak prescriptions can no longer guide our conduct.

[86] *The Ancien Regime*, 168–169; cf. SL IX:7.
[87] OC 3:1, 478; Jean Alphonse Bernard, *Tocqueville in India* (Paris: Les Éditions d'en face, 2006). Tocqueville also now sought to derive inspiration from the American model of colonization, Letter to Lieber, July 22, 1846, OC 7, 111.
[88] Letter to Corcelle, October 11, 1846, OC 15:1, 219.

PART FOUR

DEMOCRACY, IMPERIALISM, AND FOREIGN POLICY

CHAPTER 10

The Surprising M. Tocqueville: Necessity, Foreign Policy, and Civic Virtue

David Clinton

> Antecedent facts, the nature of institutions, the cast of minds and the state
> of morals are the materials of which are composed those impromptus which
> astonish and alarm us.
>
> – Alexis de Tocqueville[1]

To anyone wishing to explore the perennial debate over the issue of whether the United States can more effectively promote the cause of liberty around the world by conducting itself as the exemplar of liberty at home or by exerting itself as the vindicator of liberty abroad, an examination of the practical steps to advance liberty is as inescapable a starting point as is an understanding of the theoretical underpinnings of liberty. No one has expounded on the interplay between theory and practice more fully and more lucidly than Alexis de Tocqueville. Reflecting on his North American travels in 1830 and on the mass of documentation that he gathered on American thinking and political practice and on his observation of the fate of liberty in France and elsewhere in Europe, he made himself perhaps the greatest advocate of freedom and the most acute analyst of threats to freedom that the modern world has seen. Yet in his identification of the public policies best calculated to preserve freedom by encouraging the habits of mind that would support freedom, he returns to the realm of necessity. The circumstances in which a people live, it seems, significantly constrain the means by which it can maintain its liberty and the degree to which it can promote the liberty of others;

---

[1] *Recollections*, trans. Alexander Teixeira de Mattos, ed., J. P. Mayer (London: The Harvill Press, 1948), 68.

the choice between the roles of exemplar and vindicator is narrowed by given conditions over which that people and its leaders have little control.

The great advocate for human beings' control over their own destiny and the great scourge of all varieties of determinism, Tocqueville contends that the truths of liberty are valid at all times and places. Yet the givens of human existence, and in particular the changing realities of international politics, are facts to which he advises submission. That we have inadequately appreciated the variety of counsel that Tocqueville gives to leaders facing differing but equally unchallengeable circumstances has perhaps been a result of our neglect of Tocqueville the political actor in France as opposed to Tocqueville the author of *Democracy in America*. There is more than one Tocquevillean path to liberty, and some of the alternate routes lead over unexpected terrain. Let us unfold the complete map.

America as Exemplar

In *Democracy in America*, Tocqueville ranges far and wide over a host of aspects of society and refers to an immense variety of specific illustrations, but the work rests on a single fundamental problem: that of preserving human freedom in an age of increasing equality. Far from comfortably assuming that equality and liberty are naturally intertwined and mutually reinforcing, he finds many dangers to the preservation and advancement of liberty that are peculiarly potent in an era in which impatience with all distinctions leads to a willingness to submit to any power, and any restriction on freedom, that can erase those differences. In addition to demonstrating America's success in combining liberty with equality, he also wishes to warn his European readers of the difficulty of the task.

In Volume One of *Democracy*, Tocqueville discusses the causes that affect the chances of success of any country wishing to engage in such a delicate balancing act, and in the penultimate chapter of that volume he summarizes and characterizes these causes as circumstances, laws, and mores.[2] The first of these sets of influences, which he also terms "accidental or providential," are by definition the least subject to human control, but they are not for that reason the most powerful; instead, he ranks them least in determinative influence. All of these circumstances favorable to liberty – the fact that "the Americans have no neighbors and consequently no great wars"; the fact that "America does not have a great

---

[2] DIA I.2.ix, 264–265.

capital" that could exercise the sort of malignant centralized control that Paris held over France; the fact that the earliest settlers of British North America brought with them already formed habits of liberty, intelligence, and equality of conditions; the fact that they found waiting for them a vast, rich, and "empty country" are "independent of men's will" – indeed, they are a result of "Providence." They mean that Americans were highly fortunate in their starting point in the quest for liberty in equality; however, Tocqueville contends that other peoples (the countries of South America being his most pointed example) share many of these advantages (in particular, geographic isolation and extensive natural resources) but have not managed to preserve ordered liberty. Circumstances, then, are immensely important, but they cannot be considered definitive.

Laws, the second category of causes, are among the most amenable to conscious human direction and the least subject to chance, fortune, or fate. "The principal goal of this book was to make the laws of the United States known," Tocqueville asserts to his readers, and among these laws freely chosen by the Americans, three in particular seem "to concur more than all others to maintain a democratic republic in the New World." These include federalism, "which permits the Union to enjoy the power of a great republic and the security of a small one"; township, particularly evident in New England, which, "moderating the despotism of the majority, at the same time give[s] the people the taste for freedom and the art of being free"; and judicial review, which allows the courts "to correct the aberrations of democracy."[3] Such laws, codified in the federal Constitution in the case of federalism, implied in the Constitution and soon asserted by the Supreme Court in the case of judicial review, and evolved by relatively recent practice by the citizens of the New England states in the case of township government – the clearest example of freedom exercised in human affairs – nicely complement the unchangeable circumstances that most powerfully represent the role of necessity. Federalism allows the United States to reap the greatest benefit from its sheltered geographic position and its vast extent, and local government and judicial review buttress the more general traditions of sturdy self-government and willingness to defend one's rights that Americans inherited from "the first Puritan who landed on [American] shores."[4]

Nevertheless, the most significant of the three causes of the American success in preserving liberty lies neither in circumstances nor in laws,

---

[3] DIA I.2.ix, 274, 275.
[4] DIA I.2.ix, 267.

neither in unadulterated freedom nor in iron necessity, but in the intermediate category of mores. Tocqueville's use of the term *mores* is not
free from ambiguity – not least because the French moeurs has no exact
equivalent in English – despite his effort to explain it:

> Not only do I apply it to mores properly so-called, which one could call habits of
> the heart, but to the different notions that men possess, to the various opinions
> that are current in their midst, and to the sum of ideas of which the habits of the
> mind are formed. I therefore comprehend under this word the whole moral and
> intellectual state of a people.[5]

Mores take advantage of the possibilities opened by favorable circumstances and allow peoples to realize those possibilities; mores form the
soil in which laws grow, nourishing those favorable to freedom while
forming but rocky ground for statutes with a contrary aim. The success
of the United States in escaping the ill effects of equality and in preserving liberty even as equality has progressed further there than anywhere
else, has something to do with favored circumstances and beneficial laws
but most to do with the ideas and beliefs commonly accepted among
the people. Those ideas and beliefs predispose citizens to be vigilant in
guarding their rights and active in shaping their destiny while peaceably
accepting the authority of law. As such, they constitute the strongest bulwark of liberty. In the United States, Tocqueville sees more of these mores
than in Europe – in particular, administrative decentralization, the art of
associating together to achieve shared ends rather than simply turning
to government to do whatever needs doing, self-interest rightly understood – that is, a grasp of the truth that one's greatest self-interest lies
not in purely private gain but in the public sphere, in preserving the free
society in which one can pursue private goals – and a well-considered
patriotism, which, in contrast to instinctive patriotism, loves one's country not simply because it holds the familiar scenes in which one grew up
but because one helped to make the laws that governed it, making those
laws one's own as well. Together, such mores would guard the United
States against the erosion of liberty and the erection of soft despotism, at
least for the foreseeable future.

When Tocqueville asks himself what contributes most to "serv[ing] to
maintain a democratic republic in the United States" – that is, to combining equality with liberty and liberty with order – he accuses his fellow
Europeans of exaggerating the effect of both circumstance (the realm
of necessity) and laws (the realm most open to conscious control and

5 DIA I.2.ix, 275.

regular adjustment) and points to the middle ground of mores. Not only
do "physical causes contribute less than laws, and laws less than mores,"
but mores can even outweigh the other two factors: "I am convinced that
the happiest situation and the best laws cannot maintain a constitution
despite mores, whereas the latter turn even the most unfavorable positions and the worst laws to good account."[6] He returns to this theme of
modified freedom in the conclusion of Volume Two, when he declares,
in almost the final words of the work, "Providence has not created the
human race either entirely independent or perfectly slave. It traces, it is
true, a fatal circle around each man that he cannot leave; but within its
vast limits man is powerful and free; so too with peoples."[7]

In the case of the United States that Tocqueville witnessed when he visited North America, the relative influence of these three causes is perhaps
less of a concern than in other countries because for the Americans all
three point in the same direction. Fortunate in their circumstances, they
are also favored in their mores, which lie behind their generally beneficent laws. Sheltered geographical circumstances create no necessity for
Americans to concern themselves with the outside world. Laws favorable
to freedom domestically, such as a high degree of political decentralization under the U.S. form of federalism, make the country little suited to
an adventurous, interfering foreign policy. The mores that reinforce the
lucky inheritance of circumstance and undergird the laws will be maintained by actions and attitudes that Americans adopt among themselves –
by inculcating the doctrine of self-interest rightly understood, or continuing to practice the art of associating together, for example.[8] The role of
the United States is to serve as a textbook, from which educators such as
Tocqueville will draw their lessons for others; in that way, the practices of
ordered liberty will be spread with the greatest chance of success and not
through the exercise of the military, diplomatic, or commercial might of
the American state. Americans are free, and their freedom extends to the
leeway they enjoy to stand aside from the main currents of international
politics while they cultivate their own garden.

France as Vindicator

Such is the more familiar tale, and the more familiar Tocquevillean lesson
drawn from it. Yet neither Tocqueville's consideration of the dilemmas

[6] DIA I.2.ix, 295.
[7] DIA II.4.viii, 676.
[8] See William Donohue, "Tocqueville's Reflections on Safeguarding Freedom in a Democracy," *Tocqueville Review* 6 (1984), 389–399.

posed by the preservation of liberty in equality nor his own active involvement in the political struggles of his day ceased with the appearance of
Volume One of *Democracy in America* in 1835. Volume Two was not
published until 1840, and even more clearly than Volume One, it wrestles with the general issue of the future of liberty in societies marked by
equality, not simply the manner in which that issue manifests itself in the
United States. It has to do so because Tocqueville recognizes as well as
any of his critics that although the fundamental problem is a universal
one, the prescription for meeting it necessarily has to be tailored to each
people; in particular, he is, as has long been noted, "writing of America
and thinking of France."[9] Moreover, in the interval between the publication of Volumes One and Two, he had won election to the Chamber of
Deputies, where he would serve to the end of the Orleans Monarchy in
1848. The experience of practical politics made him even more conscious
of the difference in circumstances between his own country and the land
he had visited.

There were two major differences between France and the United
States – one established by history and the other imposed by geography –
and both therefore examples of necessity, providence, or circumstances.
In the case of the first, liberty had been established among the people
Tocqueville called the Anglo-Americans long before the taste for equality
had reached its present power. The English colonists – the Puritan of
Tocqueville's conception – had brought their ancient rights with them
to the New World; their descendants, the Americans, therefore greeted
the advent of equality with a set of mores that made them determined
to protect these familiar liberties. In France, on the other hand, equality
had been expanding for centuries before the idea of liberty gained ground
in the early, moderate stages of the French Revolution – as Tocqueville
was to argue more fully in *The Old Regime and the Revolution*.[10] It had
been an equality in servitude rather than an equality in liberty, and it had
bequeathed to the French a set of moral and intellectual attitudes little

---

[9] The literature on this subject is large, but a useful early example is Cushing Strout,
"Tocqueville's Duality: Describing America and Thinking of Europe," *American Quarterly* 21 (1969), 87–99.
[10] See OR I, especially Book Two. Volume Two of this work, had Tocqueville lived to
complete it, was to carry forward the demonstration of the consequences of the appearance of equality before liberty, in its argument that the sequence in which the two ideas
appeared in the France of the ancien regime prepared the way for the equality in servitude that the French experienced under the Napoleonic Empire. See OR II, "Notes on
the French Revolution and Napoleon."

suited to public-spirited citizens. This was the history of a distinctive people, and it could not be simply assumed away or easily overlaid with a new set of beliefs drawn from across the Atlantic. Vast though the limits of the circle of human freedom were, those limits did exist, and French history was among them.[11]

Another limit, identified by Raymond Aron, was that imposed by one's position in the international system. "Without neighbors, thus without enemies, the American state escaped the 'tyranny' of diplomacy and war, it preserved the spirit of the pioneers and also that of the first arrivals, the puritans." By contrast, "France is surrounded by neighbors who are always rivals and may at any time become enemies. She must place above all the good of external security, thus confer on the state extensive prerogatives."[12] Aron's language of necessity is matched only by Tocqueville's own: "Our situation in Europe lays down an imperative law for us in what should be a thing of choice."[13]

Neither of these historical or geographic circumstances in France would be favorable to the expedients that Tocqueville contended had served American liberty well. He admitted that a state in the cockpit of international politics could not afford to adopt decentralization, for if it did so, it would almost certainly be defeated in any armed confrontation with a centralized state. The greater taste for equality that history had given to the French made them impatient with seeming anomalies and inconsistencies that resulted when different jurisdictions made different decisions in a federal system and indifferent to the pleas for independence by an "undemocratic" institution like the judiciary. How, then, in the face of these less favorable circumstances and in the absence of the almost naturally occurring practices of liberty that Tocqueville had witnessed in the United States, were American-like mores of civic virtue to be sustained? The empire of circumstances had reasserted itself, and the limits of the circle of human freedom were revealed.

One answer, for Tocqueville, lay in the objects of government and its means of dealing with them. He took it for granted that foreign policy and national security were fundamental subjects of government action in a threatening international environment and that war was "an accident

[11] DIA II.4.viii.

[12] Raymond Aron, "Idees politiques et vision historique de Tocqueville," *Revue Français de Science Politique* X (September 1960), 518, 520. See also Centre National de la Recherche Scientifique, *Alexis de Tocqueville: Livre du Centenaire, 1859–1959* (Paris: Centre National de la Recherche Scientifique, 1960).

[13] SLPS, letter to Eugène Stoffels, October 5, 1836, 113.

to which all people are subject, democratic peoples as well as others."[14]
Lacking the unusual, providential circumstances of the United States,
France was necessarily involved in the struggles of European politics and
therefore, in an age in which Europe was extending control over the non-
European world, global politics. Here were tasks that only statesmen
could undertake – unlike the unwise actions of soft despotism, in which
government insinuated itself into the everyday lives of its people, "protecting them against every danger, supervising their every activity," and
attempting to do for them what they could and should do for themselves,
in the arena of high politics, government was necessary to promote the
collective interests of its people – that is, their safety as a people. The
United States did not have to fear war, and there the benign art of associating together accomplished desirable social objectives while preserving
the utmost freedom for individuals. France never escaped an external setting in which "force is ... one of the conditions of happiness and even of
existence of nations," and in war "a people acts like a single individual
vis-à-vis foreign peoples"; as "it struggles for its very existence," it can
afford to accept neither the restraint of administrative decentralization
nor the free play of individual self-interest.[15]

Foreign policy was more than the promotion of the strictly material
interests of the populace, however, and it was here that one came to
the manner in which international questions were approached. For Tocqueville, the abiding and frequently unmet need of nations in a democratic
age was pride. Not to be confused with the "swashbucklers' pretensions"
that he attributed to both Thiers and Napoleon III (the use of foreign
policy to strike a pose or proffer a bluff, simply to distract the people
from their domestic difficulties, often without any mature consideration
of whether one had the means of backing up such defiance), a foreign
policy of pride or grandeur was one that pursued high-minded objectives,
not bombastically but resolutely. The desired effect was to remind the
people that they were citizens and not simply shoppers, with a duty to
take part in political life and direct these historic enterprises. In other
words, a foreign policy of greatness would shake the people out of the
narrow individualism that could otherwise lull them into devoting themselves entirely to their own material well-being and forgetting to play
the active role of citizenship that could alone protect their liberties. In a
democratic age in which the universal temptation was to concern oneself

[14] DIA II.3.xxii, 617.
[15] DIA II.3.xxi; I.1.viii, 152.

with the small, the immediate, the soft, and the selfish, a properly active international attitude bracingly confronted the citizenry with the far reaching, the long term, the rigorous, and the public spirited. Bereft of the favored circumstances of the United States, France had to pursue a glorious policy abroad if it was to maintain the mores that alone could sustain liberty at home.

The end in both cases was the same – the sustaining of civic virtue. Beyond laws and circumstances, foreign policy was the most potent means of preserving freedom in an age that, because of tendencies toward mediocrity, ease, and small mindedness, was not necessarily friendly to liberty. How these mores were to be advanced, however, was heavily influenced by the uncontrollable circumstances of history and geography, as revealed most vividly in the international setting of a people. When that setting was safely protected by favored historical legacies and a protected geographical location – as was true of few countries, but was the happy lot of the United States – the country could be a worthy exemplar of liberty by its fidelity to domestic institutions and practices that encouraged these mores while largely ignoring the outside world. When a people occupied the position of France, however, the path to civic virtue lay elsewhere – through government action in general, and action internationally in particular, that "raised their sights" and reminded them to participate in the noble task of defending the regime. Under those circumstances, the conundrum of domestic liberty or foreign advocacy of freedom was a false choice; the habits of mind that would alone be compatible with the former needed the inspiration of the latter. Only if it acted in a high-minded way abroad could France cultivate the kind of citizenship that would make it an exemplar of liberty at home.[16] Mores remained in all cases the key to preserving liberty, but circumstances dictated the way in which the proper mores were to be inculcated.

Throughout his service in the Chamber of Deputies, Tocqueville sounded this activist theme. In his November 30, 1840, speech – his second on the so-called Eastern Question – he declared that among the few ties that continued to bind Frenchmen together, "there exists one, perhaps only one, which is unbroken and strong, the pride in the name that we bear" and warned that a foreign policy that tarnished that name could so undermine support for the regime that it would collapse: "Two great paths it seems to me can carry France today toward revolutions.

[16] See Doris Goldstein, "Alexis de Tocqueville's Concept of Citizenship," *Proceedings of the American Philosophical Society* 108 (1964), 39–53.

The first of these paths, I acknowledge, would be violent, unjust, revolutionary, anarchic war.... But there is another path ... that of peace without glory."[17] Shortly thereafter, when the treaty right of British naval vessels to stop French ships on the high seas to search for slaves became highly controversial in France, Tocqueville's was among the voices most passionately calling for the government to take an unyielding line with London, and in response to criticism from his liberal friends in England, he was unapologetic, telling Mill, for example, "The most elevated feeling now left to us is national pride."[18]

The point of an active foreign policy, however, was not activity for its own sake but exertion on behalf of the kind of cause that would inspire French citizens to shake themselves free from their individualistic fascination with personal enrichment and to consider the good of the country. This aim was that of promoting liberty abroad, thus, his stinging critique of what he considered Francois Guizot's indifference to the fate of liberty elsewhere, so long as French material interests were protected:

France, if she were governed as she ought to be, would feel that her principal interest, her permanent interest, is to gain the triumph of liberal institutions across the world, not only for the love of these liberal institutions, but for the care even of her own strength and her grandeur.... The great interest of France is therefore to substitute liberal institutions for despotic institutions everywhere: that is, I dare to say, the capital interest of France.[19]

France should never abandon "its glorious role as the avant-garde of the ideas of liberty."[20]

What a foreign policy that would advance the cause of liberty meant in particular may be discerned in Tocqueville's preoccupations during the years of his service as a parliamentarian in the Orleanist regime – years that were also the period of his composition of *Democracy in America*. A foreign policy of grandeur would be very careful of its reputation for vigor as well as liberalism because "any nation that readily lets go of what it has taken and withdraws peacefully of its own accord back inside its old boundaries proclaims that the golden age of its history is past. It visibly enters the period of its decline."[21] And the humiliation of international decline would sap the spirit of self-sacrifice and civic involvement – the

---

[17] OC 3:2, 300–301, translation mine.
[18] Letter to John Stuart Mill, December 18, 1840, OC 6:1, 330–331.
[19] Speech to the Chamber, January 20, 1845, OC 3:2, 426; translation mine.
[20] Article in the journal *Le Commerce* (March 1, 1845), OC 3:2, 467; translation mine.
[21] OC 3:1, 214; translation mine.

mores that bolstered a people's willingness to defend its liberties. Reputation in turn derived from an active foreign policy, whether within Europe (Tocqueville periodically pressed for an understanding between France and Britain, the liberal great powers after 1830, as a counterweight to the absolutist Eastern powers) or beyond Europe (he alternately criticized Orleanist governments for truckling to Britain in colonial disputes, as in the controversy over Tahiti in 1844).[22]

The mention of colonialism raises the issue that, for many students and even admirers of Tocqueville, calls into question the coherence of this second, externally demanded, route to the mores of liberty – whether a foreign policy of forceful conquest could in fact nurture in the citizens of the conquering state habits of mind favorable to individual freedom.[23] Tocqueville, who had "none of the bad conscience on this matter that people of the twentieth century" and later were to have, seems sincerely enough to have believed that a liberalizing imperialism could be compatible with the advance of liberal ideas at home.[24] He criticized the civil colonial administration of Algeria for a bureaucratic ponderousness that stifled the individual initiative of French settlers and damned the military administration there for its harsh and arbitrary rule. While prepared to countenance violent displacement of Arab populations in the process of establishing French control, he declared that pointless cruelties – acts that did not advance this political objective – were unjustifiable, and he publicly condemned them. For him, conquest with all its attendant horrors was the means to a new state of affairs in which colonists, having gained a new domain for enterprise without losing the civil, political, and social liberties their compatriots enjoyed at home, lived beside the conquered population, which had lost its independence but had gained in return a better ordered justice.

There would remain two peoples, not one, and the link between them would be formed by precisely that tie that Tocqueville argued was inadequate to sustain a liberal regime within France itself – self-interest:

What we owe [the indigenous peoples of Algeria] at all times is good government. By this term we mean a power which directs them not only to achieve our interests,

[22] OC 6:1, 32, letter to Henry Reeve, May 22, 1836. See also Mary Lawlor, *Alexis de Tocqueville in the Chamber of Deputies: His Views on Foreign and Colonial Policy* (Washington, DC: The Catholic University of America Press, 1959), esp. 67–99.

[23] See Melvin Richter, "Tocqueville on Algeria," *The Review of Politics* 25 (1963), 362–398; Richard Boyd, "Tocqueville's Algeria," *Society* 38 (2001), 65–70.

[24] Andre Jardin, *Tocqueville: A Biography*, trans. Lydia Davis with Robert Hemenway (New York: Farrar Straus Giroux, 1988), 318.

but their own as well; which searches in all sincerity for means appropriate to such ends; which is concerned with their well-being and their rights; which continually works with order to develop their imperfect civilization.

> It would not be very wise to believe that we can succeed in binding the natives to us by a community of usages, but we may hope to do so by building a community of interests.... The European needs the native to increase the value of his land; the Arab needs the European to obtain a higher salary. Thus interest may bring together two men otherwise far apart.[25]

Because France confronting other European powers had to act as one people, the reliance on material interest that Tocqueville attributed to Guizot failed to sustain the political involvement necessary to both individual citizenship and national greatness. Because Algerian Arabs and French colonists would remain two peoples divided into a stationary and a progressive civilization, self-interest sufficed as a basis for their interactions. Civic spirit was not required in the latter setting so long as reliable laws, order, and efficient administration produced material benefits. Circumstances were all.

Under these conditions, what mattered were less the means – that is, "the smaller violences that are absolutely necessary" – than the end, "that *great violence* of conquest" which they were intended to achieve.[26] A liberal colonialism could not succeed without bloodshed and dispossession, but once established it could be judged by its results in bringing better government and improved material conditions to a subject people that would have endured only stagnation had it been left alone. This was the test by which he wished to assess the French enterprise among the Algerians – whether it produced a colonial government "which does not believe that our task is confined to obtaining submission and taxes, and which in the final analysis governs but does not exploit them."[27] It was the test by which he found the British dominion over India wanting. Although this extension of European power and control represented the "triumph ... of Christianity and civilization," he would write at the time of the Indian Mutiny that "the English had not in a century done anything for the Indian population that might have been expected from their

[25] OC 3:1, 329. These passages come from the reports issued by the Chamber's Committee on Algerian Affairs. Tocqueville was one of four members of the committee who visited Algeria in the autumn of 1846, and he served as the committee rapporteur. See Richter, "Tocqueville on Algeria," 394, 395.

[26] LCS, 565; letter to Lamoricière, April 5, 1846, quoted in Jardin, *Tocqueville*, 318.

[27] Quoted in Richter, "Tocqueville on Algeria," 394.

enlightenment and their institutions." What might be expected was clear: "not only to dominate India, but to civilize it."[28] It was not that Tocqueville was unaware of the hardships being visited upon the Algerians by the French or the Indians by the British but that he hoped that the liberal rule that followed would make these sufferings worthwhile. In any event, whatever the costs might be, the rule of necessity prevailed. In its circumstances, the penalty that France faced if it failed to keep up in the era of colonial expansion was the decay of the public-spirited mores that would alone preserve freedom for the French; the providential considerations of its location and its history meant that a foreign policy of abstention was the surest route to despotism at home.

Such was the burden of the parliamentary and public campaign waged by Tocqueville throughout the years of the July Monarchy, and waged with particular fierceness from 1841 on, after Guizot had become the primary power in the government. Its past and its position in the international system made it impossible for France to adopt the modest international role allowed to the United States. "Fortune, which has done such particular things in favor of the inhabitants of the United States, has placed them in the midst of a wilderness where they have, so to speak, no neighbors," he had recognized in *Democracy in America*. "A few thousand soldiers are enough for them, but this is American and not democratic."[29] Free countries do not derive from their mores any immunity from the harsh necessities of international relations, including the possibility of war and the consequent need to keep up large armed forces. Such immunity comes only from their circumstances. In the case of the Americans, their circumstances have exempted them from the realities of international life. By way of contrast, France, being immersed in rather than removed from rivalries and threats, is forced to hazard centralized government and large standing armies, for simple self-defense. It can hope to preserve freedom only by employing its strength in a high-minded fashion, "raising the sights" of its citizens and thereby provoking in them a selfless dedication to the public good and an active involvement in politics that are, in their conditions, the only means of instilling the all-important mores friendly to freedom. It must accept all the risks of an interventionist foreign policy; it is not free to refuse, for that is the only path to domestic liberty that its circumstances leave open to it.

---

[28] Letter to Lord Hatherton, November 27, 1857, SLPS, 359–360. See also the unfinished work *L'Inde*, OC 3:1, 441–550.
[29] DIA II.3.xxii, 618.

Exemplar Redux

There then came another turn of the revolutionary wheel, or another stage
in that single process that Tocqueville contended had been underway
for seven centuries, had expressed itself in violent revolution in 1789,
and had not ceased to assault society with new demands for equality in
the sixty succeeding years. In February 1848, the overthrow of the July
Monarchy brought with it not only a change in governmental institutions
but also something very like a class war. The chamber of the Constituent
Assembly – whose members, including Tocqueville, had been elected in
the aftermath of the fall of Louis-Philippe to govern the country on an
interim basis and write a new constitution – was invaded by protestors in
May, an event that came to seem less threatening only in retrospect when
it was overshadowed by the June Days. These four days of fighting in
Paris between, on the one side, the government and its defenders – many
of them from the provinces – and, on the other, the proletariat of Paris
exceeded in violence anything that the country would experience between
the Terror and the Commune.[30] France emerged from the crisis with
untested and – Tocqueville feared – unworkable political institutions, its
economy in tatters, the loyalty of its armed forces in question, and its
fellow great powers on the continent aroused by fear of revolution and
determined to stamp it out, with the concurrence of the new regime or
without it.

Circumstances, in other words, had changed. By the middle of 1848,
both the power position of France and its relation to the major currents
of opinion prevalent in its counterparts in Prussia, Austria, and St. Petersburg had altered so radically from six months before that the theoretical
foundations of its foreign policy had to be relaid if it was to remain in
touch with reality. Tocqueville's bold intention to seek out threats to
liberty abroad and succor fellow liberals could no longer be sustained
with the resources at hand. Raising citizen spirit by running the risks
inherent in vindicating freedom elsewhere would accomplish nothing if

---

[30] In his *Recollections*, Tocqueville tells the story of the political revolution that took place
in February and the social revolution that nearly followed it. His viewpoint is that of
a member of the opposition under the Orleanist Monarchy who was nevertheless sad
to see the failure of an experiment in constitutional liberty, and a vigorous exponent of
suppressing the envy, hatred, and lawlessness he perceived in the "socialism" that sought
power in the June Days, who predicted with a heavy heart that fear of renewed disorder
would drive the victorious part of the nation into sacrificing its liberty to anyone who
would promise stability.

the inevitable results of such intrepidity were defeat, the discrediting of the one free government of a major continental capital, and the extension of the influence of the autocracies.

One of the earliest examples of this change in Tocqueville's thinking may be found in writings that he never intended to see the light of day. Britain and France had offered themselves as mediators in the war between Austria and Sardinia that was another legacy of the revolutionary spasm of 1848, and an international conference on the conflict was scheduled for Brussels. In October, General Cavaignac appointed Tocqueville as a French delegate, and he spent that month and the following one examining the archives in preparation for his work. Ultimately, the idea of the conference was abandoned, but at the moment, he was assembling these thoughts on the general direction of French foreign policy, Tocqueville believed himself to be on the verge of assuming a position of considerable responsibility. Perhaps this realization made him particularly conscious of the virtue of prudence; at any rate, his tone was cautious. He continued to assert that "the interest in the extension of our democratic principles is one of the great interests of our policy," but he granted that it was not the only one. How could it be furthered when the effect of war would be to place more power domestically in the hands of the "anti-republic element" – the army? His answer to this dilemma would be familiar to anyone who had read his work on America of 13 years before: "You have another means. Your example." A foreign war, even one entered into for the purpose of advancing liberty, could arouse the revolutionary faction within France that five months before he had witnessed on the streets of Paris. Supporting the cause of freedom by standing as a working manifestation of it, on the other hand, would avoid straining the hastily composed elements of the new French regime; survival of the government and testimony to its principles in action went hand in hand. He noted "the utility of peace, for liberty, for the Republic," and contrasted the present modest paths open to a liberal government of France with the grander highway that had beckoned it in its days of greater potency: "In [17]90, the means of emancipation was war, today it is peace."[31]

In his circular to the voters of his district in the elections to the newly established National Assembly, held in May 1849, Tocqueville barely mentioned foreign affairs. When he did, however, it was to make them

---

[31] OC 3:3, 249–254.

second in importance to success in the business of government at home. "France, gentlemen, knows by experience that the Republic can produce great efforts, great victories, great actions, great men; but what she has never seen produced until now is a regular government and by this material prosperity," he declared. "She ardently feels the need of these two things."[32] Such was the line he took following his election, both as a member of the National Assembly and after June 2, when he was named foreign minister. The remarks he made on June 25 were representative of his stance. In contrast to his fiery speeches of 1840, when he had advocated a readiness by France to go to war simply to show that it could not be isolated by any agreement arrived at behind its back by the other four great powers, he now termed a "black" coalition of Austria, Prussia, and Russia against France and her republican institutions a "chimera" that "does not exist!" The consequence of the absence of any pressing foreign threat was that French policy should itself not be threatening to the other powers of Europe, no matter how strongly France might disagree with their illiberal governments. And "I therefore believe that the policy useful to the country, the policy our interests urge on us, is today the policy of peace." A period of quiet could allow the new republic to take root in the affections of its citizens, while a precipitous war would certainly uproot it. Accordingly, "not only do I want [peace] in the interest of humanity, out of hatred for the evils and horrors that war brings, I want it still more in the interest of the Republic." If the newly established liberal republic could live in order at home and peace abroad, it would be "immortal." "But it is not only from the purely national point of view, by the narrow egoism of a particular nationality, that I desire peace," he added. "No, I place the source of my desire still higher: I fear war, because I believe that it could bring on, not only for us but for the whole civilized world, a hideous shipwreck."[33]

If France blundered into war in the mistaken belief that by doing so it was advancing liberty in Europe, it might in fact endanger liberty, not only from the Right, as the Eastern powers counter attacked and probably successfully put down liberty everywhere, including in France itself, but also from the Left, as the sacrifices and excitement of war would relight the revolutionary fuse just extinguished in the June Days and encourage the socialists, whose rage for economic equality far outweighed

[32] OC 3:3, 257–261.
[33] OC 3:3, 277–292.

any attachment they might have to liberty, to try once more to overthrow the liberal republic.[34]

Subject to hostility both from the illiberal Right and the revolutionary Left, a shaky liberal government in France had no alternative to a modest policy of demonstrating that liberalism could work successfully in domestic affairs. As Tocqueville put it, "It was the same isolation as before February, with the continent more hostile to us and England more lukewarm. It was therefore necessary, as it had been then, to reduce ourselves to leading a small life, from day to day."[35] The experience of guiding French foreign policy under such conditions even led him to cast a more kindly eye on the pacific stance of the Guizot years, as he asked himself whether he and his friends had "attacked the foreign policy of Louis-P[hilippe]'s government too much (although that government really did lack both shame and patriotic feeling, but its difficulties really were great, too)."[36] Indeed, some of his most despairing complaints were against French public opinion, which failed to see the consequences following inevitably from the events of 1848:

The French nation, which had made and, in a certain way, still made so great a figure in the world, kicked against this necessity of the time: it had remained haughty while it ceased to be preponderant; it feared to act and tried to talk loudly; and it also expected its Government to be proud, without, however, permitting it to run the risks which such conduct entailed. A sorry condition for a Ministry of Foreign Affairs in such a country and at such a time! [37]

The Surprising M. Tocqueville

The aim of this chapter has not been to try to catch an eminent political philosopher in contradictions, for in fact on the crucial issue of the

[34] This fear was the basis of Tocqueville's strong criticism of Palmerston's dispatch of Lord Minto to the Italian Peninsula just before 1848, with the mission of pushing the rulers there into reform. With the avowed aim of supporting liberalism, Palmerston in fact undertook "to interfere in the affairs of the Continent for the purpose of serving his own personal or party interest at home, with little regard to the consequences on the rest of Europe," although he "ought to have known in 1847 that he could not stir the inflammable elements of Rome and Naples without risking a general conflagration.... He must have known that all the Continent was mined. And he had no right to presume on his insular position and throw combustibles over the rest of the world." See Tocqueville, *Memoir, Letters, and Remains*, trans. and ed. Miss Senior, 2 vols. (London: Macmillan and Company, 1861), vol. I, 78–79.
[35] *Recollections*, 287.
[36] *Recollections*, 285.
[37] *Recollections*, 287.

considerations that ought to determine a country's foreign policy he remained consistent throughout his life: first, that the highest priority of any country's foreign policy is the preservation of its own domestic liberty through the encouragement of the proper mores among its citizens; second, that if this encouragement can be accomplished through purely domestic means, that is the safest and therefore the most desirable method; third, that one alternative method is the raising of civic spirit through an active, high-minded foreign policy; and, fourth, that the choice between these two alternatives (or among other possible alternatives, each of which would imply a corresponding kind of foreign policy) is not a free choice but instead is largely dictated by the circumstances of history and the physical and external political environment. Rather, the purpose has been to suggest that in our reading of this great exponent of human freedom we have underestimated the role that he assigned to necessity. Mores were primary in sustaining the civic virtues essential to the preservation of liberty, but circumstances defined the actions that, at a given time and place, would best strengthen those mores in a particular people.

Where the international position of a people was safely protected by a history free of the burden of Europe's past – "an immense inheritance that its fathers have willed to it, a mixture of glory and misery, of friendships and national hatred" – and by a sheltered geographical location, as was true of few countries, but was the happy lot of the United States at the time of Tocqueville's tour, the country could be a worthy exemplar of liberty by tending to the domestic mores that would underpin free laws and institutions, while largely ignoring the outside world.[38] Where a people occupied the position of France under Louis-Philippe, however, the path to virtuous mores lay elsewhere – through government action in general and acting internationally in particular that reminded them to participate in the noble task of defending the regime by supporting liberty through its international vindication. Again, where a people occupied the position of France following the Revolution of 1848, with its power much diminished and the risks of conflict very great, then, as Tocqueville the foreign minister told his ambassador in Austria at the time of the Hungarian revolt, "We can only take a passive part . . . our distance from the seat of war must impose upon us, in the present state of our affairs and of those of Europe, a certain reserve."[39]

---

[38] DIA I.2.v.
[39] Quoted in *Recollections*, 305.

The question for present policy then is one of the circumstances of the United States – whether it more nearly resembles the America that Tocqueville saw and envied; or Orleanist France, whose route to ordered liberty required the bracing vindication of freedom abroad; or Republican France, whose international and domestic exhaustion necessitated drawing back to the role of exemplar. Certainly, the contemporary United States has the same political and social history – the same legacy of having achieved liberty before equality, the same inheritance of English common-law freedoms and Puritan religion – although with a far more diverse population than the one that he found dominated by Anglo-Americans. The supporting legal practices, such as federalism and judicial review, remain, albeit much attenuated in the former case and strengthened in the latter.

Rather, it is in terms of the United States' position in the international system that one might argue that circumstances have decisively changed and that the limits on human choice have most altered. The attenuation of the protection afforded by two great oceans and comparatively weak neighbors has been a truism for two generations, a reality accentuated by the vulnerability to terrorist actions demonstrated by the events of 9/11. In responding to that threat to national and personal security, government has intruded into many areas of life previously left to individual choice or the dealings of private entities. No longer can it be said that the United States is a largely decentralized political system with minimal armed forces.

Beyond these specific developments, which were largely imposed on Americans by decisions and conditions abroad, there has been the more general shift in the position of the United States from the periphery to the center of the international system. Its complex network of alliances, its leadership in financial and other international institutions, its active diplomatic involvement in almost every major international issue, its near-universal diplomatic representation around the world, its influence on popular culture globally – all of these developments suggest a very different place in international society from the fortunate isolation of a seaboard republic, with an enormous undeveloped hinterland drawing it away from Europe. The mutual influence of the United States and the rest of the world is multifaceted, immediate, powerful, and inescapable.

Under these circumstances, one might wonder whether the better parallel for the United States of the early twenty-first century is the France of the 1830s and 1840s rather than the United States of the 1830s. As a member of the Chamber of Deputies, the Constituent Assembly, and the National Assembly, as a political publicist, and as a foreign minister, Tocqueville prescribed two very different policies for his native France. One – diplomatically active, militarily somewhat interventionist, support- ive of the imperial *mission civilatrice*, insistent on taking a leading part in the international defense of liberal values – was a policy that Tocqueville thought dictated by circumstances of relatively great external power but a certain distractedness and love of ease at home. He intended this to be a policy of inspiration and discipline. The other – diplomatically cau- tious, militarily abstentionist, intent on domestic reform and prosperity, committed to the domestic reaffirmation of liberal values – was a policy that he believed was required by circumstances of straitened international influence and popular unwillingness to run risks for the freedom of oth- ers abroad. This amounted to a policy of prudence and accommodation. Ironically, in the light of radically altered international and domestic cir- cumstances, the surprising M. Tocqueville would be less likely to counsel imitating the country ostensibly described in *Democracy in America* and more likely to point our attention toward the country for whose instruc- tion it was composed. That said, he would be the first to admit that the question of whether the France of the 1830s and 1840s should be consid- ered the analog of the United States of 2013 is not simply a matter of the free choice of American citizens, but it must be guided by a recognition of imperious necessity.

CHAPTER 11

Democracy and Domination: Empire, Slavery, and Democratic Corruption in Tocqueville's Thought[1]

Jennifer Pitts

Tocqueville's thought and political career, from his early observations in America, through his advocacy of the French colonization of Algeria, to his late preoccupations with the American political crises of the 1850s, may help us to explore two converse aspects of the relationship between democracy and empire. The first is the temptation to consolidate democratic society internally by exercising forms of domination over outsiders, as when democratic – or democratizing – societies engage in imperial ventures, as all the major European nations and the United States did in the nineteenth and early twentieth centuries.[2] Democracy in settler societies has had a particularly intimate relationship with exclusion and domination: egalitarian relations among settlers have often been fostered by a

[1] I am grateful to the audience at the University of Richmond, where an early draft of the paper was presented.

[2] Aziz Rana, *The Two Faces of American Freedom* (Cambridge: Harvard University Press, 2010); Thomas R. Hietala, *Manifest Design: Anxious Aggrandizement in Late Jacksonian America* (Ithaca, NY: Cornell University Press, 1985); Fred Anderson and Andrew R. L. Cayton, *The Dominion of War: Empire and Liberty in North America, 1500–2000* (New York: Viking, 2005); James T. Campbell, Matthew Pratt Guterl, and Robert G. Lee, eds., *Race, Nation, and Empire in American History* (Chapel Hill: University of North Carolina Press, 2007); Bruce Cumings, *Dominion from Sea to Sea: Pacific Ascendancy and American Power* (New Haven: Yale University Press, 2009); David C. Hendrickson, *Union, Nation, or Empire: The American Debate over International Relations, 1789–1941* (Lawrence: University Press of Kansas, 2009); and Richard Immerman, *Empire for Liberty: A History of American Imperialism from Benjamin Franklin to Paul Wolfowitz* (Princeton: Princeton University Press, 2010). Daniel Hulsebosch notes the "curiously reciprocal relationship between imperial expansion and constitutional liberty," in *Constituting Empire: New York and the Transformation of Constitutionalism in the Atlantic World, 1664–1830* (Chapel Hill: University of North Carolina Press, 2005).

sense of shared civilizational or racial status and by the abundance of
cheap land wrested from indigenous peoples.[3] The second is the destruction that imperial formations wreak not just on the colonized but also
on the democratic societies that sponsor them, short-circuiting or corrupting democratic processes. This can happen when forms of arbitrary
power exercised in colonies or over slaves come home to roost or when
elites co-opt democratic processes for profit or plunder abroad or at the
frontier. Jacksonian populism fostered both the rampant abrogation of
Indian treaties and the increasing stratification of American society under
the operations of the "free market"; British capitalists likewise managed
to whip the public into the jingoistic frenzy that supported the Boer War,
to the cost of many and the profit of a few.[4]

Tocqueville's work illuminates the relationship between democracy
and imperial domination not, or rather not simply, because he was one
of the foremost theorists of democracy of the period but also despite
that theoretical acumen. For all the subtlety of his analysis of democratic society in America and in France, as a political thinker, Tocqueville
was in important ways strikingly inattentive to the connections between
democracy and domination and to the dangers of empire for democracy.
Notably, Tocqueville chose early on to sequester themes of slavery and
empire from his theoretical account of democracy. He opens his chapter
on the "Three Races," the final chapter of the 1835 volume of *Democracy
in America*, with a disclaimer:

Although Indians and Negroes have come up frequently in the course of this
work, I have yet to pause to show how these two races stand in relation to the
democratic people I have been describing... these topics were tangential to my
subject: they are *American but not democratic*, and it was above all democracy
that I wished to portray.[5]

The chapter goes on to denounce America's expulsion of the Indians with
eloquence and pathos, to contrast the prosperity and vigor of free states
with the corruption and torpor of slave societies, and to lament the racism
of American whites. But such arguments remain within the framework
set out at the beginning of the chapter. However distressing or prominent

[3] Rana, *Two Faces of American Freedom*; David R. Roediger, *The Wages of Whiteness:
Race and the Making of the American Working Class* (New York: Verso, 1991); also see
Caroline Elkins and Susan Pedersen, eds., *Settler Colonialism in the Twentieth Century*
(New York: Routledge, 2005).
[4] J. A. Hobson, *The Psychology of Jingoism* (London: G. Richards, 1901) and *Imperialism:
A Study* (London: Allen and Unwin, 1902); Hannah Arendt, *The Origins of Totalitari-
anism* (New York: Harcourt Brace, 1973 [1948]), esp. 123–157, and "Home to Roost:
A Bicentennial Address," *New York Review of Books* (June 26, 1975).
[5] DIA (G) I.2.x, 365.

on the American scene, the book implies, these things have little to do with American democracy. Still, if Tocqueville chose to argue that imperial expansion and the subordination of others were tangential to, or outside the bounds of, democracy, his political career suggests otherwise. Even if he failed fully to theorize connections between democracy and empire, he drew them nonetheless: above all, by recognizing the importance of the frontier to American democratic culture and by calling for a French imperial project in Algeria as a response to what he saw as the great vulnerability of democracy in France in the wake of revolution and counterrevolution.

Indeed, Tocqueville's defense of, and worries about, democracy repeatedly intersected with his lifelong interest in questions of empire and slavery. Tocqueville's entire career was, arguably, devoted to the project of stabilizing liberal democracy in France in the face of its extreme political volatility. He hoped that a successful imperial venture in Algeria might aid this project. In placing the conquest of Algeria at the center of his political agenda during his decade as a French statesman, Tocqueville suggested that the lessons for France that he drew from America's example included lessons of and for empire – ideas, that is, about the ways in which imperial expansion might support democracy or liberty at home. Arguments to the contrary – that such forms of domination were threats to democratic society – were available not just in various traditions of imperial critique but also among Tocqueville's own circle of friends, both French and American. Still, he seems largely to have resisted such worries, anxious as he was about the prospects for freedom in France's highly uncertain future.

Tocqueville's wager that Algerian colonization might help stabilize French democracy looked like a losing one after Louis Napoleon's coup in 1851, during which Tocqueville was briefly arrested. It is perhaps no surprise that he had henceforth nothing more to say about Algeria, when it could no longer serve the domestic political purpose he had imagined. However, he remained intently interested, if increasingly bleak, about the fate of democracy in America. After the second volume of the *Democracy* was published in 1840, Tocqueville had continued an impassioned transatlantic conversation with his large and devoted circle of American friends, for the most part northern lawyers and academics who were profoundly antislavery.[6] The exchanges, about French and American politics,

---

[6] Alexis de Tocqueville, *Tocqueville on America after 1840: Letters and Other Writings*, eds. and trans. Aurelian Craiutu and Jeremy Jennings (Cambridge: Cambridge University Press, 2009).

slavery, and empire, among other topics, reached a peak of intensity in the years just before Tocqueville's death and the Civil War, as they debated the gravity, and the likely causes, of the degradation of America's public life and the country's increasing propensity for violence. In response to Tocqueville's questions and worries that equality and mass suffrage might be degrading and corrupting the character of American politics, some of Tocqueville's most astute American correspondents insisted that the gravest threats to democracy came from powerful Wall Street speculators and southern planters, from inequality and habits of domination rather than from equality and democracy. One way to wonder about what the contours of a third volume of *Democracy in America* might have been is to ask how much, and how, Tocqueville might have taken up those urgent defenses of egalitarianism and their insistence that the sources of democratic corruption lay in privilege and unequal power rather than in universal suffrage or mass immigration.[7]

Recent scholarship has suggested that the development of democracy in Europe and the United States in the nineteenth century was far more tightly bound up with empire than historians had been accustomed to believe.[8] Certainly the ideological connections were many. Democracy in Europe and the United States was repeatedly theorized or figured in contrast to a series of archetypes of colonial others as slaves, New World savages, and Oriental despots were cast as the constitutive outside of democracy. Tocqueville himself framed democratic society by the two extremes of slavery and savagery: as he put it, "The Negro exists at the ultimate extreme of servitude, the Indian at the outer limits of freedom."[9]

It was common in the antebellum United States to see the fortunes of U.S. democracy as dependent on westward expansion. Jacksonian Democrats made "Indian removal" central to their political program.[10] Northern labor advocates and their allies in the Whig and then Republican parties, for their part, saw western migration as the key route to social mobility for the working class, a means of bolstering wages in the East by reducing competition, and therefore politically stabilizing as well. As the radical Whig and then Republican Horace Greeley wrote, "The

---

[7] "Sumner to Tocqueville, 7 May 1858," in Craiutu and Jennings, *Tocqueville on America*, 289.

[8] See works cited in footnote 2.

[9] DIA (G) I.2.x, 368.

[10] Stuart Banner, *How the Indians Lost Their Land* (Cambridge, MA: Harvard University Press, 2005); Michael Rogin, *Fathers and Children: Andrew Jackson and the Subjugation of the American Indian* (New York: Knopf, 1975).

public lands are the great regulator of the relations of Labor and Capital, the safety valve of our industrial and social engine."[11] Western land made possible the society of independent farmers that Lincoln praised – those who "[ask] no favors of capital on the one hand, nor of hirelings and slaves on the other."[12] The dependence of this apparently self-reliant society on the expropriation of Indians went largely unmentioned, despite the increasing prominence of the West in the national imaginary.

Tocqueville arrived in America in May 1831, a year after President Jackson signed into law the Indian Removal Act. Tocqueville was an eloquent eyewitness to the expulsions unleashed by the act, having shared a steamboat on the frozen Mississippi River with a group of Choctaws being exported west. He had little respect for Jackson, whom he called a "man of violent character and middling ability."[13] As he wrote to his mother on Christmas Day 1831, reporting on the scene of the "old people, women, children, with baggage" boarding the riverboat:

What a splendid thing is logic. When the Indians found themselves a little too near their white brethren, the president of the United States sent them a message explaining that, in their own interest naturally, they would do well to retreat slightly westward. . . . Throw in gifts of inestimable value, calculated to buy the Indian's compliance: casks of whisky, glass-bead necklaces, earrings and mirrors. What clinches the argument is the insinuation that if Americans meet with a refusal, force may be applied.[14]

Tocqueville recognized this phenomenon as imperial expansion. "Residents of the United States," he wrote, "are filtering into Texas daily

---

[11] See Eric Foner, *Free Soil, Free Labor, Free Men* (New York: Oxford University Press, 1970), 27ff.; on the centrality of land ownership to the Jeffersonian republican tradition, see especially Foner, "Radical Individualism in America," *Literature of Liberty* 1 (1978):5–31; and on Jefferson's policies of land acquisition, Anthony F. C. Wallace, *Jefferson and the Indians: the Tragic Fate of the First Americans* (Cambridge, MA: Harvard University Press, 1999).

[12] Abraham Lincoln, "Annual Message to Congress," December 3, 1861, in Lincoln, *Speeches and Writings 1859–1865* (New York: Library of America, 1989), 296.

[13] DIA (G) I.2.ix, 320.

[14] "Letter to Louise de Tocqueville, 25 December 1831," OC 14: 157–161; translation by Frederick Brown in "Letters from America," *Hudson Review* 62 (2009), 357–397. Cf. Rogin, *Fathers and Children*, 173: "In attempting to secure treaties in 1816 with Cherokees, Choctaws, and Chickasaws, 'Jackson employed the two weapons which dominated all his later Indian treaties.' The treaties would not have succeeded, he wrote, 'unless we addressed ourselves feelingly to the predominant and governing passion of all Indian tribes, *i.e.*, their avarice and fear.'" [citing R. S. Cotterill, *The Southern Indians: The Story of the Civilized Tribes before Removal* (Norman: University of Oklahoma Press, 1954), 98–201; and "Jackson to Secretary of State James Monroe," July 8, 1816, AJC, II, 252–253)].

and . . . founding an empire there. . . . The province of Texas is still under Mexican rule, but before long Mexicans will have vanished, as it were, from the vicinity. . . . The English race will not stop at lines traced by treaty, imaginary barriers that cannot resist the onrushing tide."[15]

It was typical of the Jacksonians to deny any responsibility for the horrors and mass deaths of the Indian expulsions. As one U.S. agent had written in 1816: "A disposition to migrate seems to pervade the whole eastern part of the United States. . . . The tendency is as uniform as the law of gravitation. It can no more be restrained *until the shores of the Pacific Ocean make it impossible to go further.*"[16] Tocqueville himself resisted the suggestion that impersonal forces were at work and that American settlers and governments could not be blamed: "The European *forced* the Indian tribes to flee into the remote wilderness, thereby condemning them to a wandering, vagabond existence filled with unspeakable miseries," he wrote.[17] However, for all his criticism of the Americans' hypocritical use of treaties and legal proceedings to carry out their conquest – as he put it, "[t]o destroy human beings with greater respect for the laws of humanity would be impossible" – Tocqueville shared the Jacksonian Democrats' depiction of the Indians' destruction as an inevitable result of the encounter between savagery and civilization.[18] He lamented this destruction, but he did not exactly condemn it, for he could imagine no alternative. Indeed, he claimed: "There is something providential about this gradual and steady progress of the European race toward the Rocky Mountains: it is like a human flood, rising steadily and daily driven on by the hand of God."[19] There are echoes, here, of his claims that democratic society, too, was providential.

Tocqueville recognized that the limitless availability of land – land seized from the Indians, although described by Tocqueville as God given – had profound consequences for the equality of conditions that in his view was the essential characteristic of American society. It underwrote

[15] DIA (G) I.2.x, 472.
[16] Cherokee agent R. J. Meigs, quoted by Michael Rogin, *Fathers and Children*, 244–245. "R.J. Meigs to Secretary of War William Crawford, Nov 8, 1816," *American State Papers, Indian Affairs* [ASPIA], II:115.
[17] DIA (G) I.2.x, 367.
[18] On "how settler communities and their legislatures manipulated laws of property and civil law better to fit the project of indigenous dispossession and of property development," see Lisa Ford, *Settler Sovereignty* (Cambridge: Harvard University Press, 2010), 85 and ff.
[19] "No power on earth can keep [Anglo-American] immigrants out of this fertile wilderness, which offers so many inducements to industry and refuge from every manner of misery," DIA (G) I.2.x, 473 and 437.

social mobility, which in turn signaled the end of paternal authority, as well as the turning of hierarchical class relations between master and servant into contractual and basically egalitarian ones.[20] The social and mental habits distinctive of democracy were also exaggerated in the West – reliance on one's own judgment, but also faith in public opinion as the only authority. "In the West," he wrote, "it was possible to observe democracy pushed to its ultimate limit." Not only were there none of the usual hierarchies of "great names and great wealth"; also absent was the "natural aristocracy [of] enlightenment and virtue" that made New England politics so admirable in his view.[21] Westward expansion was a lynchpin of Jacksonian populism for just such reasons. Jackson himself, born on the Carolina frontier and orphaned early, exploited the imagery of boundless opportunity for all on unlimited Western land. He also, as Tocqueville obliquely recognized, made his military and political career on his triumphs in Indian wars.[22] Tocqueville worried about the vulgarity of Western politicians like Jackson and about what he called the "disorderly, passionate, [almost] feverish" quality of public life in the Western territories, which he saw as the result of extreme egalitarianism on the frontier – the absence of that natural aristocracy that tamed democracy in the East.[23] General Jackson, he wrote, "is the slave of the majority: he obeys its wishes and desires and heeds its half-divulged instincts; or, rather, he . . . anticipat[es] its desires before it knows what they are in order to place himself at its head."[24]

Both Tocqueville and the Jacksonians, however, exaggerated the equality of the American West.[25] Land speculation was rife in frontier society, as Tocqueville himself recognized when he called it a "swarm of adventurers and speculators."[26] He later saw such speculation as deeply

[20] DIA (G) I.2.ix, 325; I.1.iii, 55–56; and II.3.v, 673.
[21] DIA (G) I.1.iii, 58.
[22] See DIA I.2.ix, 322, noting the dangers of "military glory" for democracy and citing Jackson as the archetype, although without noting that the Jackson's military glory was a result of campaigns of expansion; cf. Rogin, *Fathers and Children*, ch. 3.
[23] DIA (G) I.2.ix, 355.
[24] DIA (G) I.2.x, 453.
[25] Edward Pessen, *Jacksonian America; Society, Personality, and Politics* (Urbana: University of Illinois Press, 1985), ch. 5, adduces evidence that "not equality but disparity of condition was the rule in Jacksonian America" (81), that the disparities increased markedly during the period, and that there was far less social mobility than Tocqueville imagined.
[26] DIA (G) I.2.v, 229. Cf. DIA (G) II.2.xix, 647, where Tocqueville notes that "it is unusual for an American grower to settle permanently on the land he occupies. In the new provinces of the West especially, a man will clear a field in order to resell it and not to harvest a crop from it."

threatening to the stability of French Algeria.[27] The fortunes made, as well as the spread of slave ownership, meant that the society of the American West, even if it was chaotic and unstable, was stratified and not egalitarian.[28] It might be more accurate to describe the American West not as a society at the democratic extreme, as Tocqueville did, but as what he called a revolutionary society.[29] Like Tocqueville's France, as he describes it in *Democracy*, the American West was turbulent and volatile but unequal. It was threatened, arguably, not by mass politics or excessive equality but rather by the machinations of those who enjoyed disproportionate but unstable power.[30] This was precisely the condition that made Tocqueville deeply fearful for French liberty. Perhaps if he had recognized the same qualities on the American frontier and in American cities, he would have been less tempted by it as a model for a French imperial project.

For Tocqueville seems to have concluded from his American journey that France's democratic society had much to learn not just from the example of American democracy but also from American empire: from the self-reliance of the frontiersmen, the self-government of new communities, and the heroism of making one's way in a hostile new world. On first sight of Algiers, he wrote, "This whole world moves about with an activity that seems feverish.... On all sides, you see nothing but recent ruins, buildings going up; you hear nothing but the noise of the hammer. It is Cincinnati transported onto the soil of Africa."[31]

Tocqueville's democratic hopes for Algeria were initially two. First, he believed that France needed a grand undertaking to convince the people that their collective political project was worthwhile, something to raise French politics above its usual pettiness, an antidote to stagnation. He wrote in *Democracy* that the "greatest danger today" was neither anarchy nor despotism so much as the root cause of both, which was "apathy"; it was this apathy, this disengagement from politics, that he hoped a grand imperial enterprise might combat.[32] And second, in his more sanguine moments he hoped that the European settlements on the

---

[27] DIA (G) I.2.v, 229 and OC 3:1, 384–386; WES, 178–179.

[28] As Rogin and others have noted, Jackson himself was a land speculator who conveniently but highly misleadingly presented himself as a populist fighting Eastern elites.

[29] DIA (G) II.3.v, 678.

[30] On the political dominance of the wealthy, see Pessen, *Jacksonian America*, 97–100.

[31] "Entry of 7 May 1841," OC 5:2, 191; WES, 36.

[32] DIA (G) II.4, note xxvii, 869.

Algerian frontier might serve as laboratories of self-government on the model of the New England townships he so admired – schools of self-reliance for a country all too dependent on the central government for any initiative. Tocqueville remained committed to French rule in Algeria throughout his parliamentary career, even though he grew increasingly disgusted by its violence and abandoned any hope that its French colonists would ever blossom into New England townspeople.

As France consolidated the conquest of Algeria through notoriously brutal assaults on the indigenous people, Tocqueville made himself one of the legislature's most vocal advocates of the two key facets of the imperial project as he saw it: complete subjugation of the natives and European settlement of the territory, or in Tocqueville's words, domination and colonization. Whereas his lamentations over the fate of the Indians in *Democracy in America* might lead us to think that he would condemn France's brutality in the course of the conquest, in fact he took a self-consciously aggressive stance on this question. He argued that the French had to accept that the Algerians were, for the foreseeable future, enemies with whom the only possible relationship was one of domination. As France proceeded to secure its rule through ruthless assaults on the civilian population, he wrote to his friend Claude (Francisque) de Corcelle, "I think that we will never do all the great things we set out to do in Algeria, and, all things considered, we have quite a sad possession there. But, on the other hand, I remain more convinced than ever . . . that there is no middle ground between complete abandonment and . . . total domination."[33] The tone of lamentation is familiar from *Democracy in America*. Here, however, instead of writing as an outside observer about an inevitable process in which he played no part, Tocqueville was a legislator actively pressing for continued domination.

By the time of his second voyage to the colony in 1846, Tocqueville seems to have concluded that French Algeria would never become a successful democratic experiment on the American model. Still, he remained one of the legislature's most forceful advocates of a program of domination and colonization. In a letter written from Algiers, Tocqueville conceded to Corcelle, a far greater critic of the conquest and someone whose humanitarian concerns about French treatment of the native Algerians seem to have troubled Tocqueville without altering his views, that "it is not only cruel, but absurd and impracticable, to try to force back or

---

[33] "Letter of 26 September 1840, to Corcelle," OC 15, 151.

exterminate the natives," and he lamented the "hatred that rules between the two races," the "mistrust and anger [that] still fill the hearts of our officers," who saw the Arabs as dangerous beasts.[34] However, he also wrote in a parliamentary report that the French must avoid giving the Algerians "exaggerated ideas of their own importance" – they must not be allowed to think they deserved to be treated "as though they were our fellow citizens and our equals."[35] Here too Tocqueville may have drawn lessons from America. Some have argued that the nineteenth-century United States should not be considered an empire because it fully incorporated its new territories as equal states.[36] But Indians and later Mexicans were annexed not as equal citizens but as subordinated populations. Political membership in the American West was highly racialized: many of the new states and territories gave voting rights to "free whites" even if they were not citizens; at the same time, Indiana, Illinois, Iowa, and Oregon prohibited free blacks from entry altogether.[37] Similarly, in the new constitution following the 1848 Revolution, France incorporated Algeria as an integral part of the French state, unlike any of France's later African colonies. However, as in the United States, the indigenous population remained legally subjugated, without the rights of citizens. Tocqueville himself served on the constitutional committee, and his own writings suggest that this was exactly the arrangement he supported: total incorporation of the European colonists into French democracy on equal terms, along with subordinate status for the natives. The lessons from America, again, seem to have been not just democratic but imperial.

As we have noted, with Louis Napoleon's coup in 1851 France's experiment in democratic government collapsed and with it Tocqueville's concern with Algeria. However, he remained profoundly interested in the fate of American democracy, which in this period seemed more than

---

[34] "Letter of 1 Dec 1846, from Algiers, to Corcelle," OC 15, 224.
[35] See "First Report on Algeria," OC 3:1, 324; WES,141.
[36] E.g., Anthony Pagden, "Imperialism, Liberalism and the Quest for Perpetual Peace," *Daedalus* (2005), 54; however, early Americans themselves embraced the term as appropriate to their ambitions for extensive territory; see Robert W. Tucker and David Hendrickson, *Empire of Liberty: The Statecraft of Thomas Jefferson* (New York: Oxford University Press, 1990), and Norbert Kilian, "New Wine in Old Skins? American Definitions of Empire and the Emergence of a New Concept," [1976] in *Theories of Empire 1450–1800*, ed., David Armitage (Aldershot: Ashgate, 1998), 307–324.
[37] See Rana, *Two Faces of American Freedom*, 114–120; Alexander Keyssar, *The Right to Vote: The Contested History of Democracy in the United States* (New York: Basic Books, 2000), 44–49; Eric Foner, *The Story of American Freedom* (New York: Norton, 1998), 76–77; and Rogers Smith, *Civic Ideals: Conflicting Visions of Citizenship in U.S. History* (New Haven, CT: Yale University Press, 1997).

ever bound up with forms of empire and domination, as the United States conquered the southwest, annexed the Oregon territory, and saw, in effect, the nationalization of slavery with the passage of the Fugitive Slave Act. Tocqueville's later correspondence shows the deep and careful interest with which he followed these developments. He posed urgent questions to his American friends – questions focused squarely on corruption, inequality, and social power: How do financial misdeeds and crises threaten democracy? Do democratic conditions themselves degrade social mores? And how does slavery corrupt democracy? Tocqueville worried about the increasing violence in American public life – especially reports of urban riots and of the brutality of American high politics, epitomized by the crippling attack on his friend, the abolitionist senator Charles Sumner (1811–1874), by the South Carolina congressman Preston Brooks. Brooks beat Sumner unconscious on the floor of the Senate after Sumner's May 1856 speech on the "Crime against Kansas," in which Sumner spoke of slavery as a "harlot" kept by his southern colleagues and summoned what Sumner called the "aroused masses . . . not only to vindicate Right against Wrong, but to redeem the Republic from that Oligarchy which prompts, directs, and concentrates the distant wrong" in Kansas.[38] Sumner spent three years recuperating from the attack, some of it in France, where he visited Tocqueville.[39]

In addition to Sumner himself, Tocqueville's chief correspondents on questions of American politics in the 1850s included the senator's brother George Sumner (1817–1863); the lawyer Theodore Sedgwick (1811–1859); the Prussian-born political scientist Francis Lieber (1798–1872), who in 1856 left South Carolina College for Columbia University; and Jared Sparks (1789–1866), the historian and president of Harvard and one of his important sources for *Democracy in America*.[40] Some of the richest exchanges in Tocqueville's American correspondence are with a wealthy but little known New York businessman named Nelson Marvin

[38] Charles Sumner, *The Works of Charles Sumner* (Boston: Lee and Shepard, 1870–1883), 4:125 ff.
[39] See "Sumner to Tocqueville, letter of 4 August 1857," in Craiutu and Jennings, *Tocqueville on America*, 246; William James Hull Hoffer, *The Caning of Charles Sumner: Honor, Idealism, and the Origins of the Civil War* (Baltimore, MD: Johns Hopkins University Press, 2010).
[40] James Farr has discussed Lieber's complex political position at this time as one of South Carolina's rare Unionists and once a close friend of Sumner but also a slave owner while he lived in the South and an abolitionist after he moved to the North, in James Farr, "Tocqueville and Lieber on Antebellum America," paper presented at American Political Science Association annual meeting, Toronto, September 2009.

Beckwith (1807–1889), whose letters to Tocqueville are long, sophisticated, and sometimes quirky political essays. Tocqueville praised his "penetrating and original mind."[41] Beckwith lived in Europe in the early 1850s and came to know the Tocquevilles well during the winter of 1852–1853 when he and his family were in Paris. He went to Hong Kong in 1857 as a managing partner of Russell and Co., the most important American trading house in China in this period; this engaging and worldly correspondent was unusual in Tocqueville's circle in being neither an author nor an academic.

Tocqueville pointedly interrogated his American correspondents about the sources of the spike in violence and the corruption of democracy it seemed to portend. Tocqueville was tempted by explanations that blamed the influence of the democratic masses; these worries about the increasing influence of "the people" in public life – that class of Americans with "violent mores and uncouth habits [that] increasingly sets the tone for the rest" – might be thought to echo his earlier concerns about the tyranny of the majority.[42] Some American friends, including Sumner and Beckwith, emphatically rejected such speculations and argued, to the contrary, that the dangers to American democracy came not from democracy itself but from forms of hierarchy and domination, not from the many but from the few: Wall Street financiers, slave-owning southern elites, and those (especially the southern elites) with imperial aspirations in Mexico and the Caribbean.[43]

---

41 "Letter of September 7, 1858," in Craiutu and Jennings, *Tocqueville on America*, 294. Beckwith was a friend and client of Theodore Sedgwick, who introduced him to Tocqueville. See Henry Hall, ed., *America's Successful Men of Affairs: an Encyclopedia of Contemporaneous Biography* (New York: New York Tribune, 1895–1896), reproduced in the American Biographical archive, at http://db.saur.de/WBIS/basicSearch.jsf. Also see James Parton, Bayard Taylor, Amos Kendall, et al., *Sketches of Men of Progress* (Cincinnati: Greer, 1870–1871); Robert B. Forbes, *Personal Reminiscences* (Boston: Little, Brown and Co., 1882); and John Murray Forbes, *Letters and Recollections of John Murray Forbes* (Boston: Houghton Mifflin, 1899).

42 "Tocqueville to Lieber, October 9 1857," in Craiutu and Jennings, *Tocqueville on America*, 261.

43 On the particular imperial ambitions of the slave-holding South, see Horace Greeley, *The American Conflict* (New York: O.D. Case & Co., 1864); Robert E. May, *Manifest Destiny's Underworld: Filibustering in Antebellum America* (Chapel Hill: University of North Carolina Press, 2002) and *The Southern Dream of a Caribbean Empire, 1854–1861* (Baton Rouge: Louisiana State University Press, 1973); Adam Rothman, *Slave Country: American Expansion and the Origins of the Deep South* (Cambridge, MA: Harvard University Press, 2005); David C. Hendrickson, *Union, Nation, or Empire: The American Debate over International Relations, 1789–1941* (Lawrence: University Press

Tocqueville's letters of the late 1850s suggest that in analyzing England, France, and America, he saw each society as exemplifying extreme versions of its characteristic historical tendencies, and he perhaps did not attend enough to continuities across them of the kind Beckwith pointed out, in which various powerful groups undermined liberty by abusing their positions of power. England's troubles, Tocqueville said after a visit there in 1857, were caused by its being still dominated by a small body of aristocrats.[44] Second Empire France was a "formidable mixture of socialism and absolutism," in which the government, especially after the assassination attempt on Emperor Napoleon III, repressed opposition with impunity and appeased the poor with handouts.[45] Tocqueville's diagnosis of France's troubles focused on the poisonous interaction between an absolutist monarchy and the desperate masses.

America, he thought, was exhibiting the dangers of extreme license, a lowered tone of public life, the corruption of public officials, and the failure to incorporate so many new immigrants, and so was losing its sense of national character. He began to imagine that the American public too was becoming a desperate mass: his inclination, in pondering the conspicuous violence of American society in the 1850s, was to blame the ill effects of universal suffrage and mass immigration. He worried that the election of judges under universal suffrage was undermining the justice system and leading people to resort to personal violence instead of the courts.[46] He wondered whether democracies value human life less than other societies. He warned Jared Sparks that America had "nothing to fear but from itself, from the excesses of democracy, the spirit of adventure and conquest, the sentiment of an the excessive pride in its strength."[47]

---

of Kansas: 2009), 115–117; and Brian Schoen, *The Fragile Fabric of Union: Cotton, Federal Politics, and the Global Origins of the Civil War* (Baltimore: Johns Hopkins University Press, 2009), 201–222.

[44] See, e.g., his "Letter to Kergorlay of 4 August 1857," LCS, 1255–1256.

[45] "Letter to Nassau Senior," LCS, 1221.

[46] See the "Letter to Lieber, 9 October 1857," in Craiutu and Jennings, *Tocqueville on America*, 261. These were different worries than he had expressed in *Democracy*, where he had argued that the distinctively democratic form of corruption was the use of public office for personal gain by men trying to get wealth and power quickly; there he had worried that the conniving of public officials would infect the public, when ordinary people saw men no richer or better than themselves gaining prominence through vice, DIA (G) I.2.v, 251–253.

[47] "Tocqueville to Jared Sparks, 11 December 1852," in Craiutu and Jennings, *Tocqueville on America*, 139.

Sparks agreed that the popular appetite for conquest posed a great danger to American political stability:

Your apprehensions of the tendencies of the popular mind are not without foundation. The history of the last few years, the acquisitions of Texas and California, prove that the spirit of adventure and conquest excites the aspirations and moves the will of the people. Perhaps it is inherent in the democratic element. The clamor for acquiring Cuba springs from the same spirit; and a slight cause could carry the arms of the United States again into Mexico. Where will this end, and how are such vast accessions and discordant materials to be held together in a confederated republic? But the slave question presents the most formidable problem.[48]

Likewise, Harvard president Edward Everett wrote Tocqueville that Americans "push [their freedoms] so far beyond their legitimate exercise that their abuse threatens to become a more unbearable evil than their total absence."[49]

Others, however, insisted instead that the threat to democracy came from the powerful: Wall Street speculators and above all the southern plantocracy, whose culture of violence and love of overweening power increasingly infected national public life. These friends tried to check Tocqueville's apparent readiness to doubt the political and moral stability of egalitarianism. Nelson Beckwith responded to Tocqueville's worries about riots and mass politics with a resounding endorsement of "the people" as not a threat to democracy but rather America's chief hope against the dangers posed by those with disproportionate political and economic power.[50] He downplayed Tocqueville's worries about street violence – the greatest bodily danger in America, he said, was the risk of being run over by an omnibus in New York. Instead he attributed the violence of American public culture squarely to the corrupt mores and power hunger of the slaveholding class, and more broadly to inequalities and habits of domination. "The corrupting and enormous influence of slavery" as he put it, was the primary cause of the depravity that Tocqueville worried about:

The spirit of violence born on the plantation is ... like poison introduced into the heart of the nation at Washington, and flows into the arteries and out into all the veins, tainting the whole system. . . . It becomes fashionable and looks lucky

---

[48] "Jared Sparks to Tocqueville, 13 June 1853," in Craiutu and Jennings, *Tocqueville on America*, 145.

[49] "Letter of December 8, 1857," in Craiutu and Jennings, *Tocqueville on America*, 269.

[50] The questions were posed in a missing letter that, judging from Beckwith's response, must have put questions similar to those in the letter to Lieber; see "Beckwith, undated," Craiutu and Jennings, *Tocqueville on America*, 314.

and jaunty to carry a pistol and a knife, cock the hat on one side, sport cigars and kid gloves – he's not afraid, not he; he can help himself, he is independent of judges and constables – they are for women and weak people – he can take care of himself, he is a sovereign, and delights in a row. But of course he is on the straight road to barbarism.... Slavery is the cause, I do not say the sole cause, but cause enough obvious and certain, to produce the progressive demoralization you have indicated.[51]

Beckwith's views closely approach those of Charles Sumner, the most emphatically abolitionist of Tocqueville's friends, who, much like Beckwith, argued that it was slavery that had "degraded" Americans and "demoralized our government [with] vulgar principles of force."[52] These men saw slavery as the single issue of overriding political importance in their day, and they adamantly fought the westward extension of slavery, although some, like Beckwith, continued to distinguish themselves from strict abolitionists by refusing to use what they saw as unconstitutional means to fight slavery where it already existed.[53] Unlike Tocqueville, Beckwith wrote that he "never could see any danger in immediate emancipation."[54] And again unlike Tocqueville, who feared that incorporation of freed slaves into the American people was impossible, Beckwith wrote that "[i]f we can live with savage slaves, we can surely live with the same race when civilized and free." This

[51] "Undated letter," in Craiutu and Jennings, *Tocqueville on America*, 316.
[52] Sumner: "Be assured that many of those things by which we are degraded are caused by slavery, even in states where slavery does not exist" (289). Apart from the abolitionist Sumner, Tocqueville's correspondents, though staunch critics of slavery, seem largely to have been free-soilers. Tocqueville himself shared that view, as he wrote to Sedgwick in 1857: "I am unwilling to admit that any contract whatsoever could include among its terms the annihilation of the right and the duty that the present generation has to prevent the most horrible of all social evils from spreading over millions and millions of people belonging to future generations" (226).
[53] For his part, Tocqueville professed that he "never believed in the possibility of destroying slavery in the old states" but saw extension of slavery into new territories as "one of the greatest crimes that human beings could commit against the general cause of humanity"; "Letter to Theodore Sedgwick, 10 January 1857," in Craiutu and Jennings, *Tocqueville on America*, 195. Contrast both of these positions with that of Sedgwick, a friend of both men, who saw the spread of slavery to lands suited to produce cotton and sugar as inevitable, and who believed there were greater dangers to the North than slavery: financial speculation, moral corruption, "lack of discipline"; "Letter to Tocqueville, 5 February 1857," in Craiutu and Jennings, *Tocqueville on America*, 201.
[54] It should be noted, however, that he also thought the "negroes...not fit for freedom" and believed a forty-year period of acclimatization to freedom would be preferable to immediate emancipation. "Dec 18, [1857?]," in Craiutu and Jennings, *Tocqueville on America*, 271 and 270.

coexistence, he insisted, must be "on the terms of liberty and justice to all."[55]

Beckwith professed the kind of faith in the basic integrity and good sense of popular judgment that Tocqueville sometimes indulged in but more often yearned for. In response to Tocqueville's worries that universal suffrage was undermining the judicial system, he wrote, America's evils stemmed not from liberty or democracy but from "the corrupting and enormous influence of slavery" and that "I rely on 'the people' to do, what nothing else could do, which is to exterminate slavery."[56] He added that careful observers would see "nothing in the existing disorders to the discredit of free institutions, but will perceive that *universal suffrage* is the sole possible remedy"; "we never go so right as when that *vulgar* voice ["the voice of the people"] is listened to."[57] And just as he insisted that America's culture of violence should be blamed on the slave power and not on the lower classes, he argued that the greatest danger to property in America came not from riots, as Tocqueville feared, but from what he called the "modern 'pirate on change'": stock exchange speculators who were conspiring to manipulate property values for quick profits. He linked all of these to imperial violence in a letter that conveys a sense of the global crisis of modern American and European society as the Civil War loomed and the British brutally suppressed the Sepoy Rebellion in India.

Here is Beckwith again: "Looking at the venality which prevails at Washington, the rascality of Wall Street . . . the savage war in Algeria, the homicides in India and the murders in China – the moral aspect of things is not cheering – and worst of all these are the peoples claiming to be the most advanced in Christian civilization."[58] Unlike Tocqueville, Beckwith

---

55 Sumner: "Be assured that many of those things by which we are degraded are caused by slavery, even in states where slavery does not exist" (289). Tocqueville himself shared the free-soil view: as he wrote to Sedgwick in 1857: "I am unwilling to admit that any contract whatsoever could include among its terms the annihilation of the right and the duty that the present generation has to prevent the most horrible of all social evils from spreading over millions and millions of people belonging to future generations" (226).

56 "Beckwith to Tocqueville, undated," in Craiutu and Jennings, *Tocqueville on America*, 316–317.

57 "[T]he people has no object in going wrong, desires to go right and in general when it appears to go wrong – only *appears* so, because its wishes are willfully perverted and turned aside by a captious and arrogant government" (202). Note that Beckwith believed that "much as they may hate slavery," the various Northern factions and interests would never be united against it until they recognized the dangers it posed for them (167).

58 "Beckwith to Tocqueville, 20 September 1857," in Craiutu and Jennings, *Tocqueville on America*, 257.

saw the evils of slavery not as sequestered in a dying southern society that was fundamentally aristocratic but as bound up with an array of abuses of power in and by modern societies.

It is noteworthy that Tocqueville had discussed slavery in *Democracy* in the context of a discussion of the three races; he was interested above all in race prejudice and race relations and in the persistence – and in his view, the increase – of white racism after the abolition of slavery in the North. He was struck by the far greater economic dynamism of free as opposed to slave societies; he believed slavery was shrinking in American South, and he clearly did not anticipate in 1835 the struggles over slavery in the West. The fight over slavery was, for Tocqueville, a moral and humanitarian rather than a political struggle.[59] That is, he had relatively little to say about slavery's political consequences for the nation, such as the disproportionate political power that Constitution's three-fifths provision granted to slave holders.[60] The question of slavery's distortion of democratic politics at the national level, which so preoccupied his American friends in the 1850s, had left next to no trace in *Democracy*. Similarly, his own letters of the 1850s suggest that he regarded the Kansas crisis primarily as a question about whether slavery would occupy more territory, not, as the Americans saw it, over democracy's future.[61]

For his part, despite his own deeply felt opposition to slavery, Beckwith rejected abolition as a "breach of faith" and an inappropriate intervention into the affairs of, in his words, "*sovereign* states." He saw the question of the expansion of slavery as more consequential for America's future than that of slavery per se because it was the slave owners' only way to entrench their wildly disproportionate political power and their stranglehold on the majority.[62] He called the three-fifths provision "the most

---

[59] Cheryl Welch, "Creating Concitoyens: Tocqueville on the Legacy of Slavery," in *Reading Tocqueville: From Oracle to Actor*, eds. Raf Geenens and Annelien De Dijn (Basingstoke: Palgrave Macmillan, 2007), 31–51.

[60] He was concerned to make a few counterintuitive points: that "habits are milder and more tolerant" toward blacks in the South than in the North, and that abolition in the North had been for the interests of whites and not blacks, DIA (G) I.2.x, 396–397.

[61] Tocqueville to Edward Vernon Childe: "I hope that the abolitionist cause will triumph in Kansas . . . in the interest of the whole of mankind" (January, 23, 1858, 282); to Charles Sumner, "Will Kansas be condemned to the horrors of slavery?" (March 28, 1858, 286).

[62] He told Tocqueville that he had bought substantial land in Kansas as a means of keeping out slave holders; similarly, his friend and business associate John Murray Forbes sent money and arms to northerners fighting slavery in Kansas. Unitarian encyclopedia: http://www25.uua.org/uuhs/duub/articles/johnforbes.html. See *Letters and Recollections of John Murray Forbes*, ed. Sarah Forbes Hughes (Boston: Houghton Mifflin, 1899), vol. 1, 177, 182;

fatal mistake and the most vicious bargain in the whole American system" but added, "[b]ut the bargain was made and we don't ask to break
it; we intend to keep the agreement and beat them besides."[63] This was
the position of almost all antislavery leaders, including, most famously,
Lincoln: most radical republicans were not abolitionists in the strict sense.
The abolitionist, Beckwith wrote Tocqueville, is "one who acts upon the
principle of the slave holder in this, that like the slave owner, he would
be a law to himself, and would enforce his will as law upon others, in
their own sphere, in their own dominions." These are sovereign states, he
wrote: "I claim no more right to meddle in the affair, than in the affairs of
Naples or Greece or Turkey or Russia or Persia."[64] Although we might
disagree with this equation of slave holding and abolition and of states in
the American union and sovereign countries, Beckwith's worries about
domination exercised in the name of justice are worth considering, especially in light of the civilizing imperial rule that the British in India and the
French in Africa purported to exercise. And abolitionism forged its own
pathway to imperialism. British abolitionists of this period were among
the most vocal supporters of the expansion of British influence and rule
in West Africa, and American abolitionism would later contribute to U.S.
colonial rule in Philippines.[65]

Thanks to his keen sense of rivalry with Britain, Tocqueville was often
less skeptical about American expansion than his American friends were.
They tended to see the depredations of slavery as nefariously bound
up with imperial expansion in ways that Tocqueville did not.[66] They

---

[63] "Beckwith to Tocqueville, 18 December 1857," in Craiutu and Jennings, *Tocqueville
on America*, 274.

[64] "Beckwith to Tocqueville, 18 December 1857," in Craiutu and Jennings, *Tocqueville
on America*, 271.

[65] See Thomas Fowell Buxton, *The African Slave Trade and its Remedy* (London: John
Murray, 1840), a "prospectus of the society for the extinction of the slave trade and
for the civilization of Africa"; Derek R. Peterson, ed., *Abolition and Imperialism in
Britain, Africa, and the Atlantic* (Athens: Ohio University Press, 2010); Ralph Austen
and Woodruff D. Smith, "Images of Africa and British Slave-Trade Abolition: the Transi-
tion to an Imperialist Ideology, 1787–1807, *African Historical Studies*, 2 (1969), 69–83;
Deirdre Coleman, *Romantic Colonization and British Anti-slavery* (Cambridge: Cambridge University Press, 2005); and Michael Salman, *The Embarrassment of Slavery:
Controversies over Bondage and Nationalism in the American Colonial Philippines*
(Berkeley: University of California Press, 2001).

[66] Northerners tended to object to the spread of slavery and the "slave power" or to
worry about the feasibility of holding together such an extensive territory acquired so
quickly rather than to oppose American territorial expansion on principle. As Aziz Rana

worried about President Buchanan's plots to seize Cuba from Spain as further slave territory.[67] Earlier, in the 1840s, Tocqueville had been keen to see America triumph in its struggles with Britain over the Oregon territory, and he believed it was in France's self-interest to further America's maritime presence as a counterbalance against British hegemony. Tocqueville's own worries about expansion were centered squarely on Britain. As he said, "If [Britain] had, as is the case with the peoples on the Continent, the possibility of limitless [military] recruitment, I believe the entire world would end by being the object of its covetousness."[68] European imperial and commercial expansion as such did not worry him; on the contrary, he regarded them with awe and, in certain moods (or perhaps to British correspondents), was willing to extend that awe even to Britain's conquests.[69] As he wrote to his English friend Lord Hatherton during the Sepoy Rebellion, "I have never for an instant doubted your triumph, which is that of Christianity and civilization."[70] Tocqueville "admit[ted]" to Hatherton that he was disappointed by the English failure to govern India better. However, from the time of his study of India in 1843 through the Sepoy Rebellion, Tocqueville continued to regard the incursion of Europe into Asia as a basically beneficial uprooting of enervating custom and despotic rule, and for all his disappointment in its

writes, northerners and southerners alike believed the settler community "possessed an imperial prerogative power that made both indigenous sovereignty and existing borders provisional – dependent exclusively on internal social needs," Aziz Rana, *Two Faces of Freedom*, 111; also see Robert May, *Southern Dream*, 21.

[67] As Sumner wrote: "Why will not Spain follow the example of European powers – and now of Russia – and declare emancipation in her colonies? This would do more to settle the slavery question than any blow ever before struck. It would at once take Cuba from the field of Mr. Buchanan's lawless desires and destroy the aliment of filibusters" ("Sumner to Tocqueville, 7 May 1858," in Craiutu and Jennings, *Tocqueville on America*, 289). On filibusters, the private adventurers, mostly from the South, who launched military expeditions to the West and in Central America, see May, *Manifest Destiny's Underworld*.

[68] "Tocqueville to Beckwith, February 6 1858," in Craiutu and Jennings, *Tocqueville on America*, 283.

[69] As in his claim in 1840 that "the old Asiatic world is vanishing, and in its place the European world is rising. Europe in our times does not attack Asia only through a corner, as did Europe in the time of the crusades: She attacks...from all sides, puncturing, enveloping, subduing." OC 3.ii 290; translation from Seymour Drescher, *Tocqueville and England* (Cambridge: Harvard University Press, 1964), 156.

[70] November 27, 1857; Tocqueville, *Oeuvres Complètes*, ed. Gustave de Beaumont (Paris, 1860) 6:422; SLPS, 359. The English had not done "anything for the Indian populations that might have been expected from their enlightenment and their institutions. I think that more could have been expected from them."

execution, he continued to approve English rule over the Hindus, whom he called "men with the hearts of sheep."[71]

Judging from Beckwith's reply to a missing letter from Tocqueville, Tocqueville had worried about English "oppression and misrule" in India and had wondered whether Christianity could be introduced into the colony through violence. In contrast to Tocqueville's mild critique of English methods and pride, Beckwith was categorically opposed to imperial rule (in part, it should be said, on the grounds that racial mixing was, providentially, unlikely to work). He declared that "one people should never govern another people: what business have the English in India?" and wrote, "I see nothing for the future of India but slaughter, destruction of property, interruption of industry, famine, pestilence and rapid depopulation."[72] He scoffed at the idea that the English had any Christian motives in India: the British government, he wrote, "has never read the New Testament; it takes its religion and its policy from the old," in which "conquest and revenge are the divine right of the strongest party." Tocqueville's pious letter to Hatherton was dated two months after Beckwith's to Tocqueville, so these stinging judgments must have been fresh in his mind.

As a prominent American businessman about to leave for China to open it further to American shipping, Beckwith had his own complex interests and biases, not to be discounted. These may have included his own sense of rivalry with Britain and a typically American preference for informal, so-called free-trade imperialism. He gives us little to go on about his own motives or interests in these letters or in a series of letters that he wrote from Hong Kong to a business partner in Japan.[73] But they suggest that he was exploring the affinities among imperial violence, the autocratic habits of American slave owners, and the economic power of certain financiers as connected abuses of power and threats to democratic society. Tocqueville admired Beckwith's political judgment, but his instincts were interestingly different.

Tocqueville's writings of the late 1850s suggest that as he sought to understand the causes of the abuse of liberty that seemed to him to

---

[71] See "Letter to Eugénie de Grancey, 8 October 1857," in LCS, 1267. "I believe, after all [that has happened], that this [English] government is infinitely superior, in equity and mildness, to that of the Muslim princes that preceded it and that India has never in the past three centuries been more tranquil and less hardly treated than it is today."

[72] "Beckwith and Tocqueville," in Craiutu and Jennings, *Tocqueville on America*, 252.

[73] Massachusetts Historical Society, Franklin Gordon Dexter Papers, Ms N-1117, boxes nos. 3, 4, and 5.

be America's most salient feature at that moment; his inclination was to blame a leveling down of tastes and habits, as in his lamentation over what he called the "follies and vulgarities that liberty gives rise to."[74] He did not look first to persistent inequalities or abuses of power by the privileged. This may have been in part because he continued to see the evils of slavery as essentially confined to the South, as he had done in *Democracy in America*. In part, perhaps, it was because he was determined to see distinctively democratic features – that is to say, those rooted in the equality of conditions and the love of equality – as responsible for both America's advantages and its ills. Tocqueville himself had recognized in the second volume of *Democracy* that he may have overemphasized the dangers of equality: "I chose to speak out publicly about the dangers that equality poses to human independence because I firmly believe that those perils are the most formidable that the future holds, as well as the least anticipated. But I do not believe that they are insurmountable."[75] However, if he himself was rarely as attentive to American democracy's imperial features, his writings and those of his contemporaries may yet help us to think through the ways in which democracy both invites and is corrupted by empire.

---

[74] "Tocqueville to Francis Lieber, 1 September 1856," in Craiutu and Jennings, *Tocqueville on America*, 184. Tocqueville repeatedly used Hobbes's phrase "robust child [*puer robustus*]" to describe America.

[75] DIA (G) II.4.vii, 830.

CHAPTER 12

Tocqueville and the Napoleonic Legend

Richard Boyd

Introduction

Arguably no figure in the modern world better personifies the agonies and ecstasies of empire than Napoleon Bonaparte. With his stunning military victories over the various coalitions of European powers; his liberalizing reforms of the Continental legal system; and his advocacy of religious toleration for Jews, Catholics, and Protestants, Bonaparte can plausibly be construed as the architect of a uniquely modern vision of empire that promised legal emancipation and civilization to all those falling under its power. Nonetheless, the emperor's insatiable lust for conquest and the devastation his military campaigns wrought on the peoples of Europe, Russia, and the Middle East cast him in a much less flattering light. His personal legacy is every bit as multivalent as the peculiar brand of imperialism he ushered onto the political stage in the nineteenth century.

What is even more confounding are the wildly disparate responses Bonaparte elicited from contemporaries – republicans, liberals, and monarchists alike. Among the emperor's many observers, Alexis de Tocqueville captures this ambivalence as well as any commentator in the first half of the nineteenth century. Tocqueville is usually cast alongside early nineteenth-century French liberals such as Benjamin Constant and Germaine de Staël as a trenchant critic of Bonaparte's despotic rule. There is undeniable truth to this characterization, as we will see, but in this chapter I want to complicate the standard view of Tocqueville as a whole-hearted critic of Bonapartism.[1]

---

[1] Although Tocqueville's liberal critique of Napoleonic rule is a running – albeit under-developed – theme in the Tocqueville scholarship, the view of Tocqueville as being

My discussion of Tocqueville's ambivalent relationship to the Napoleonic tradition builds upon Sudhir Hazareesingh's insights into the considerable range and ambiguity of "liberal" responses to the Napoleonic legend in mid-nineteenth-century France.[2] Although Tocqueville condemned Napoleon's illiberal domestic policies, he is nonetheless drawn – even against his broader liberal sympathies – to the ideals of grandeur, heroism, power, conquest, and national greatness represented by the First Empire. As we will see, Tocqueville's writings on France's domestic life in the 1840s and 1850s testify to his growing sense of a nation in decline and his frustration with the pettiness and mediocrity of bourgeois society. His colonial writings of the same period show a nostalgic longing for France's lost greatness and offer glimpses of an imperial alternative that represents France's best hope for recapturing the power and grandeur of the First Empire. Appealing to Bonaparte's aims and imperial accomplishments – while simultaneously distancing himself from Napoleon's personal legacy of despotism – Tocqueville shares much in common with subsequent nineteenth-century interpreters such as Stendhal, Émile Zola, and Friedrich Nietzsche.

This chapter advances three main claims. First, by fleshing out the full range of French attitudes toward Napoleon in the first half of the nineteenth century, I argue that we can better understand how Bonaparte can simultaneously appear as anathema and apotheosis of liberalism. Secondly, this intellectual context allows us to appreciate Tocqueville's position midway between the liberal vision of Napoleon as despot and usurper and a subsequent and a more nostalgic Napoleonic legend of the second half of the nineteenth century that saw the First Empire as the high tide of French political grandeur. Lastly, and most importantly, I want to suggest that Tocqueville's embrace of certain aspects of the Napoleonic legacy has both practical and moral implications for our

particularly concerned with the problem of Bonapartism has been explored most exhaustively by Melvin Richter, "Tocqueville, Napoleon, and Bonapartism," in Shmuel Eisenstadt, ed., *Reconsidering Tocqueville's "Democracy in America"* (New Brunswick: Transaction Publishers, 1988), 110–145; and Richter, "Tocqueville and French Nineteenth-Century Conceptualizations of the Two Bonapartes and their Empires," in Baehr and Richter, eds., *Dictatorship in History and Theory: Bonapartism, Caesarism, and Totalitarianism.* (Cambridge: Cambridge University Press, 2004), 83–102.

[2] Especially Sudhir Hazareesingh, *The Legend of Napoleon* (London: Granta Books, 2004); Hazareesingh, *The Saint-Napoleon: Celebrations of Sovereignty in Nineteenth-Century France* (Cambridge, MA: Harvard University Press, 2004); and Hazareesingh, "Memory, Legend and Politics: Napoleonic Patriotism in the Restoration Era," *European Journal of Political Theory* 5 (January 2006), 71–84.

own understanding of empire, international relations, and the frontiers of democracy.

Nineteenth-Century Liberalism and the Critique of Napoleon

From the vantage of much of nineteenth-century liberalism, Napoleon Bonaparte was a despotical usurper who preyed upon the anarchy and instability of the French Revolution. For Madame de Staël, Benjamin Constant, and others who found themselves on the wrong side of Bonaparte's aspirations, he was legendary only for his perfection of the art of tyranny. His insatiable ambition, his cultivation of the art of propaganda, his plebiscitarian manipulation of public opinion, the ruthless censorship and other inroads he made against political liberty, his abduction and execution of the Duke of Enghien, his ready use of conscription, and the eagerness with which he appropriated the Revolution's baneful instrument of exile – all of this made him the very personification of modern despotism. Liberals hardly monopolized this vision of Bonaparte as amoral tyrant, warmonger, and usurper; their criticisms were widely shared across the political spectrum of post-revolutionary France, particularly by conservatives such as Chateaubriand.[3]

Staël's loathing of Bonaparte runs throughout her works, especially her 1818 *Considerations on the Principal Events of the French Revolution*. "Never had a man the art of multiplying the ties of dependence more ably than Bonaparte," Staël complains. "He surpassed everybody in his knowledge of the great and the little means of despotism."[4] She credits herself with being among the first to suspect that Napoleon's designs as First Consul were in no way an extension of the legitimate liberal reforms of the Revolution but imperialistic, unprincipled excuses for war and expansion that served no other purpose than advancing the ambitions of Bonaparte and his followers. "It was military glory which intoxicated the nation while the nets of despotism were spread out by some men whose

---

[3] On the variety of reactions to Napoleon, across the political spectrum, see especially Pieter Geyl, *Napoleon: For and Against* (New Haven: Yale University Press, 1948) and Hazareesingh, *Legend of Napoleon*. For an impassioned and lengthy list of Napoleon's offenses, see François-René de Chateaubriand, *De Buonaparte et Des Bourbons* (Paris: Mame Frères, 1814).

[4] Germaine de Staël, *Considerations on the Principal Events of the French Revolution*, ed. Aurelian Craiutu (Indianapolis: Liberty Press, 2008), 490.

meanness and corruption cannot be sufficiently emphasized," she bitterly notes.[5]

Her antipathy was as much personal as political. Napoleon was "natural only when he commands."[6] Even his physiognomy stamped him as a creature made for war.[7] He had already perfected the "system" of domination, as he was later to do with "every other mode of subjugating men by degrading them."[8] Unrestrained by any moral principle or scruple, he found France atomized and disturbed by internecine struggles. Displaying an "uncommon ability" for "dominion," his method consisted of "satisfy[ing] men's interests at the expense of their virtues," "deprav[ing] public opinion by sophisms," and most disastrously, "giv[ing] the nation war for an object instead of liberty." Bonaparte found himself with "nothing but the mass of the nation to manage," as French society had been reduced to individual existence and servile dependency.[9] While the nation was only too eager to go along with his despotism, his own "fatal genius" was ultimately to blame.[10]

Undoubtedly, Staël and other liberals were alarmed by the domestic face of Bonaparte's tyranny, but there is also a keen understanding of how his inroads against political liberties were linked with his mania for imperial conquest. She notes that "from the moment that his soul became so miserable as to see no grandeur except in despotism, it was perhaps impossible for him to do without continual wars; for what would a despot be without military glory in a country like France?" Arguing that domestic instability necessitates foreign conquest, Staël wonders whether a nation could be "oppressed in the interior without giving it the fatal compensation of ruling elsewhere in its turn?"[11] Every French government since the Constituent Assembly has "perished by yielding to this seduction under some pretext or other."[12] As we will see, Staël's sense of the dangerous allure of foreign empire for a nation unable to establish liberty at home stands as a sharp counterpoint to Tocqueville's much

---

[5] Staël, *Considerations*, 490.
[6] Staël, *Considerations*, 416.
[7] Staël, *Considerations*, 410.
[8] Staël, *Considerations*, 411.
[9] Staël, *Considerations*, 444.
[10] Staël, *Considerations*, 441.
[11] Staël, *Considerations*, 484.
[12] Staël, *Considerations*, 484.

warmer views of the therapeutic benefits of imperial conquest under the July Monarchy and Second Republic.

For his part, Benjamin Constant's relationship to Napoleon was less categorically negative. After denouncing Napoleon's usurpation in terms that were every bit as forceful as Staël's, Constant eventually agreed to serve under Napoleon during the Hundred Days. This pragmatic attempt to moderate Bonaparte's personal authority by drafting a liberal constitution was surprising, however, given Constant's scathing condemnation of Bonapartism in his 1814 work *Of the Spirit of Conquest and Usurpation and Their Relation to European Civilization.*

Constant accuses Napoleon of inventing a wholly new form of modern tyranny known as "usurpation." Usurpation is infinitely worse than earlier forms of monarchical absolutism. While a monarch ascends nobly to the throne, the "usurper slithers onto it through blood and muck, and when he takes his place on it, his stained robe bears the marks of the career he has followed."[13] Usurpation is crowned by deceit, perfidy, exploitation, injustice, corruption, and greed – vices hardly confined to the usurper himself but that pollute the whole regime.[14] Absolute monarchs of earlier ages may have compelled obedience with threats of physical violence, but usurpation "profanes liberty" by compelling individuals to participate actively in the process of their own domination. Whereas despotism "rules by means of silence, and leaves man the right to be silent," usurpation "condemns him to speak, it pursues him into the most intimate sanctuary of his thoughts, and, by forcing him to lie to his own conscience, deprives the oppressed of his last remaining consolation."[15]

Like Staël, Constant sees a necessary link between Bonaparte's national and foreign despotisms. Because the diffusion of truth and critical thinking are weapons against usurpation, only perpetual warfare made Bonaparte's manipulation of public opinion sustainable. "Had France remained at peace," Constant notes, "her peaceful citizens, her idle warriors would have observed the despot, would have judged him, and would have communicated their judgments to him... Usurpation would not have long withstood the influence of truth."[16] It was necessary for Napoleon to "distract public attention by bellicose enterprises."[17] A

---

[13] Benjamin Constant, *Political Writings*, ed. Biancamaria Fontana (Cambridge: Cambridge University Press, 1988), 89.
[14] Constant, *Political Writings*, 89.
[15] Constant, *Political Writings*, 95–97.
[16] Constant, *Political Writings*, 163.
[17] Constant, *Political Writings*, 163.

"usurper's sole resource is uninterrupted war," which captivates the public mind, blocks the free flow of information, and dispels to "distant shores" whatever "part of the French nation that still had some real energy."[18] Moreover, rather than imperial conquest transporting civilization into the midst of barbarism, as its apologists would contend, Napoleon's foreign conquests did precisely the opposite: "Since he could not bring ignorance and barbarism to the heart of Europe, he took some Europeans to Africa, to see if he could succeed in forming them in barbarism and ignorance; and then, to maintain his authority, he worked to make Europe go backward."[19] The conceit that France was waging war to bring her principles of liberty and equality to other parts of the world represented the vilest sort of "pretext" and hypocrisy.[20]

Against this backdrop of post-revolutionary liberal hostility to Napoleon, it has been tempting to portray Tocqueville as essentially in the same camp as Staël, Constant, Guizot, Lamartine, and other liberal critics. Among Tocqueville scholars, Melvin Richter has perhaps done most to flesh out this view of Tocqueville as an anti-Bonapartist liberal. Richter perceptively notes the many ways in which Bonapartism came to represent a categorically new form of modern despotism, born of revolutionary conditions but based on an unprecedented degree of political centralization and the concentration of power.[21] Of the two likely paths for democracy outlined by Tocqueville in the *Democracy*, with one leading toward equality under liberty and the other culminating in the despotism of a single man, Tocqueville came to believe that the latter scenario best described the France of his day: "From the 18th century and the Revolution, as from a common source, emerged two rivers: the first carried men to free institutions, whereas the second drew them toward absolute power." Like a switchman between these two channels, Napoleon shifted the course of French history from the former to the latter: "Led by him, the French found themselves even further from liberty than they had been at any period in their history."[22]

Following Constant's typology of usurpation, Tocqueville concurs that the worst feature of Napoleon's rule was that it found a sanction for absolutism in the will of the people themselves, a form of oppression that

[18] Constant, *Political Writings*, 163.
[19] Constant, *Political Writings*, 100.
[20] Constant, *Political Writings*, 65.
[21] Especially Richter, "Tocqueville and French Nineteenth-Century Conceptualizations of the Two Bonapartes and their Empires," 83–102.
[22] OC 16, 263.

Richter characterizes as "plebiscitarian democracy." In Tocqueville's own words: "If an absolute government were ever established in a country as democratic in its social conditions and as demoralized as France, there would be no conceivable limits on tyranny. Under Bonaparte we have already seen one specimen of such a regime."[23]

Although he never managed to compose as sustained a treatment of the First Empire as he offered of the ancien régime, the Revolution, or the July Monarchy, Tocqueville's scattered criticisms of Bonaparte's domestic despotism are revealing and seem at first glance to fall squarely in the liberal tradition outlined earlier. Whereas Bonaparte in many ways "personified and continued the French Revolution," he was nonetheless one of the "greatest enemies ever known to human liberty."[24] Tocqueville's 1842 address at his inauguration into the Académie francaise has done much to confirm this impression of Tocqueville as an anti-Bonapartist in the tradition of Staël and Constant. In this speech, Tocqueville denounces Napoleon's genius for centralizing and remaking French society, the way in which he preyed upon the egalitarianism and individualism already rampant in France, and how he studiously cultivated the image of a defender of liberty by extending civil liberties even while making unprecedented inroads into political liberties.

All that being said, and despite Tocqueville's profound misgivings about Bonaparte's illiberal stratagems and despotical legacy, his portrayal of Napoleon himself was deeply ambivalent: less polemical and more rhetorically nuanced than Constant's or Staël's. Without denying either Napoleon's faults or genius in perfecting despotism, the leitmotiv of Tocqueville's comments on Bonapartism is to stress continuities between Napoleon's actions and the Revolution that came before him. Whereas for Staël and Constant, Napoleon interrupted the French Revolution, for Tocqueville, Napoleon merely completed the potential for democratic despotism that was latent in it from the very beginning. Appearing at the "supreme moment" when the French Revolution had introduced disorder and weakness into French society, Napoleon laid his hands on

all the scattered remnants of power, formed an administration, established a system of justice, and organized on a single and uniform framework all civil and political legislation; he drew, in a word, from beneath the ruins that the Revolution had left behind, a new society, better linked together and stronger

---

[23] Tocqueville, "Letter to Kergolay, January 1835," OC 13:1, 373.
[24] OC 16, 234.

than the former society which had been destroyed, and unveiled it at a stroke before all the eyes of France, who no longer even recognized herself.[25]

Whether for good or ill, French society found itself ecstatic at the magnitude of his accomplishment.

While he never goes so far as to apologize for Napoleon's tragic ambition or fatal genius, neither does Tocqueville unequivocally condemn the Empire. "One must neither praise nor blame Napoleon for having concentrated in his own hands virtually all administrative powers," Tocqueville notes, "for after the sudden disappearance of the nobility and the upper classes, these powers came to him by themselves; it would have been almost as difficult for him to relinquish them as it was to take them up."[26]

Napoleon may have bequeathed a new form of despotism to the world, but in his own lifetime this was in some sense overshadowed – if not justified – by his own personal charisma and energy. Tocqueville concedes that

the singularity of his genius justified and legitimated to some degree in the eyes of his contemporaries their extreme dependency. The hero concealed the despot. People were able to imagine that in obeying him, they were submitting less to his power than to his person. But after Napoleon had ceased to light up and inspire this new world that he had created, nothing remained of him but his despotism: the most perfect despotism that had ever come to weigh on a nation the least prepared to retain its dignity in servitude.[27]

And with grudging admiration mingled with criticism: "The person who founded and maintained this Empire was the most extraordinary phenomenon to appear for many centuries. Napoleon was as great as a man can be without virtue."[28] While the achievements of the Empire were estimable, its "grandeur" was in some measure a result of events beyond its control, the product of accidents rather than any intrinsic virtues of itself or its leader. Napoleon's task was deceptively simple: "The Revolution had brought France to its feet; Napoleon made it march."[29]

Not only are Tocqueville's criticisms of Napoleon muted, but they differ in key respects from those of the preceding generation. For Constant, Staël, Chateaubriand, and others, Napoleon's chief crimes were

[25] OC 16, 258.
[26] OC 16, 258 note 7.
[27] OC 16, 264.
[28] OC 16, 263.
[29] OC 16, 263.

those inflicted against French citizens via censorship, the manipulation of public opinion, the centralization of power, confiscation, conscription, the assassination of the Duke d'Enghiens, exile, and so forth. As we have seen, however, he is equally culpable in their eyes for the casualties of the Napoleonic Wars. His imperialism was inextricable from his domestic tyranny, and both were thoroughly objectionable. Their liberal critique is anti-imperial as much as anti-Bonapartist. Mirroring in fascinating ways the anti-imperial "volte-face" in nineteenth-century liberal thought so ably documented by Jennifer Pitts, Tocqueville's critique of Napoleon comes to focus almost exclusively on his domestic despotism, whereas the broader project of empire of which Napoleon was the chief agent emerges unscathed.[30] The grandeur of Napoleon's accomplishments was ultimately hollow, in Tocqueville's view, because it represented an illusory product of a single man's amoral ambitions. However, this does not mean that the pursuit of imperial grandeur is of no value. What is required is to make the pursuit of imperial glory an expression of the collective will of the French people rather than leaving the nation to bask in the hollow, refracted glory of a single charismatic individual. Unlike Staël and Constant before him, Tocqueville finds no contradiction in being anti-Bonapartist and pro-imperial.

Tocqueville's "Bonapartism" Reconsidered

As Sudhir Hazareesingh has shown in his masterful work on the development and transformation of the "Napoleonic legend" throughout the nineteenth century, liberal understandings of Napoleon were by no means as clear-cut as the preceding typologies might suggest. Liberals came to differ greatly in their opinion of Napoleon's personal accomplishments and legacy. There were at least two distinctive narratives in play. The first and most familiar was the one upon which we have mainly focused so far – what Hazareesingh calls the "black legend" of Napoleon – which portrayed Bonaparte as a "violent and despotic ruler" who hijacked the French Revolution and subordinated its liberalizing reforms and lofty

---

[30] Jennifer Pitts, *A Turn to Empire: The Rise of Imperial Liberalism in Britain and France* (Princeton: Princeton University Press, 2006), esp. 165–203. As Pitts notes with respect to the Napoleonic legacy: "Napoleon's imperial ambitions in Europe and beyond – including his brief foray into Egypt – were remembered with great ambivalence by many Frenchmen, who sought to retain the national confidence imparted by Napoleonic military victories while distancing themselves from 'Bonapartism.'" (165).

aspirations to his own imperial ambitions. The second and less familiar was the subsequent "countermyth" of "liberal Bonapartism," which
lionized Napoleon as the great systematizer and reformer and maintained
that the emperor had been a closet liberal all along.[31]

In the remainder of this chapter, I want to reconsider Tocqueville's
relationship to the two rival visions of Napoleon sketched out earlier.
Respectfully disagreeing with Richter and others, I hope to establish
that Tocqueville's relationship to Bonapartism is both more complex
and ambivalent than has generally been acknowledged. To accomplish
this I will examine, first, three key aspects of Tocqueville's own ideas
that seem to have an affinity for the counter myth of liberal Bonapartism.
Secondly, I want to suggest that his ideas are comprehensible in light of a
general dissatisfaction with bourgeois society discernible among a variety
of European political and literary thinkers in the second half of the nineteenth century. Above and beyond this particular axis of the Napoleonic
legend – that is, the distinction between liberals who vilified Napoleon as
illiberal and antidemocratic and those who adored him for what they perceived to be his deeper liberal credentials – there is a subsequent tradition
of European thinkers who were drawn to Napoleon precisely because of
the ways in which his person and accomplishments called attention to
the limitations and shortcomings of bourgeois liberal society. My claim
is that Tocqueville shares as much with later nineteenth-century critics of
malaise, decline, and decadence of French society under the regimes that
succeeded Napoleon as he does with post-revolutionary liberals such as
Staël and Constant.

Grandeur and the Imperial Project

In terms of Tocqueville's own ideas, there are three dimensions to his
thought that demonstrate affinities for Bonapartist ways of thinking. The
first is his complex embrace of empire – a dimension that, as Jennifer
Pitts has demonstrated in great depth and detail, clearly distinguishes
Tocqueville from earlier French liberal thought, which had been decidedly
anti-imperialistic.[32]

Tocqueville's position on French imperialism is admittedly nuanced –
and arguably shifts over the course of his engagement with the Algerian
question from an initial optimism about peaceful coexistence to an advocacy of brutal military conquest – but one constant is his fascination with

---

[31] Hazareesingh, *The Legend of Napoleon*, 156.
[32] Pitts, *A Turn to Empire*, esp. ch. 6.

"grandeur."[33] Confronted by the increasingly privatistic, self-interested, and demoralized French society of Louis Philippe and the July Monarchy, Tocqueville came to view the imperial project as the most promising way of reestablishing the standing of the French nation in the eyes of other nations around the world. Although he remained sufficiently dubious of the spiritual lassitude, civic apathy, and bourgeois effeminacy of his contemporaries as to doubt whether France was in any position – at least at this juncture of history – to reenact the heroic exploits of the First Empire, he was nonetheless wary of his contemporaries' willingness to squander what little international standing France continued to enjoy.

Emphasizing a theme that runs consistently through his writings on the Algerian question, Tocqueville argued strenuously in his 1841 "Essay on Algeria" that France's compromised position in European affairs gave it no way to relinquish safely its imperial conquests in Algeria. As Tocqueville warned:

In the eyes of the world, such an abandonment would be the clear indication of our decadence. It would be far less disturbing to see our conquests taken from us forcibly by a rival nation. A people in all its vigor and in the course of expanding its power can still be unlucky in war and so lose provinces. . . . But if France shrank from an enterprise in which she faced nothing but the natural difficulties of the terrain and the opposition of little barbarous tribes, she would seem in the eyes of the world to be yielding to her own impotence and succumbing to her own lack of courage. Any people that easily gives up what it has taken and chooses to retire peacefully to its original borders proclaims that its age of greatness is over. It visibly enters the period of its decline.[34]

As I have argued at greater length in another context, Tocqueville's preoccupation with grandeur comes to dominate his thinking on foreign affairs, constituting the antipode of the bourgeois decadence and mediocrity from which he sought to rescue France.[35] After having been defeated in her conquests on the European continent, losing virtually all of her territories in the Americas, and being pushed back within her territorial borders, France's new Algerian colonies afford one last chance to demonstrate her relevance in foreign affairs. With courage, will, and a bit of good

---

[33] On the need for French colonies to support grandeur, greatness, and national pride, see, WES, esp. 24, 59, 206–207.

[34] Tocqueville, "Essay on Algeria" (1841), in WES, 59.

[35] Richard Boyd, "Imperial Fathers and Favorite Sons: J. S. Mill, Alexis de Tocqueville, and Nineteenth-Century Justifications of Empire," in Jill Locke and Eileen Botting, eds., *Feminist Interpretations of Alexis de Tocqueville* (University Park: Penn State University Press, 2008), 225–252.

fortune France might establish some lasting monument to her greatness on the northern coasts of Africa. "This future appears to be in our hands," Tocqueville exhorts, "and I assure you that with time, perseverance, competency, and justice I have no doubt that we have the power to erect on the coast of Africa a grand monument to the glory of our nation."[36]

While generally positive or affirmative, Tocqueville's nationalistic obsession with France's standing in the eyes of other nations, particularly Britain, was clearly tinged with something of the ressentiment described by contemporary scholars of nationalism.[37] As John Stuart Mill chides Tocqueville in one of their last exchanges on the subject, a petty concern for national standing and superiority is a vulgar sign of insecurity. Even "the most stupid & ignorant person knows perfectly well that the real importance of a country in the eyes of foreigners does not depend on the loud & boisterous *assertion* of importance, the effect of which is an impression of angry weakness, not strength."[38]

Every bit as important as demonstrating France's continued relevance in the world of international relations was the hope of civic regeneration and psychic renewal. Demoralized and sunken into domestic malaise by its humiliation in the Napoleonic Wars, France needed to regain confidence in her own power and mission in the world. This was to be accomplished by rising above a merely domestic or commercial point of view and embracing the project of empire from the standpoint of "the political" itself.[39] In his many writings on the Algerian question, Tocqueville regarded the national interests of the French as preeminent and those of the Algerians as secondary. Although he entertained hopes that the interests of France could be harmonized both with the peaceful civilization of France's colonial subjects in Algeria and the requirements of international law and humanity, he also made it clear that when push comes to shove, the interests of France – military, political, psychological, and existential – were paramount.

Tocqueville's enthusiastic defense of the French imperial conquest of Algeria brings to light an illiberal and antidemocratic aspect of his

---

[36] OC 3:1, 151.
[37] I have developed this point about the necessarily other-directed character of Tocqueville's imperialism at greater length in Boyd, "Imperial Fathers and Favorite Sons," 244–246. On the psychological roots of nationalism in ressentiment, see especially Liah Greenfeld, *Nationalism: Five Roads to Modernity* (Cambridge, MA: Harvard University Press, 1992).
[38] "Letter from Mill to Tocqueville, August 9, 1842," OC 6:1, 337–338.
[39] OC 3:1, 254.

political theory that has, at least in the past, been too readily glossed
over by defenders who have chosen to focus exclusively on his liberal
writings on France, Britain, and the United States.[40] Yet in addition to
noting the apparent moral contradictions within Tocqueville's thought, it
is also important to consider how Tocqueville's advocacy of empire rests
upon ideals that seem to have a recognizably Bonapartist lineage. Ideals of
grandeur that are to be manifested through military successes; an expansionist notion of France's borders; a preoccupation with France's standing in the world relative to other European powers with whom France is
engaged in a life-and-death struggle; a heightened sense of competition
with England and other European nations; the call to self-sacrifice, transcendence, courage, heroism, glory, honor, and other martial dispositions
that are not self-evidently democratic – Tocqueville's rhetoric of empire
is steeped in all of these appeals. At the risk of exaggeration, all that
seems to distinguish Tocqueville from the Napoleonic vision of the First
Empire is his conviction that in order for this glory to be meaningful and
therapeutic for French civic life, imperial grandeur needs to become the
authentic representation of the will of the whole French nation.

Imperialism as Universalizing the Ideals of the French Revolution

To observe that Tocqueville's defense of imperialism was nationalistic
and expansionist in the same manner as Bonapartism brings to light an
important linkage between the two thinkers. This is not to say, of course,
that Tocqueville supports Bonaparte's imperial legacy root and branch.
As for Staël and Constant, the aspects of Bonapartism that seem most
objectionable to Tocqueville are the domestic effects of his despotism.
The problem with the First Empire is not that the imperial project was
mistaken but that the glory and grandeur it represented were in some
sense tainted, inauthentic, or mediated because this new glory was not
France's own so much as Napoleon's personal achievement. As we have
seen, this cavil is fully consistent with Tocqueville's broader acceptance

---

[40] Among those who have emphasized the alleged contradiction between Tocqueville's
liberalism and colonialism, see especially Melvin Richter, "Tocqueville and Algeria"
Review of Politics 25 (1963), 362–398; Roger Boesche, "The Dark Side of Tocqueville:
On War and Empire," *Review of Politics* 67 (2005), 737–752; Cheryl Welch, "Colonial
Violence and the Rhetoric of Evasion," *Political Theory* 31 (2003): 235–264; Pitts,
A Turn to Empire. Those who find a theoretical consistency in Tocqueville's position
include Richard Boyd, "Tocqueville's Algeria," *Society* 38 (September/October 2001),
65–70; Stéphane Dion, "Durham et Tocqueville sur la colonisation libérale," *Journal
of Canadian Studies* 25 (1990), 60–77; and Tzvetan Todorov, *On Human Diversity*
(Cambridge, MA: Harvard University Press, 1993), 191–207.

of the legitimacy – indeed desirability – of the pursuit of imperial glory and grandeur through military conquest.

All that said, Tocqueville's defense of empire is considerably more nuanced than a vulgar celebration of the Nietzschean "will to power" or Machiavellian *raison d'état*. Military exploits may be necessary for imperial grandeur, but they are clearly not sufficient. Indeed, Tocqueville's defense of empire reminds us that there was more to the Revolutionary and Napoleonic Wars than the naked pursuit of power, grandeur, and conquest for its own sake. As did Napoleon, the self-proclaimed "liberator of Italy," Tocqueville understands French imperialism as linked to the project of disseminating the liberal democratic ideals of the French Revolution throughout the world. Although this dimension of his colonialism tends to recede into the background, overshadowed by his realism with respect to the Algerian question, his writings on France's colonies in the Americas show a conviction that France's imperialism represents a way of propagating ideals of liberty and equality. Previously, Staël and Constant had rejected such principled or idealistic justifications of empire as little more than hypocritical window dressing, but Tocqueville takes seriously the notion that honor, greatness, and grandeur have as much to do with remaining faithful to France's vocation as the Enlightenment nation par excellence as they do with manifesting martial virtues on the battlefield.

In what is ultimately a nationalistic argument on behalf of humanitarian ends, Tocqueville contends that France's failure to abolish slavery in her remaining colonies in the Caribbean will mark her abandonment of the revolutionary ideals of liberty and equality for which she once served as the vanguard. If France fails to carry through in this project of abolishing slavery, the mantle of these revolutionary ideals will fall into the hands of England or other European nations.[41] Discussing the question of the abolition of slavery, Tocqueville describes the spread of Enlightenment ideas of freedom and equality as more or less inevitable given the "general movement of the century."[42] Nonetheless, the efficient cause that succeeds in ending slavery in any given locality depends to some degree on an "accident." Once the English abolished slavery in their colonies, France must either follow suit or face the danger of abandoning her own professed ideals. Contrasting the situation of France with other European nations "among whom the new institutions and mores have not yet established their empire" but who have nonetheless already

---

[41] "Emancipation of Slaves" (1843), in WES, 207.
[42] "Emancipation of Slaves" (1843) in WES, 201.

managed to abolish slavery, Tocqueville wonders how it can possibly be
that the "freest and most democratic nation of the European continent"
has not yet succeeded in bringing her own colonists under the "empire"
of progressive liberal ideals?

The proud historical fact of the French having been the purveyors –
even at the head of the armed columns of la Grande Armée – of revolutionary ideals of liberty and equality looms large in Tocqueville's defense
of the abolition of slavery in the colonies:

These notions of freedom and equality that are weakening or destroying servitude
everywhere: who spread them throughout the world? This sentiment, disinterested
and yet impassioned with the love of men, which all at once made Europe hear
the cries of slaves – who propagated it, directed it, illuminated it? We were the
ones. Let us not deny it. It was not only our glory, but our strength... Thanks to
us, these ideas have become the symbol of the new politics. Shall we desert them
now, when they are triumphant?... If so, [France] must resign herself to letting
that standard of modern civilization that our fathers first raised fifty years ago
pass into other hands, and she must finally renounce the great role that she had
the pride to take up, but that she does not have the courage to fulfill.[43]

Tocqueville's conviction here that empire might be part of a civilizing
project of spreading Enlightenment ideals to other parts of the world –
a notion that also makes a brief appearance in his 1837 "Letters on
Algeria" – casts light on an aspect of Napoleon's First Empire too often
obscured or dismissed as hypocritical by critics such as Staël and Constant. Amidst the litany of complaints about the centralizing and ratio-
nalizing aspects of Napoleon's domestic tyranny and the horrific scale
of bloodshed the Napoleonic Wars inflicted on all of Europe, one tends
to forget Napoleon's practical efforts to foster governments based on
liberal ideals of freedom and equality in parts of Europe, Russia, and
Africa where these principles were unknown. The moral ironies of the
First Empire are nowhere more evident than in Francisco Goya's haunt-
ing images of the events of May 1808, depicting the tragic spectacle of
thousands of Spaniards sacrificing their lives to the Napoleonic army and
its liberalizing reforms while defending the restoration of the bloodthirsty
absolutist King Ferdinand VII. Without discounting the manifold ways in
which Bonaparte's reign was despotical and the horrible cost his policies
of conscription imposed on the French nation and the horrors of war for
all of Europe, the ostensible promise of the First Empire was that of combining the grandeur and national interests of France with the disinterested

---

[43] "Emancipation of Slaves" (1843) in WES, 207.

and benevolent transmission of her ideals of liberty and equality to other European nations whose masses groaned in ignorance and poverty under the boot heels of dynastic empires and monarchies.

Energy, Will, and Greatness as Alternatives to Bourgeois Decadence and Malaise

I have suggested already that Tocqueville's imperialism cannot be dis-aggregated from his sense of its therapeutic benefits for French society. That is to say that Tocqueville's defense of empire is inseparable from his critical diagnosis of the languor, impotence, boredom, privatization, and commercialization under the July Monarchy. It is unclear whether Napoleon himself shared this disgust with modern bourgeois society. What is certain, however, is that no sooner had the emperor's blood-shed receded into historical memory than subsequent nineteenth-century political thinkers, novelists, and intellectuals began appealing back to the legend of Napoleon and the Empire – some explicitly, others only implic-itly – as a way of critiquing the decadence and decline they saw gripping nineteenth-century European society.[44]

For his part, Tocqueville complains mightily about the perils of decline and decadence into which France has drifted in the past two decades, particularly under the reign of Louis-Philippe. This darker side of bour-geois society is conspicuous in the *Recollections*, in which Tocqueville worries that a "taste for well being...easily comes to terms with any government that allows it to find satisfaction."[45] Political allegiance in Louis-Philippe's France rests on nothing more than crude self-interest, clientelism, and place seeking.[46] The "universal calming down and lev-eling off that followed the July Revolution" left Tocqueville lamenting, until the events of 1848, that he was "destined to live [his] life in an enervated tranquil society."[47]

In contrast to a U.S. society blessed with a rich network of civic associa-tions, decentralized government, and traditions of political liberty, France

---

[44] Once Napoleon's "victims' curses, their cries of pain, their howls of anguish, are heard no more" and "a weary France no longer offers the spectacle of women plowing her soil" or "conscription lists stuck up at street corners," even the likes of Chateaubriand is tempted to indulge in a bit of nostalgia, *Mémoires d'Outre-Tombe* cited in Geyl, *Napoleon: For and Against*, 25.

[45] Alexis de Tocqueville, *Recollections*, ed. J. P. Mayer and A. P. Kerr (New Brunswick: Transaction Publishers, 1997), 78.

[46] *Recollections*, 32–33.

[47] *Recollections*, 11.

is the legatee of traditions of centralization and civic apathy.[48] Tocqueville
notes that he had "spent the best years of [his] youth in a society that
seemed to be regaining prosperity and grandeur as it regained freedom."
However, the bourgeois Louis-Philippe's attempt to "drown revolutionary passions in the love of material pleasures" led only to further revolution, leaving France destined "to spend a wretched life between alternate
swings to license and to oppression."[49] "Political life itself" in France
was abbreviated and repressed. Any remaining vestiges of the political
were colored with "languor, impotence, immobility, and boredom."[50]
Not even the increase of national wealth with the triumph of the bourgeoisie in 1830 could disguise "a sort of rapid shrinkage" or "marked
lull" of "every political passion." "The spirit peculiar to the middle classes
became the general spirit of government; it dominated foreign policy as
well as home affairs," Tocqueville complains. Left to its own devices –
unalloyed with aristocratic grandeur and inattentive to lower class energies – the bourgeoisie "treated government like a business, each member
thinking of public affairs only in so far as they could be turned to his
private profit."[51]

The French colonial project in Algeria, including what he repeatedly
calls the "domination and subjugation" of the Algerian people, by whatever means necessary, are remedies to this bourgeois "malaise." Only by
participating in a project larger than himself can the individual's sense
of citizenship and public life be reawakened. Grandeur and the monu-
mental political undertakings of conquest, domination, and the martial
virtues are prescriptions against the very sort of pacified and demilitarized
commercial society. The narrow commercial spirit of France can only be
overcome by thinking in terms of a political scale of values that is incom-
mensurable with and irreducible to the self-interested calculations of the
bourgeois.[52] "I know very well," Tocqueville notes, "that metropolitan
commerce and industry will complain that we are sacrificing them; that

[48] Challenging this "Tocquevillian myth" of French civic apathy, centralization, and lack
     of a vibrant public life, Hazareesingh points out that nineteenth-century French society
     was in fact quite capable of conjuring up forms of civic engagement and participation,
     many of which took place spontaneously and locally. See especially, *The Saint-Napoleon*,
     13–14.
[49] *Recollections*, 64–65.
[50] *Recollections*, 10–11.
[51] *Recollections*, 5.
[52] In turning to empire, Tocqueville "sought a *passion* that would draw humans out of
     their small, circumscribed, private interests." Michael Hereth, *Alexis de Tocqueville:
     Threats to Freedom in Democracy* (Durham, NC: Duke University Press, 1986), 162.

the main advantages of a colony are to furnish an advantageous market for the mother country and not to come into competition with it." However, what this narrowly commercial viewpoint overlooks is that in the "current state of things, it is not from a commercial, industrial or colonial point of view that one must consider Algeria." It must be seen rather from an "even higher perspective," that of "a great political interest that dominates all the others."[53]

Nineteenth-Century Defenders of Napoleon: Stendhal, Zola, and Nietzsche

The preceding sheds light on three aspects of Tocqueville's political theory that are outliers within his more general orientation of centrist liberalism. First, there is Tocqueville's advocacy of empire as the collective pursuit of glory, grandeur, and honor. Second, there is his critical preoccupation with the malaise, decadence, and civilizational decline of modern bourgeois society. Third, there are the implicit parallels between Tocqueville's defense of colonialism and empire and the more messianic aspirations of the French Revolutionary Wars and First Empire. These features of his social and political thought seem to distinguish him categorically from his liberal forbearers. Without denying Tocqueville's profound debts to a long line of liberal thinkers such as Burke, Staël, Constant, and Guizot before him, he also anticipates the radical critics of modern bourgeois society who came after him and for whom the legend of Napoleon served as a critical reference point. As for the novelists Stendhal, Balzac, Victor Hugo, and Zola, the Napoleonic Wars come to symbolize social mobility, greatness, and national prosperity – ideals against which the subsequent regimes of the Bourbon Restoration, July Monarchy, Second Republic, and Second Empire fall decidedly short.[54]

Stendhal's admiring 1817–1818 *Life of Napoleon* provides the early outlines of his own critical view of French society, with the Napoleonic era representing in hindsight an age of energy, social mobility, natural excellence, dynamism, spirit, and greatness. Bonaparte was, in Stendhal's view, "the finest man to have appeared since Caesar," and while "tainted by some of the essential vices of a conqueror," he was "no more prodigal

[53] OC 3:1, 254.
[54] See, for example, Maurice Descotes, *La Légende de Napoléon et les écrivains français du XIXe siècle* (Paris: Minard, 1967); Saint-Paulien [M. Y. Sicard], *Napoléon, Balzac, et l'Empire de la Comédie Humaine* (Paris: Albin Michel, 1979); and Geyl, *Napoleon: For and Against*, 24–32; Hazareesingh, *Legend of Napoleon*, 200–202.

of blood, nor indifferent to humanity than men like Caesar, Alexander, or Frederick the Great."[55] By way of contrast, according to Stendhal, France of the subsequent decades was sapped of all masculinity, courage, spontaneity, and individuality.[56] Social mobility all but ceased under the Bourbon Restoration. Like his protagonist Julien Sorel who secretly worships a photo of his hero Napoleon, Stendhal mocks the remnants of French civilization and looks fondly back to the age of Napoleon as a time when natural excellence was given space to rise up; when courage, vitality, and public spirit were at their peak; and when military valor and intellectual energy were legitimate modes of social advancement.

Stendhal was only one among many critics to juxtapose the Restoration aristocracy – who traded in their martial courage for salon manners – with the bold adventures of the First Empire. The imperial ideal served as a counterpoint to the boredom, loss of spontaneity, and blocked social mobility of the Restoration years.[57] "The young Parisians I know," Stendhal complains in his *Souvenirs*,

appear rather *effeminate* to me, concerned only with the cut of their clothes, the elegance of their hats, or the question how to tie their cravats. It is hard for me to conceive of a man without a little *manly energy*, without some depth and constancy in his ideas, all of which are as rare in Paris society as a vulgar turn of speech, or, for that matter, a harsh statement.[58]

As the *Red and Black*'s Mathilde de la Môle ponders:

Is it my fault if the young people around the court today are so devoted to the *conventional*, and pale at the mere idea of a very minor adventure the very least bit out of the ordinary? A short trip to Greece or Africa is for them the height of audacity, and even then they'll go only in a crowd. As soon as they see they stand alone, they become afraid, not of the Bedouin's lance, but of ridicule, and that fear drives them wild.[59]

Nostalgia for the First Empire only accelerated with the coup d'état of Napoleon III and the birth of the Second Empire. Documenting France's

55 Stendhal, *A Life of Napoleon* (New York: Howard Fertig, 1977), 183–184.
56 I have discussed Stendhal's critique of modern bourgeois society at greater length in Richard Boyd, "*Politesse* and Public Opinion in Stendhal's *Red and Black*," *European Journal of Political Theory* 4 (Fall 2005), 367–392.
57 Geyl, *Napoleon, For and Against*, 25–26, 32.
58 Stendhal, *Memoirs of Egoism*, ed. Matthew Josephson (New York: Lear Publishing, 1949), p. 93. Original emphasis. cf. 93, 122, 161, 172, 184, 196, 227–229.
59 Stendhal, *Red and the Black*, 252; H. F. Imbert, *Les Métamorphoses de la Liberté* (Paris: Librairie José Corti, 1967), 501, 529, notes the irony of contrasting these "little voyages" with the true military conquests of the Napoleonic Wars and the imminent French conquest and colonization of North Africa.

humiliating defeat at the hands of the Prussians in the Franco-Prussian War of 1870–1871, Emile Zola's *The Debacle* vividly dramatizes the differences between the First and Second Empires. The heroic efforts of France's armies – indeed, the entire nation – in support of the First Empire are juxtaposed to the corruption, pusillanimity, and general lack of will enveloping Napoleon III, his generals, and the whole French nation. France's officers are incompetent, her soldiers undisciplined and insubordinate, and her population cowardly and self-serving. And all of this emanates, for Zola, from the ineffectual person of the emperor himself. His equivocation, inability to inspire the troops, and general incompetence are open objects of ridicule. One look at the emperor's ashen face is enough for Jean Macquart and his fellow soldiers to dismiss him as a "goner." "Damn bad luck for an army to have a chief like that!" Jean concludes.[60] By way of contrast, old-timers and stalwarts from the Grande Armée or the Algerian campaigns are what hold the army together.

Zola's damning indictment of Napoleon III and his generals in *The Debacle* proved controversial for its apparent lack of patriotism, but the more general theme of sickness, malaise, and decadence in bourgeois society runs throughout the whole Rougon-Macquart series of novels. There is a direct continuity between France's military humiliation at the hands of the Prussian army and the broader pathologies of moral decadence, malaise, infirmity, and sexual impotence that are all clearly linked by Zola to the triumph of the bourgeoisie. Novels as different as *Pot-Bouille, Au Bonheur des Dames, La Bête Humaine,* and *Nana* offer a stark contrast between the sterility, vanity, hypocrisy, and empty pretensions of the newly ascendant bourgeoisie and the furious sexual and political energy of the lower classes.[61]

---

[60] Emile Zola, *The Debacle* (New York: Penguin, 1972), 77.
[61] In *Pot-Bouille*, for example, "respectable" middle-class wives are either frigid or adulteresses, impregnated by energetic young shop clerks on the make. *Au Bonheur des Dames* reveals the frenzies and pathologies – mental illness, obsession and compulsion, shoplifting, and so forth – associated with modern consumer society. In *La Bête Humaine*, bourgeois marriage proves so stultifying that an adulterous couple must engage in murder to inject energy and spirit into their lives. And the prostitute Nana, that "poisonous flower of the ghetto," devours every last vestige of aristocratic and middle-class respectability. On Zola as critic of the bourgeois, see Brian Nelson, *Zola and the Bourgeoisie: A Study of Themes and Techniques in Les Rougon-Macquart* (New York: Macmillan, 1983). For a more extensive discussion of the trope of bourgeois degeneration, see especially Daniel Pick, *Faces of Degeneration: A European Disorder, ca. 1848–1918* (Cambridge: Cambridge University Press, 1989).

Although the two otherwise make for an unlikely pairing, Tocqueville's
rousing defense of conquest, energy, vitality, and grandeur even shares
something with later radical thinkers such as Georges Sorel, for whom
a Bergsonian *élan vital* and "myth of revolutionary violence" came to
represent the last possible strategy for energizing the masses of French
society and shaking off the torpor and humiliation France had suffered in
1870. Sorel compares the modern radical technique of the "general strike"
to the overwhelming force of the Napoleonic battle.[62] As for Tocqueville,
Zola, and other critics, the common problem was political apathy, love
of creature comforts, privatism, and spiritual enervation associated with
the bourgeois lifestyle.

Maybe the most extreme nineteenth-century fascination with
Napoleon as part and parcel of the critique of bourgeois society comes
in the writings of Friedrich Nietzsche, for whom Napoleon appeared
like a "signpost to the *other* path," as the "most isolated and late-born
man there has even been," in whom "the problem of the *noble ideal as
such*" is "made flesh."[63] It is Napoleon, the "synthesis of the *inhuman*
and *superhuman*," who managed to coax the final gasp of greatness and
courage from a Europe otherwise sliding into bourgeois decadence and
nihilism.

One last point of qualification: I have suggested that Tocqueville shares
with later, more radical critics of bourgeois society both a sense of
Napoleon's greatness as well as the conviction that something about
his imperial project represents a preferable alternative to bourgeois mediocrity and decline. In this view, the Napoleonic legend is both critical
and potentially therapeutic. However, it is also important to stress that
one of the distinguishing features of Tocqueville's political theory is his
sense of the importance of political moderation and his awareness of the
dangers of excessive political passions.[64] Despite his affinities for subsequent and more radical versions of the Napoleonic legend, Tocqueville
ultimately stands anchored – politically at least – within the penumbra
of the liberal myth of Napoleon. While sharing many critical misgivings
about bourgeois society and entertaining potentially illiberal fascinations

[62] Georges Sorel, *Reflections on Violence* (Glencoe, IL: Free Press, 1950), 48, 106–107,
208, 269, 277–278.
[63] Friedrich Nietzsche, *On the Genealogy of Morals*, ed. Walter Kaufmann (New York:
Vintage, 1989), First Essay, Section 16, 54.
[64] For a more systematic study of Tocqueville's centrism and moderation, see especially
Aurelian Craiutu, "Tocqueville's Paradoxical Moderation" *Review of Politics* 67 (Fall
2005), 599–629.

with the Napoleonic project, Tocqueville would almost certainly reject as politically irresponsible the aesthetic radicalism of Stendhal, Zola, Sorel, Bergson, or Nietzsche.

Conclusion: Bonapartism and the Frontiers of Democracy

It is admittedly controversial to supplant the traditional narrative of Tocqueville as legatee of post-revolutionary liberalism with the revisionist counter-narrative of Tocqueville as progenitor of nineteenth-century radical anxieties about bourgeois malaise. Nonetheless, placing Tocqueville in the latter camp highlights aspects of his social and political theory commonly overshadowed by the traditional reading. It also and more importantly raises broader issues about the moral, existential, and political frontiers of democracy.

First, Tocqueville's defense of imperialism draws attention to democracy's internal or psychological frontiers. We may reject Tocqueville's normative claims on behalf of empire, but his empirical insights are telling nonetheless. In particular, his therapeutic endorsement of empire assumes that a nation's political life extends well beyond the strictly physical limits of its territorial borders or the mechanical workings of its domestic political institutions. Existential feelings of national pride, honor, and grandeur actually matter, even to the point that they set the horizons within which democracy either flourishes or languishes. There is an intimate link between how other nations in the world see us and how we ultimately think of ourselves. Is it possible, Tocqueville wonders, for citizens to manifest that legitimate spirit of pride, honor, patriotism, and civic engagement requisite to healthy democratic institutions when one's nation is either dishonored or reviled by the rest of the world? Concepts such as honor, national character, collective memory, and political psychology have fallen out of favor in the social sciences, and perhaps with good reason, but the psychic character of nations does seem to have a bearing on the vitality and viability of democratic politics.

Rather than being able to shake off widespread international attitudes of anti-Americanism (or anti-Sinoism, anti-Russianism, anti-Europeanism, etc.), these sentiments affect how citizens themselves conceive of their own domestic political institutions. Ignominious defeat in war; the imposition of humiliating terms of surrender or reparations; the experience of being conquered and occupied by a foreign power; the legacies of authoritarianism, colonialism, decolonization, or revolution – how can these experiences fail to reverberate in the domestic political life of a nation? It is a gigantic leap of logic, of course, to argue that self-respect is sufficiently important that it could ever justify building an empire or conquering other nations, but Tocqueville does have a point in connecting international standing with domestic politics, existential feelings of national pride with the well-functioning of democratic political institutions. The paradoxical bottom line seems to be that a healthy democracy may rest on feelings of national pride – or indeed even national superiority – that are less than purely democratic.

Conversely, the flip side of Tocqueville's logic is that humiliating other nations – say, by conquest or occupation ostensibly to make them free – can have profound psychological repercussions for their ability to establish liberal democratic institutions for themselves. Might the scars of occupation, humiliation, and colonial tutelage forever plague their native aspirations to democratic self-rule? As Tocqueville observes so poignantly in his chapter on the "Point of Departure of the Anglo-Americans," rather than being blank slates or tabula rasa, nations – like individuals – "always bear some marks of their origin."[65] The circumstances that bring a nation into being leave indelible stamps on its collective memory and may exert a kind of path dependency on its future political development. If Tocqueville is right about this, then it seems to present a powerful rejoinder to the project of a liberalizing empire. There is something paradoxical, or even self-defeating, about one nation dominating another to help it achieve its freedom and dignity. Exceptional cases such as West Germany and Japan may give cause for optimism, but ordinarily liberal democracy begotten at the gunpoint of an occupying army seem much less likely to take root and flourish than indigenous democratic movements arising organically from within.

Lastly, Tocqueville's defense of empire raises decisive ethical questions about the legitimate transnational frontiers of democracy. As we have seen, the preponderance of Tocqueville's argument hinges on the therapeutic effects of imperial glory for the conquering nation. However, at least under certain circumstances, there may be a case for the salutary effects of empire on nations that are conquered. If one accepts that democracy and human rights are universal goods – let alone the stronger claim that their antithesis in the form of authoritarianism and genocide ought to be resisted whenever possible – then democratic nations have a presumptive responsibility to facilitate their transmission to other parts of the world. And yet the vocation of expanding the frontiers of democracy may

[65] DIA (L) I.1.ii, 31.

sometimes require violating the territorial sovereignty of other nations, interfering in their domestic politics, and deploying military force.

These agonistic conflicts appear from time to time at the margins of contemporary political life – in far-flung places such as Iraq, Afghanistan, Somalia, Sudan, Libya, Syria, or Cote d'Ivoire – and thus they are easy to dismiss as exceptions that prove a more general liberal rule of noninterference. Upon closer examination, however, these and other cases of international intervention revolve around the same basic moral conundrums raised by Tocqueville's imperialism. The grim reality is that military force may sometimes be a necessary means to spread freedom and equality to nations either unwilling or unable to respect the basic norms of liberal democracy.

Like Staël and Constant before them, contemporary liberals will complain that imperialists such as Napoleon and Tocqueville are entirely too sanguine about the possibility of spreading democracy and human rights by military conquest and that initiatives like these too often serve merely to rationalize the interests of the colonizer. There is much to these criticisms. However, the reality that international intervention is often self-serving does not mean that there are never times when it might be ethically appropriate to intervene forcefully in another nation's political life. Although democracy is in some sense premised on the existence of fixed national borders, one of the most singular aspects of the contemporary world is how these carefully delineated borders are regularly elided by an international juridical system that represents – as Michael Hardt and Antonio Negri have suggested – a veritable "empire."[66] One ought to be leery of Tocqueville's justification of colonialism, obviously, but his empirical insights do serve to blur the psychological, moral, and geopolitical frontiers of democracy, stretching the concept beyond its strictly legal, institutional, or political connotations.

[66] Michael Hardt and Antonio Negri, *Empire*. (Cambridge, MA: Harvard University Press, 2000).

PART FIVE

DEMOCRACY'S OLD AND NEW FRONTIERS

CHAPTER 13

Tocqueville, the Problem of Equality, and John Ford's Stagecoach

Robert Pippin

I

I must begin with a disclaimer: as readers will no doubt realize, I do not quite belong with the Tocqueville experts in this volume. I do not write or, as we now must say, do research, on Tocqueville, and my main acquaintance with *Democracy in America* consists in teaching it nearly every year for the past 17 years in the Classics Core at the University of Chicago. However, Tocqueville shares a lot with a philosopher whom I do know something about – Hegel – and he raises issues that also concern a visual poet whom I also have some interest in – that great mythologizer of America's idea of itself, John Ford. So I entertain the hope that out of this mix of overlapping interests, I might have something to contribute to the discussion.

What Tocqueville and Hegel share, I want to say, is an approach to political matters. Neither of them directly asks the central question of classical political philosophy: What is the best human regime? Neither is indifferent to the question of the worthiness of some regime or other, but they do not propose to address that issue by wondering how best to approximate some ideal paradigm. Both, that is, do not separate the question of political philosophy itself from political actuality, where that especially means historical actuality. So let me start with a general remark about that issue and then discuss how that frames the way Tocqueville and Ford address the question of equality and its worthiness.

II

Any human social world is obviously finite, limited in resources and space, composed of agents whose pursuit of individual ends unavoidably must limit what others would otherwise be able to do, and often directly conflicting with such other pursuits. This situation forces the issue of power: Who will be subject to whose will? Who will subject whom? However, these individual agents are finite as well – unable to achieve most of their ends without forms of cooperation and dependence. The biology of human development ensures a profound familial dependence throughout childhood, and the variety and breadth of the distribution of human talent and the frailty and vulnerability of human life all ensure that various forms of social dependence will be impossible to avoid. So it has long been acknowledged that a human society is both deeply conflictual and competitive, as well as necessarily cooperative and communal. Our natures ensure a constant tension between a self-regarding desire for independence and freedom from subjection to the will of other self-regarding agents, as well as a powerful need to achieve some stable form of dependence and relative trust. The major, although not at all exclusive, arena where solutions to this basic problem are proposed and tried out is commonly known as the political.

Even if we presuppose a great deal of agreement at some time within some community about the proper form of the political (already a great idealization), we cannot ever be sure of the trustworthy compliance of everyone with the basic rules and procedures. So all political life involves the use of violence and the coercive threat of violence by one group of people against another. The claim that there is such a thing as political life amounts to the claim that, while there is such violence and coercion, its exercise is legitimate and rational and that power may be justifiably exercised over those who may in fact resist such an exercise. Those who, like Marx and Nietzsche, reject the idea that there really is such a thing as politics deny this claim and so argue that what some call political power is just a disguised version of the exercise of violence by one group against another or by one type against another. On some versions of such a critique, like Alexandre Kojève's, there never are rulers and subjects, representatives and citizens – never even human beings as such. Until the final bloody revolution ensures classlessness, there are always and everywhere only masters and slaves, those who subject the will of others to theirs and those whose will is subject to the will of others.[1]

---

[1] Alexandre Kojève, *Introduction to the Reading of Hegel*, trans. J. H. Nichols, Jr., ed. Alan Bloom (New York: Basic Books, 1969).

Those who defend the claim to legitimacy, the claim that there is politics, argue in familiar ways. An ancient claim is that no true human excellence may be achieved without hierarchical relations of power and that without such coercive constraint, the baser instincts of human beings would reign, and nothing worthwhile could be collectively achieved. Such baser passions, it is claimed, are not subject to persuasion or argument, and there are some human beings in whom such passions are paramount. These people (sometimes said to be most people) must be constrained from above just as any one individual's passions must be ruled rather than allowed to rule. The appeal to this sort of argument in the project of European colonialism – and the long history of male exercise of power over "naturally inferior" or "emotional" or "irrational" women – has rightly made it difficult for any such possible claim to be entertained now without the suspicion that it must be an apology for the brute exercise of self-interested power, masquerading in the form of such an argument. Postcolonialism, we are much more suspicious either that anyone or any class or type is ever free of such putatively tyrannical passions and so that the natural rulers always present the same danger as the naturally ruled or that what looks base and nearly inhuman to one might look perfectly fine, a high culture even, to another.

One might argue that everyone would simply be better off under some system of political rule, perhaps better off with respect to necessary common goods that no one could reasonably reject or perhaps better off merely by avoiding a state of such anarchy that no sane person could reasonably prefer it. Those inclined to think this way often think that even if there are a few who are very much better off, a coercive use of violence to preserve such an order is acceptable if everyone is at least better off than they would be otherwise. This kind of argument has its colonial echoes, too. (Yes, we got fabulously wealthy, but we gave them the gift of English, or French schools, or developed industrial societies. Think how much better off they are.) Or one might argue that what appears as coercion really is not – that *inuria non fit volenti*, and everyone can be presumed to have reasonably consented to such an arrangement. Or they would consent if they were rational agents. On an extension of this approach, one could argue that the use of force to protect basic human entitlements – human rights – is not only permissible but required and that no claim for the existence of such rights would be coherent unless measures, even violent and coercive measures, could be taken to protect and enforce them. There is no loss of freedom when one is constrained from doing what he may not do or is compelled to do what he must: what is a universal and rational obligation.

This is all familiar and proceeds as classical and modern political philosophies always have: by assuming that the question of legitimacy (or the goodness, the value) of some form of rule involves a search for a rationale, an argument, a demonstration by force of the better case, in favor of some arrangement of power and against some others – all in the service of resolving the original tension noted at the outset. However, I have sketched this set of issues in its abstract forms to stress that these familiar ways of looking at the issue are abstract. In order for philosophy to get a grip on the core problem of dependence and independence, a great abstraction must be made from, let us say, the complex psychological stake that individuals have in achieving and maintaining independence and the ways they come to care about and understand their varieties of mutual dependence. They are rarely, if ever, in any position to assess rationally how important some sort of independence is and what sort of compromise to make with the requirements of dependence, and they are never in a position simply to decide what they care about. Of course, some or all of this might inevitably have something to do with what can be rationally defended, justified without reliance on particular interest or bias. We can certainly come to care about such a standard a great deal and base a great deal on it. However, there is no a priori reason to think that such a consideration always and everywhere trumps other ways of mattering, other stakes and investments, and there is no reason to think that we could ever agree on what counts as the actualization of such a standard. Its persuasive trumping power might be illusory or might stem simply from its abstractness. To add to the problem, these different ways of caring and kinds of investments vary a great deal across different communities and across historical epochs.

And all of this makes philosophical abstraction both understandable and problematic. One wants some view of the resolution of this tension or problem that can be shared, and there is no reason to believe that one's particular investment or the way things happen to matter to one (or to one's group) will or can be shared. The assumption of a rational standpoint, entertaining considerations that rely on no particular point of view, would appear the only way to proceed.

But this comes at a high price. Because no one actually occupies such a rational standpoint (it is artificial, a fiction for the sake of argument), it is unclear what can be expected about its results for finite, concrete agents. We cannot simply assume that, no matter their particular attachments and investments – their parents, their children, their group, their status, the motherland, or their God – these agents care more about what reason demands the greatest good for the greatest number, what form of law is consistent with pure practical reason, the supreme importance of avoiding the state of nature, what they must be assumed to have consented to, and so forth. None of these considerations has any obvious or inherent psychological actuality, and it seems absurd to wave away such concerns with actuality as a matter of mere irrationality that cannot concern philosophers. That approach threatens to turn political philosophy into a mere game, operating under initial abstraction conditions so extreme that they allow no actual role other than as ideals that we might hope to approach asymptotically, if even that. Indeed, an insistence of the putative purity of such ideal considerations – the claim that the philosophical cogency of an argument form is one, wholly distinct thing, its possible application in a colonial project another – is just what inspires suspicions that the argument form itself is mere ideology.[2] What can be said about such a situation?

One thing one might claim in the face of such an issue is to proclaim, as Tocqueville in effect did, that there is now, or now dawning, such a thing as a democratic form of life, and the question of how such a new form of life might concentrate and distribute and exercise political power – the monopoly on legitimate coercive violence enjoyed by the state – must from the start take its bearings from such a political actuality. I at least count this as Tocqueville's great contribution to the Western intellectual tradition. As everyone knows, Tocqueville concluded that one issue above all rises to prominence in the American experience when things are approached this way: what could generally be called the problem of equality, especially in its relation to liberty. But to address Tocqueville's treatment of that theme, I want to take a detour through John Ford's 1939 film, *Stagecoach*.

III

Stagecoach has a simple enough plot. A group of seven strangers has to crowd into a stagecoach in the town of Tonto and, for seven different reasons, make a journey across dangerous Indian territory to the town of

[2] I discuss this problem in these terms, applied to a different context, i.e., the novels of J. M. Coetzee, in "The Paradoxes of Power in the Novels of J. M. Coetzee," in *J.M. Coetzee and Ethics*, ed. Peter Singer and Anton Leist (New York: Columbia University Press, 2010), 19–42. The discussion here is also an expansion of chapter one of my *Hollywood Westerns and American Myth. The Importance of Howard Hawks and John Ford for Political Philosophy* (New Haven: Yale University Press, 2010).

Lordsburg. We are not far into the narrative before any reasonably attentive viewer begins to notice several signs of a far greater ambition than a
standard adventure story. For one thing, the characters seem deliberately
representative and deliberately matched and contrasted in a way that goes
beyond the colorfully psychological. There is a haughty and respectable
but pompous banker, Gatewood, who, we will soon learn, is a thief, and
his opposite number, a shady, shoots-people-in-the-back, disreputable
gambler, Hatfield, a former southern "gentleman" who is traveling on
the stage solely to act as the southern gentlewoman's protector and who
turns out to be genuinely chivalrous and capable of sacrifice and nobility.
There is a meek, gentle, and respectable whiskey salesman, the absolute
bourgeois, Peacock, who turns out to be made of much sterner stuff than
we appreciate at first, and he is paired with his all-time best customer,
an alcoholic, disgraced physician, Doc Boone, who can summon back his
skill and dedication when the situation calls for it. There is a prostitute,
Dallas, who by conventional movie logic we expect to be wise with a heart
of gold but who, in a brilliant turn by Claire Trevor, is a nervous, edgy,
somewhat whiny and bitter woman, who, of course, finally does have a
heart of gold, paired and contrasted with a genteel, pregnant southern
woman, Lucy Mallory, who is at first contemptuous of her lower-class
traveling companion but who comes to appreciate the worth and dignity
of Trevor's character and even to admire her. So we have avatars of bourgeois rectitude and their anti-bourgeois companions – a spirits peddler, a
banker and a loyal wife, a drunk, a gambler, and a prostitute – and many
of them come to transcend and even invert their early (and perhaps our)
class and typological prejudices.

In the middle of it all (literally in the cramped stagecoach and fig-
uratively as the story's pivotal character) is John Wayne's ambiguous
character, the Ringo Kid, who joins the group en route and who has
escaped from jail and is out on a mission of private revenge that the
sheriff, traveling with them, has pledged to stop. (Ringo had been sent
to jail as a 16-year-old, framed by the Plummer brothers, the murderers

Dallas is being run out of town by a women's morality league, and
one sees the relevance of Tocqueville immediately in this comically visual
presentation of the tyranny of the majority. That is, it is important that
Ford plays this scene for laughs, making the women so physically ugly
and crudely narrow minded that one cannot believe they represent or will
ever represent "the real America." (Perhaps if Ford had lived through the
eight years of the Bush presidency he would not have been so sanguine.)
(See Figure 1.)

FIGURE I.

of his father and brother). Ford introduces him to the narrative with a spectacular shot zooming up and close in as Ringo waits by the side of the road (Figure 2).

This issue in itself, as in many Westerns, elevates the plot and marks out a theme of elemental importance. The difference between mere private revenge and the justice demanded by law is at least as old as Aeschylus's *Oresteia*, and the introduction of this ancient question gives us another clue about the point and the ambiguous ending of the film. (The sheriff, the representative of law, fails to stop the revenge killing; he hardly even makes a serious try, actually, and even aids the extralegal attempt by Ringo.)

Once we realize how archetypal rather than merely individual the treatment of character and the theme of justice is, it also becomes clear that their journey itself is just as representative. The film has thrown together people from very different backgrounds and from very different social and economic classes. Most of them either must get to Lordsburg or cannot return to Tonto; they are driven inexorably forward with the same force and power as the stagecoach itself – an image Ford uses to propel the

FIGURE 2.

film itself forward at a compelling, often thrilling pace, all as if representative of the pressure and power of the great historical force Tocqueville alludes to.[3] And this setup clearly poses a familiar and frequently asked question about the United States, clearly in the back or sometimes near the front of Tocqueville's curious mind: *can* such a collection of people without much of a common tradition or history, without much of what had been traditionally assumed to be the social conditions of nationhood, become in some way or other a unity capable of something greater than the sum of its parts? This turns out to be not just a question about social cooperation but a higher and more complicated unity, something like a political unity. In the film, votes are taken about whether to go on; political metaphors are frequent – Dallas asks Doc if her expulsion is legitimate, consistent with natural right, "Haven't I any right to live? What have I done?"; the banker pontificates about the state of politics; the question of whether Ringo should leave his grievances to the law or not is present throughout the film. We come to realize that Ford is asking whether this kind of a group of people could ever be said to form a nation. He reminds us, by including a southern ex-officer and a woman of the Old South, that America failed catastrophically at its first try at nationhood and that this failure has left a bitter legacy, affecting for the coach riders even the question of what the "rebellion" should be called. But the heart of his question here is of class and social hierarchy in such a nation and so, by contrast, the quintessentially American political ideal

---

[3] The exception is Peacock, the whiskey salesman, who keeps reasonably protesting that the crossing is much too dangerous. He is the only one, we might say, whose fate is determined by the force of the common or democratic will of the group. He even seems to understand this and, while protesting, to sign on to the common fate that they have come to share.

FIGURE 3.

of equality, the (potentially) binding force of such a norm: How could it be an effective and unifying norm in the face of such inequalities? We are shown that there are very wide open spaces in this setting and, so it would appear, room to avoid such questions, room for some psychological and social distance between such political citizens. There is, that is, the grandeur and emptiness of Monument Valley, but also its hostility, the vastness and indifference of nature to the puny human attempts at civilized life (Figure 3). But fate has now crammed them together in an absurdly small coach, suggesting that the illusion of some escape to isolated independence is just that, an illusion (or soon will be). Their being so tightly packed into the coach makes visually clear their necessarily common fate (Figure 4).

Inside this enforced dependence, the narrative mostly concerns the dissolution, the growing lack of credibility, of class and even putative moral distinctions, and so we get a mythic representation of the American aspiration toward a form of politically meaningful equality – a belief or aspiration that forms the strongest political bond, such as it is, among Americans.

In a way, set up like this, the film seems almost designed to answer Tocqueville's famous remarks on and worries about American

FIGURE 4.

egalitarianism. Although Tocqueville once noted a "manly" egalitarianism that he approved of (everyone aspiring to "greatness"), he was
famously deeply uneasy about what he took to be the American and, he
thought, more material version. As far as he could see, such a passion
was too close to envy and resentment and would prove the great Achilles
heel of the American experiment, inclining Americans to restrictions on
liberty if inequalities emerged, as they inevitably would. Here is his claim:

> But the human heart also nourishes a debased taste for equality, which leads the
> weak to want to drag the strong down to their level and which induces men to
> prefer equality in servitude to inequality in freedom. It is not that peoples with
> a democratic social state naturally scorn freedom; on the contrary they have an
> instinctive taste for it. But freedom is not the chief and continual object of their
> desires; it is equality for which they feel an eternal love; they rush on freedom with
> quick and sudden impulses, but if they miss their mark they resign themselves to
> their disappointment; but nothing will satisfy them without equality, and they
> would rather die than lose it.[4]

Ford's film is a compelling visual alternative, a picture of an aspiration
to equality that Tocqueville did not seem to understand well – a claim to

[4] DIA (L) I.1.3, 57.

moral equality, the equal dignity and worth, the "inestimable" value of each individual as such, as Kant put it, following Rousseau. For all the inequalities in talent and accomplishment, no human life can be said to be worth more than any other because no price or measure of value can be fixed on inherent human worth or worth or dignity based on the fact that each is a free rational agent – that each person's life must be led and uniquely led by each subject.

Such an appreciation is suggested by how matters develop as the narrative unfolds. Things start off with plenty of inequality, made visible in a beautifully choreographed dance of distancing at one of the way stations where they stop for a meal. Everyone except Ringo (and Peacock, we assume; he appears indifferent to these issues, Christian that he is) jockeys for a seat that will avoid the presumably unclean Dallas. Ringo, in jail for almost all his youth, has no idea what is going on and sits next to Dallas, assuming that people are trying to avoid him, an escaped convict. This is another Tocquevillean point. The scene aptly reflects Tocqueville's puzzlement about the intensity of American obsession with sexual mores. They know nothing about Ringo except that he is an escaped criminal convicted of murder, and it is the prostitute they are concerned with (Figure 5).

The collapse of the elaborately staged pretense to hierarchy, and something like the collective realization of the truth of this form of moral equality, occurs at another way station where the southern gentlewoman gives birth to her baby, and the common, shared human aspirations to peace, health, domestic intimacy, and the common frailty and finitude of the human body are experienced by almost everyone in the party. Or at least, as both Tocqueville and Hegel would have realized, we see manifested what would be assumed unquestionably shared in a bourgeois form of life. We also see here that there is an elaborate American send-up of the pretensions of social hierarchy and class. When the way station owner's wife, clearly Indian, comes in and Peacock screams that there is a savage in the room, the owner good-naturedly replies, "Si, Señor; she is a little bit savage, I think."

There is of course controversy about this. Some critics see Dallas as accepting a subservient, not an equal, role, simply catering to the gentlewoman Lucy, as redeemed from the life of prostitution only because she accepts a traditional woman/mother/class role.[5] However, the baby

[5] See William Rothman, "Stagecoach and the Quest for Selfhood," in *John Ford's Stagecoach*, ed. Barry Keith Grant (Cambridge: Cambridge University Press, 2003), 161.

FIGURE 5.

unites all of them, not just Dallas; the baby reminds all of them of some dimension of commonality and some common aspiration for familial life and security. Rather than serving Lucy, Dallas actually "becomes" the mother, holding the baby far more often and, in some sense, shames the rest of them by challenging their whorish assumptions about her (Figure 6).

The push in the group toward an even more egalitarian form of mutual acknowledgment comes from Ringo's constant and somewhat naïve but clearly morally motivated insistence on drawing Dallas back into the society that has expelled her and finally as well from the peddler Peacock, who asks for "a little Christian charity one for the other." The banker is a hopeless windbag throughout; the agents of this realization – agents of the (equally frail) body one might say – are the doctor and the prostitute. This is a different view than the Jeffersonian idealization of frontier or yeoman democracy as the condition most responsible for a more egalitarian, less Europeanized (i.e., class conscious) society. The assumption behind this depiction is more Rousseauean and Kantian; it is an appeal to a natural equality that needs only some proper condition to manifest its truth and appeal. (Indeed, it is in a frontier town, in

FIGURE 6.

achieved civilization, Tonto, that the stark class divisions have so clearly reappeared.)[6]

And the film shows this in a way that continues the archetypal, representative, or even mythic framework suggested by many of its elements from the very beginning – in this case a representative tale of the revelation of the insubstantiality and unreality of class hierarchies. Moreover,

---

[6] See the remarks below on Frederick Jackson Turner. This is hardly the end of the story. The tension in the American desire for the eventual refinement of civilized life and the fact that such refinement was not possible without reintroducing a social hierarchy, and one that was often portrayed in Westerns as enervated and potentially corrupt and hypocritical, is portrayed in many Westerns (*My Darling Clementine* is an interesting case) and has been much discussed. See especially Henry Nash Smith, *Virgin Land. The American West as Symbol and Myth* (Cambridge: Harvard University Press, 2005), 215; and with regard to *Stagecoach*, Tag Gallagher, *John Ford. The Man and his Films* (Berkeley and Los Angeles: University of California Press, 1986), 161; Robin Wood, "Shall We Gather at the River?: The Late Films of John Ford," *Film Comment*, Fall (1971), 31–32; Barry Keith Grant, "Two Rode Together: John Ford and James Fenimore Cooper" in *John Ford Made Westerns. Filming the Legend in the Sound Era*, eds. Gaylyn Studler and Matthew Bernstein (Bloomington: Indiana University Press, 2001) on Natty Bumpo, Cooper, and Ford, 207 ff.; and Gaylyn Studler, "'Be a Proud, Glorified Dreg': Class, Gender and Frontier Democracy in John Ford's *Stagecoach*" in *John Ford's Stagecoach*, 145.

as is the case in many Westerns with this sort of ambition – within these sweeping and mythic explorations of the fate of politics in America – there is often a reflective, distancing, uneasy resolution that is not really a resolution suggested, and that is certainly true in this film. In *Stagecoach*, everything moves toward a revenge killing that we are led to hope will be final and transformative. The bad guys will have been eliminated, and a new start – a new civilized, political order – is possible. However, in the first place, as in many Westerns, this resolution is extralegal and private. It is a kind of resolution that would not have been possible inside the civilized order it is helping to found. It thus also raises the question of the justice of such origins: its legitimacy. But that new order is also figured in this film in the Ringo Kid's love for the prostitute, Dallas. And in an odd, somewhat bizarre twist, he does not seem to realize, ever, despite her best efforts to drag him through the world she lives in, that she is a prostitute. This, of course, is left ambiguous. A case could be made that he knows, perhaps that he always really knew. In any event, even his professed naïveté is quite odd and unique among all the characters in the film.[7]

Ringo also shows that he never does become a fully integrated and committed member of this group. During the final Apache raid on the stagecoach, he saves, at great risk to everyone else, three precious bullets for his private revenge quest, and he lies brazenly to the sheriff about it. So, the possibility of some hope for a truly new beginning – a genuinely (that is, moral or natural) egalitarian political order in these conditions – seems to depend on a level of naïveté that borders on the ludicrous, as if anticipating a Tocquevillean skepticism. Moreover, and even more significantly, they cannot establish such a new homeland here in the States; Ringo and Dallas must "escape" to Mexico. It almost seems as if America needs its own America, its own New World, if it is to continue to be America – obviously a doomed hope. Ringo thinks he is turning himself in and going back to prison. However, the sheriff and Doc Boone

---

[7] See Rothman, "Stagecoach and the Quest for Selfhood," 159. Gilberto Perez, *The Material Ghost. Films and Their Medium* (Baltimore: Johns Hopkins University Press, 1988) suggests that Ringo knows, and he notes that, when Dallas had asked Ringo to give up his revenge quest and go off with her, he had, contrary to many stereotypes of Ford and Westerns, *agreed* (hardly the "masculinist" answer). It is also important that Lucy's baby is a girl. Cf. 238–239. This issue of the relation between self-sufficient independence and domestic dependence will return frequently in later Westerns. See the discussion of *The Man Who Shot Liberty Valance* in Pippin, *Hollywood Westerns and American Myth*, Chap. 3.

FIGURE 7.

bring him a buckboard. Ringo chastely shakes Dallas's hand good-bye, and she climbs in, on the pretense of "riding a while with him" back to prison. But then the sheriff and Doc Boone gleefully shoo the horses into a gallop, allowing Ringo and Dallas to escape to Mexico (Figure 7).

The doctor's closing lines of the movie – "There's two more *saved* from the blessings of civilization" – are, obviously, portentously ambiguous.[8]

Moreover, the most concrete expression of the possibility of a transcendence of class barriers is clearly supposed to be the acknowledgment by Lucy Mallory that Dallas is not only "as good as she is," but perhaps better, in a humanist, Christian sense. Yet when the coach arrives in Lordsburg, and we are in effect set up for that acknowledgment, Lucy refrains from a public acknowledgment when surrounded by the gentlewomen of the town, and even when alone with Dallas, can only start to express her gratitude. "If there is ever anything I can do..." And she stops, and lowers her eyes. Dallas, again taking the much higher ground,

---

[8] See the contrasting accounts of Nick Browne, "The Spectator-in-Text: The Rhetoric of Stagecoach," *Film Quarterly*, 34, No. 2, (1975), 26–38, and T. Gallagher, *John Ford: The Man and his Films*, 153–160, and Rothman's summation in "Stagecoach and the Quest for Selfhood," 174–176.

FIGURE 8.

simply says "I know," as if she means, "I know that you want to do
something, say something, but this promise of a morally equal society
is, we both know, a fantasy, and that I can never be anything but an
ex-whore. At least in this country." She then places her cloak over Lucy
as the latter is carted away. We are shown a promise of a reconciliation
and a new moral order but then also shown its unreality (Figure 8). This
is an extraordinarily deflationary moment in a film by a director who is
often (stupidly) taken to be a jingoistic nationalist. The movie, after all,
ends with the suggestion that the realization of this egalitarian American
ideal can only plausibly take place outside the United States.

Or one might say that Ford's raising the possibility of a form of equality
that Tocqueville did not consider should not be understood as any sort
of potential criticism of the French aristocrat. Given the multiply ironic
ways Ford treats that possibility, he might in fact be suggesting that the
aspiration to such a collectively held value requires the level of naiveté
and blindness typified by the Ringo Kid; that, in actuality, Tocqueville
is right – such an aspiration is inseparable from more material concerns,
the social conditions of any actual status as free and equal citizens. Or at
least it helps us see that the kind of abstraction from the realities of social
and political power, and the effects of its exercise, required to keep faith
with the moral equality is not a socially living actuality but a sustaining
fantasy and that we would be better off seeing it for what it is.

CHAPTER 14

The Poetry of Democracy

Paul Berman

In 2008, the editors of *Dissent* magazine invited a number of writers to comment on the jury system, which the editors regarded as, in their phrase, "probably the original form of participatory democracy."[1] *Dissent* is a New York magazine with solid liberal and socialist roots reaching back to the 1950s and memories reaching back even earlier into the mists of the workers' movement of the nineteenth century. From the viewpoint of a magazine with roots and archaic memories of that sort, participatory democracy seemed distinctly an ideal – maybe the magazine's loftiest ideal of all, the name of its desire. The *Dissent* editors of 2008 fretted about their ideal, however. They wanted to know how participatory democracy has fared in the United States of our own time. They had their worries. And they came up with a clever way of conducting an inquiry.

They turned to Alexis de Tocqueville and his account of the jury system in *Democracy in America*. Tocqueville's discussion appears in the little section called "The Jury in the United States Considered as a Political Institution," which concludes chapter VIII of *Democracy in America*'s Volume One, Part Two. The editors quoted the opening sentence, from a 1966 translation by George Lawrence: "My subject having led me to discuss the administration of justice in the United States, I shall not leave it without speaking of the jury."[2] Tocqueville composed his sentence in a pointedly offhand style, as if the jury system were merely something

---

[1] "We the Jury," *Dissent*, Vol. 55, No. 1, 19–20.
[2] Unless otherwise noted, all citations from Tocqueville are taken from *Democracy in America*. Translated by George Lawrence. Edited by J. P. Mayer (New York: Harper & Row) I.2.viii, 249–253.

to mention in afterthought – an idiosyncrasy of American life that, like fast food and tobacco chewing, European travelers might feel obliged to mention but not something to dwell upon. Tocqueville was sly, though, and juries were not, for him, an afterthought.

The *Dissent* editors quoted a number of other sentences, drawn from later in the chapter, emphasizing the importance of this particular topic: "To regard the jury simply as a judicial institution would be taking a very narrow view of the matter, for great though its influence on the outcome of lawsuits is, its influence on the fate of society itself is much greater still." "Juries teach men equity in practice. Each man, when judging his neighbor, thinks that he may be judged himself." "Juries teach each individual not to shirk responsibility for his own acts, and without that manly characteristic no political virtue is possible." And so forth, with the various quoted lines striking the sonorous tones of philosophical grandeur, from deep to deeper, that Tocqueville knew how to sound as if with no effort at all. Then, having quoted a sufficient number of sentences, the *Dissent* editors invited the magazine's contributors to comment.

I was one of the invited writers, and, in my zeal for the topic, I set aside the excerpted lines and George Lawrence's translation and turned, instead, to the chapter in its original version, "Du jury aux États-Unis considéré comme institution politique." I read with enthusiasm. I even reread, and rereading proved to be instructive. I noticed a distinctive quality in Tocqueville's chapter, which is perhaps not unique to that one portion of the book. His observations and argument, which are wonderfully astute, bear precisely on the anxieties of the *Dissent* editors over matters of civic spirit and egalitarian citizen participation. Rereading, however, led me to notice something else. This was Tocqueville's style of presentation – the shape he gave to his argument, and not just the argument itself.

The chapter seemed to me self-consciously rhythmic. And the rhythms appeared to be arranged in an orderly fashion that could plausibly be described as a kind of prosody. Only, what was the prosody? I was curious, and my curiosity led me to recall an experiment conducted some years ago by the American poet William Everson – a distinguished figure in what used to be called the San Francisco Renaissance, a California poetry movement of the mid-twentieth century. The San Francisco Renaissance revered Walt Whitman. Everson was especially enthusiastic, and, in a reverent spirit, he decided to focus his attention on one of Whitman's strangest and knottiest compositions. This was the preface to the original edition of *Leaves of Grass*, in 1855. Whitman's 1855 preface is fairly difficult to read – a preface written ostensibly in prose yet without the simple lucidity that one normally expects of prose. Whitman himself may have felt less than satisfied with his preface, given that, in later editions of his book, he dropped the preface altogether.

Everson entertained the idea, however, of taking the 1855 preface and rearranging the layout of its sentences to convert the prose into free verse. The Viking Press in New York published the results as a small book under the title *American Bard* in 1982, and the book proved to be wonderfully illuminating. Everson's newly laid-out version demonstrated that Whitman's knotty prose did follow a rhythm, and the rhythm corresponded pretty much to the dominant verse rhythms of *Leaves of Grass*. The 1855 preface, rearranged as free verse, turned out to be easy to read instead of difficult. It was as if, in composing his preface, Whitman had made the mistake of imagining that he was writing prose, when, in truth, he was writing verse. Otherwise he had written an excellent preface. Such was Everson's argument, and he proved his case by presenting the preface in verse form.

Now, Tocqueville and his own prose have almost nothing in common with Walt Whitman and his gnarly sentences. Tocqueville's writing is famously lucid. Never are Tocqueville's sentences knotty or difficult to read – even if his readers like to quarrel with one another over his ultimate meaning. Still, with Everson's example in mind, I set out to rearrange, at least in my imagination, the layout of Tocqueville's chapter on juries, and I did this in precisely the manner that Everson had adopted for Whitman's preface. I redesigned the paragraph indentations in Tocqueville's chapter as line breaks, as in poetry. In this fashion, each new paragraph was transformed into a line of verse – sometimes a fairly short line, other times a rather long line, as in prose poetry. Groups of paragraphs ended up looking like stanzas or strophes of one sort or another.

My readers should bear in mind that, like free markets and free speech, free verse is never entirely free. A free verse poem is merely a poem that, instead of following one of the established forms of conventional verse, establishes an idiosyncratic structure of its own and then conforms to the newly established structure, or departs from it, with pleasing effects. The idiosyncratic structure may even hint at formal verse – a typical element in what is called free verse. No one can read Whitman, for instance, without hearing echoes of the King James Bible and seventeenth-century blank verse. In the case of Tocqueville's chapter, once I had rearranged the sentences and paragraphs as a kind of free verse, I noticed right away that a verse structure of sorts did seem to exist. And the free verse structure hinted, now and then, at the rhythms of formal verse.

I will describe. Tocqueville's section on the jury opens with five short paragraphs. If you lay out those opening paragraphs as verse lines, you will notice that a structure indisputably emerges – a simple and visible structure, although not a rigid one. The structure takes the form of steadily expanding rhythms, advancing from the narrow to the wide, like an opening angle bracket, or <.

Paragraph one is a single sentence. This is the sentence that, in George Lawrence's translation, declares, "My subject having led me to discuss the administration of justice in the United States, I shall not leave it without speaking of the jury." The sentence is flat and lawyer-like, and this is the case both in Lawrence's translation and in the French original. Still, I point something out. In French verse, a classically composed stanza may typically be a quatrain of Alexandrine or twelve-syllable lines, which, all in all, makes a unit of forty-eight syllables. A classical stanza of that sort, if composed correctly, will subdivide into symmetrical or nearly symmetrical subunits. And the symmetries will generate a modulated and musical tone.

Tocqueville's opening paragraph contains, by contrast, forty-two syllables in the French original. The difference between forty-two syllables and forty-eight is significant, and it shows that, in composing his paragraph, Tocqueville was certainly not trying to mimic a conventional quatrain or stanza. Still, he managed to produce a paragraph that remains within the metric universe of a classical quatrain. And then, as if he were, in fact, writing verse, he divides his paragraph more or less in the middle, with a comma supplying the caesura, or break, to give the paragraph a symmetrical shape and a modulated tone.

Paragraph two is a single sentence. In my translation, "It is necessary to distinguish between two things in the jury: a judicial institution and a political institution." Again the sentence is cut in roughly the middle, with the caesura supplied this time by a colon. The sentence is slightly shorter than the previous one. Then again, the colon creates a pause that is sharper than a comma's, which causes the sound to linger a little longer in the ear.

Paragraph three is a single sentence. This time the sentence consists of fifty-six syllables, which makes it significantly longer. The sentence is more complex, too. I will not quote the sentence, but I remark that it contains four main components, instead of two, which maintains the sense of symmetry.

Paragraph four is a single sentence. This new sentence is longer still. And yet its basic structure remains faithful to the form established by each of the three preceding, one-sentence paragraphs. The new paragraph is broken in the middle, more or less, this time by a semicolon. Each of the halves is likewise broken into halves, in this case by commas. In this fashion, Tocqueville continues to maintain the pattern of symmetry, even as he increases the size of his sentences.

The parallel structure of these four one-sentence opening paragraphs, together with their growing length and complexity, builds a feeling of suspense. And the suspense, having mounted step by step, spills at last into the fifth and climactic paragraph. The fifth paragraph is altogether different. It consists of five sentences of varied complexity, containing two colons and three semicolons – a paragraph of rich tones, expressing a conversational ease instead of the stentorian and symmetrical quality of the one-sentence paragraphs that have come before. It is as if, in the opening four paragraphs, Tocqueville has spoken in a sort of declamatory verse, and now, in the fifth and climactic paragraph, he has allowed his voice to subside into prosaic conversation.

Next comes a transitional bridge of three sentences, announcing a change of topic. "But let us leave this subject." And then comes an unmistakable recapitulation of the opening strophe. There are three short one-sentence paragraphs (or, in the case of the second paragraph, a very short, two-sentence paragraph, corresponding to the second, colon-broken paragraph of the opening strophe). The short paragraphs grow in length and complexity. And the rising tension spills at last into a full-length conversational paragraph of multiple sentences and complicated rhythms followed by yet another such paragraph. The five paragraphs of the opening strophe are, in sum, followed, after a short transitional bridge, by a second, parallel strophe, likewise of five paragraphs.

Even if you do not consciously take note of what Tocqueville is doing, you would have to be poetically deaf to fail to register the disciplined rhythm of those opening passages. And then, having declaimed his first strophe and his second strophe, Tocqueville moves to an entirely new section, employing a different rhythmic style altogether. The entire progression, until this point, follows a sonata form of A, A, B.

I will not go through the whole chapter, except to note that it consists of various combinations of one-sentence paragraphs and conversational multi-sentence paragraphs, arranged in such a way as to oscillate between emphatic declarations and conversational tranquility. If you want to see an example of a one-sentence paragraph in an emphatic tone, you might reexamine one of the sentences that I have quoted earlier from the George

Lawrence translation: "Juries teach each individual not to shirk responsibility for his own acts," and so forth.

I am not fond of the translation, however. The original goes like this: "Le jury apprend à chacque homme à ne pas reculer devant la responsabilité de ses propres actes; disposition virile, sans laquelle il n'y a pas de vertu politique." Now, in the case of this particular one-sentence paragraph, if you count the syllables, they add up to a round forty-eight – that is, so long as you grant the hint of a second syllable in "actes," before the caesura. The sentence, regarded as verse, would make a perfect Alexandrine quatrain, or very nearly so – except that, at the end of the first Alexandrine, the word *reculer* would have to be divided, in contradiction to the classical rules of verse. The resemblance to a proper Alexandrine quatrain is close enough, though – closer than in any other paragraph of the chapter. By remarkable coincidence, in this same perfectly syllabled paragraph you also happen to find the nub of Tocqueville's argument about the beneficial consequences of civic participation. Here is his grand argument in favor of what the *Dissent* editors describe as "participatory democracy." The paragraph that achieves most perfectly a classical French poetry rhythm turns out to be, in sum, the paragraph that expresses most perfectly his central point.

Am I foolish to detect these kinds of structures in Tocqueville's chapter? Allow me to point to the chapter's conclusion: his last five paragraphs. The first of those five paragraphs is two sentences long, containing two periods, a semicolon, and a colon plus five commas, not to mention a footnote asterisk. It is a paragraph written in a tranquil conversational prose tone without any of the symmetries or musical qualities of conventional verse. Then comes a still larger paragraph, which happens, however, to be only a single, complicated sentence. Then follow three more paragraphs, each of which is, in fact, a single sentence. The three single-sentence paragraphs become progressively simpler.

The very last paragraph turns out to be a straightforwardly brief and classically constructed sentence. It begins with a three-word introduction, "Thus the jury . . . " – and then, having begun, it is neatly broken in the middle by a comma serving as caesura. It is a one-sentence paragraph that manages to recapitulate the shape and style of the one-sentence paragraph at the very start of the chapter: "Thus the jury, which is the most energetic means of allowing the people to reign, is also the most efficacious way of making them learn to reign."

The ending is remarkable, if you recall the format of the chapter as a whole. The chapter begins, as I say, in the shape of an opening angle bracket, or <, advancing over the course of a five-paragraph strophe from one-sentence declamations to a multi-sentence conversational paragraph. And the chapter concludes with a five-paragraph strophe that goes the other way, in the shape of a closing angle bracket, or >. The chapter's opening line and closing line turn out to be rhythmically identical, too, or nearly so: an opening line of forty-two syllables matched by a closing line of forty-one syllables.

Readers who make their way through the chapter will experience, at the end, a pleasurable click of satisfaction. The readers might tell themselves that Tocqueville's chapter on the jury system is an example of his genius for lucid exposition, and the click of satisfaction expresses the readers' pleasure at fully understanding his argument. But the satisfying click also comes from something else. Tocqueville has cleverly arranged his sentences in such a way that, at the end, we have no alternative but to experience the satisfying click – a click that has been produced by the mathematical symmetries and their variations throughout the chapter. And then, as if to outdo himself, he presents in his final sentence an extravaganza of symmetries.

In that concluding sentence, the jury turns out to be not only "the most energetic means of allowing the people to reign" but also "the most efficacious way of making them learn to reign." The repetition of "to reign" conforms to the epigrammatic style of a certain kind of French philosophy, but repetition and rhyme are, above all, poetic devices. And so, the chapter concludes with a perfect sentence, triply symmetrical (because it matches the opening sentence of the chapter; because it divides into equal halves; because it balances the two uses of "to reign"). The triply symmetrical perfect sentence argues that democracy itself has a perfect quality in regard to the jury system (because the institution that allows the people to reign also instructs them how to do so in a wise and responsible manner). The musical perfection of the chapter and especially of its last sentence expresses the institutional perfection of a democracy that relies on a jury-based system of justice. And the click of satisfaction resounds still more satisfactorily. You feel the click not only because Tocqueville's argument is so lucidly presented and the metrical rhythms are so cleverly manipulated and maintained, but also because democracy itself, his ultimate theme, turns out to have elegant symmetries.

Tocqueville never doubted that a good thinker must be a good writer, attentive to the rules of composition. In a private letter on literary style, he specified that good writing can always be defined by what he called, as if shrugging at the simplicity of it all, "good sense." But *Democracy in America* is not merely well written. It is beautiful. This poses a question. Does the aesthetic quality of the book convey any sort of political or philosophical meaning of its own, apart from what is stated directly in the text? Are there additional significances to the book, which can be understood only in connection to the style in which it has been written?

I think that, yes, there are – although, in making this claim, I do not mean to suggest that *Democracy in America* contains any sort of hidden code or esoteric implication, invisible to the unaided eye. Still, in the 1830s, when Tocqueville was composing the book, matters of poetry and formal composition tended to carry an unusual weight of meaning for the most eagerly alert of readers and writers, and the meanings spread outward from the world of literature to the world of political philosophy. There is much to say on this point, and I hope to lay out some of the argument on another occasion. For the moment, however, I would like to propose a simple biographical observation.

Tocqueville was born in 1805 into an aristocratic family with Catholic royalist views and bitter memories of extreme suffering under the revolutionary Terror, not to mention the years that followed. Young people who were born around 1800 constituted a distinct generational cohort. They were, in Musset's phrase, "children of the century." The children from royalist backgrounds were still more distinctly marked. Rousseau and other philosophers dominated the age, intellectually speaking. The young people from royalist backgrounds tended to shy away from philosophy, though, and this was because, given the traumas of the 1790s, philosophy appeared, in their eyes, to be fatefully allied with the horrors of the age.

Literary-minded Catholic royalists tended to be, instead, readers and even writers of poetry. Poetry was the queen of the arts. But it was also the queen of the moral and social sciences. Matters of poetry and matters of political philosophy were entirely intertwined – an old principle in the Catholic world of Versailles, dating back a hundred years earlier to Fénelon or even further back. Tocqueville's uncle by marriage, Chateaubriand, demonstrated the up-to-dateness of the same idea in his renowned and learned tract of 1802, *Le Génie du Christianisme*, which everyone read in those days.

The old-fashioned emphasis on poetry also led to some political implications in the years that followed. Chateaubriand himself remained a sturdy champion of the Bourbon family, apart from a brief and soon regretted period when he fell under Napoleon's seduction. The younger generation of Catholic royalists, the children of the century, ended up chafing at the Bourbons, though. They talked about poetry, but their discussions evolved. The year 1823 is said to have been, for those people, a turning point (said, that is, by the great historian of French literature Paul Bénichou). And, in 1830, a significant group of the brightest of the young literary royalists broke away from royalist legitimacy. They came out in favor of the revolution that overthrew Charles X, the Bourbon king.

But they also came out in favor of a revolution in poetry – a necessary thing to do, given the link between poetry and politics. The first major sign of this took place in the world of theatre. Victor Hugo, at age 28, was one of the young Catholic royalists, an ardent follower of Chateaubriand, and already the literary leader of his generation. In 1830, Hugo composed the verse play *Hernani* about a rebel who wants to kill a king, and the play caused a riot at its opening nights – the most famous artistic riot of world history, I would think. A "riot," in this instance, means an outbreak of booing and anti-booing.

In the opening line of the play, Hugo violated one of the established laws of French poetry. His play was composed in proper Alexandrines, but the opening sentence spilled over from the first line into the second – which is to say, Hugo enjambed his sentence from one line to the next. The syllabic rhythm remained correct, and the rhyme, perfect, but to anyone dedicated to literary traditional, the enjambment could only jar the ear, like an ugly discord. The enjambment was a deliberate provocation, and, by placing it in the opening words of the play, the playwright guaranteed that everyone heard it, and no one could suppose that young Hugo had merely awkwardly stumbled. The legitimist royalists in the audience were naturally outraged, and they expressed themselves. Here was a turning point in French literature. It was also a turning point in the history of French liberalism (if I may use the word *liberalism* a little loosely), given that Hugo soon enough ceased to be a literary champion of Catholic royalism and the counterrevolution. He defected, instead, to the democratic and republican left, in a fashion strictly devoted both to humanitarianism and the rights of man.

Chateaubriand's nephew began to write *Democracy in America* a year later, with its sometimes-ostentatious echoes of verse. I will hold off from expounding what I think are the implications of his poetic thinking (although you can dig up certain of these implications for yourself in the chapter on poetry in *Democracy in America*). However, I will remark that participatory democracy, which the editors of *Dissent* admire and revere, and which I, too, admire and revere, is not just an institutional matter. The questions raised by participatory democracy touch on literary matters, too. At least the political questions and the literary questions used to merge together in the past, and not only in France. Allow me to recall that Whitman likewise considered poetry and the democratic precepts of the United States to be inextricably bound together. This was the whole point of his preface to the 1855 edition of *Leaves of Grass*. He wrote, "The United States themselves are essentially the greatest poem" – a strange thing to say. He said it, though. Ideas about poetry and democracy and the United States were plainly floating about in the mid-nineteenth-century air. Do those ideas still float about? Of course they do – at least in the degree that books like *Leaves of Grass* remain alive in our present age. The same is true of *Democracy in America*.

CHAPTER 15

Tocqueville and the Local Frontiers of Democracy

Robert T. Gannett, Jr.

> To be free one must have the capacity to plan and persevere in a difficult undertaking, and be accustomed to act on one's own; to live in freedom one must grow used to a life full of agitation, change, and danger; to keep alert the whole time with a restless eye on everything around: that is the price of freedom.
>
> – Alexis de Tocqueville, 1835[1]

As a community organizer in Chicago, I work to define, strengthen, and give political structure to democracy's community borders, or what we might call its local frontiers. It will not surprise readers of Alexis de Tocqueville's *Democracy in America* that the philosophical origins of my profession of community organizing, dedicated as it is both to freedom and equality, are embedded in his writings and reflections. So when I imagine the young Tocqueville equipped with his red bandana, hunting knife, and six-shooter on America's frontier during his great voyage from 1831 to 1832, I see members of my own profession standing with our own weapons of vigilance and resistance on America's contemporary local frontiers. The pivotal question in both Tocqueville's case and our own, of course, is just what frontiers do we seek to define, preserve, or expand with our weaponry? For whom are we establishing such frontiers? Against whom are we protecting them? Are we working to advance what Tocqueville would call in his book "the triumphal progress of civilization across the wilderness"?[2] Or are we seeking to block or retard it, and if

[1] Alexis de Tocqueville, JEI, 116.
[2] DIA (L) I.2.ix, 280.

so, for what reasons? Finally, given the location of our conference in the same American Midwest whose virgin forests helped shape Tocqueville's own experience of the American frontier, how might his nuanced view of frontier freedom help us understand Chicago today? For Chicago, I will argue, is a city that has repeatedly sacrificed local political frontiers and robust freedom in the name of "triumphal progress" and servile order.

America's frontiersmen – the Daniel Boones of history and Natty Bumppos of literature – have stirred the American imagination for generations, epitomizing adventure, ingenuity, and courage. Tocqueville predicted our enduring fascination with such pioneers, anticipating that they would serve as one great source of future American (and democratic) poetry: "The American people see themselves marching through wildernesses, drying up marshes, diverting rivers, peopling the wilds, and subduing nature."[3] In Tocqueville's telescopic view, however, such an elevated vision might lead future democrats to dream of eliminating borders and assimilating all mankind within "one vast democracy,"[4] thus planting seeds of despotism as their democratic governments quietly worked behind the scenes to appropriate the bordered, independent, free spaces that nurtured potent sources of resistance. Tocqueville hated governments and their agents who sought to eliminate borders (administrative tutors in the Old Regime, demagogic egalitarians in the French Revolution, and master architects of empire in Napoleonic times), just as he hated religions and their leaders who sought to do the same (pantheists, including American Unitarians, who subverted doctrinal borders, and Islamic imams and their followers who dispensed altogether with the crucial frontier between church and state). To counter such engineers of despotism, Tocqueville extolled those who recognized, created, and/or protected borders – New England's Puritans (America's first frontiersmen), lawyers and jurists, association builders of all kinds, and (I like to think) community organizers.

Tocqueville argued for not one but two democratic tracks to make democracy work: a national one and a local one, each distinguished by its own clearly defined mission and appropriate set of responsibilities. At the national level, a central government must provide such essential needs for its citizens as national security, general police regulations, a unified justice system, and a nationwide infrastructure to promote commercial integration and economic independence. Tocqueville called this

3 DIA (L) II.1.xvii, 485.
4 DIA (L) II.1.xvii, 486.

"governmental centralization"[5] and insisted on its very specific prerogatives and powers: "what I want is a central government energetic in its own sphere of action," he wrote his friend Eugène Stoffels in October 1836.[6] However, at the same time, he argued for the importance of a second local track that would be equally energetic in its own sphere of action. This second track consisted of Tocqueville's famous cross section of local associations – permanent ones (towns, villages, and other local governments), voluntary political ones, voluntary civil ones, small private ones, and various hybrids such as juries and social movements. Each set of associations contributed in its own way to building the power and independence of the second track by educating citizens for freedom: voluntary political associations were "great free schools," political parties were "rough school[s]," a jury was "a free school which is always open," and local towns served as the "primary schools" where citizens first learned their political ABCs.[7] Such schools on democracy's second track strengthened democratic citizenship and fostered its essential qualities: fearless trust in one's own powers, respect for the voices and rights of all, skill at deliberation and negotiation, economic enterprise, self-discipline, and the ability "to keep alert the whole time with a restless eye on everything around."[8] In concert with religion, associations on democracy's second track helped forge America's principal moral doctrine of self-interest properly understood.[9] Most importantly, they strengthened the needed skills for citizens to hold democracy's first track accountable through constant vigilance, periodic resistance, and occasional wary partnership. Citizens – and only citizens – could work to protect borders, even as their governments sought to abolish them.

To properly grasp Tocqueville's understanding of the importance of democracy's local frontiers, we must grasp his formulation of their

---

[5] DIA (L) I.1.v, 87.
[6] "Tocqueville to Eugène Stoffels, October 5, 1836," SLPS, 113.
[7] DIA (L) II.2.vii, 522, I.1.ii, 33, I.2.viii, 275, I:1.v, 63. For a more detailed discussion of Tocqueville's educational curriculum for citizenship, see Robert T. Gannett, Jr., "Tocqueville and Local Government: Distinguishing Democracy's Second Track," *Review of Politics* (Fall 2005): 721–736.
[8] Tocqueville, JEI, 116. For Tocqueville's view of economic enterprise, see Christine Dunn Henderson, "'Plus ça change...': Innovation and the Spirit of Enterprise in America," *Review of Politics* (Fall 2005): 753–774. As epigraph to her essay, Henderson uses the same Tocquevillean quote regarding freedom that I have used for this essay: she applies it to the spirit of American commerce while I apply it to the spirit of American local frontier freedom. Tocqueville invites either reading.
[9] DIA (L) II.2.viii–ix, 525–530.

intellectual underpinnings prior to his arrival in America on May 9, 1831. François Furet first outlined the philosophical contours of such a preliminary Tocquevillean "voyage in America" of 1825–1831 and correctly situated it within the context of Tocqueville's complex relationship with France's preeminent modern historian and celebrated liberal political star François Guizot.[10] Building on Furet's recognition of Tocqueville's "continuous intellectual and political exchange [with Guizot] marked by a mixture of complicity and hostility,"[11] I find the most revealing source for Tocqueville's early intuitions about democracy to be his reflections contained in correspondence and lecture notes responding to Professor Guizot's sixty-three famous lectures delivered at the Sorbonne in 1828, 1829, and 1830. Escaping his day job as an unpaid *juge auditeur* at Versailles, Tocqueville often attended these Saturday morning lectures at the Sorbonne. For the lectures he missed, he depended on notes from his friends or the published copies rushed into print to satisfy the immense interest of France's young liberal intelligentsia.[12] It is widely understood by scholars that the young Tocqueville was infatuated with Guizot's historical method, both in terms of its "truly *prodigious*" formulation of ideas and lucid articulation of them.[13] However, Tocqueville also possessed profound political reservations about Guizot's arguments, all based on his early preoccupation with the importance of borders.

What so disturbed the young Tocqueville in Guizot's historical account? In Guizot's sweeping view, civilization in Europe and France was engaged during a dozen centuries in an inexorable march of progress leading to the triumph of his great heroes – the bourgeoisie or the third

---

[10] François Furet, "Naissance d'un paradigme: Tocqueville et le Voyage en Amérique (1825–1831)," *Annales* 39/2 (1984): 225–239. Furet repeated and expanded his argument in "The Intellectual Origins of Tocqueville's Thought," *La Revue Tocqueville/Tocqueville Review* 7 (1985–1986): 117–129.

[11] François Furet, *Interpreting the French Revolution*, trans. Elborg Forster (Cambridge and Paris: Cambridge University Press and Maison des Sciences de l'Homme, [1978] 1981), 135.

[12] François Guizot, *Histoire générale de la civilization en Europe depuis la chute de l'Empire romain jusqu'à la revolution française* (Paris: Pichon et Didier, 1828) [lecture cycle #1] and François Guizot, *Histoire de la civilization en France depuis la chute de l'Empire romain jusqu'en 1789* (Paris: Pichon et Didier, 1829–1832) [lecture cycles #2 and #3]. Guizot's European lectures of 1828 "soon became one of the most popular books in nineteenth-century France, a true best-seller," Aurelian Craiutu, "Introduction" to François Guizot, *The History of the Origins of Representative Government in Europe* (Indianapolis, IN: Liberty Fund, 2002), x. In her introductory footnote to Tocqueville's lecture notes, Françoise Mélonio indicates that fraudulent transcriptions of Guizot's lectures quickly became available at Parisian bookshops as well, "Notes on Guizot's course on the history of civilization in France," OC 16, 441 n. 1.

[13] "Tocqueville to Gustave de Beaumont, August 30, 1829," OC 8:1, 80.

estate. The bourgeoisie received their start in the medieval towns or communes that existed alongside the church and the feudal system as the
three great pillars of the medieval world. Winning their charters often
by fiery rebellion against oppressive feudal lords, Guizot's feisty burghers
excelled at establishing borders and thus exercised a measure of local
self-government:

> Let us enter into the commune itself . . . we are in a kind of fortified place defended
> by armed burghers: these burghers tax themselves, elect their magistrates, judge
> and punish, and assemble for the purpose of deliberating upon their affairs. All
> come to these assemblies; they make war on their own account against their lord;
> and they have a militia. In a word, they govern themselves; they are sovereigns.[14]

So far, so good – indeed, we can see in Guizot's description here the very
attributes that Tocqueville will discover and trumpet with such gusto in
Democracy in America in his assertion that America's first founding took
place in its New England's towns. But local liberty in such communes
was turbulent, Guizot proceeded to say, and he carefully catalogued in
his later lectures the reasons for both their rise and eventual chaotic fall
during the eleventh to fifteenth centuries, showing how at the end of this
period they succumbed to a sweeping process of royal centralization that
united the nation and facilitated the emergence of representative institutions. Royal centralization stripped the towns of their independence and
self-government, with the third estate's own *légistes* conspiring with the
king to establish a legal basis for his powers at the expense of their own
local freedoms. "In these towns," Guizot calmly, objectively, and dispassionately noted, "political freedom was absent." In its place, a new spirit
took root among its inhabitants, one that would become the "dominant
character" of the French bourgeoisie and that Guizot described as "not
very ambitious, not very enterprising, timid even, and scarcely entertaining the thought of definitive and violent resistance, but honest, a friend
of order, of rule, persevering, attached to its rights, and skillful enough
sooner or later to make those rights recognized and respected."[15] While
regretting the loss of local freedom in this trade-off with the crown, Guizot
made no apologies for what he saw as its larger benefits: "Therefore I am

[14] Guizot, *The History of Civilization in Europe*, ed. Larry Siedentop, trans. William Hazlitt
(London: Penguin Classics, 1997), 121.
[15] Guizot, *Histoire de la civilisation en France*, 10th ed., 4 vols. (Paris: Didier, 1868),
4:86–87. In his notes, Tocqueville recorded Guizot's description of the bourgeois spirit
in the following terms: "honest, a friend of order, an enemy of tumult and even of sound,
a partisan of authority still more from love than from fear, a spirit that is excessively
timid by nature and that takes fright at the very idea of energetic resistances," OC 16,
532–533.

convinced that on the whole the centralization that characterizes our history obtained for our France much greater prosperity and grandeur [and] happier and more glorious destinies than she would have obtained if local institutions, local freedoms, and local ideas had remained sovereign or even preponderant."[16]

Guizot thus posed in particularly provocative fashion for his most precocious student the question of the importance of local borders. Tocqueville never doubted where he stood on this question, during these lectures of 1828–1830, his trip to America from 1831 to 1832, or his subsequent political and scholarly careers, ever fused as complementary means to dispel his "anxiety that he would fail to make a difference with his life."[17] He was distressed and would always be distressed by civilized man's impatience, condescension, derision, and willingness to sacrifice local governments and local borders. Three months after the conclusion of Guizot's first cycle of lectures in June 1828, writing a lengthy series of ruminations to Gustave de Beaumont on English history, he sarcastically described "civilization's first fruit" that elevated "one man's standard" and "led all peoples to throw themselves, bound hand and foot, into the power of their rulers."[18] In his lecture notes of 1829 and 1830, he injected such pejorative descriptions as "equality under a master," "tutelary influence [of the crown] that watches unceasingly over [its royal communes]," and "the calm of servitude" to describe the bourgeoisie's surrender of their freedom in the face of such royal power.[19] Writing to his

---

[16] Guizot, *Histoire*, 4:93. Tocqueville rendered Guizot's verdict as follows: "As for me, Messieurs, I believe and am not afraid to state that the loss by the towns of their independent freedom was, all things considered, a blessing for France. It was necessary for us to undergo great modern centralization in order to become one people unified and compact in all its parts [and] in order to achieve in our vast territory but a sole and immense commune acting for one goal, stirred by the same ideas, agitated by the same passions, finally marching as one man to overcome the same obstacles," OC 16, 534. Guizot had offered a similar description of the bourgeois spirit and rendered a similar beneficial verdict on the loss of local freedoms in 1828 in his first lecture cycle, *The History of Civilization in Europe*, ed. Siedentop, 131–133 and 188–189.

[17] Leo Damrosch, *Tocqueville's Discovery of America* (New York: Farrar, Straus and Giroux, 2010), 72.

[18] "Tocqueville to Beaumont, October 5, 1828," JEI, 38. Both Furet ("The Intellectual Origins," 121–122) and André Jardin, the editor of Tocqueville's correspondence with Beaumont (OC 8:1, 57 note 21), detect Guizot's potent presence in Tocqueville's reflections while writing this letter.

[19] OC 16, 516, 523, and 531. For a valuable discussion of additional layers of discomfort expressed by Tocqueville with respect to Guizot's "alliance of freedom and power" (OC 16, 475 note), see Cheryl B. Welch, "Tocqueville's Resistance to the Social," *History of European Ideas* 30 (2004): 104–106.

friend Charles Stoffels during this same period, he memorably described in pointed fashion the effects of such obsequious servitude:

In the case of a society that has achieved a high degree of civilization, the social body has taken charge of everything: the individual has to take responsibility for being born; for all else, society places him in the arms of its wet nurse, supervises his education, opens before him the paths of fortune. Society supports him on his way, brushes aside the dangers from his head. He advances in peace under the eyes of this second providence. This tutelary power that protected him during his life watches over the burying of his ashes as well: that's the fate of civilized man. Individual energy is almost extinguished.[20]

Central rulers and democratic despots of all stripes, Tocqueville believed, had become and would continue to become ever more adept at extracting this Faustian trade-off from their own citizens: they supplied private comfort and servile order in exchange for the surrender of local frontiers and the voluntary relinquishment of public responsibilities. To counter such democratic enfeeblement leading to despotism, Tocqueville turned throughout his career to associations of citizens: they could best protect their local freedoms by strengthening local ambition, local enterprise, local courage, local accountability, and local "energetic resistances" – all of which Tocqueville believed Guizot had blithely surrendered.[21]

Tocqueville thus arrived in America in May 1831 with a recognition of the need, honed in Guizot's lectures, for not one but two powerful and independent tracks that would serve as dueling frontiers within a democracy. Four months later in Boston, he discovered to his surprise the New England town with its unique tradition of local participatory democracy that had endured for over 200 years. Guizot's bourgeois *légistes*, it turned out, had not succeeded in throttling all spirit from democracy's new citizens: a whole English bourgeois contingent had escaped to America and voilà, Tocqueville proclaimed, look at their accomplishments: participation in enacting their own laws, free voting of their taxes, the ability to hold local officials accountable to them, individual freedom in their personal affairs, and recognition of their duties to provide for the poor, maintain their roads, keep sound order, and furnish universal public education. The Puritans even "marvelously combine[d] . . . the

---

[20] "Tocqueville to Charles Stoffels, April 21, 1830," in DIA (Nolla), 1369–1370.
[21] OC 16, 533. For a broader discussion of Guizot's failure to pass Tocqueville's liberty test, see Robert T. Gannett, Jr., *Tocqueville Unveiled: The Historian and His Sources for "The Old Regime and the Revolution"* (Chicago: University of Chicago Press, 2003), 1–3, 18–25.

spirit of religion and the *spirit of freedom*,"²² constituting the essential communal counterweight or border to both brazen political ambition and excessive individual materialism. New England towns thus served as incubators for freedom properly understood. At the same time, they exported that freedom westward as their villagers restlessly extended the American frontier. Tocqueville marveled at how tiny Connecticut could be home state to thirty-six members of the United States Congress in 1830,²³ supporting his claim that "New England civilization has been like beacons on mountain peaks," spreading its light "to the farthest limits of the horizon."²⁴ It remains for us to assess how well those beacons of local freedom have continued to illuminate that horizon's farthest limit: Chicago.

Community Organizing on Chicago's Local Frontier

In 2008, in my capacity as a community organizer in Chicago during the past thirty-plus years, I had reason to bring a group of neighborhood residents to a meeting with one of Chicago's finest – no, I am not referring to a police officer but a local alderman. These were residents whom I had met by doing what community organizers do – knocking on their doors, talking with a broad cross section of them, inviting them to meetings, challenging them to engage in their own energetic resistances, and teaching them how to pierce through the bureaucratic and political fog they inevitably encounter. You might say – in fact I like to say – that we help residents establish Tocquevillean "primary schools" of local democracy in their local neighborhoods. After two and one-half years of such schooling, these particular residents had developed a plan for their community – one that called both for a major commitment from the city of 500 of its 2,000 city-owned vacant lots for local affordable homes and a major commitment from local residents to establish a local Housing Trust Fund with their own tax dollars. Residents insisted on one stipulation for the fund – they wanted the right to elect community representatives to a governing commission in biannual elections that would determine exactly how their tax dollars would be spent to meet the fund's objectives. Residents had vetted their proposal at numerous community meetings. They had placed it on an official election ballot in 2004 and

²² DIA (L) I.1.ii, 47.
²³ DIA (L) I.1.ix, 282.
²⁴ DIA (L) I.1.ii, 35.

received more than 18,500 positive votes (better than 85%) in favor of it. And they had convened a Blue Ribbon Committee of lawyers and affordable housing experts to help them craft an ordinance incorporating their principles and demands.[25]

When we met with this particular alderman, she did not mince any words in dismissing her constituents' work and rejecting any chance that she would ever support their proposed ordinance. "Let me explain to you how Chicago works," she calmly, objectively, and dispassionately announced:

Chicago politics is like a medieval feudal system, where Mayor Daley is king and we aldermen are the lords and ladies of our wards. Now we are not in the business of standing up to the king. And in return, the king allows us to run our wards as we see fit. Your ordinance is unacceptable to me because you are attempting to tie my hands in how I want to run my own ward.[26]

Having educated her constituents about the city's modern-day feudal structure, she proceeded to warn the group's members that they should put aside any hopes that they could curry aldermanic favor for their ordinance by splitting the four local aldermen one from another: "We realize that to preserve our own local powers, we must maintain a united front in the face of any local resistance." Seven days later, true to her word, all four local aldermen appeared at a community meeting attended by 250 local residents and indeed stood shoulder to shoulder in opposition to their constituents' wishes.

While some might give credit here for refreshing aldermanic candor, I am reminded instead of Tocqueville's account of Madame Duchâtelet in *The Old Regime and the Revolution* who "felt no embarrassment at undressing in front of her servants, as she was not convinced that valets were men."[27] Following Guizot, Mayor Richard Daley and our aldermen have made the Faustian trade-off to advance civilization and ensure their power in their realm. To the extent that the trade-off is made with "the lords and ladies of [the] wards," rather than the bourgeoisie, so much the better, because it means that the aristocracy itself has now

---

[25] For greater detail on each of these activities, see Housing Bronzeville's Web site at http://www.standupforbronzeville.org/HBhome.htm.

[26] Housing Bronzeville was evidently not the only group with whom this particular alderman used this analogy. See Derek S. Hyra, *The New Urban Renewal: The Economic Transformation of Harlem and Bronzeville* (Chicago: University of Chicago Press, 2008), 120.

[27] OR I, 227.

joined in surrendering its own local freedoms – a trait Tocqueville also described in *The Old Regime and the Revolution* as the king had attracted to Paris the largest number of France's own lords and ladies, a major royal miscalculation in Tocqueville's view that helped precipitate the French Revolution.[28] The mayor and the aldermen are of course quick to cite the benefits of their particular mutual pact: planters in our streets, wrought-iron fences in our parks, a bean in our new Millennium Park, a spiffy downtown pressing ever outward into blighted neighborhoods in the name of civilization's latest progressive march, a proliferation of Tax Increment Financing (TIF) districts to eradicate that blight, and a proposed Olympic Games in 2016.

These are the acknowledged goods we have gained from our Chicago Guizotian trade-off. The unacknowledged "goods" (in quotes) are less likely to be highlighted, but each has received national and international attention in 2008-2009. I will conclude by citing three of them.

Corruption

In Tocqueville's view, corruption is more "coarse and vulgar" in a democracy than in an aristocracy, because "stealing from the public purse or selling the favors of the state for money – those are matters any wretch can understand and hope to emulate in turn."[29] However, in a democracy, he adds, there is also more hope to resist such corruption: "In democracies, the people, constantly occupied as they are with their affairs and jealous of their rights, prevent their representatives from deviating from a general line indicated by their interests."[30]

It is precisely this democratic vigilance – both by the populace as a whole of its elected officials and by elected officials of each other – that we have surrendered in Chicago given mayoral-aldermanic collusion and the absence of any borders provided by a two-party political system. As cited in Derek Hyra's *The New Urban Renewal*, a South Side Bronzeville community leader says it well:

[Chicago] is the most unusual city in the country. No other city functions like this. I've lived in Cincinnati, in New York City, and in Boston. In these places your representatives actually . . . sit down [with you] and act like they work for

[28] OR I, 180–192.
[29] DIA (L) I.2.v, 221.
[30] DIA (L) I.2.vi, 233.

you. Here nobody works for you, you work for them, you know, so that's the way it is.[31]

We accept this Chicago Way; in a perverse fashion, we applaud it for efficiency's sake. Mirroring Guizot, we view the loss by local communities of their individual freedoms as, all things considered, a blessing for Chicago. Our disgraced former governor expressed his own pride in the Chicago Way in the *New York Times*, boasting that "I come out of the alleys of Chicago politics."[32] However, it is precisely the web of unlit, unwatched, unrecorded, and unacknowledged deals and deceit hatched in those alleys that has infected the very pores (the mores in Tocqueville's terms) of our city, our state capital in Springfield, and, if my aldermanic sources are correct, Chicago's 2016 Olympic Committee as well.

Community Organizing

If corruption is our first unacknowledged Guizotian good, community organizing is our second, serving as its reverse mirror image and one potent response to it. No observer of urban America can be surprised that community organizing originated in Chicago and has always had its deepest roots here, harking back to the work of Saul Alinsky. For where corruption extinguishes beacons of local freedom, thrives in a climate of secrecy, and operates in back alleys, community organizing lights those beacons, demands transparency, and does its work on front porches. Where corruption appeals to people's venal interest, community organizing aims for their self-interest properly understood. Where corruption feeds upon citizen apathy, community organizing combats apathy by engaging precisely those citizens whom Tocqueville viewed as freedom's champions – those who loved freedom for "its own peculiar charm, independent of its benefits: . . . the pleasure of being able to speak, act, and breathe without constraint, under the sole government of God and the laws."[33] Where corruption seeks to eliminate the second democratic track through deception, co-option, or intimidation, community organizing fights to protect it and build it. Where corruption isolates people, freezing their souls, community organizing brings them together.

[31] Hyra, *New Urban Renewal*, 118.
[32] Monica Davey, "Blagojevich Has His Final Say, Making Day of It," *New York Times*, January 30, 2009, sec. 1A, p. 14.
[33] OR I, 217.

Where corruption justifies its democratic bona fides by pointing to every citizen's right to vote every four years and then works to silence them in the electoral interim, community organizing insists on day-to-day vigilance and participation, reflecting Tocqueville's maxim that "one should never expect a liberal, energetic, and wise government to originate in the votes of a people of servants."[34] Where corruption embraces Guizot's tendency to sell off local liberties at a bargain price, community organizing follows Tocqueville in seeking to cancel that sale.

A *Chicago Tribune* centerpiece on Chicago's native son Saul Alinsky correctly identified him as "the father of community organizing," adding that "Chicago is probably the only place that had the combination of ingredients that shaped Alinsky: sociology, socialism, and the syndicate."[35] Missing from this list is the most important factor that shaped Alinsky and has shaped all of Chicago's great organizers: the fear that our citizens are becoming sheep, school children, or slaves, to use Tocqueville's terminology, as Alinsky frequently did. "In the last analysis," Alinsky wrote in 1969 in his own defense of local frontiers,

democracy is preserved and strengthened by maintaining differences and variations. When – as is happening in our cities – all strong, local vested interests are obliterated, when these differences are removed, then I too see what Tocqueville saw as the major peril to our democracy: an egalitarian society that may have the look and forms of democracy, but is its very opposite.[36]

Barack Obama

Chicago's third Guizotian "good" is Barack Obama. Drawing on his Chicago experience, President Obama has positioned himself in 2009 as the simultaneous master of not one but both democratic tracks in the United States – our national and local ones. We can point to an earlier partisan of democracy's second track who similarly did much to support and sustain it early in his career, similarly found himself subsequently elevated to his nation's first track, and then wrestled with all the questions of the proper relation between the two tracks. I am referring, of course, to Tocqueville, elected a national deputy for three terms during the July Monarchy, elected a member of the Constituent Assembly after

34 DIA (L) II.4.vi, 694.
35 Ron Grossman, "Activism for Alinsky a Hope-Based Pursuit," *Chicago Tribune*, January 30, 2009, sec. 4, p. 1.
36 Saul D. Alinsky, "Afterword" to *Reveille for Radicals* (New York: Vintage Books, [1946] 1969), 218.

the 1848 Revolution, elected by his peers within the Assembly to the Committee to rewrite the French Constitution, and plucked by the new President Louis-Napoleon Bonaparte to be France's foreign minister for five months in 1849 as the result of his rising national power and stature. In his case, Tocqueville consistently saw the two tracks as mutually reinforcing but essentially distinct. They were mutually reinforcing in the sense that Tocqueville viewed freedom properly understood as operating on a continuum: when a national government – be it Prussia, the papal states of Pope Pius IX in Italy, or France – lacked what he called "great political freedom," it might be encouraged to move in that direction by its citizens' exercise of "all of [their] secondary freedoms."[37] The tracks were essentially distinct, however, in the sense that they had distinct foundings, distinct structures, distinct rules and roles and responsibilities, distinct opportunities with which to engage their common citizenry, and distinct benefits they provided to the democratic system as a whole. They were separate but hopefully equal, designed to preserve accountability and vigilance and thus inject healthy tension within the democratic system as a whole.

President Obama possesses a different view of the two tracks, seeing them as essentially intertwined and seamless, capable of being subsumed by the same political leader into a single overarching vision. They need not be separate, they need not be equal, they are collapsible, we could say – useful for national political campaigns and useful for governing on the first track. Indeed, on January 17, 2009, the president institutionalized his new group, Organizing for America, as a "special project" of the Democratic National Committee.[38] This was the group that after the November elections consulted its membership by holding 4,800 house meetings and receiving 500,000 surveys providing guidance for its future plans and functions. It has become the group that now serves as the official repository of the president's email list, consisting of 13 million addresses of supporters. It may be the group finally to solve the "organizers' dilemma" that has bedeviled community organizing since Alinsky's days: how, as the president formerly expressed it, do you help people "start to get higher horizons" so that they will "link up winning that stop sign or getting that home equity with the larger trends, larger movements in the city or

[37] "Tocqueville to Louis de Kergorlay, October 10, 1836," OC 13:1, 407–408.
[38] Chris Cillizza, "Obama Announces Grass-Roots Lobby," *Washington Post*, January 18, 2009, sec. 1A, p. 8; Jim Rutenberg and Adam Nagourney, "Retooling a Grass-Roots Network To Serve a You Tube Presidency," *New York Times*, January 26, 2009, sec. 1A, 1, 12.

country."[39] Tired of community organizing's inability or unwillingness to address this dilemma, President Obama summarily overturned the whole discussion by introducing his new paradigm: a new brand of inclusionary organizing directed from the first track that collapsed both tracks and all borders within it.

Conclusion

The image developed for our conference marking the 150th anniversary of Tocqueville's death takes us back to the young Tocqueville in America, poised to do battle on the frontiers of democracy. In *Democracy in America*, Tocqueville reconceived and recalibrated those frontiers, providing multiple frames to help future democrats understand both democracy's great promise and its great peril. In my chapter, I have chosen to focus on just one of those frames on democracy's frontier – that of the connection and interconnection, in Tocqueville's mind and experience and our own, of democracy's two great tracks. Whom was Tocqueville fighting on this particular frontier? We have identified several of the targets for his knife and gun: Guizot, who failed to pass muster on Tocqueville's liberty test; administrative centralizers of all stripes and their indispensable allies, the bourgeois *légistes*; and all those who question the validity, corrupt the mores, or compromise the independence of democracy's second track.

In his penultimate chapter in *Democracy in America*, Tocqueville offered his prognosis for us – "the men [and women] living in the democratic centuries into which we are entering." "[They will] have a natural taste for freedom," he says:

> By nature they are impatient with putting up with any regulation. They get tired of the duration even of the state they have chosen. They love power but are inclined to scorn and hate those who wield it, and they easily escape its grasp by reason of their very insignificance and changeableness. These instincts will always recur because they result from the state of society, which will not change. For a long time they will prevent the establishment of any despotism, and they will furnish fresh weapons for each new generation wanting to struggle for human freedom.[40]

We will recognize and confront our own enemies on democracy's future frontiers, Tocqueville here predicts, thanks to our possession of our

[39] Comments of Barack Obama, "Organizing in the 1990s: Excerpts from a Roundtable Discussion," in *After Alinsky: Community Organizing in Illinois*, ed. Peg Knoepfle (Springfield, IL: *Illinois Issues* of Sangamon State University, 1990), 133.
[40] DIA (L) II.4.vii, 702.

own quotient of frontier freedom. Properly recognized, properly defined, and properly combined with that of others through effective organization, our natural taste for freedom can lead us to preserve and protect it on our local frontiers, thus sustaining the democracy in which we live.

Epilogue: New Frontiers, Old Dilemmas

Richard Boyd

As we have seen in preceding chapters, the concept of a "frontier" has multiple connotations.[1] Some frontiers are tangible, referring to actual places or lines of demarcation, whereas others are purely metaphorical. In contemporary French, *une frontière* is literally a territorial border between nation-states. We usually think of political borders as concrete, identifiable lines on maps corresponding to geographical features such as rivers, mountains, or oceans. These natural barriers are often embellished by man-made checkpoints, guards, or walls. What could be more self-evident than, say, the border between Mexico and the United States or the frontiers of the European Union? And yet looking more closely we find that territorial borders between nation-states are historically unstable and frequently contested. One need only glance at maps of Europe from the seventeenth century to the present to appreciate just how susceptible national borders are to being redrawn.

Even when territorial boundaries are relatively static, however, the political frontiers between nation-states regulate the flow of populations, goods, capital, cultures, and discourses only imperfectly, if at all. International trade, technology, financial crises, and the forces of globalization render national borders increasingly porous. Linguistic, religious, and ethnic communities spill across national borders; refugees, clandestines, and criminals evade the most determined efforts at control. Observing these and related phenomena, many influential "cosmopolitan" critics such as Seyla Benhabib or Martha Nussbaum go so far as to conclude

---

[1] I'm grateful to Ewa Atanassow for her careful reading, detailed suggestions, and incisive criticisms of earlier drafts of this essay.

that national frontiers are losing significance in terms of how citizens of the world understand their identities and organize their lives.

Whether it is a question of immigration to the United States or Western Europe, the effects of globalization, or the spread of democracy and human rights – some of the most heated philosophical and political controversies of our day hinge on the question of frontiers. Yet these and other dilemmas presented by frontiers are hardly new. Since at least the days of Herodotus, Aristophanes, Plato, and Aristotle, political thinkers have pondered whether frontiers are natural or socially constructed, morally repugnant or politically indispensable. Even so, the most basic of questions remain.

The nineteenth-century American frontier that Tocqueville and Beaumont sought in their westward foray across the continent was, at least in principle, a tangible geographic place. Inspired by the novels of Chateaubriand and Cooper or the lectures of François Guizot, the two young Frenchmen half expected to find a clear-cut demarcation between lands settled by Europeans and a pristine wilderness inhabited by indigenous peoples untouched by European civilization. Yet as the distinguished historian Frederick Jackson Turner observed in his classic 1893 essay, "The Significance of the Frontier in American History," the American frontier differed from traditional European notions of a discrete line or "fortified boundary line running through dense populations." In Turner's view, the American frontier was best understood as the "hither edge of free land," a "meeting point between savagery and civilization," the "outer edge of a wave" or evolutionary process that indelibly stamped the American character with vitality.[2]

Indeed, as Tocqueville and Beaumont discovered over half a century earlier, the westernmost territories of the United States were places where "the extreme limits of civilization and nature abandoned to itself are brought face to face."[3] The frontier is a space of confrontation and exchange where familiar moral distinctions between civilized Europeans and barbarous native peoples become blurred. For Tocqueville, the American frontier also carried tragic overtones, spelling the end of the native inhabitants' way of life as a result of their assimilation of the vices as

---

[2] Frederick Jackson Turner, "The Significance of the Frontier in American History" in *The Early Writings of Frederick Jackson Turner*, ed. Everett B. Edwards. (Madison, WI: University of Wisconsin Press, 1938), 187.

[3] *Journey*, 332–333; OC 5.1, 346.

well as virtues of European civilization. Nonetheless, and more optimistically, the frontier appears as a laboratory of democratic equality, where different human possibilities and forms of life "mingle and confuse their labors."[4]

The fascinations of Tocqueville, Chateaubriand, and other nineteenth-century European observers are perfectly understandable, as America's western frontier symbolizes the ambiguities of frontiers more generally. Frontiers have a dual and paradoxical nature; they simultaneously function to create and elide distinctions. On the one hand, a frontier marks off a categorical distinction between places or states of being. In the eighteenth and nineteenth centuries, for example, oceans established the frontier between Old and New Worlds. In the second half of the twentieth century, outer space became the "final frontier." To stipulate a frontier is to initiate a gulf – spatial, political, historical, or existential – between two alien social conditions. On the other hand, however, frontiers are notorious for their hybridity. The frontier (as distinguished from what lies beyond it) is a fluid and dynamic zone where different worlds meet, blur, and intermingle. One thinks of the American "Wild West," where traditional categories of race, gender, or social class were either relaxed or suspended under rough-and-tumble conditions. Frontiers are moral nether-lands, neither strictly here nor there.

This paradox of frontiers as simultaneously constituting and blurring difference is nicely captured by the French anthropologist Arnold van Gennep. In his 1909 classic *The Rites of Passage*, van Gennep observes that "liminal" points marking the edges between worlds are typically ritualized in ways that serve to dramatize, or even exaggerate, transitions from one condition to another.[5] In the life cycle of individuals, for example, symbolic deaths, surrenders, or breaks put an end to previous identities or states of being. Likewise, the new condition is celebrated as akin to a rebirth, graduation, founding, or baptism. This applies to transitional points between physical places – entryways to cathedrals, palaces, or amusement parks; border checkpoints separating East and West Berlin, Mexico and the United States, or Israel and the West Bank – no less than to time periods, regimes, or conditions of being, for example, antebellum, post-revolutionary, turn-of-the-century, and so forth.

[4] *Journey*, 356–357; OC 5.1, 368–370. For a more developed consideration of Tocqueville's views of the American wilderness, see Ewa Atanassow, "Fortnight in the Wilderness: Tocqueville on Nature and Civilization," *Perspectives on Political Science* 35 (2006), 22–30.
[5] Arnold van Gennep, *The Rites of Passage*. (Chicago: University of Chicago Press, 1961).

Identifying something as a frontier also imparts a moral valence, whether positive or negative, to that which lies on the other side. Denizens of frontiers can be the subjects of scorn, condescension, fear, curiosity, mystery, or romance. People who cross frontiers are adventurers, celebrated but also potentially fugitives or outlaws liable to censure. Regardless of whether the effect is one of moral attraction or repulsion, frontiers serve to render discrete states of being unfamiliar to one another, replacing transparency with obstruction, in the words of Jean Starobinski.[6] Accordingly, one possible complaint about the notion of a frontier of democracy is that it obfuscates our sense of what lies beyond democracy. Without the possibility of genuine understanding, the frontier becomes a blank slate, a metaphorical canvas or mirror onto which we transpose our deepest prejudices, aspirations, and fears.[7]

Nothing illustrates this better than the two mutually antithetical characterizations of the western frontier that coexisted in the American imagination around the time of Tocqueville's visit. Maybe the most influential is the Puritan vision of the wilderness as home to the barbarous, wicked, and savage. In the Puritan view, the wilderness symbolized an antipolitical abandonment to the sinful gravity of human nature.[8] Fittingly, the political community's heretical or heterogeneous were exiled beyond the frontier, as with Roger Williams or Anne Hutchinson, and there was constant anxiety about the baneful moral influence of the untamed wilderness on the faithful who remained. Early Puritan communities were physically designed to maximize differences between the public space of the common, where Christian liberty and discipline reigned, and the hinterlands that lay beyond the farthest edges of the cleared fields.

Nathaniel Hawthorne's 1835 allegory "Young Goodman Brown" dramatizes the Puritan anxiety about the fine line separating Christian civilization from moral depravity.[9] Venturing reluctantly into the wilderness

---

[6] Jean Starobinski, *Jean-Jacques Rousseau: Transparency and Obstruction.* (Chicago: University of Chicago Press, 1988).

[7] On this phenomenon of the non-Western or non-democratic "other" as a mirror into ourselves, see especially Edward Said, *Orientalism.* (New York: Vintage, 1979); Roxanne Euben, *Enemy in the Mirror: Islamic Fundamentalism and the Limits of Modern Rationalism.* (Princeton University Press, 1999).

[8] On this Puritan wariness of the wilderness and frontier, see Wilson Carey McWilliams, *The Idea of Fraternity in America* (Berkeley: University of California Press, 1973), esp. 162–163.

[9] Nathaniel Hawthorne, *Young Goodman Brown and Other Tales*, ed. Brian Harding (New York: Oxford World Classics, 2009).

one night to sell his soul, Young Goodman Brown is shocked to discover all the leading citizens of Salem cavorting with the devil. This revelation leads him to lose his proverbial "Faith" in mankind. And yet the subversive thrust of Hawthorne's short story – as for virtually all of his fiction, including his masterpiece *The Scarlet Letter* – stems from the lesson that human wickedness is found on both sides of the frontier and that the only thing separating the self-righteousness of civilization from the barbarism of untamed nature is a thin veneer of hypocrisy.

In contrast to this bleak Puritan view of the wilderness, James Fenimore Cooper's *Leatherstocking Tales*, published between 1820 and 1841, offer a more flattering contrast between the frontier and civilization.[10] From Cooper's vantage, civilized society itself is the source of wickedness and war. The frontier constitutes a natural refuge from the corruptions of civil society as well as a native font of republican virtue, simplicity, courage, independence, and freedom. Wilderness dwellers such as Natty Bumppo and his loyal Mohican sidekick Chingachgook personify stolid republican virtues and natural freedom. Cooper's romanticization of the natural freedom, equality, and moral purity of the American wilderness is of a piece with much romantic European theorizing, from Rousseau to Chateaubriand.[11]

These two competing visions of the American frontier are timeless elements of American political culture. From the Lincolnian myth of the frontiersman as paragon of republican citizenship, to Manifest Destiny and the imperialistic vocation of subduing the American Continent, to Mark Twain's rendering of Huck Finn and his apostasy of "sivilization" to "light out for the Territories," to the Westerns of John Ford – what lies beyond the frontier is the subject of equal parts literary fascination and moral contestation.

Above and beyond their historical significance, these familiar tropes surrounding the American frontier are chock full of insights into the contemporary frontiers of democracy. Latter-day commentators on the fate of democracy face similar interpretive challenges as Tocqueville's nineteenth-century philosophical forbearers. As in these earlier attempts to theorize the American frontier, rather than trying to figure out where,

---

[10] James Fenimore Cooper, *The Leatherstocking Tales: The Library of America Edition*, ed. Blake Nevius. (New York: Modern Library, 2012).

[11] For a more qualified view of Cooper's romanticism, see McWilliams, *Idea of Fraternity*, 230–232.

concretely, such a frontier of democracy might be located, it is crucial to understand the work being done – either implicitly or explicitly – by the concept itself.

First, and most importantly, the very notion of a frontier of democracy serves to validate democratic ways of life. As in the case of nineteenth-century European civilization, the ostensible superiority of democracy is established over and against its antithesis in the form of authoritarianism, illiberality, or social inequality. Often being democratic is defined not in terms of positive attributes or characteristics but in terms of what one is not: a monarchy, oligopoly, violator of human rights, derogator of women or minorities, and so forth. Democracy derives its meaning and purpose by virtue of the existence of a frontier between itself and some other condition of being. The contradiction justifies the democratic vocation of bringing democracy to the world. Moreover, as in the case of the American frontier, hypothesizing a frontier of democracy implies the transitory and fleeting nature of this condition of being. What are frontiers except points of difference that exist to be immanently breached? So the most immediate consequence of postulating a frontier of democracy is to valorize the democratic sense of mission, struggle, destiny, or vocation. We would hope that this conceptualization is ultimately positive, in the sense of strengthening the cause of democracy. And yet as we have seen in the foregoing chapters, a potential side effect of the concept of a frontier of democracy – as with nineteenth-century notions of civilization – is that it may blur over into a kind of messianic universalism or cultural imperialism.

Second, and very much on this point, the presence of identifiable populations who reside (either voluntarily or against their will) on the other side of a frontier can be a source of anxiety. As for the Puritans, or nineteenth-century Europeans, the nondemocratic other is regarded with suspicion if not antipathy. One thinks of the treatment of Muslims (both outside but especially within Western democratic nations such as France, Germany, or the United States) or members of religious or cultural minorities whose practices are something less than purely democratic. Even where there is no overt hostility, a sense of alterity envelops the undemocratic other. We wonder (sometimes out loud but mostly silently) about the kinds of people who would choose (or merely tolerate) undemocratic cultural practices or systems of government. Even the most well-intentioned permutations of the rhetoric of democratization are laden with this sense of suspicion, misapprehension, and inscrutability. Is a given nation really a viable soil for democracy? If so, how could it have tolerated dictatorship or authoritarian regimes for so long? Will such and such a people about to cross the frontier of democracy be up to the task of self-government? Are those born into undemocratic nations, cultures, or religions readily assimilable by democratic nations? In all of these cases, one of the dangers of stipulating a frontier of democracy is the way it weaves a fabric of mutual incomprehension between ourselves and nondemocratic others.

A third set of questions revolve around the future of this putative democratic frontier. Skeptics might object that the concept of a frontier of democracy conceals more than it illuminates. For all of its ambiguity, the metaphor seems to postulate two categorically different and mutually incompatible states of being: the democratic and something alien to democracy. But is this really a tenable distinction? As we have seen, Tocqueville himself can be accused of exaggerating the absolutism of the break between aristocracy and a new democratic age. And yet even the most democratic societies are not without certain pre-democratic or undemocratic institutions. Conversely, it is not as if many of those societies that Western democratic nations would relegate to the category of the nondemocratic world are altogether lacking intimations of moral equality, self-government, or individual liberty. In practice, the frontier between the democratic and nondemocratic is far murkier than the metaphor suggests. Rather than deploying the concept of a frontier of democracy to erect stark barriers between democracy and what lies on the other side, we would do well to keep in mind the other sense of a frontier as a meeting point, encounter, or zone of hybridity.

Lastly, assuming that the concept of a frontier of democracy does capture something meaningful about the contemporary world and that nations fall (however imperfectly) on one or the other side of this line, a different set of questions emerge. Can the frontier between democracy and non-democracy be overcome? Should it be overcome, and if so, what lies beyond it? Presumably the universalization of democracy will relegate this particular frontier to the dustbin of history alongside the Wild West or the Cold War. But once the frontier of democracy has been abolished, what, if anything, will replace it? Is it really possible, we may wonder, to live in a world that is frontierless? As preceding chapters have argued, Tocqueville thought this cosmopolitan vision of a world without distinctions was chimerical. Human beings need moral horizons to orient their lives and identities, and when such frontiers are not readily available as part of a coherent historical tradition, they will simply invent them anew.

If Tocqueville is right about the evidence of history and people really cannot live without frontiers, there is still the question of what novel frontiers are destined to replace the frontiers of democracy. If every nation in the world were to become fully democratic in the political sense tomorrow, other social frontiers of race, gender, social class, ethnicity, religion, or civilization would no doubt persist. Supposing these most tenacious of frontiers were someday overcome, would they not be supplanted by other, vaster frontiers, such as that between the capitalist and noncapitalist, human and nonhuman, sentient and nonsentient, as Marxists, animal rights activists, or environmentalists might insist? The riddle of the twenty-first century is not so much the question of where the frontiers of democracy are properly located, as for example, between East and West or along the putative fault lines of so-called civilizations. Nor is it strictly a matter of how they are constituted and maintained: by culture, religion, tradition, force, or consent. Rather, the most pressing questions of our day pertain to what lies beyond these frontiers.

Bibliography of Works Cited

Alagappa, Muthiah. "Civil Society and Political Change: An Analytical Framework," in Muthiah Alagappa (ed.), *Civil Society and Political Change in Asia: Expanding and Contracting Democratic Space* (Stanford: Stanford University Press, 2004), 25–60.

Alinsky, Saul D. *Reveille for Radicals* (New York: Vintage Books, 1969 [1946]).

Allen, Barbara. "Racial Equality and Social Equality," in Craiutu and Gellar (eds.), *Conversations with Tocqueville*, 85–116.

Allen, Barbara. *Tocqueville, Covenant and the Democratic Revolution: Harmonizing Earth with Heaven* (Lanham, MD: Lexington Books, 2005).

Anderson, Fred and Andrew R. L. Cayton. *The Dominion of War: Empire and Liberty in North America, 1500–2000* (New York: Viking, 2005).

Antoine, Agnès. *L'impensé de la démocratie: Tocqueville, la citoyenneté et la religion* (Paris: Fayard, 2003).

Arendt, Hannah. "Home to Roost: A Bicentennial Address," *New York Review of Books*, June 26, 1975.

Arendt, Hannah. *The Origins of Totalitarianism* (New York: Harcourt Brace Jovanovich, 1973 [1948]).

Aron, Raymond. "Idées politiques et vision historique de Tocqueville," *Revue français de science politique* 10 (1960), 509–526.

Aron, Raymond. *Les Étapes de la pensée sociologique* (Paris: Gallimard, 1967).

Aron, Raymond. *Main Currents in Sociological Thought*, 2 vols. (New York: Anchor Doubleday, 1968–1970).

Atanassow, Ewa. "Fortnight in the Wilderness: Tocqueville on Nature and Civilization," *Perspectives on Political Science* 35 (2006), 22–30.

Atanassow, Ewa. "Tocqueville and the Question of the Nation." PhD diss., University of Chicago, 2007.

Augustine. *City of God*, trans. Henry Bettenson (New York: Penguin Books, 1984).

Austen, Ralph A. and Woodruff D. Smith. "Images of Africa and British Slave-Trade Abolition: The Transition to an Imperialist Ideology, 1787–1807," *African Historical Studies* 2 (1969), 69–83.

Bachrach, Peter. *The Theory of Democratic Elitism: A Critique* (Lanham, MD: University Press of America, 1980).

Baïanov, B., Y. Oumanski, and M. Chafir. *La Démocratie socialiste soviétique* (Moscow: Editions du progrès, 1969).

Balibar, Étienne. *La crainte des masses: politique et philosophie avant et après Marx* (Paris: Galilée, 1997).

Banner, Stuart. *How the Indians Lost Their Land* (Cambridge, MA: Harvard University Press, 2005).

Barber, Benjamin. *Jihad vs. McWorld: How Globalism and Tribalism are Reshaping the World* (New York: Crown Books, 1995).

Bargemont, Villeneuve. *Economie politique chrétienne, ou recherche sur la nature et les causes du paupérisme en France et en Europe et sur les moyens de le soulager et de le prévenir* (Paris: Paulin, 1834).

Barrera, Guillaume. "Espagne," in Catherine Volpilhac-Auger and C. Larrère (eds.), *Dictionnaire Montesquieu* (2008). http://Dictionnaire-Montesquieu. ens-lsh.fr. (accessed November 8, 2012).

Beaumont, Gustave de. *Marie, ou l'esclavage aux États-Unis: tableau de moeurs américaines* (Paris: Librairie de Charles Gosselin, 1840).

Beitz, Charles. "Cosmopolitanism and Global Justice," *Journal of Ethics* 9 (2005), 11–27.

Bell, Daniel A. and Hahm Chaibong (eds.). *Confucianism for the Modern World* (Cambridge: Cambridge University Press, 2003).

Bender, Thomas. *Rethinking American History in a Global Age* (Berkeley: University of California Press, 2002).

Bendix, Reinhard. *Embattled Reason: Essays on Social Knowledge*, Vol. 1 (New Brunswick, NJ: Transaction Publishers, 1988).

Benhabib, Seyla. *The Rights of Others: Aliens, Residents, and Citizens* (Cambridge: Cambridge University Press, 2004).

Benoît, Jean-Louis. *Comprendre Tocqueville* (Paris: Armand Colin, 2004).

Benoît, Jean-Louis. "Relectures de Tocqueville," *Le Banquet* 16 (2001), 1–9.

Bernard, Jean Alphonse. *Tocqueville in India* (Paris: Les Editions d'En Face, 2006).

Blanqui, Auguste. "Letter to Maillard, June 6, 1852," in *Oeuvres complètes 1, Ecrits sur la révolution (Textes politiques et lettres de prison)* (Paris: Ed. Galilée, 1977).

Boesche, Roger. "The Dark Side of Tocqueville: On War and Empire," *Review of Politics* 67 (2005), 737–752.

Boesche, Roger. *The Strange Liberalism of Alexis de Tocqueville* (Ithaca, NY: Cornell University Press, 1987).

Boesche, Roger. *Tocqueville's Road Map: Methodology, Liberalism, Revolution, and Despotism* (Lanham, MD: Lexington Books, 2006).

Boyd, Richard. "Imperial Fathers and Favorite Sons: J. S. Mill, Alexis de Tocqueville, and Nineteenth Century Visions of Empire," in Locke and Botting (eds.), *Feminist Interpretations of Alexis de Tocqueville*, 225–252.

Boyd, Richard. "*Politesse* and Public Opinion in Stendhal's *Red and Black*," *European Journal of Political Theory* 4 (2005), 367–392.

Boyd, Richard. "Tocqueville's Algeria," *Society* 38 (2001), 65–70.

Briant, Pierre. "Montesquieu, Mably et Alexandre le Grand: aux sources de l'histoire hellénistique," *Revue Montesquieu* 8 (2005–2006), 151–185.

Brogan, Hugh. *Alexis de Tocqueville: A Life* (New Haven: Yale University Press, 2006).

Browne, Nick. "The Spectator-in-the-Text: The Rhetoric of *Stagecoach*," *Film Quarterly* 29 (1975–1976), 26–38.

Brubaker, Rogers. *Citizenship and Nationhood in France and Germany* (Cambridge, MA: Harvard University Press, 1992).

Burke, Edmund. *Reflections on the Revolution in France*, ed. J. C. D. Clark (Stanford: Stanford University Press, 2001).

Burke, Edmund. *Réflexions sur la Révolution française* (Paris: Hachette Pluriel, 1998).

Buxton, Thomas Fowell. *The African Slave Trade and Its Remedy* (London: John Murray, 1840).

Callahan, William. "Comparing the Discourse of Popular Politics in Korea and China: From Civil Society to Social Movements," *Korea Journal* 38 (1998), 277–322.

Campbell, James T., Matthew Pratt Guterl, and Robert G. Lee (eds.). *Race, Nation, and Empire in American History* (Chapel Hill: University of North Carolina Press, 2007).

Capdevila, Nestor. *Le concept d'idéologie* (Paris: Presses universitaires de France, 2004).

Capdevila, Nestor. "Marx ou Tocqueville: capitalisme ou démocratie," *Actuel Marx* 46 (2009), 150–162.

Capdevila, Nestor. *Tocqueville et les frontières de la Démocratie* (Paris: Presses universitaires de France, 2007).

Carrithers, David. "Montesquieu and Tocqueville as Philosophical Historians: Liberty, Determinism, and the Prospects for Freedom," in Rebecca Kingston (ed.), *Montesquieu and His Legacy* (Albany: State University of New York Press, 2009), 149–177.

Ceaser, James. "Alexis de Tocqueville on Political Science, Political Culture, and the Role of the Intellectual," *American Political Science Review* 79 (1985), 656–672.

Ceaser, James. *Liberal Democracy and Political Science* (Baltimore: Johns Hopkins University Press, 1990).

Centre National de la Recherche Scientifique. *Alexis de Tocqueville: Livre du Centenaire, 1859–1959* (Paris: Éditions du Centre National de la Recherche Scientifique, 1960).

Chaibong, Hahm. "The Cultural Challenge to Individualism," *Journal of Democracy* 11 (2000), 127–134.

Chaibong, Hahm. "Family versus the Individual: The Politics of Marriage Laws in Korea," in Bell and Chaibong (eds.), *Confucianism for the Modern World*, 334–359.

Chaihark, Hahm. "Constitutionalism, Confucian Civic Virtue, and Ritual Propriety," in Bell and Chaibong (eds.), *Confucianism for the Modern World*, 31–53.

Chan, Adrian. "In Search of a Civil Society in China," *Journal of Contemporary Asia* 27 (1997), 242–251.

Chan Sin Yee, "The Confucian Conception of Gender in the Twenty-First Century," in Bell and Chaibong (eds.), *Confucianism for the Modern World*, 312–333.

Chateaubriand, François-René de. *De Buonaparte et Des Bourbons* (Paris: Mame Frères, 1814).

Cho, Hein. "The Historical Origin of Civil Society in Korea," *Korea Journal* 37 (1997), 24–41.

Christophersen, Jens Andreas. *The Meaning of "Democracy" as Used in European Ideologies* (Oslo: Univesitetsforlaget, 1966).

Churchill, Winston S. *The Gathering Storm* (Boston: Houghton Mifflin, 1948).

Cillizza, Chris. "Obama Announces Grass-Roots Lobby," *Washington Post*, January 18, 2009, sec. 1A, p. 8.

Clinton, David. *Tocqueville, Lieber, and Bagehot: Liberalism Confronts the World.* (New York: Palgrave Macmillan, 2003).

Coleman, Deirdre. *Romantic Colonization and British Anti-Slavery* (Cambridge: Cambridge University Press, 2005).

Commager, Henry Steele. *Commager on Tocqueville* (Columbia: University of Missouri Press, 1993).

Confer, Vincent. *France and Algeria* (New York: Syracuse University Press, 1966).

Constant, Benjamin. *Political Writings*, ed. Biancamaria Fontana (Cambridge: Cambridge University Press, 1988).

Cooper, James Fenimore. *The Leatherstocking Tales: The Library of America Edition*, ed. Blake Nevius. (New York: Modern Library, 2012).

Cotterill, R. S. *The Southern Indians: The Story of the Civilized Tribes Before Removal* (Norman: University of Oklahoma Press, 1954).

Craiutu, Aurelian. "Introduction" to François Guizot, *The History of the Origins of Representative Government in Europe* (Indianapolis, IN: Liberty Fund, 2002).

Craiutu, Aurelian. "Tocqueville's Paradoxical Moderation," *Review of Politics* 67 (2005), 599–629.

Craiutu, Aurelian and Sheldon Gellar (eds.). *Conversations with Tocqueville: The Global Democratic Revolution in the Twenty-First Century* (Lanham, MD: Lexington Books, 2009).

Cropsey, Seth and Arthur Milikh. "Democracy in Egypt: Applying the Tocqueville Standard." *World Affairs* (May/June 2011). http://www.worldaffairsjournal.org/articles/2011-MayJun/full-Cropsey-MJ-2011.html (accessed July 21, 2011).

Cumings, Bruce. "The Abortive Abertura: South Korea in the Light of Latin American Experience," *New Left Review* 173 (1989), 5–32.

Cumings, Bruce. *Dominion from Sea to Sea: Pacific Ascendancy and American Power* (New Haven: Yale University Press, 2009).

Damrosch, Leo. *Tocqueville's Discovery of America* (New York: Farrar, Straus and Giroux, 2010).

Davey, Monica. "Blagojevich Has His Final Say, Making Day of It," *New York Times*, January 30, 2009, sec. 1A, p. 14.

De Bary, William. "Why Confucius Now?" in Bell and Chaibong (eds.), *Confucianism for the Modern World*, 361–372.

De Bary, William and Tu Weiming (eds.). *Confucianism and Human Rights* (New York: Columbia University Press, 1998).

Deneen, Patrick. *Democratic Faith* (Princeton: Princeton University Press, 2005).

Descotes, Maurice. *La Légende de Napoléon et les écrivains français du XIXe siècle* (Paris: Minard, 1967).

Desjobert, Amédée. *L'Algérie en 1846* (Paris: Guillaumin, 1846).

Diamond, Larry and Marc F. Plattner (eds.). *Democracy in East Asia* (Baltimore: Johns Hopkins University Press, 1998).

Dijn, Annelien de. *French Political Thought from Montesquieu to Tocqueville* (Cambridge: Cambridge University Press, 2008).

Ding, X. L. "Institutional Amphibiousness and the Transition from Communism: The Case of China," *British Journal of Political Science* 24 (1994), 293–318.

Dion, Stéphane. "Durham et Tocqueville sur la colonisation libérale," *Journal of Canadian Studies* 25 (1990), 60–77.

Dion, Stéphane. "La conciliation du libéralisme et du nationalisme chez Tocqueville," *La Revue Tocqueville/The Tocqueville Review* 16 (1995), 219–227.

Disraeli, Benjamin. "Vindication of the English Constitution," in *Whigs and Whiggism: Political Writings*, ed. William Hutcheon (London: J. Murray, 1913), 111–222.

Donohue, William. "Tocqueville's Reflections on Safeguarding Freedom in a Democracy," *Tocqueville Review* 6 (1984), 389–399.

Drescher, Seymour. *Dilemmas of Democracy: Tocqueville and Modernization* (Pittsburgh: University of Pittsburgh Press, 1968).

Drescher, Seymour. "Introduction" to *Tocqueville and the French*, ed. Françoise Mélonio (Charlottesville: University of Virginia Press, 1998).

Drescher, Seymour. *Tocqueville and England* (Cambridge: Harvard University Press, 1964).

Drescher, Seymour. "Who Needs *Ancienneté*? Tocqueville on Aristocracy and Modernity," *History of Political Thought* 24 (2003), 624–646.

Duara, Prasenjit. *Culture, Power, and the State: Rural North China, 1900–1942* (Stanford: Stanford University Press, 1988).

Duncan, John. "The Problematic Modernity of Confucianism: the Question of 'Civil Society' in Chosŏn Dynasty Korea," in Charles K. Armstrong (ed.), *Korean Society: Civil Society, Democracy, and the State* (London: Routledge, 2002), 36–56.

Dunn, Susan. *Sister Revolutions: French Lightning, American Light* (New York: Faber and Faber, 1999).

Dworkin, Ronald. *La vertu souveraine* (Paris: Emile Bruylant, 2008).

Elkins, Caroline and Susan Pedersen (eds.). *Settler Colonialism in the Twentieth Century* (New York: Routledge, 2005).

Elster, Jon. *Alexis de Tocqueville, The First Social Scientist* (Cambridge: Cambridge University Press, 2009).

Euben, Roxanne. *Enemy in the Mirror: Islamic Fundamentalism and the Limits of Modern Rationalism* (Princeton University Press, 1999).

Fairbanks, Charles H., Jr. "The British Campaign Against the Slave Trade: An Example of a Successful Human Rights Policy," in Fred E. Baumann (ed.), *Human Rights and American Foreign Policy* (Gambier, OH: Public Affairs Conference Center, Kenyon College, 1982), 87–135.

Farr, James. "Tocqueville and Lieber on Antebellum America." Paper presented at the Annual Meeting of the American Political Science Association, Toronto, September 2009.

Field, John. "Social Capital," in Jan Peil and Irene van Staveren (eds.), *Handbook of Economics and Ethics* (Northampton, MA: Edward Elgar Publishing, 2009), 509–515.

Foner, Eric. *Free Soil, Free Labor, Free Men* (New York: Oxford University Press, 1970).

Foner, Eric. "Radical Individualism in America," *Literature of Liberty* 1 (1978), 5–31.

Foner, Eric. *The Story of American Freedom* (New York: Norton, 1998).

Forbes, John Murray. *Letters and Recollections of John Murray Forbes*, ed. Sarah Forbes Hughes (Boston: Houghton Mifflin, 1899).

Forbes, Robert B. *Personal Reminiscences* (Boston: Little, Brown and Co., 1882).

Ford, Lisa. *Settler Sovereignty* (Cambridge, MA: Harvard University Press, 2010).

Fowler, Robert Booth, Allen D. Hertzke, Laura R. Olson, and Kevin R. den Dulk. *Religion and Politics in America: Faith, Culture* (Oxford: Westview Press, 2004).

Franklin Gordon Dexter Papers. Massachusetts Historical Society, Boston, MA.

Friedman, Edward. "Democratization: Generalizing the East Asian Experience," in Friedman (ed.), *The Politics of Democratization: Generalizing East Asian Experiences*, 19–60.

Friedman, Edward (ed.). *The Politics of Democratization: Generalizing East Asian Experiences* (Boulder, CO: Westview Press, 1994).

Fukuyama, Francis. *Trust: The Social Virtues and the Creation of Prosperity* (New York: Free Press, 1995).

Fullinwider, Robert K. *Civil Society, Democracy, and Civic Renewal* (Lanham, MD: Rowman & Littlefield, 1999).

Furet, François. "The Intellectual Origins of Tocqueville's Thought," *La Revue Tocqueville/The Tocqueville Review* 7 (1985–1986), 117–129.

Furet, François. *Interpreting the French Revolution*, trans. Elborg Forster (Cambridge and Paris: Cambridge University Press and Maison des Sciences de l'Homme, 1981).

Furet, François. *In the Workshop of History* (Chicago: University of Chicago Press, 1984).

Furet, François. *Le passé d'une illusion. Essai sur l'idée communiste au XXe siècle* (Paris: Robert Laffont / Calmann-Lévy, 1995).

Furet, François. *Marx et la révolution française* (Paris: Flammarion, 1986).

Furet, François. "Naissance d'un paradigme: Tocqueville et le Voyage en Amérique (1825–1831)," *Annales* 39 (1984), 225–239.

Gallagher, Tag. *John Ford: The Man and His Films* (Berkeley: University of California Press, 1986).

Gallie, Walter Bryce. "Essentially Contested Concepts," *Proceedings of the Aristotelian Society* 56 (1955–1956), 167–198.

Gannett, Robert T., Jr. "Tocqueville and Local Government: Distinguishing Democracy's Second Track," *Review of Politics* (2005), 721–736.

Gannett, Robert T., Jr. "Tocqueville as Politician: Revisiting the Revolution of 1789," in Svetozar Minkov (ed.), *Enlightening Revolutions* (Lanham, MD: Lexington Books, 2006), 235–258.

Gannett, Robert T., Jr. *Tocqueville Unveiled: The Historian and His Sources for "The Old Regime and the Revolution"* (Chicago: University of Chicago Press, 2003).

Gannett, Robert T., Jr. "Village-by-Village: What Seeds for Freedom," in *Tocqueville on China: A Project of the American Enterprise Institute* (April 2009). http://www.aei.org/papers/society-and-culture/village-by-village-democracy-in-china/ (accessed November 8, 2012).

Gargan, Edward. *Alexis de Tocqueville: The Critical Years, 1848–1851* (Washington, DC: Catholic University Press, 1955).

Gellner, Ernest. *Conditions of Liberty: Civil Society and Its Rivals* (New York: Viking, 1994).

Gellner, Ernest. *Nations and Nationalism* (Ithaca, NY: Cornell University Press, 1983).

Geyl, Pieter. *Napoleon: For and Against* (New Haven: Yale University Press, 1948).

Gobineau, Arthur de. *The Inequality of Human Races* (New York: Howard Fertig, 1999).

Goldberg, Chad Alan. "Social Citizenship and a Reconstructed Tocqueville," *American Sociological Review* 66 (2001), 289–315.

Goldhammer, Arthur. "Translating Tocqueville: The Constraints of Classicism," in Welch (ed.), *The Cambridge Companion to Tocqueville*, 139–166.

Goldstein, Doris. "Alexis de Tocqueville's Concept of Citizenship," *Proceedings of the American Philosophical Society* 108 (1964), 39–53.

Goldstein, Doris. *Trial of Faith: Religion and Politics in Tocqueville's Thought* (New York: Elsevier, 1975).

Grant, Barry Keith (ed.). *John Ford's Stagecoach* (Cambridge: Cambridge University Press, 2003).

Grant, Barry Keith. "Two Rode Together: John Ford and James Fenimore Cooper," in Gaylyn Studler and Matthew Bernstein (eds.), *John Ford Made Westerns: Filming the Legend in the Sound Era* (Bloomington: Indiana University Press, 2001), 193–219.

Greeley, Horace. *The American Conflict* (New York: O.D. Case & Co., 1864).

Greenfeld, Liah. *Nationalism: Five Roads to Modernity* (Cambridge, MA: Harvard University Press, 1992).

Grossman, Ron. "Activism for Alinsky a Hope-Based Pursuit," *Chicago Tribune*, January 30, 2009, sec. 4, p. 1.

Guellec, Laurence. "Tocqueville à travers sa correspondance familiale," in L. Guellec, F. R. Ankersmit, and A. Antoine (eds.), *Tocqueville et l'esprit de la démocratie*, Bicentenary Issue, *The Tocqueville Review / La revue Tocqueville* 25, No. 1 (2005): 383–409.

Guellec, Laurence. "The Writer Engagé: Tocqueville and Political Rhetoric," trans. Arthur Goldhammer, in Welch (ed.), *The Cambridge Companion to Tocqueville*, 167–187.

Guizot, François. "De la démocratie dans les sociétés modernes," *Revue française* 3 (1837), 139–225.

Guizot, François. *De la démocratie en France* (Paris: Victor Masson, 1849).

Guizot, François. *General History of Civilization in Europe*, ed. George Wells Knight (New York: D. Appleton and Co., 1896).

Guizot, François. *Histoire de la civilization en Europe*, "Fourth Lecture" (Paris: Didier, 1857).

Guizot, François. *Histoire de la civilisation en France*, 10th ed., 4 vols. (Paris: Didier, 1868).

Guizot, François. *Histoire de la civilization en France depuis la chute de l'Empire romain jusqu'en 1789* (Paris: Pichon et Didier, 1829–1832).

Guizot, François. *The History of Civilization in Europe*, ed. Larry Siedentop, trans. William Hazlitt (London: Penguin Classics, 1997).

Hadari, Saguiv A. *Theory in Practice: Tocqueville's New Science of Politics* (Stanford: Stanford University Press, 1989).

Haddock, B. A. *A History of Political Thought: 1789 to the Present* (Malden, MA: Polity Press, 2005).

Halévi, Ran. "La pensée politique de l'honneur," in Hervé Drévillon and Diego Venturino (eds.), *Penser et vivre l'honneur à l'époque modern* (Rennes: Presses universitaires de rennes, 2011), 109–126.

Hall, Henry (ed.). *America's Successful Men of Affairs: An Encyclopedia of Contemporaneous Biography* (New York: New York Tribune, 1895–1896).

Hancock, Ralph. "The Uses and Hazards of Christianity in Tocqueville's Attempt to Save Democratic Souls," in Ken Masugi (ed.), *Interpreting Tocqueville's "Democracy in America"* (Savage, MD: Rowman and Littlefield, 1991), 348–393.

Hand, Jonathan B. "Tocqueville's 'New Political Science': A Critical Assessment of Montesquieu's Vision of a Liberal Modernity." PhD diss., University of Chicago, 2002.

Hardacre, Helen. "Japan: The Public Sphere in a Non-Western Setting," in Wuthnow (ed.), *Between States and Markets*, 217–242.

Hardt, Michael and Antonio Negri. *Empire* (Cambridge, MA: Harvard University Press, 2000).

Harrison, Lawrence. "After the Arab Spring, Culture Still Matters," *The American Interest* (September 1, 2011). http://www.the-american-interest.com/article.cfm?piece=1021 (accessed January 4, 2012).

Harrison, Lawrence. "Want Democracy in Iraq? Culture Matters." *Christian Science Monitor* (July 1, 2008). http://www.rath.us/random-stuff/interesting-articles/want_democracy_in_iraq__culture_matters.txt (accessed July 5, 2011).

Harrison, Lawrence and Samuel Huntington (eds.). *Culture Matters: How Values Shape Human Progress* (New York; Basic Books, 2000).

Hartz, Louis. *The Liberal Tradition in America* (New York: Harcourt Brace & Co., 1955).

Hawthorne, Nathaniel. *Young Goodman Brown and Other Tales*, ed. Brian Harding (New York: Oxford World Classics, 2009).

Hazareesingh, Sudhir. *The Legend of Napoleon* (London: Granta Books, 2004).

Hazareesingh, Sudhir. "Memory, Legend and Politics: Napoleonic Patriotism in the Restoration Era," *European Journal of Political Theory* 5 (2006), 71–84.

Hazareesingh, Sudhir. *The Saint-Napoleon: Celebrations of Sovereignty in Nineteenth-Century France* (Cambridge, MA: Harvard University Press, 2004).

Helgesen, Geir. "The Case for Moral Education," in Bell and Chaibong (eds.), *Confucianism for the Modern World*, 161–180.

Henderson, Christine Dunn. "'Plus ça change . . .': Innovation and the Spirit of Enterprise in America," *Review of Politics* 67 (2005), 753–774.

Hendrickson, David C. *Union, Nation, or Empire: The American Debate over International Relations, 1789–1941* (Lawrence: University Press of Kansas, 2009).

Hereth, Michael. *Alexis de Tocqueville: Threats to Freedom in a Democracy* (Durham: Duke University Press, 1986).

Hietala, Thomas R. *Manifest Design: Anxious Aggrandizement in Late Jacksonian America* (Ithaca, NY: Cornell University Press, 1985).

Hirschman, Albert. *The Passions and the Interests: Political Arguments for Capitalism Before Its Triumph* (Princeton: Princeton University Press, 1977).

Hobsbawm, Eric. "Introduction" to *The Communist Manifesto: A Modern Edition*, Karl Marx and Friedrich Engels (London: Verso, 1998).

Hobson, J. A. *Imperialism: A Study* (London: Allen and Unwin, 1902).

Hobson, J. A. *The Psychology of Jingoism* (London: G. Richards, 1901).

Hoffer, William James Hull. *The Caning of Charles Sumner: Honor, Idealism, and the Origins of the Civil War* (Baltimore, MD: Johns Hopkins University Press, 2010).

Hont, Istvan. *Jealousy of Trade* (Cambridge, MA: Harvard University Press, 2005).

Horowitz, Irving Louis. *Behemoth: Main Currents in the History and Theory of Political Sociology* (New Brunswick, NJ: Transaction Publishers, 1999).

Howard, Marc Morjé. *The Weakness of Civil Society in Post-Communist Europe* (Cambridge: Cambridge University Press, 2003).

Hsieh, John Fuh-Sheng. "East Asian Culture and Democratic Transitions, with Special Reference to the Case of Taiwan," *Journal of Asian and African Studies* 35 (2002), 29–42.

Huet, Père. *Histoire du commerce et de la navigation des anciens* (Paris: Fournier, 1716).

Hulsebosch, Daniel. *Constituting Empire: New York and the Transformation of Constitutionalism in the Atlantic World, 1664–1830* (Chapel Hill: University of North Carolina Press, 2005).

Hwang, Kyung Moon. "Country or State? Reconceptualizing *Kukka* in the Korean Enlightenment Period, 1896–1910," *Korean Studies* 24 (2000), 1–24.

Hyra, Derek S. *The New Urban Renewal: The Economic Transformation of Harlem and Bronzeville* (Chicago: University of Chicago Press, 2008).

Ignatius, David. "A War of Choice, and One Who Chose It," *Washington Post*, November 2, 2003, p. B01. http://www.washingtonpost.com/wp-dyn/articles/A49310-2003Oct31.html (accessed July 20, 2011).

Imbert, H. F. *Les Métamorphoses de la Liberté* (Paris: Librairie José Corti, 1967).

Immerman, Richard. *Empire for Liberty: A History of American Imperialism from Benjamin Franklin to Paul Wolfowitz* (Princeton: Princeton University Press, 2010).

Janara, Laura. *Democracy Growing Up: Authority, Autonomy, and Passion in Tocqueville's "Democracy in America"* (Albany: SUNY Press, 2002).

Jardin, André. *Alexis de Tocqueville, 1805–1859* (Paris: Hachette, 1984).

Jardin, André. *Tocqueville: A Biography*, trans. Lydia Davis with Robert Hemenway (New York: Farrar Straus Giroux, 1988).

Jardin, André. "Tocqueville et l'Algérie," *Revue des Travaux de l'Académie des sciences morales et politiques* 115 (1962), 61–74.

Jaume, Lucien. *Tocqueville* (Paris: Fayard, 2008).

Jones, David Martin. "Democratization, Civil Society, and Illiberal Middle Class Culture in Pacific Asia," *Comparative Politics* 30 (1998), 147–169.

Juntao, Wang. "Confucian Democrats in Chinese History," in Bell and Chaibong (eds.), *Confucianism for the Modern World*, 69–89.

Kahan, Alan S. *Alexis de Tocqueville* (London: Continuum, 2010).

Kahan, Alan S. "Aristocracy in Tocqueville," *The Tocqueville Review* 27 (2006), 323–348.

Kant, Immanuel. "Idea for a Universal History with a Cosmopolitan Purpose," in *Political Writings*, ed. H. S. Reiss (Cambridge: Cambridge University Press, 1991), 41–53.

Kant, Immanuel. "Perpetual Peace," in *On History*, ed. Lewis White Beck (New York: Macmillan Publishing Co., 1963), 85–136.

Kaplan, Fred. *Lincoln: The Biography of a Writer* (New York: HarperCollins Publishers, 2008).

Keyssar, Alexander. *The Right to Vote: The Contested History of Democracy in the United States* (New York: Basic Books, 2000).

Kilian, Norbert. "New Wine in Old Skins? American Definitions of Empire and the Emergence of a New Concept," in David Armitage (ed.), *Theories of Empire 1450–1800* (Aldershot: Ashgate, 1998), 307–324.

Kim, Samuel S. (ed.). *Korea's Globalization* (Cambridge: Cambridge University Press, 2000).

Kojève, Alexandre. *Introduction to the Reading of Hegel*, ed. Allan Bloom, trans. J. H. Nichols, Jr. (New York: Basic Books, 1969).

Kolakowski, Leszek. *Main Currents of Marxism* (Oxford: Oxford University Press, 1978).

Koo, Hagen. "Strong State and Contentious Society," in Hagen Koo (ed.), *State and Society in Contemporary Korea* (Ithaca, NY: Cornell University Press, 1993).

Krause, Sharon. *Liberalism with Honor* (Cambridge, MA: Harvard University Press, 2002).

Laffont, Pierre. *Histoire de la France en Algérie* (Paris: Plon, 1980).

Lambert, Frank. *The Barbary Wars* (New York: Hill and Wang, 2005).

Lamberti, Jean-Claude. *Tocqueville et les deux démocraties* (Paris: Presses universitaires de France, 1983).

Laponneraye, Albert. *Mélanges d'économie sociale, de littérature et de morale* (Paris: Dépôt central, 1835).

Larrère, Catherine. "Introduction" to *Réflexions sur la Monarchie universelle*, in Patrick Andrivet and Catherine Volpilhac-Auger (eds.), *Oeuvres completes*, Vol. 2 (Oxford: Voltaire Foundation, 2000).

Larrère, Catherine. "L'empire, entre federation et république," *Revue Montesquieu* 8 (2005–2006), 111–136.

Larrère, Catherine. "L'histoire du commerce dans *L'Esprit des lois*," in Michel Porret and Catherine Volpilhac-Auger (eds.), *Le Temps de Montesquieu* (Geneva: Droz, 2002), 319–336.

Lawler, Peter Augustine. "End of History 2000," in Peter Augustine Lawler and Dale McConkey (eds.), *Faith, Reason, and Political Life Today* (Lanham, MD: Lexington Books, 2001), 95–112.

Lawler, Peter Augustine. "*Lost in the Cosmos*: Walker Percy's Analysis of American Restlessness," in Joseph M. Knippenberg and Peter Augustine Lawler (eds.), *Poets, Princes, and Private Citizens: Literary Alternatives to Postmodernism* (Lanham, MD: Rowman & Littlefield, 1996), 169–190.

Lawler, Peter Augustine. *The Restless Mind: Alexis de Tocqueville on the Origin and Perpetuation of Human Liberty* (Lanham, MD: Rowman & Littlefield, 1993).

Lawlor, Mary. *Alexis de Tocqueville in the Chamber of Deputies: His Views on Foreign and Colonial Policy* (Washington, DC: Catholic University Press, 1959).

Lear, Jonathan. *Radical Hope: Ethics in the Face of Cultural Devastation* (Cambridge, MA: Harvard University Press, 2006).

Lee, Kwang Kyu. "Confucian Tradition in the Contemporary Korean Family," in Slote and De Vos (eds.), *Confucianism and the Family*, 249–261.

Lerner, Ralph. *Playing the Fool: Subversive Laughter in Troubled Times* (Chicago: University of Chicago Press, 2009).

Lerner, Ralph. *Revolutions Revisited: Two Faces of the Politics of Enlightenment* (Chapel Hill: University of North Carolina Press, 1994).

Lerner, Ralph. *The Thinking Revolutionary: Principle and Practice in the New Republic* (Ithaca, NY: Cornell University Press, 1988).

Levenson, Joseph R. *Confucian China and Its Modern Fate: A Trilogy. Vol. 3, The Problem of Historical Significance* (Berkeley, CA: University of California Press, 1965).

Lincoln, Abraham. "Annual Message to Congress," December 3, 1861, in *Speeches and Writings 1859–1865* (New York: Library of America, 1989).

Locke, Jill and Eileen Hunt Botting (eds.). *Feminist Interpretations of Alexis de Tocqueville* (University Park: Penn State University Press, 2009).

Locke, John. "An Essay Concerning the True Original, Extent, and End of Civil Government," in Peter Laslett (ed.), *Two Treatises of Government* (Cambridge: Cambridge University Press, 1960).

Lüthy, Herbert. *France Against Herself*, trans. Eric Mosbacher (New York: Meridian Books, 1968).

Ma, Shu-Yun. "The Chinese Discourse on Civil Society," *The China Quarterly* 137 (1994), 180–193.

Manent, Pierre. "Christianity and Democracy: Some Remarks on the Political History of Religion, or, on the Religious History of Modern Politics," in Daniel J. Mahoney and Paul Seaton (eds. and trans.), *Modern Liberty and Its Discontents* (Lanham, MD: Rowman & Littlefield Publishers, 1998), 97–116.

Manent, Pierre. *La raison des nations* (Paris: Gallimard, 2006); trans. Paul Seaton as *Democracy Without Nations?* (Wilmington: ISI Books, 2007).

Manent, Pierre. *Tocqueville and the Nature of Democracy*, trans. John Waggoner (Lanham, MD: Rowman & Littlefield, 1996).

Manent, Pierre. *Tocqueville et la nature de la démocratie* (Paris: Fayard, 1993).

Manin, Bernard. "Montesquieu, la république et le commerce," *Archives européennes de sociologie* 42 (2001), 573–602.

Mannheim, Karl. *Ideology and Utopia: An Introduction to the Sociology of Knowledge* (London: Routledge, 1936).

Mansfield, Harvey C. and Delba Winthrop. "Tocqueville's New Political Science," in Welch (ed.), *The Cambridge Companion to Tocqueville*, 81–107.

Martel, André. "Tocqueville et les problèmes coloniaux de la Monarchie de Juillet," *Revue d'Histoire Economique et Sociale* 32 (1954), 369–376.

Marx, Karl. *Das Kapital* (Berlin: Dietz Verlag, 1989).

Marx, Karl. "Economic and Philosophical Manuscripts of 1844," in Marx and Engels, *The Marx-Engels Reader*, ed. Robert Tucker, 66–125.

Marx, Karl. "The Indian Revolt," *New-York Daily Tribune*, September 16, 1857.

Marx, Karl. "On the Jewish Question," in Marx and Engels, *The Marx-Engels Reader*, ed. Robert C. Tucker, 26–52.

Marx, Karl and Friedrich Engels. "Manifesto of the Communist Party," in *The Marx-Engels Reader*, ed. Robert C. Tucker, 469–500.

Marx, Karl and Friedrich Engels. *The Marx-Engels Reader*, ed. Robert C. Tucker (New York: W.W. Norton & Co., 1978).

Mason, Sheila. "Montesquieu, Europe and the Imperatives of Commerce," *Journal for Eighteenth Century Studies* 17 (1994), 65–72.

May, Robert E. *Manifest Destiny's Underworld: Filibustering in Antebellum America* (Chapel Hill: University of North Carolina Press, 2002).

May, Robert E. *The Southern Dream of a Caribbean Empire, 1854–1861* (Baton Rouge: Louisiana State University Press, 1973).

McWilliams, Wilson Carey. *The Idea of Fraternity in America* (Berkeley: University of California Press, 1973).

Meigs, R. J. "Letter to Secretary of War William Crawford, November 8, 1816." *American State Papers: Indian Affairs* [ASPIA], II:115.

Melon, Jean François. "Essai politique sur le commerce," in Eugène Daire (ed.), *Economistes et financiers du XVIIIe siècle* (Geneva: Slatkine Reprints, 1971).

Mélonio, Françoise. "L'idée de nation et idée de démocratie chez Tocqueville," *Littérature et nation* 7 (1991), 5–24.

Mélonio, Françoise. "Nations et Nationalismes," *La Revue Tocqueville/The Tocqueville Review* 18 (1997), 61–75.

Meyer, Jean. *Histoire de la France coloniale: des origines à 1914* (Paris: Armand Colin, 1991).

Mitchell, Harvey. *America After Tocqueville: Democracy Against Difference* (Cambridge: Cambridge University Press, 2002).

Mitchell, Harvey. *Individual Choice and the Structures of History: Alexis de Tocqueville as Historian Reappraised* (Cambridge: Cambridge University Press, 1996).

Mitchell, Joshua. *The Fragility of Freedom: Tocqueville on Religion, Democracy and the American Future* (Chicago: University of Chicago Press, 1999).

Mitchell, Joshua. "It is Not Good for Man to Be Alone," in John von Heyking and Richard Avramenko (eds.), *Friendship and Politics: Essays in Political Thought* (Notre Dame, IN: University of Notre Dame Press, 2008), 268–284.

Mo, Jongryn. "The Challenge of Accountability: Implications of the Censorate," in Bell and Chaibong (eds.), *Confucianism for the Modern World*, 54–68.

Mo, Jongryn. "Political Culture and Legislative Gridlock: Politics of Economic Reform in Precrisis Korea," *Comparative Political Studies* 34 (2001), 467–489.

Montchrétien, Antoine de. *Traicté de l'oeconomie politique*, ed. Théophile Funck-Brentano (Paris: Plon, 1889).

Montesquieu. *Persian Letters*, trans. C. J. Betts (London: Penguin, 1973).

Montesquieu. *The Spirit of the Laws*, trans. Anne Cohler, Basia Miller, and Harold Stone (Cambridge: Cambridge University Press, 1989).

Moon, Katharine. "Strangers in the Midst of Globalization: Migrant Workers and Korean Nationalism," in Kim (ed.), *Korea's Globalization*, 147–169.

Mosher, Michael. "Montesquieu on Conquest: Three Cartesian Heroes and Five Good Enough Empires," *Revue Montesquieu* 8 (2005–2006), 81–110.

Nelson, Brian. *Zola and the Bourgeoisie: A Study of Themes and Techniques in Les Rougon-Macquart* (New York: Macmillan, 1983).

Nicholas, Michael A. *America Uncensored: A Nation in Search of Its Soul* (Victoria, BC: Trafford Publishing, 2004).

Nietzsche, Friedrich. *On the Genealogy of Morals*, ed. Walter Kaufmann (New York: Vintage, 1989).

Nisbet, Robert. *The Sociological Tradition* (New York: Heinemann, 1966).

Nolla, Eduardo. *Liberty, Equality, Democracy* (New York: New York University Press, 1996).

Nora, Pierre. "Nation," in François Furet and Mona Ozouf (eds.), *A Critical Dictionary of the French Revolution*, trans. Arthur Goldhammer (Cambridge: Harvard University Press, 1989), 742–753.

Nugent, Jim. "John Murray Forbes," in *Dictionary of Unitarian & Universalist Biography*. (Unitarian Universalist History & Heritage Society, 1999). http://www25.uua.org/uuhs/duub/articles/johnforbes.html (accessed November 8, 2012).

Oren, Michael. "Early American Encounters in the Middle East," in *Power, Faith, and Fantasy: American in the Middle East, 1776 to the Present* (New York: Norton, 2007), 17–100.

"Organizing in the 1990s: Excerpts from a Roundtable Discussion," in Peg Knoepfle (ed.), *After Alinsky: Community Organizing in Illinois* (Springfield, IL: Sangamon State University, 1990), 124–152.

Pagden, Anthony. "Imperialism, Liberalism and the Quest for Perpetual Peace," *Daedalus* 134 (2005), 46–57.

Pagden, Anthony. *Lords of All the World* (New Haven: Yale University Press, 1995).

Pagden, Anthony. *Peoples and Empires* (New York: The Modern Library, 2001).

Parton, James, Bayard Taylor, Amos Kendall, E. D. Mayo, and J. Alexander Patten. *Sketches of Men of Progress* (Cincinnati: Greer, 1870–1871).

Perez, Gilberto. *The Material Ghost: Films and Their Medium* (Baltimore: Johns Hopkins University Press, 1988).

Pessen, Edward. *Jacksonian America: Society, Personality, and Politics* (Urbana: University of Illinois Press, 1985).

Peterson, Derek R. (ed.). *Abolition and Imperialism in Britain, Africa, and the Atlantic* (Athens: Ohio University Press, 2010).

Pharr, Susan and Frank J. Schwartz (eds.). *The State of Civil Society in Japan* (Cambridge: Cambridge University Press, 2003).

Pick, Daniel. *Faces of Degeneration: A European Disorder, ca. 1848–1918* (Cambridge: Cambridge University Press, 1989).

Pippin, Robert. *Hollywood Westerns and American Myth: The Importance of Howard Hawks and John Ford for Political Philosophy* (New Haven: Yale University Press, 2010).

Pippin, Robert. "The Paradoxes of Power in the Novels of J.M. Coetzee," in Peter Singer and Anton Leist (eds.), *J.M. Coetzee and Ethics* (New York: Columbia University Press, 2010), 19–42.

Pitts, Jennifer. *A Turn to Empire: The Rise of Imperial Liberalism in Britain and France* (Princeton: Princeton University Press, 2006).

Platania, Marco. "Dynamiques des empires et dynamiques du commerce: inflexions de la pensée de Montesquieu (1734–1802)," *Revue Montesquieu* 8 (2005–2006), 43–66.

Plattner, Marc and Larry Diamond (eds.). "Democracy in the World: Tocqueville Reconsidered," *Journal of Democracy* 11, no. 1 (2000).

Putnam, Robert. *Making Democracy Work* (Princeton: Princeton University Press, 1993).

Pye, Lucian. *Asian Power and Politics: The Cultural Dimensions of Authority* (Cambridge, MA: Harvard University Press, 1985).

Rahe, Paul. *Soft Despotism: Democracy's Drift* (New Haven: Yale University Press, 2009).

Rana, Aziz. *The Two Faces of American Freedom* (Cambridge, MA: Harvard University Press, 2010).

Raynal, Guillaume-Thomas. *Histoire philosophique et politique des établissements et du commercer des Européens dans les deux Indes* (Ferney-Voltaire: Centre international d'études du XVIIIe siècle, t. I, 2010).

Richter, Melvin. "Comparative Political Analysis in Montesquieu and Tocqueville," *Comparative Politics* 1 (1969), 129–160.

Richter, Melvin. "Tocqueville and French Nineteenth-Century Conceptualizations of the Two Bonapartes and their Empires," in Peter Baehr and Melvin Richter (eds.), *Dictatorship in History and Theory: Bonapartism, Caesarism, and Totalitarianism* (Cambridge: Cambridge University Press, 2004), 83–102.

Richter, Melvin. "Tocqueville, Napoleon, and Bonapartism," in Shmuel Eisenstadt (ed.), *Reconsidering Tocqueville's "Democracy in America"* (New
Brunswick: Transaction Publishers, 1988), 110–145.

Richter, Melvin. "Tocqueville on Algeria," *Review of Politics* 25 (1963), 362–
398.

Richter, Melvin. "The Uses of Theory: Tocqueville's Adaptation of Montesquieu," in Melvin Richter (ed.), *Essays in Theory and History: An Approach
to the Social Sciences* (Cambridge: Harvard University Press, 1970), 74–102.

Robin, Corey. *Fear: The History of a Political Idea* (Oxford: Oxford University
Press, 2004).

Robin, Corey. "Why Do Opposites Attract? Fear and Freedom in the Modern
Political Imagination," in Nancy Lusignan Schultz (ed.), *Fear Itself: Enemies
Real and Imagined in American Culture* (West Lafayette, IN: Purdue University
Press, 1999), 3–22.

Robison, Richard. "Indonesia: Tensions in State and Regime," in Kevin Hewison,
Richard Robison, and Garry Rodan (eds.), *Southeast Asia in the 1990s* (Sydney:
Allen & Unwin, 1993), 39–74.

Roediger, David R. *The Wages of Whiteness: Race and the Making of the American Working Class* (New York: Verso, 1991).

Rogin, Michael. *Fathers and Children: Andrew Jackson and the Subjugation of
the American Indian* (New York: Knopf, 1975).

Rothman, Adam. *Slave Country: American Expansion and the Origins of the
Deep South* (Cambridge, MA: Harvard University Press, 2005).

Rothman, William. "Stagecoach and the Quest for Selfhood," in Grant (ed.),
John Ford's Stagecoach, 158–178.

Rozman, Gilbert. "Center-Local Relations: Can Confucianism Boost Decentralization and Regionalism?" in Bell and Chaibong (eds.), *Confucianism for the
Modern World*, 181–200.

Rutenberg, Jim and Adam Nagourney. "Retooling a Grass-Roots Network To
Serve a You Tube Presidency," *New York Times*, January 26, 2009, sec. 1A,
1, 12.

Saich, Tony. "The Search for Civil Society and Democracy in China," *Current
History* 93 (1994), 260–264.

Said, Edward. *Orientalism* (New York: Vintage, 1979).

Saint-Paulien [M. Y. Sicard]. *Napoléon, Balzac, et l'Empire de la Comédie
Humaine* (Paris: Albin Michel, 1979).

Salman, Michael. *The Embarrassment of Slavery: Controversies over Bondage
and Nationalism in the American Colonial Philippines* (Berkeley: University of
California Press, 2001).

Sang-Jin, Han. "The Public Sphere and Democracy in Korea: A Debate on Civil
Society," *Korea Journal* 37 (1997), 78–97.

Schleifer, James T. *The Making of Tocqueville's "Democracy in America"*
(Chapel Hill: University of North Carolina Press, 1980).

Schmitt, Carl. *Land and Sea* (Washington: Plutarch Press, 1977).

Schneider, Robert A. "Self-Censorship and Men of Letters: Tocqueville's Critique
of the Enlightenment in Historical Perspective," in Robert M. Schwartz and
Robert A Schneider (eds.), *Tocqueville and Beyond: Essays on the Old Regime*

in Honor of David D. Bien (Cranbury, NJ: Rosemount Publishing, 2003), 192–225.

Schoen, Brian. *The Fragile Fabric of Union: Cotton, Federal Politics, and the Global Origins of the Civil War* (Baltimore: Johns Hopkins University Press, 2009).

Seok-Choon, Lew, Chang Mi-Hye, and Kim Tae-Eu. "Affective Networks," in Bell and Chaibong (eds.), *Confucianism for the Modern World*, 201–217.

Seung-sook Moon. "Overcome by Globalization: the Rise of a Women's Policy in South Korea," in Kim (ed.), *Korea's Globalization*, 126–146.

Shklar, Judith. *American Citizenship: The Quest for Inclusion* (Cambridge, MA: Harvard University Press, 1991).

Shklar, Judith. *Montesquieu* (Oxford: Oxford University Press, 1987).

Shulman, Robert. *Social Criticism and Nineteenth-Century American Fictions* (Columbia: University of Missouri Press, 1987).

Slote, Walter H. and George A. De Vos (eds.). *Confucianism and the Family* (New York: State University of New York Press, 1998).

Smith, Adam. *Wealth of Nations*, ed. Edwin Cannan (Chicago: University of Chicago Press, 1976).

Smith, Henry Nash. *Virgin Land: The American West as Symbol and Myth* (Cambridge, MA: Harvard University Press, 2005).

Smith, Jay M. *Nobility Reimagined: The Patriotic Nation in Eighteenth-Century France* (Ithaca, NY: Cornell University Press, 2005).

Smith, Rogers. "Beyond Tocqueville, Myrdal, and Hartz: The Multiple Traditions in America," *American Political Science Review* 87 (1993), 549–566.

Smith, Rogers. *Civic Ideals: Conflicting Vision of Citizenship in U.S. History* (New Haven, CT: Yale University Press, 1997).

Sorel, Georges. *Reflections on Violence* (Glencoe, IL: Free Press, 1950).

Spector, Céline. *Montesquieu et l'émergence de l'économie politique* (Paris: Honoré Champion, 2006).

Spector, Céline (ed.). "Montesquieu et l'empire," special issue of *Revue Montesquieu*, no. 8 (2005–2006).

Spector, Céline. *Montesquieu: Pouvoirs, richesses et societies* (Paris: P.U.F., 2004; repr. Hermann, 2011).

Staël, Germaine de. *Considerations on the Principal Events of the French Revolution*, ed. Aurelian Craiutu (Indianapolis: Liberty Press, 2008).

Stand, David. "Protest in Beijing: Civil Society and the Public Sphere in China," *Problems of Communism* 39 (1990), 1–19.

Starobinski, Jean. *Jean-Jacques Rousseau: Transparency and Obstruction.* (Chicago: University of Chicago Press, 1988).

Steinberg, David I. "Civil Society and Human Rights in Korea: On Contemporary and Classical Orthodoxy and Ideology," *Korea Journal* 37 (1997), 145–165.

Stendhal. *A Life of Napoleon* (New York: Howard Fertig, 1977).

Stendhal. *Memoirs of Egoism*, ed. Matthew Josephson (New York: Lear Publishing, 1949).

Stone, John and Stephen Mennel. "Introduction" to *Alexis de Tocqueville on Democracy, Revolution, and Society*, ed. John Stone and Stephen Mennel (Chicago: University of Chicago Press, 1980).

Stora, Benjamin. *Algeria 1830–2000: A Short History*, trans. Jane Marie Todd (Ithaca, NY: Cornell University Press, 2001).

Strong, Tracy B. "Seeing Differently and Seeing Further: Rousseau and Tocqueville," in Peter Dennis Bathory and Nancy L. Schwartz (eds.), *Friends and Citizens* (Lanham, MD: Rowman & Littlefield, 2001), 97–122.

Strout, Cushing. "Tocqueville's Duality: Describing America and Thinking of Europe," *American Quarterly* 21 (1969), 87–99.

Studler, Gaylyn. "'Be a Proud, Glorified Dreg': Class, Gender and Frontier Democracy in John Ford's *Stagecoach*," in Grant (ed.), *John Ford's "Stagecoach,"* 132–157.

Sullivan, Kathleen S. "Toward a Generative Theory of Equality," in Locke and Botting (eds.), *Feminist Interpretations of Alexis de Tocqueville*, 199–224.

Sumner, Charles. *The Works of Charles Sumner* (Boston: Lee and Shepard, 1870–1883).

Swedberg, Richard. *Tocqueville's Political Economy* (Princeton: Princeton University Press, 2009).

Talmon, J. L. *The Origins of Totalitarian Democracy* (London: Secker and Warburg, 1952).

Terrel, Jean. "A propos de la conquête: droit et politique chez Montesquieu," *Revue Montesquieu* 8 (2005–2006), 137–150.

Tessitore, Aristide. "Alexis de Tocqueville on the Incommensurability of America's Founding Principles," in Peter Augustine Lawler (ed.), *Democracy and Its Friendly Critics: Tocqueville and Political Life Today* (Lanham, MD: Lexington Books, 2004), 59–76.

Texier, J. "Marx, penseur égalitaire?" *Actuel Marx* 8 (1990), 45–66.

Thomson, Ann. "Arguments for the Conquest of Algiers in the Late Eighteenth and Early Nineteenth Centuries," *The Maghreb Review* 14 (1989), 108–118.

Tocqueville, Alexis de. *The Ancien Regime* (London: J. M. Dent, 1988).

Tocqueville, Alexis de. *The Ancien Régime and the French Revolution*, trans. Gerald Bevan (London: Penguin Books, 2008).

Tocqueville, Alexis de. *De la démocratie en Amérique* (Paris: Garnier Flammarion, 1981).

Tocqueville, Alexis de. *De la démocratie en Amérique* (Paris: Gallimard, 1961).

Tocqueville, Alexis de. *L'ancien régime et la révolution: Fragments et notes inédites sur la revolution*, ed. André Jardin (Paris: Gallimard, 1953).

Tocqueville, Alexis de. "Letter to Louise de Tocqueville, December 25, 1831," trans. Frederick Brown, in "Letters from America," *Hudson Review* 62 (2009), 357–397.

Tocqueville, Alexis de. *Manuscrits de 1857–1858 (Grundrisse)* (Paris: Editions sociales, 1980).

Tocqueville, Alexis de. *Memoir, Letters, and Remains*, 2 vols., trans. and ed. Miss Senior (London: Macmillan and Company, 1861).

Tocqueville, Alexis de. *Oeuvres Complètes*, ed. Gustave de Beaumont (Paris, 1860).

Tocqueville, Alexis de. *Recollections*, ed., J. P. Mayer, trans. Alexander Teixeira de Mattos, (London: The Harvill Press, 1948).

Tocqueville, Alexis de. *Recollections*, ed. J. P. Mayer and A. P. Kerr (New Brunswick: Transaction Publishers, 1997).

Tocqueville, Alexis de. "Speech on the Right to Work," in Seymour Drescher (ed.), *Tocqueville and Beaumont on Social Reform* (New York: Harper Torchbooks, 1968).

Tocqueville, Alexis de. *Sur la démocratie en Amérique, Fragments inédits* (Paris: Crété, 1959).

Tocqueville, Alexis de. *Tocqueville on America After 1840: Letters and Other Writings*, eds. and trans. Aurelian Craiutu and Jeremy Jennings (Cambridge: Cambridge University Press, 2009).

Tocqueville, Hervé de. *Coup d'œil sur le règne de Louis XVI, depuis son avènement à la couronne jusqu'à la séance royale du 23 juin 1789, pour faire suite à l'Histoire philosophique du règne de Louis XV* (Paris, 1850).

Todorov, Tzvetan. *On Human Diversity*, trans. Catherine Porter (Cambridge, MA: Harvard University Press, 1993).

Touraine, Alain. *What Is Democracy?*, trans. David Macey (Boulder, CO: Westview Press, 1997).

Trollope, Frances. *Domestic Manners of the Americans* (London: Penguin Classics, 1997).

Tsai, Lily L. "Solidary Groups, Informal Accountability, and Local Public Goods Provision in Rural China," *American Political Science Review* 101 (2007), 355–372.

Tucker, Robert W. and David Hendrickson. *Empire of Liberty: The Statecraft of Thomas Jefferson* (New York: Oxford University Press, 1990).

Turner, Frederick Jackson. "The Significance of the Frontier in American History" in Everett B. Edwards (ed.), *The Early Writings of Frederick Jackson Turner* (Madison, WI: University of Wisconsin Press, 1938), 183–232.

Twing, Stephen W. *Myths, Modes, and U.S. Foreign Policy* (Boulder: Lynner Reinner Publishers, 1998).

Van Gennep, Arnold. *The Rites of Passage.* (Chicago: University of Chicago Press, 1961).

Volpilhac-Augur, C. "Introduction" to *De l'esprit des loix (manuscrits), Oeuvres complètes de Montesquieu*, Vol. 4 (Oxford: Voltaire Foundation, 2008), 766–767.

Volpilhac-Auger, C. (ed.) *Montesquieu. Manuscrits inédits de La Brède* (Naples: Liguori, 2002).

von Hoffman, Nicholas. "Our Idealist in Chief Promotes a Lovely War," *The New York Observer*, November 17, 2003. http://www.observer.com/2003/11/our-idealist-in-chief-promotes-a-lovely-war/ (accessed July 20, 2011).

Wakeman, Frederic, Jr. "The Civil Society and Public Sphere Debate: Western Reflections on Chinese Political Culture," *Modern China* 19 (1993), 108–138.

Wallace, Anthony F. C. *Jefferson and the Indians: The Tragic Fate of the First Americans* (Cambridge, MA: Harvard University Press, 1999).

Wallerstein, Immanuel. *European Universalism: The Rhetoric of Power* (New York: The New Press, 2006).

Walsh, David. *The Growth of the Liberal Soul* (Columbia: University of Missouri Press, 1997).

Watanabe, Hiroshi. "The Old Regime and the Meiji Revolution." Paper delivered at the Colloque international commémorative du Bicentennaire de la naissance d'Alexis de Tocqueville, Tokyo, June 2005.

Weber, Eugen. *Peasants into Frenchmen: The Modernization of Rural France, 1870–1914* (Stanford: Stanford University Press, 1976).

Welch, Cheryl B. (ed.). *The Cambridge Companion to Tocqueville* (Cambridge: Cambridge University Press, 2006).

Welch, Cheryl B. "Colonial Violence and the Rhetoric of Evasion: Tocqueville on Algeria," *Political Theory* 31 (2003), 235–264.

Welch, Cheryl B. "Creating Concitoyens: Tocqueville on the Legacy of Slavery," in Raf Geenens and Annelien De Dijn (eds.), *Reading Tocqueville: From Oracle to Actor* (Basingstoke: Palgrave Macmillan, 2007), 31–51.

Welch, Cheryl B. "Tocqueville on Fraternity and Fratricide," in Welch (ed.), *The Cambridge Companion to Alexis de Tocqueville*, 303–336.

Welch, Cheryl B. "Tocqueville's Resistance to the Social," *History of European Ideas* 30 (2004), 83–107.

Whittington, Keith. "Revisiting Tocqueville's America: Society, Politics, and Association in the Nineteenth Century," in Bob Edwards, Michael W. Foley, and Mario Diani (eds.), *Beyond Tocqueville: Civil Society and the Social Capital Debate in Comparative Perspective* (Hanover, NH: University Press of New England, 2001), 21–31.

Wilbur, Richard. "Icarium Mare," in *Collected Poems, 1943–2004* (San Diego: Harcourt, 2004), 94–95.

Wills, Garry. "Did Tocqueville 'Get' America?" *The New York Review of Books*, April 29, 2004.

Wolin, Sheldon. *Democracy Incorporated: Managed Democracy and the Specter of Inverted Totalitarianism* (Princeton and Oxford: Princeton University Press, 2008).

Wolin, Sheldon. *Politics and Vision* (Princeton and Oxford: Princeton University Press, 2004).

Wolin, Sheldon. *The Presence of the Past: Essays on the State and the Constitution* (Baltimore: Johns Hopkins University Press, 1989).

Wolin, Sheldon. *Tocqueville Between Two Worlds: The Making of a Political and Theoretical Life* (Princeton: Princeton University Press, 2003).

Wood, Robin. "Shall We Gather at the River? The Late Films of John Ford," *Film Comment* 7 (1971), 8–17.

Wuthnow, Robert (ed.). *Between States and Markets: The Voluntary Sphere in Comparative Perspective* (Princeton: Princeton University Press, 1991).

Yun-Shik, Chang. "Mutual Help and Democracy in Korea," in Bell and Chaibong (eds.), *Confucianism for the Modern World*, 90–123.

Zetterbaum, Marvin. *Tocqueville and the Problem of Democracy* (Stanford: Stanford University Press, 1967).

Zhiguang, Liu and Wang Suli, "Cong qunzhong shehui zouxiang gongmin shehui" [From mass society to civil society], *Zhengzhixue yanjiu [Political Research]* 5 (1988), 1–5.

Zola, Emile. *The Debacle* (New York: Penguin, 1972).

Index

aristocracy, 10, 33, 37, 41, 49, 64, 78,
112, 115, 326, 338
elements of, 34, 51, 57, 66–67, 73
French aristocracy, 56, 68
impossibility to return to, 9, 39, 69
"natural aristocracy," 64, 249
"new aristocracy," 5, 50, 73
Tocqueville's account of, 10, 64–73,
92, 106, 113, 181–182, 196
"aristocratic age," 60, 67, 140, 144
"aristocratic honor," 60, 64
"aristocratic man," 133
Aristophanes, 333
Aristotle, 333
Aron, Raymond, 165, 229
"art of association," 171, 227, 230
Asia, 6, 8, 18, 119, 121, 124, 126,
129, 207, 220, 261
Asian moeurs, 119–120
democracy in, 121
paternalistic conceptions of power
in, 119
unlikely democratization in, 119
Asia Minor, 209
associational culture. *See* civil society
associations, 72, 73, 114, 116, 142,
170, 171, 172, 173, 174, 175,
216, 279, 318, 319, 323
in Asia, 117–118, 121–122
freedom and, 28, 123–124,
170–171, 319, 323
in Old Regime France, 116–117
Tocqueville on, 114–115
and "spirit of exclusion," 172
Atanassow, Ewa, 1, 19, 178
Athena, 198
Athens, 209, 210
Atlantic Ocean, 157, 176
Au Bonheur des Dames (Zola), 284
Austria, 236, 237, 238, 240

Baath Party, 136
Baghdad, 145, 146
Baghdad College, 146
Balzac, Honoré de, 281
Barbary states, 189
Bastille, 11

Bayle, Pierre, 85, 86
Beaumont, Gustave de, 25, 35, 36,
164, 322, 333
Beckwith, Nelson Marvin, 253, 254,
255, 256, 257, 258, 259, 260,
262
Bedouin, 282
Beitz, Charles, 154
Bell, Daniel, 125
Bendix, Reinhard, 155
Benhabib, Seyla, 332
Bergson, Henri, 285
Berlin Wall, 11, 35, 134
Berman, Paul, 26, 27, 307
Black Sea, 187
Blanqui, Louis Auguste, 48
Blue Ribbon Committee, 325
Boer War, 244
Boesche, Roger, 5, 175
"bois-brûlé," 35
Bonaparte, Napoleon, 23, 53, 189,
264–287, 315
as alternative to bourgeois society,
281–285
as enemy to human liberty,
266–269, 270, 278
Tocqueville's relation to, 269–281
Boone, Daniel, 318
Boston, 326
Boston Tea Party, 11
Bourbon Restoration, 10, 63, 281,
282
Bourbons, 11, 63, 315
bourgeois, 48, 49
Boyd, Richard, 1, 23, 264, 332
Brahmanism, 105
Britain, 78, 80, 217, 219, 233, 237,
260, 261, 262, 275, 276
British East India Company, 194
British Empire, 182, 199
Brooks, Preston, 253
Brussels, 237
Buchanan, James, 261
Bugeaud, Thomas Robert, 217
Burke, Edmund, 11, 74–83, 161, 281
Burma, 6
Bush, George W., 1, 3

Bénichou, Paul, 315

Cabet, Étienne, 48
Caesar, 103, 281, 282
California, 256
Caliphate, 100
Calvinists, 97, 98
Canada, 207
Capdevila, Nestor, 8, 9, 33, 201
Caribbean, 188, 207, 254, 277
Carthage, 210
caste system, 105, 106, 107
Catholic Church, 55
Catholicism, 14, 15, 98, 115, 125
Cavaignac, Louis Eugène, 237
Ceaser, James, 173
centralization, 11, 127, 269, 280, 321,
    322
  egalitarian society and, 114, 116,
    120–121, 125, 127, 200
Chaibong, Hahm, 125, 128, 130
Chamber of Deputies, 228, 231, 241
Chan Sin Yee, 130
Channel, 79
Charlemagne, 204
Charles X, 315
Chateaubriand, François-René de, 25,
    27, 266, 271, 314, 315, 333,
    334, 336
Chicago, 27, 28, 317, 318, 324, 325,
    326, 327, 328
Chicago Tribune, 328
Chile, 18
China, 6, 18, 117, 120, 124, 125,
    254, 258, 262
Chinese, 118
Chingachgook, 336
Cho, Hein, 127
Choctaws, 247
Chosŏn dynasty, 126, 127
Christendom, 89, 102
Christian dogma, 103
Christianity, 14, 15, 89–91, 95, 97,
    100–101, 103, 104, 107, 109,
    261, 262
  and democratic values, 14, 61, 103
  history vs. ideal of, 101–102

church and state, 94, 99, 101, 109,
    114
Church of Rome, 115
Churchill, Winston, 84
Cincinnati, 250, 326
civil society, 1, 13, 16, 17, 121, 122,
    123, 124, 130. *See also*
    associational culture
Civil War, 246, 258
civilization, 5, 25, 35, 36, 37, 159,
    185, 186, 193, 199, 207, 212,
    234, 248, 261, 264, 269, 278,
    302, 305, 317, 320, 322, 323,
    325, 326, 333, 336, 337, 339
  Christian civilization, 258, 335
  democratic civilization, 37
  European civilization, 333, 334,
    337
  French civilization, 282
  Indian civilization, 103
  melding of civilizations, 188
  "modern civilization," 278
  "Muslim civilization," 70
  New England civilization, 324
  vs. nature, 35, 36, 37, 299, 333
  "one equal civilization," 198
"civilizing mission," 218
Clinton, Bill, 1
Clinton, David, 22, 223
Clinton, Hillary, 148
Colbert, Jean-Baptiste, 207, 209
Cold War, 35, 37, 38, 133, 338
"collective individualism," 108
colonialism, 5, 14, 22, 29, 194–195,
    233, 234, 277, 281, 286, 287,
    293
colonization, 20, 70, 188, 194, 203,
    207, 213, 220, 251
  of Algeria. *See* Algeria
  ancient Roman, 192
  commercial, 203, 208, 219
  effects of, 194–196, 213
  of India. *See* India
  modern American, 192
Columbia University, 253
Commager, Henry Steele, 162
communism, 5, 35, 49, 201

honor in, 180, 182, 217–218
instrumental view of religion in, 109
intended readership of, 90, 116
international relations in, 184
jury chapter in, 307–313
liberty and equality in, 227–228
Montesquieu's legacy in, 202–203, 211–213
philosophical grandeur in, 308
poetics in, 309–313
providential language in, 60–62
qualified optimism of, 114
religion in. *See* Religion
rhetorical strategies in, 124–125
theory and politics in, 48, 161–162
Three Races in. *See* Race(s)
two paths for democracy in, 269
women in, 129
"democracy without nations," 184
"democratic age," 9, 140, 142, 144, 147, 149, 230
"democratic man," 44, 45, 71, 133, 142, 144, 163
democratic process, 28, 62, 64, 65, 71, 72, 179
"democratic tyranny," 62
democratization, 2, 3, 4, 7, 8, 10, 12, 13, 16, 17, 22, 23, 27, 111, 113, 119, 127, 132, 153, 157, 158, 165, 179, 181, 183, 200, 337
dialectical dynamic of, 200
in East Asia. *See* East Asia
East European, 121
irreversible and undetermined, 113
local communities and, 27
in Old Regime France, 116–117
political vs. social, 17–18
rhetoric of, 337
Deneen, Patrick, 168
Desjobert, Amédeé, 189
despotism, 8, 56, 92, 97, 100, 103, 109, 112, 114, 128, 168, 172, 174, 175, 176, 204, 205, 213, 214, 215, 235, 250, 265, 266,

267, 268, 269, 270, 271, 272, 276, 318, 323, 330
democratic, 8, 103, 215, 225, 270
Napoleon and, 265, 266, 269
soft or administrative, 127, 172, 230
determinism, 30, 107, 224
Detroit, 158
Dey of Algiers, 218
Dilemmas of Democracy: Tocqueville and Modernization (Drescher), 4
Dissent magazine, 307, 308, 312, 315
"doctrine of fatality," 98
Doha, 134
domination, 5, 23, 100, 103, 192, 196, 209, 213, 214, 218, 220, 246, 251, 253, 254, 256, 260, 268
colonial, 214
European, 197
French domination, 103
habits of, 246, 256
Napoleon's "system" of, 267
as threat to democratic society, 245
Drescher, Seymour, 4, 7
Duara, Prasenjit, 117
Duke d'Enghiens, 266, 272

East and West Indies, 208
East Asia, 16, 111, 112, 117, 119, 121, 122, 123, 124, 128, 129, 131
democracy in, 111, 122–123, 128
Eastern Europe, 8, 13
Egypt, 139
Egyptian Revolution, 2
Emirates, 18
Emperor. *See* Bonaparte, Napoleon
empire, 2, 23, 204, 216, 219, 243, 245, 246, 248, 250, 252, 253, 263, 264, 265, 267, 271, 272, 275, 278, 279, 281, 285, 286, 287, 318
British model of, 209, 210, 220
of circumstances, 229
of Europe, 187, 197

political culture of. *See* political
culture
politics and poetry in, 316
Stendhal's critical view of, 281–282
as the paradigmatic Enlightenment
nation, 217, 277, 278
Tocqueville's view of, 81, 108, 111,
116, 124, 213, 216–217,
218–219, 228–229, 265, 270,
274, 276, 279, 280, 329
Franco-Prussian War, 283
Frederick the Great, 282
free verse, 309–310
freedom, 98. *See also* Liberty
egalitarian taste for, 113
empire and, 197–198, 210, 212,
233, 286
frontier freedom, 318, 330
local freedom, 27–28, 321, 322,
324, 325, 327
natural freedom, 91, 336
"old freedoms," 79
political vs. economic, 17–18, 111
preconditions for, 94, 115, 175,
226–227
religion and. *See* religion
"fear of freedom," 165, 166
"great political freedom," 329
"secondary freedoms," 329
French Revolution, 11, 149, 318, 326
child of the absolute monarchy, 56
irreligious fury of, 55
lasting principles of, 56
liberal democratic ideals of, 277
légicentrisme of, 55
and Napoleon, 270–271
Tocqueville's views of, 54, 75–83,
98
Friedman, Edward, 120, 121
Front de Libération Nationale, 200
frontier(s)
ambiguities of, 33, 34, 334
American frontier, 25, 35–37, 158,
164, 244, 250, 317, 324, 333,
336, 337
America's contemporary local
frontiers, 317

and democratic culture, 245,
304–305
extreme egalitarianism on, 249
Jeffersonian idealization of, 302
as laboratory of democratic
equality, 334
Puritan vision of, 335–336
Tocqueville on, 333–334
between aristocracy and democracy,
9, 53. *See also* frontiers of
democracy
between church and State, 318
between the aristocratic past, 59
contestability of, 34
meaning of, 33–34, 35, 42, 51–333
moral valence of, 334–335
Tocqueville on, 153–154, 178, 181,
318, 322–323
frontiers of democracy, 4, 9, 24, 27,
28, 34, 44, 46, 49, 51–52, 183,
285, 286, 287, 330, 335, 336,
338
Algerian, 251
concept of, 336–337
dueling frontiers, 323
external, 40, 45, 47
"final frontier," 183, 188, 198,
200
future, 330, 338
internal, 40–42, 45, 48, 51
local, 317, 319, 323
main, 51
in Tocqueville, 33, 51–52
Fugitive Slave Act, 253
Fukuyama, Francis, 13, 18
Furet, François, 126, 320
Fénelon, François de Salignac de la
Mothe, 314

Gannett, Robert, 27, 28, 75, 82, 317
Gatewood (*Stagecoach*), 296
Gauls, 74, 81, 209
Gellar, Sheldon, 6, 7
Gellner, Ernest, 13
"general ideas," 161
"generative fact," 62, 65, 179
"gentilhomme," 118

democratic revolution, 10–11, 12, 49, 51, 61, 62, 65, 149. *See also* Democracy
the final, 292
Industrial, 215
in poetry, 315
preceeding the Revolution itself, 56
psychic, 83
socialist revolutions in the Middle East, 144
Tocqueville's fear of, 215, 231, 280
Rhodes, 209
Rice, Condoleezza, 3
Richter, Melvin, 5, 7, 269, 270
right to work, 48, 82
Rites of Passage (Gennep), 334
Rocky Mountains, 248
Rome, 204
Rousseau, Jean-Jacques, 203, 301, 314, 336
Russia, 6, 18, 238, 260, 264, 278

Saginaw, 35, 36, 164
Saint-Lambert, Jean-François, 217
Salem, 336
"San Francisco Renaissance," 308
San-Jin, Han, 121
Sardinia, 237
Saudi Arabia, 18
The Scarlet Letter (Hawthorne), 336
Second Empire, 255, 281, 282
Second Republic, 22, 267, 281
Second Treatise of Government (Locke), 143
Second World War, 84
Sedgwick, Theodore, 253
self-government, 6, 13, 85, 111, 113, 114, 116, 250, 251, 321, 338
self-interest, 230, 233, 234, 279
self-interest rightly understood, 227, 319, 327
Sepoy Rebellion, 194, 195, 258, 261. *See also* Great Mutiny Of 1857
Shklar, Judith, 22
Singapore, 18
slavery, 5, 22, 23, 246, 258
in the US, 253, 256–258, 261

Tocqueville on, 196, 216, 259, 263, 277–278
Smith, Adam, 18, 138, 140, 142
Smith, Rogers, 22
"social instincts," 114, 116
social state, 71, 72, 113
socialism, 8, 35, 48, 142, 255, 328
"soft despotism," 226
Somalia, 287
Sorbonne, 320
Sorel, Georges, 284, 285
South America, 225
South Carolina, 253
South Carolina College, 253
South Side Bronzeville, 326
Souvenirs (Stendhal), 282
Soviet Union, 8
Spain, 204, 209, 261
Spanish conquista, 185
Sparks, Jared, 253, 255
Spector, Céline, 20, 21, 202
"spirit of liberty," 164
"spirit of religion," 164
The Spirit of the Laws (Montesquieu), 95, 202, 203, 204, 206, 207, 209, 211, 212, 213, 215, 217
Springfield, Illinois, 28, 327
St. Jerome, 92, 93
St. Petersburg, 236
Stagecoach, 26, 295, 304
Starobinski, Jean, 335
state of nature, 62, 143, 295
Steinberg, David, 119, 120
Stendhal, 265, 281, 282, 285
Stoffels, Charles, 323
Sudan, 139, 287
Sulaimani, 134
Sumner, Charles, 253, 254, 257
Sumner, George, 253
Sun King, 83
"superstitious terror," 36
Syria, 287

tabula rasa, 56, 107, 286
Tacitus, Publius Cornelius, 86
Tahiti, 233

5

240, 241, 247, 253, 256, 276,
298, 307, 310, 316, 332, 333,
334, 337
  democratic society par excellence,
    185
  as exemplar of liberty, 231
  foriegn policy of, 2–3, 223, 240
  United States Congress, 324
  U. S. Constitution, 185, 225
  U.S. colonial rule, 260
  U.S. State Department, 148
universalism, 9
  democratic, 9, 20, 33, 44–45, 47
  European, 46
  messianic, 337
  national limits of, 45
  Tocqueville's critique of, 162,
    166
University of Chicago, 291
"unsocial sociability," 201
USAID, 148
Usbek (*Persian Letters*), 54

van Gennep, Arnold, 334
Varanesi, 108
Versailles, 314, 320
Viking Press, 309
violence, 23, 185, 193, 246, 253, 254,
    255–258, 262, 295
  in American public life, 253
  and colonial rule, 193–194, 234
  integral to political life, 292
  of June Days, 1848, 236
  legitimacy of, 292–293, 294
  "revolutionary violence," 284
  Tocqueville on violence, 214
  vs. liberty, 268
von Hoffman, Nicholas, 2

Wall Street, 23, 246, 254, 256, 258
"Washington Consensus," 127
Washington, DC, 28, 256, 258
Wayne, John, 296
Wealth of Nations (Adam Smith), 138
Weber, Max, 19
Welch, Cheryl, 5, 16, 111
West Africa, 260
West Bank, 334
West Berlin, 334
West Germany, 286
Western Europe, 6, 16, 333
Western territories, 25, 249
Westernization, 17, 135, 136, 138,
    187
Westerns, 297, 304
Whitman, Walt, 27, 308, 309, 316
Whittington, Keith, 172
Wilbur, Richard, 153
Wild West, 334, 338
"will to power," 277
William and Mary, 81
Williams, Roger, 335
Wills, Gary, 57
Wolfowitz, Paul, 2, 3
Wolin, Sheldon, 39, 154, 161
World Affairs, 2
Writings on Empire and Slavery
    (Tocqueville), 5

Yemen, 139
Young, Arthur, 74, 78
"Young Goodman Brown"
    (Hawthorne), 335
Yun-Shik, Chang, 126

Zeus, 198
Zola, Émile, 265, 281, 283, 285